BIKING BRITAIN & BEYOND

Robert Adams

This book is dedicated to my family. Each one has, in their own way, encouraged these tours and supported or tolerated the time and computer monopolization involved recording them in this book. Some of them even read its predecessor 'Panniers, Pedals and Pubs'. I wish also to acknowledge that my most enduring friends are British, cyclists or both.

COVER: The cover photograph is courtesy of that passionate photographer, Mari Adams, who also happens to be my wife. We discovered this excellent restaurant on Fossgate in York during a joint cycling holiday in 1992. Then known as the Cockatoo Crêperie, it is now the Blue Bicycle. Its quality and popularity have been maintained but prices have soared. Nevertheless, the Blue Bicycle has nourished me, as a rare treat, on subsequent solo tours and its image captures two essentials of them: cycling and food.

Published in 2014 by FeedARead.com Publishing – Arts Council funded
Copyright © Robert Adams

First Edition

A CIP catalogue record for this title is available from the British Library.

BIKING BRITAIN AND BEYOND

A personal love story spanning six decades between man, bike, Britain and more recently, France. Serenity, exhilaration, challenge and frustrations are the ingredients of the ten, mainly solo, long-distance cycle tours in the book. Amusing anecdotes, eccentric characters, historical notes and scenic information enrich this personal journal. A separate section provides detailed daily routes for each tour.

Cycle Path alongside 1932 replica of 16th century Smock Mill at Rye, East Sussex, one of two 'antient townes' supporting the Cinque Ports

FOREWORD

Solo cycle touring in idyllic countryside is one of my favourite activities and it makes possible indulging my other favourite- reading history or mysteries accompanied by tea and pastry as the opportunities arise. I can be flexible about what to do, where, when and how long to stop. The consultation and compromise of group travel doesn't exist and interaction with potentially interesting others is less constrained. I have a strong bias for Britain and France as good cycling countries and a long-nurtured aversion to spending too much.

The latter characteristic reflects a just post-depression, small town childhood, missionary grandparents and a Scots-Irish banker father. These factors shaped my care with money, a condition that controls most of my thoughts and actions including what seemed important to include this book. I've severely weeded out the non crucial parsimonious bits so those that remain are essential to be genuine, accurate and faithful to my experiences and motivations. Despite looming large for me, excessive references to food have also been purged.

Why Cycling?

A well-made bicycle is a marvellous machine, versatile, practical, fun and efficient. Even before the introduction of super light carbon fibre to cycle building, a bike made of steel was judged more efficient than any other creature or form of transport (see Appendix).

The initial idea of a human powered machine is attributed to Jacques Ozanam in a famous book *Récréations Mathématiques et Physiques* published in 1696. Nearly two hundred years passed before a machine came along that looked similar to our modern road bikes. The Rover cycle, introduced then in Britain was known as a safety bicycle compared to the earlier, well-known Ordinary or Penny Farthing which was anything but safe. The Ordinary's saddle sat over a huge front wheel that was pedalled tricycle style, contributing to many 'head over wheel' tumbles. The Rover introduced equal sized wheels, centrally located pedals and a chain rotating the rear wheel. An 1879 poster for the Rover proclaimed it as 'an ever-saddled horse which eats nothing.' Much, if not most, of the cycle's evolution over that two hundred years occurred in France and Britain, with an early major contribution from Germany.(1)

Cycling opened up the countryside and expanded social opportunities for the average person. Clubs developed, and women participated. Suitable clothing had to be developed for women cyclists, freeing them of some restrictions and indirectly fostering other emancipative progress. Susan B. Anthony, the famous US suffragette, reportedly said that the bicycle was the most important factor in women's emancipation.

I did not know any of that history when I got my first bike at age nine. It was a blood-red, bare-bones, single-speed, coaster brake bike that cost $39.95. Nearly ten times (inflation adjusted) more expensive, my current bike is a custom tourer built in traditional style with a flat top tube, Brooks saddle, mudguards and, in a break with tradition, disk brakes and stainless-steel couplers. The latter, theoretically allow the bike to be dismantled and easily packed for shipping by air.

Cycling can be vigorous or relaxed, thrilling or sedate; it offers greater opportunities to explore and is less tiring than walking. There is joy in downhill speed and pride in negotiating the bends with skill. Long distance, fully loaded and unassisted touring adds a sense of self-reliant accomplishment. I'm not competitive; communing with nature at a moderate but reflective pace is my objective, not speed. The path I've taken and its diversions are far more important than how quickly I reach the destination.

My first tour, at 15, covered 1100 km in the eastern US. The second and third at 16 and 18, also self-guided, were in Britain. Later, while living in England with my family, a Sunday ride ending in a countryside pub garden was one of my wife's and my favourite pastimes. When our children matured and we had returned to North America, we enjoyed van-assisted, luxury tours in New England, then more basic, self-guided ones in France and England. In 1990, I realized my long-held dream of a solo tour the length of Britain. Now, such tours are the highlight of my years and the subject of this book.

Britain

My interest in Britain was kindled by a several week trip to Europe with my younger brother, Byron, in 1957. We financed that trip ourselves, from newspaper route earnings, and by necessity as well as inclination, travelled as cheaply as we could. Observing Britain and Europe's different approaches to life made me question the assumption by US citizens of their country's 'superiority.' This is such a part of the ether there that one absorbs it unconsciously growing up with almost every breath. The following year, I entered Edinburgh University, lived with British students and found it difficult, often impossible, to explain the functioning of the US political system or to combat their challenges of my remaining assumptions. I'd swallowed the line without proof or questions. Then, Britain had only just exited the final phase of WW II rationing. Life was still frugal, with few luxuries. Consequently, it was, in this aspect, more home than foreign.

My attachment to Britain lay latent while finishing university in the US, marrying, and starting a career. Later at graduate school, during the job interview season one of my interviewers had by chance just returned from a seven-year assignment in London. Inspired by his experience, when his company offered me a position, I asked to be sent overseas and was immediately posted to Britain. We prolonged this assignment for six years, cementing my affection for Britain. Since then we have lived 90% of our lives in Commonwealth countries. I adopted and continue British habits and restrict my choice of films and books mainly to those produced in Britain. Consequently, I have attempted to write this book in British English. Remaining errors are the remnants of what my Edinburgh English tutor described as the disastrous effects of my North American education.

While there is no doubt that I am a committed anglophile—my love is mainly for the British countryside, its ample green space, its rural villages that appear all of a sudden without preliminary kilometres of hoardings, fast food shops and automotive dealers to announce them. Britain's contributions to literature and science, so much more than her proportion of the world's population, justify admiration for the erudition of its educated classes. Britain's influence in the world, though now diminished, remains considerable. But, I'm not blind to the country's problems. The class structure continues to shape attitudes and behaviour, often with destructive effect. Britain has one of the worst records among the industrialized world for keeping its children in school beyond normal leaving age. Ambition and self-reliance have been squashed for many by a too broad social safety net, creating an entitlement culture that seems to span generations and foster antisocial behaviour. Alcohol abuse is a major problem. These all distress me greatly but don't diminish Britain's tremendous cycling environment.

France
More recently, I have developed a growing interest in France. Moving to Canada over 30 years ago as a latter-day Loyalist and now as a recently minted (2003) Canadian, I have a great interest in our founding cultures. French and British rivalries formed our history and continue to colour our daily lives. So, expanding my tours to France seemed a natural progression and was intensified by the discovery that both Britain and France were the principal pioneers in bicycle development.

Canada retains elements of the Anglo/French divide with the often politically irritating Quebec. But, its people are gregarious and vital, its major cities are appealing to visit and it has the best bike network in North America. Quebec is a favourite holiday destination for many of us. In this, it mirrors the strong appeal that France has for the British. Many of them have chosen to settle down in France, drawn by the life style and more reasonable housing costs.

This reverse invasion is relatively new. Certainly French and British relations since the Norman invasion in 1066 were mainly violent, suspicious and negative. Some resentment and disdain lingers, but it isn't powerful enough to keep the British away. On my last tour, while traversing the Black Perigord region of France, there were a number of newsagents that carried three or four different British papers. One day, the Daily Telegraph ran an article about the popularity and safety of tourist locations for British travellers. France ranked as the most popular and the safest.

I have laboured for years, with little success, to become capable in French. The result is a mongrel, corrupt 'Franglais' that quickly falls back on English at the slightest difficulty or indication that the other person speaks English. I'm still working at it.

Finally, I confess that this book builds on my previous 'Panniers, Pedals and Pubs', adding five subsequent tours to its five. Each tour provided challenges, frustrations, interesting people, places and adventure, contentment and a strong sense of accomplishment. A summary of bicycle development is new and there is also a separate chapter of map-case sized daily routes for each of the tours should any reader want to duplicate my travels.

END TO END TOUR

BRITAIN

END-TO-END TOUR

Cycling the length of Britain was a long time ambition and my six-year old Sakai Tourer needed only pannier racks and a tune-up to be ready. An upcoming job transfer provided a perfect opportunity to slot my full annual holiday between the two positions. But work demands wouldn't permit any serious training. I did join the Cycle Touring Club(CTC) of Britain, obtained their official route by snail mail and reworked it to run north to south. Why I did that I don't know, perhaps just a perverse wish to be different. It was tedious work and ignored the avoiding headwinds rationale of the south to north original.

The Route

As the map shows, my route ran mainly along the west of Britain starting from John O' Groats in north-east Scotland down to Land's End, the most south-westerly point in England. I deviated even from my reversed official route adding some 180 km more than the distance the CTC was willing to acknowledge on my completion certificate. And, after finishing the End-to-End, I added more distance travelling east through southern England to Gatwick Airport for the flight home.

Arrival

My adventure began at Prestwick, a former military airport perhaps sixty kilometres south west of Glasgow. Needing to get into Glasgow for a train to the Scottish north coast for the start of my top to bottom version of the End to End, I collected my gear and approached a waiting taxi. The fare would have been the mind-numbing equivalent of C$50, over half my daily budget! Then the bus driver refused to take me, saying 'you cannae take a bike in a bus—it's against the law.' This reception, added to the lack of sleep, robbed the day of its sunny warmth.

Retreating back inside the terminal, I sought the help of a very pleasant and efficient matronly tourist information attendant. She booked B&B's for me tonight in Perth and tomorrow in Thurso as well as arranging and paying for a taxi to take me to a nearby station. where trains left for Glasgow. Her kind help erased the blues and I was soon basking in the sun on the railway platform marvelling at the scenery with five minutes to spare before the train arrived.

Lost in a jet-lagged, warm and contented mental lull, I failed to notice a train arriving on the opposite platform or to hear the announcement that it was the Glasgow train. Somehow, I came to my senses at the last moment and ran madly up the steep steps of the platform bridge over the tracks. My demented dash lugging a still-boxed cycle, duffel bag and a rucksack up and down those steps had to be hilarious to any observer. Thank goodness, the train driver was one of them and held up the train for a couple of minutes.

The train pulled into a festive Glasgow Central Station filled with travellers in good spirits. It looked well managed and in good condition with appealing shops. Glasgow had been chosen the 1990 cultural centre of Europe and the city was being freshened up for celebrations later in the year. My train to Perth departed from nearby Queen Street station. This transfer was eased by apparently different legislation in Glasgow that allowed buses to carry a boxed cycle! (Perhaps it was bloody mindedness in Prestwick rather than legislation.)

On that brief journey to Queen Street, I was impressed by Glasgow's human-scaled and architecturally consistent cityscape. With its fresh paint and newly scrubbed facades, it looked friendly and impressive —well worth a return visit. At Queen Street, the ticket agent informed me that reservations were necessary for cycles at the particular time I wished to travel and reservations were now closed! I was quickly learning that this type of trip requires resourcefulness, a willingness to act independently and perhaps a bit of personal bloody-mindedness. Rushing to grab an earlier train to Perth and pausing just long enough to buy a sandwich and coffee for the journey and ignoring the possible need for a reservation.

Then, as the train pulled out of Glasgow, I felt that the trip had really started. Much of the close-in residential area was uniformly bleak, grey and without relief but soon we were in lovely countryside with rolling hills and green pastures dotted with sheep and cattle.

At Perth, a porter helped to put my cycle box in the left luggage room and made special arrangements for me to collect the cycle in the morning for the trip to Thurso as the left luggage facility would be closed tomorrow--a Sunday.   I bought my ticket, made a cycle reservation and set off for the B&B.

I found it facing a huge park with lovely gardens set off by a massive honeysuckle with coral and yellow flowers. It is a very British park with broad playing areas, borders of grand old trees, a pond for canoeing, a trampoline centre, miniature golf and a lawn bowling green. As no one was yet home at the B&B, I chose a park side bench across the road to watch a wedding party emerging from the nearby church. The aged Bentley limousines, kilted males and photography choreography provided entertainment until my landlady arrived.

My room had three beds, a strong smoke smell, colour television and tea making facilities.   So, my first cuppa on the 'old sod' I made myself. The cup was Pyrex, manufactured in Corning, New York – just 29 km from my birthplace! Thus fortified, I went out, exploring the town and finding dinner in the food department of Marks and Spencer (then Britain's largest department store chain).

By six p.m., my body and mind were telling me 'get to bed.' It had been 39 hours since I was last in one.   Back at the B&B, my sandwiches and yoghurt were washed down with another cuppa and I was soon fast asleep.

The final leg of the rail journey to Thurso involved an hour's wait at Inverness. Taking advantage of this delay, I unpacked the cardboard box and reassembled my bike, attracting considerable interest from other cyclists who came over to chat. Two men had just returned from a month in Florida and three RAF men were in training for an attack(two wheeled variety) on the Pyrenees in August.

Overcast skies and cold showers greeted my 7 p.m. arrival in Thurso. The B&B was a long way from the station so I got soaked in transit. The weather was so miserable that I had no interest in venturing out again for a meal and made do with my host's complimentary supper of tea and sandwiches about nine.   This Scottish custom was a nostalgic reminder of my Edinburgh digs while at university and proved to a godsend a number of times on this tour.

Next morning, mounting the cycle for the first time of the tour, I pedalled east in a light mist, with the temperature about 7 C. It shouldn't have been surprising. Thurso's latitude is about 58.5°, slightly north of Moscow. This chilling baptism lasted nearly two hours before I was able to take temporary refuge in the tourist shops at John O' Groats.

The balance of this chapter relates experiences that I found amusing, interesting or both along the way. These are told in approximately chronological order.

Daughter's Room
Depressed by the consistently gloomy wet weather and the tawdriness of the tourist-focused tearoom/gift shop at Drumnadrochit, I cycled west in drizzling rain along the northern shore of Loch Ness determined to take the first B&B that appeared. It was a cottage set high up on the slope opposite the lakeshore, operated by Valerie with Pam, her 16-year-old daughter. Since the prospect of continuing to cycle in that rain was totally unappealing, I accepted their only room, a double, and persuaded Valerie to allow me to share their evening meal.

While she prepared the meal, we chatted about naturopathy and her ability to read people's allergies and other afflictions from simply having them hold different types of food. Dinah, her black and white cat, deposited herself contentedly in my lap, completing the domestic scene. Later, as we were concluding the meal and Pam was serving the pudding, a couple arrived looking for accommodation. After a few minutes of hushed conversation in the front hall, Valerie returned to the kitchen to ask if I would mind sleeping in Pam's room. Perhaps because males are subject to occasional fantasies, I initially misunderstood. The salesman and farmer's daughter stories of my youth flooded to mind. I should have known better.

The meal together, Dinah's acceptance and sleeping in Pam's bed room made me feel almost one of the family, but one without

15

background. Next morning, at breakfast, Valerie filled me in on her life as an abused child, contracting multiple sclerosis and recovering through homeopathic medicine. She also suffered from the class divide as her husband's family rejected her because her attendance at a grammar school and subsequent employment by a bank made her a snob intellectual!

Old Cyclist

The Glen Albyn A82 runs in a narrow valley between two mountain ranges along the eastern shore of Loch Lochy. A cold, strong headwind chilled me and the lorries passing on the other side of the road created a frighteningly magnetic draught sucking me towards them. Cycling into the wind was difficult; the horizon stretched to infinity, making the distance seem formidable and unending. I was uncomfortable and feeling sorry for myself, when a voice called out behind me. Drawing alongside was another cyclist—a man, perhaps twenty years my senior, dressed more for a mountain hike than cycling. Clad in heavy boots, his gear was stowed in a wooden box strapped to the luggage rack. He too, was doing the End-to-End but to benefit the blind. We talked for a while, but after less than ten minutes, he said 'I can't keep on at this pace, I'll have to say goodbye now' and sped ahead. Talk about a demoralising experience!

Loch Linnhe

One of the things I learned on this trip is that arranging accommodation in advance definitely enhances the experience. Doing so doesn't guarantee comfort or interesting places but it saves considerable time and frustration. Today, after strolling through Fort William, I left about five planning to do another 8 km before stopping for the night. All the B&B's disappeared after 5 km. Another 13 km produced a tiny village with five different B&B's each displaying a vacancy sign and each one of them telling a fib!

By the time I had knocked hopefully on all their doors and left rejected, it was half past six and raining again. The map indicated that the next village was 20 km further. Then, all of a sudden, there, gracing the sea-fed Loch Linnhe shore, was a small, white, red-roofed bungalow sporting a B&B sign.

This time there really was a vacancy. The couple running the B&B were about 70 and looked as if they needed to squeeze every penny until the Queen protested. Again, I decided to rely on the Scottish supper tradition rather than brave the weather again searching for a restaurant. In this household, however, supper was limited to tea and a single digestive biscuit, with no sandwiches or anything else.

I went to bed very hungry in a cold, cold room that could be tolerated only when under the goose down duvet. Next morning at breakfast, rather than turn on an electric fire to take off the chill, the husband wore a wool shirt over heavy underwear and topped it off with a quilted jacket. His wife was as ecstatic as an aged and polite Scot can be when I asked for a low cholesterol breakfast, letting Mari's admonitions overrule my hunger. My breakfast became two wee tomatoes on toast, no bacon or eggs or anything extra to compensate. I imagined her celebrating silently, 'Hoot Mon, there's an extra fifty pence profit on this client!'

The husband talked of his youth when he would regularly cycle 80 km after tea during the week and as much as 200 on a Sunday—all of this on a fixed-speed cycle. My daily distances on this tour are averaging considerably less than 100 km. Cycling clearly was much more a part of people's lives here in mid-century than in North America both for regular transportation and for recreation.

Glen Falloch Farm
Heading east from Loch Linnhe, I made a pleasant stop at the Glencoe Centre for a much needed lunch and to see a short film on the Glencoe Massacre. This massacre happened in 1692 when a company of soldiers under a Campbell commander killed more than 40 MacDonalds that had given them hospitality for nearly a fortnight. The Campbells got up early, in a snowstorm, to begin the massacre and killed Mac Ian, the chief of the MacDonalds. His sons escaped to the hills with other survivors.

Also known as the Glen of Weeping, Glencoe runs between magnificent mountains. After the film, I braved the wind tunnel created by those mountains and struggled against the wind and unceasing climb. With my ankles and backside screaming, I felt the agony would never stop as the slope and the wind made it feel like sitting still, going nowhere. So, I was very surprised to find that my speed was averaging 10 km per hour. Still at that pace, it would take me until 6 pm just to reach Crianlarich.

Given the conditions, I decided to be satisfied with the 60 km day that Crianlarich would represent. Just then, my odometer quit, adding to the sense of no progress until I realized that the historical small tombstone-like, white stone road markers were placed a mile apart could be my odometer. Within just a little while, Bridge of Orchy arrived on the horizon at 2.30 leaving only 18 more kilometres, perhaps two hours, before Crainlarich.

Unfortunately, this provided an excuse to stop for a beer and sandwich at the nearest pub. I should have anticipated the effect of the beer on my cycling efficiency and without any sunshine, the scenery became oppressive, remote, dark and deserted.

Then again, at Crianlarich, very few B&B's bothered to indicate 'no vacancy' outside, so I lost several minutes at each only to wind up rejected. At Crianlarich's final possibility, the landlady had no vacancy but suggested a 10 km distant farm called Glen Falloch. At this hour, I suggested it might be wise to first check by telephone whether Glen Falloch had a vacancy. Her response was, 'Ach no, I couldnae do that. It's a different exchange and I wouldna ken the number.' I suspect the real reason was the cost of the call. There was no option but to cycle on.

The ride to Glen Falloch was at that beautiful time of evening in Britain when the sun makes perhaps its first appearance of the day, producing a soft angled golden glow on the landscape. The road ran gently downhill crossing many gurgling streams rushing over rocky beds. The pace and setting were serenely uplifting, just what was needed to overcome an otherwise dismal day.

Glen Falloch was very much a working farm. Loud, up close, barking from three of the twenty working dogs diligently guarding their territory greeted my arrival. The farmer was busy moving buckets of some vile liquid down to the barn so he passed me on to his wife.

Yes, they had a single room. She led me up a narrow staircase to my room and its orange coverlet draped bed. The single window had a loose pane held in place with a bent nail leaving a significant gap that ensured round the clock, all season air conditioning. Although my hostess has said nothing, I was counting on Scottish supper as it was too late to back to Crianlarich for a meal. Finally, at 8.30 she called up to say that there was a cup of tea ready. Another guest, a gardener for the National Trust on a walking holiday, joined me.

She took us into the lounge where an open coal fire generated a warm, cosy atmosphere but intensified the odour of wet dog permeating the room. Unlike my experience at Loch Linnhe, this supper included a tiered plate stacked with sandwiches and cakes. Our landlady joined us for conversation and we soon discovered a couple of connections. Her niece had lived in my town of Oakville, Ontario and a New Zealand girl that had worked on the farm is now back in Dunedin where my family lived in the mid-seventies.

The farmer came in about 9, his day's work on this 17,000 acre, 5,000 sheep farm finally done. After a full day's work he badly needed a shower. Nevertheless, he immediately joined us. The room's odour slowly acquired additional natural barnyard nuances. When his wife asked what her guests wanted for tomorrow's breakfast, I said 'no eggs, please; my wife doesn't want me to have more than one a week to reduce my cholesterol.' The farmer exploded: 'There'd be hell to pay in this place if that happened to me.'

My egg-free breakfast was served in a front parlour thankfully devoid of dog odour and was more substantial than Loch Linnhe provided, with an addition of baked beans to the tomatoes on toast. Another guest, Bill, bragged that he avoids income tax by forming a new company annually to take advantage of the special low tax rate that applies only to new companies.

Gretna Green
Gretna Green nestles near the eastern edge of Solway Firth, conveniently close to the English border and enjoys a good tourist trade for its history as a place where clandestine marriages could be performed. England made marriage illegal without parental consent

for young people in the middle of the eighteenth century but for over 100 years neither such consent nor even residency was necessary in Scotland. Scotland later established a minimum three-week residency for one of the parties before marriage. Until 1940, the local blacksmith could perform the ceremony. Today, the blacksmith shop is a popular location for wedding photos and weddings with benefit of clergy.

As I arrived, a freshly minted couple was having a picture taken next to the town sign and the shop itself was full of German tourists. The setting is lovely----more English than Scottish in ambiance. The streets here are winding, there are stonewalls and generally a bit more affluence and optimism than I had seen in Scotland so far.

Further south and now in Brampton, England just west of Carlisle, I stopped to book a B&B at the tourist office located in the village centre clock tower. Climbing to the first floor as the clock got its daily winding, my ankles screamed from days of pedalling. So, I chose the nearest available B&B-an ancient working dairy farm called Gelt Hall in the nearby village of Castle Carrock.

The Gelt Hall B&B sign was attached to a dairy storage building abutting the road just at a bend and I almost missed seeing it. As I rode up, a woman called out to instruct her preteen daughter as she set off to make village milk deliveries on foot. 'That's for the vicar and...that's for', I did not hear the rest, but was delighted with the sense that here, in 1990, time had stood still.

Their white stone house was attached to the farm buildings. Real log beams support the upper floor and there were many lovely antique pieces amidst the awful overstuffed sofa and chairs of the guest lounge. My attic-like room is quite large with a single and double bed. Annie diplomatically instructed me to use the small bed as I am only paying for a single.

After a shower, I hobbled across the road for a pub meal. There are two pubs but The Weary Sportsman seemed more appropriate. It is small and cosy with low ceilings, beams and window seats. I chose one of these next to a retired Welsh couple who just finished a damp holiday in Scotland. Their mechanical and desultory conversation, was mainly about the weather or if she should have the raspberry pavlova. She seemed particularly eager to expand the scope of conversation and bravely spoke to the strange man (me) when hers went to the washroom. It was a short-lived improvement for her after he returned as he enthusiastically began a riveting description about the pebbledash finish for houses that he had used as a builder.

Back at Gelt Hall, I strategically positioned myself in the guest lounge to read, hoping to be offered a cup of tea before bed. Having left Scotland, this might not be her custom but about 9, Annie asked if I would like a 'cuppa.' When this arrived, it was accompanied by a cheese and tomato sandwich and a small chocolate bar. Success! Later she joined me to tell a sad and complicated tale about her extended family and an awkward division of an estate that created resentment. A visitor wishing to borrow a hat for a wedding interrupted our conversation. Sensing this to be a lengthy interruption, I escaped to my room.

Whitehaven

When he fell to his death from a skyscraper under construction, his wife, an English friend of Mari's moved to Cumbria to be close to family. At the time, we thought Oakville was nearly perfect and found it hard to imagine someone choosing to move. Mari asked me to take a detour from my route to see what her friend's new town looked like.

Whitehaven, in north west Cumbria, was considerably off route so I decided to go by train. Foxfield, the tiny but closest station to my route, provided a new experience. There was no way to buy tickets or snacks and no train stopped at Foxfield on a regular basis. One just stood on the platform and flagged down the train as it rolled by.

Most of the passengers were young people dressed in their party clothes for a Friday night out in Whitehaven's bright lights. The northward journey hugged the coast, passing ramshackle beach huts that people hire in the summertime. To my eye they looked as if they should be condemned. The route also passes the famous school of the films—St Bee's--as well as the ominous looking cooling towers of Calder Hall nuclear power station. Calder Hall's reactors were the first in the world to be used to generate electricity on a commercial scale. Overall, the scenery and the mindless high-spiritedness of my fellow passengers were depressing.

Once in Whitehaven, I rode round the town looking for B&B signs. When one finally appeared and the landlady offered me dinner, I felt fortunate, as it was too late for a pub meal. This feeling quickly evaporated when dinner was served. It had been intended for her husband and been sitting in the cooker awaiting his long overdue return from the pub. She managed to punish us both by denying him his dinner and by serving me the dried out roast beef, boiled potatoes and desiccated mass of mushy peas that clung to my plate. The only partially redeeming feature was the ice cream and fruit that owed nothing to culinary skill. Next morning, contradicting my dinner experience, I discovered her catering diploma proudly gracing the dining room wall. It was obvious that her catering school does not have a continuing education requirement. Perhaps understandably, her husband never showed up.

I took a few pictures in the town and checked property prices at the estate agents to be able to report something about Whitehaven to Mari but didn't discover the pleasant residential areas claimed by the *AA Illustrated Guide to Britain*---'a town of great character developed in Wren style in the seventeenth and eighteenth centuries…Lowther Street, in particular, has some elegant old houses….'

Ships from North Africa entered the harbour bearing phosphate rocks for the detergent chemical works on the hill above which reportedly dumps their untreated crap right into the sea. John Paul Jones had set boats on fire in the harbour in 1788. Then, Jones was a privateer, not a hero of war between Britain and the US.

By midmorning, I was ready to leave and re-board the train back to Foxfield. The day continued in demoralizing fashion as the cycle pedal jammed into the back of my leg cutting it badly while I was carrying the bike down steep steps to the platform. The bike was fully loaded and too heavy to control properly. Later that day I collected a nasty stinging nettle rash on the other leg.

The day was very warm; perspiration streamed down my face blurring my vision. My old style helmet had no cooling vent holes so it was like a sauna up there. I took it off and tied it to the back rack. Soon after this the road plunged down and I was racing at over 50 km/h. The vibration knocked the helmet off so that it bounced on the rear tyre scorching a great black skunk groove down the centre of my yellow helmet----a fitting end to an almost totally unpleasant diversion.

Page Hall

The new day was cool but dry—perfect for cycling! It was to be an easy day with Penrith, my objective, little more than an hour away. The B6413/2 route ran almost due south from Castle Carrock. A good mix of up and down roads provided both exercise and thrills. One downhill had me screaming along briefly at 58 km an hour! Traffic was light with only about one vehicles for every two kilometres. The countryside boasted stone or vegetation hedges, stone houses and rolling meadows with that particularly British semicircular sweep of majestically broad deciduous trees which mark parks and country estates like monster mushrooms. Sheep and cattle flourished, streams ran under single lane hump back bridges, and villages emerged frequently. Kirksowald was one of these; stereotypically perfect with its meandering main street running gently downhill with a pub at each bend. I stopped in the Crown Inn for an early tea and scones and extended the stop for an hour to write a few postcards.

Penrith was immediately interesting with winding streets, narrow alleys and pubs. The Tourist Information Centre booked me into Page Hall, an old farmhouse now surrounded by the town. Ken, my amiable host, was painting the outside windows as I arrived. He is an avid cyclist and an early retired forester who is now actively encouraging the growth of natural native British flora. Ken has catalogued 68 varieties in his garden without counting any trees.

Since it was early, Ken suggested I take a 15-minute hike to the Beacon —a spot on the hill where fires were lit in Elizabethan times to warn of danger. My still swollen ankles made each step painful, stretching his fifteen minutes to thirty. The forest footpath wound amidst tall pines on very rocky terrain offering a complete vista of the valley and town with the misty bunched clumps of Lakeland's mountains to the west. Perched at the top was a small tower called the Pike that had been reconstructed in 1712.

Penrith is an ancient city that originally was the capital of Cumbria and Strathclyde. The abundance of sandstone suggests that its name could mean Red Hill. After a pub dinner I walked back to Page Hall where Ken showed me some more of his garden. Although it was after 9 p.m., light was still adequate. We retired to the sun porch where his wife set out tea and biscuits for supper. The temperature was cool but soon warmed with Ken's passionate conversation about a variety of topics that quickly established him as decidedly left of centre. He is obviously intelligent and feels cheated by the lack of a university education. His family was very poor and required him to leave school to help them. A government grant would have made university possible and he clearly resents that it wasn't available.

At breakfast, I met John, a mature photography student from South Wales who was completing a project on the horse fair at nearby Appleby. This is an annual Gypsy (Traveller, Tinker) event that draws gypsies from all over. Horses are the focus of the several day events that feature swapping, selling and buying. On a later trip I purposefully scheduled a visit to Appleby while the fair was on and saw men riding bare back galloping up and down narrow lanes to show off their horses. Money changed hands somewhat covertly from great wads of notes stuffed in shirt pockets.

The park opposite the Penrith railway station provided yet another example of military monuments are almost everywhere—this time dedicated to the Boer War. War memories loom large in the British psyche. One man, noticeably under the influence, stopped me as I was about to enter a pub for lunch. He just had to tell me his war history, pulling off his cap to show me the shrapnel scar on his scalp! Germany's motives are still suspect, particularly now in 1990, with German reunification on the horizon. This persistence of this war 'top of mind' aspect of life 45 years after VE day is surprising as is the lack of evidence here on the edge of Lakeland of honour for Wordsworth or its other famous poets.

Oakvillians

A few days later following learning about the Oakville connection at Glen Falloch, I booked into a lovely B&B in Kirkby Lonsdale, Cumbria. My gracious hostess had worked for nine months in Oakville as a physiotherapist. On a later trip I returned to Kirkby Lonsdale and stayed with her again. Sadly, in the few years between, she had become a widow and was wondering what her life would have been like had she accepted an offer of marriage from a Canadian doctor while she was in Oakville.

After my first night in Kirkby Lonsdale, some distance further south, I had great difficulty in finding a place to stay. Still bed-less at 8.30 p.m., my Presbyterian upbringing made me feel certain that I had somehow transgressed and didn't deserve any accommodation. The offending action had to be glancing through an issue of the nudist magazine, *Health and Efficiency,* which I found the previous day. Compared to *Playboy*, it was dull stuff.

Waiting much longer might also have meant going without dinner, so I stopped in the Three Horseshoes pub for a late meal at about nine p.m.. The publican took pity on me and phoned to book me a spot at nearby Sambrook Farm. Darkness descended before I finished my meal and I was concerned that, without lights, finding the farm would be difficult and dangerous. Another gentleman, also booked at the farm, overheard me and intrigued by my voice, asked me to 'talk some more.' He initially mistook me for an American, but while still technically correct in 1990, it didn't fit my loyalties. When I said I'm from Canada he had to know my town. When he heard Oakville, he said, 'Oh, do you know Mary Clark? She lives on Trafalgar Road and was here just two weeks ago.' I followed his taillights on a slow drive to Sambrook Farm.

Near the end of this tour I had another Oakville experience in a Penzance laundrette. Still immersed in my book waiting for the machine to complete its cycle I noticed a woman staring at the address tag on my laundry bag. Realizing she had been caught spying, she somewhat shamefacedly introduced herself as a former Oakville resident, resident for the last several years in Saudi Arabia. Her husband is to retire in December but now they are off on a three to four month cycle tour of New Zealand. So we had plenty to talk about. Her husband arrived later and we had a good chat about cycles and touring. These coincidences add so much interest to these tours.

Church Stretton, Cheddar and Beyond

The morning at Sambrook Farm broke beautifully with fleecy clouds and bright sunshine. I took photos of the colourfully expansive garden through my attic bedroom window because the window would have fallen off if opened. After breakfast, at the invitation of my hosts, I cycled a short distance to the Sambrook Mill—a period house with ponds, streams, hump bridges and a pretty garden. My hostess gave me a complete tour of this restored and re-purposed mill whose sitting room featured grinding blocks and assorted machinery. A small window looked onto the turning millstone.

Back on the bike, at Acton Burnell, I stopped to collect one of the required post office date stamps that will prove to the CTC that I completed this ride. While there, I saw a sign for Church Stretton, only 13 kilometres away and decided to take a nostalgic side trip. Church Stretton was the home of my one and only pen pal, Andrew Hensman. My younger brother, Byron and I stayed with his family briefly in 1957 during our summer European tour. I clearly remember this first stay in an English home, my pal Andrew's fun with the conversational confusion caused by his dog also being called Bob and being told to sit down because I looked untidy standing up.

Andrew's father was a clergyman and their financial situation must have been very tight as his mother asked if we would mind reusing the same sheets when we returned for another brief visit a few weeks later. She wanted to avoid the cost of laundering them in the interim. I had never been aware of anyone that had to be quite so careful with money before. Now, I reflect back on that visit with some guilt. Feeding two extra people for a couple of days must have been difficult and we did not have the common courtesy to take a gift of any kind. We had no relevant experience to draw on. Virtually all our social experiences had been with relatives; reciprocal visits substituted for gifts, not that I then even thought about these aspects.

The road to Church Stretton became dirt and other brown material contributed by cattle. I was held up, along with other traffic, while cattle were put back to pasture after milking. Several wore silver face plates with spikes attached to their noses. The farmer told me the plate is to stop them sucking the other cows' udders but he was probably having a laugh at my expense.

The road quickly narrowed to barely a track and was so completely overgrown that it felt like being immersed in a tunnel of vegetation. At the side of the road, the ground rose sharply and steeply and the road was littered with fallen rocks.

Once out of the tunnel, it was very pleasant valley scenery with rolling green hills in the distance--good cycling country but not particularly memorable. Church Stretton had more interest than my memory recalled but my search for Andrew father's church where we had attended a harvest festival was unsuccessful. Another church, St. Laurence's, was very peaceful and inviting. Twenty years later, after re-establishing contact with Andrew, he told me that it was now known as the United Reform Church which did not exist as a denomination in 1957.

I pressed on south towards Ludlow where I had booked a B&B for tonight. After my experience yesterday, accommodation certainty was crucial tonight. Of course, once arriving in Ludlow, the place was stuffed with B&B's, most of which had vacancies.

Ludlow has a few very ancient hotel buildings. Most notable of these is the Feathers with its renowned elaborate Elizabethan driftwood like timbered front, where a single room was £60--about four times what I have been paying.

Pretty Woman
This day began badly and continued much the same but ended well. Most of the day was wet. That and the terrain slowed my progress. I took refuge from the morning mist in a laundrette at Leominster, Shropshire for a couple of hours to take care of my accumulated dirty clothes. Of course, when finished, the heavens opened, soaking my fresh laundry and me.

Immediately after drying out from this shower, the rain came again. To ward off the misery, I kept promising myself tea and cakes and finally found a dry and likely spot at Ross on Wye at a park built into the sweep of a granite hill. The tea and cakes worked their regular magic but the not very bright waitress could not help with directions and had to enlist the help of a visiting Italian!

The route then went from Ross into the Forest of Dean offering all sorts of side-trip attractions such as Goodrich Castle and Symonds Yat but I didn't have the energy for a diversion. Heading to Coleford, some 18 km beyond Ross on Wye and passing many inviting looking B&B's along the way, I stoically ignored them to achieve my self-imposed goal. Once there, the first B&B had no single room, the next showed a vacancy sign but was full. After that, I found a superb looking place but it was also full. These last people sent me to the Forest Hill Hotel at the far end of the village, near the cinema.

Pretty Woman was showing at the cinema, a film that was just the sort of light-hearted tonic I needed. The hotel was expensive but I was in no mood to keep looking. There was just enough time to clean up quickly, cross the road to a supermarket for some supper snack items and get back to the cinema in time for the first showing.

It was only about 60% full, populated by middle-aged couples and young people. There were about twenty minutes of ads, some of which were cleverly inventive while others were very amateurish. Usually, I would bristle at the delay but tonight this interval before the film prolonged the experience and was strangely relaxing. The audience talked all the way through these ads but was immediately silent when the film started. It was a luxurious experience--a dry soft seat in a warm room after today's cold, wet ride. Back at the Forest Hill, with my snack items, a cup of tea and a book,concluded my day perfectly.

The following day was again wet. I followed the CTC route as far as the Severn Bridge but once across the bridge couldn't find the route again. No route signs or place names matched. The wind and wet made it impossible to check my map, so I crawled under some bushes. With misted glasses, low visibility and blurred images on my damp map, I mistakenly headed south for Olveston instead of east towards Alveston.

Otherwise, I could have avoided the worst of Bristol. It was cold. Rain streamed down my glasses, blocking vision and both the bike and passing traffic splashed me, compounding my general soaking. This initial impression of Bristol made me grateful that Mari and I had chosen, after our wedding, to decline our acceptance at the University of Bristol in favour of the University of Hawaii.

Road signs were ambiguous and infrequent. I stopped a van driver to ask directions and got a lift through the city. It would have been impossible for me to duplicate his route. I was demoralized by the on again--off again rain and decided to cut the day short at Cheddar.

Despite feeling miserable at day's end, the kind van driver and two interesting stops today in Wales before crossing the Bristol Channel helped improve the day's balance. The first was a station on the old Tintern Railway now functioning as a tourist destination. Old railcars are converted to shops and the station is a tearoom. Noisy, excited children doing exploratory searches to complete a school treasure-hunt style quiz energized the scene. I also stopped outside Tintern Abbey, considered one of the finest relics of Britain's monastic age. This is a Cistercian Abbey founded in 1131 and rebuilt in 1288 with a splendidly open setting in a quiet meadow at a bend of the Wye overlooked by wooded hills. It was one of the victims of Henry VIII's campaign of suppression in 1536. Mari and I had visited here with her mother over twenty years ago so I simply absorbed the scene for a few minutes from the perimeter.

Refuge that night was found at the Laurels B&B, a Victorian house with an extensive, pleasant garden and most un-British like interior. Constructed in a pine and stone North American cottage-style, green dominated all surfaces the walls, the carpet and bath fixtures.

The new day was beautifully bright and bracing with strong sunshine and winds. After breakfast, I rode into Cheddar Gorge but did not visit the caves on the principle of avoiding the path beaten by tourists.

This popular destination is heavily developed. The entrance to the gorge was chock-o-block with cafes and gift shops but also had a pleasant garden and a cycle path alongside some small falls.

In the early afternoon, I stopped for an expensive but excellent cream tea at a farm operation that offered dairy, fish and meat products, including sheep's milk and ice cream, bakery goods, spreads and runner bean chutney. A dairy exhibit showed how everything is used from milk to cheese to butter with the whey going to the pigs and a methane unit.

The sunshine and dry conditions made the day glorious, enhancing the tremendous mixture of desolate high moorland above North Molton, Devon with distant finely sculpted fields in shades of gold and green. The road was just a narrow ribbon of tarmac and even though it was so steep that I had to walk--the 'top of the world' isolation, sharp, clear air and absence of civilization's clamour invigorated me.

Grazing sheep and babbling brooks bathed in the watery, weak evening sunshine, improved the visual experience, creating an almost spiritual atmosphere. Emotionally uplifting, yes, but with an underlying tingle of possible danger. The remoteness made me a bit uneasy. Without a mobile, there was no way to summon help if needed and there weren't any people let alone any places to stay. It was after eight p.m. before I found a place--completing my longest daily distance of the entire trip –116 kilometres.

Land's End
I dined last night in the pleasant Nelson Bar of the Union Hotel at Truro, Cornwall. In operation at the time of the defeat of the Armada in 1588, it one time featured both a theatre and a cockfighting pit. Nelson memorabilia filled every nook and cranny; it was warm, quiet and very cosy. I sat immediately under Nelson's bust enjoying a Beef in Guinness pie, chips and salad along with my book.

Breakfast time was shared with a young, newly married man from London who had just moved to Truro to manage a men's clothing store and was staying in the B&B until he could find a house. He broke off our conversation abruptly, nervous and eager to create a good impression by getting to work early. My other breakfast companion was a young woman doing a charity walk for African relief. She took shelter in the B&B after getting soaked in her tent.

I set out towards Penzance with the signs indicating 22 miles (nearly 36 km) from Truro. My actual distance was 50 km, a flagrant misrepresentation! The TIC found me a single room where I ditched my panniers and headed for Land's End, The vegetation became almost tropical with uncommon flowers and succulent leaves. Small stone houses crowd the edge of the hilly, winding and narrow road. In spots, vegetation canopies covered the road and the earth banks at the side rose steeply, sometimes higher than my head.

It began to mist and become cold. I wasn't dressed warmly enough and became concerned about getting back to Penzance soaked and thoroughly chilled but no, I had to press on, this was the final leg of the End to End. Without realizing it, I had chosen the long route – more than twice as long as necessary. Then, finally, there it was-the south western tip of mainland Britain-Land's End: a small theme park with a lifeboat, an old pirate boat to play on, a hotel, restaurant and an exhibition. As it was late in the day, the guard allowed me in without any fee. I went out as far as the rocks allowed, took a few obligatory photos to document my being here and left. It was nearly closing time anyway and very cold.

The return to Penzance was an exhilarating fast run on a different route. Slope made a tremendous difference--over two hours to get to Land's End but only 39 minutes to get back. The gold at the end of this tour's rainbow was a bit tawdry but I've finally cycled the full length of Britain!

The Scillies

Next morning, a cacophony of seagulls immediately above me shattered my slumber at 4.30. My attic room's window in the roof gave them direct access to annoy. Their squawking continued without abatement so I finally give up the fight for sleep to make tea and read.

This landlady was totally organised. She even had me complete a form selecting my breakfast choices and time in advance. Each table in the dining area was numbered to correspond with the bedroom numbers. Without knowing the system, I chose to sit at the correct table. Her portions were just adequate –a two cup pot of tea, two pats of butter, etc. The room showed similar loving care. There was one teabag, two packets of sugar and a single tiny container of milk. Everything possible was labelled with some instruction about its use, energy conservation or times. She talked incessantly about trivia and called everyone 'love' or 'pet' but I don't think she really liked people.

I was booked on a boat to the Scillies, islands to the southwest of Land's End that were former Prime Minister Harold Wilson's favourite holiday spot in the Sixties. Fog, nearly obscuring St Michael's Mount off to the east, delayed departure from the lighthouse pier by twenty minutes. The ship's horn sounded an ominous constant warning and seagulls hovered menacingly alongside at upper deck level. I sat outside, ostensibly reading, but really observing my fellow passengers. One of them was particularly intriguing--an old man in a dilapidated yellow plastic fisherman's hat, red tartan tie, non-coordinated wide tartan jacket, and contrasting waistcoat, eating Mars bars!

The ship called at St. Mary's, one of the several islands in the Scillies, for long enough to have a meal, take a brief hike and acquire souvenirs. Typically, the shops were popular and the immediate first stop for most of the passengers. Lemming like, I was part of this surge until I took hold of myself mentally and reversed direction to see as much of the island as possible in the time allowed. The sun made an appearance, staying in sight long enough to grace my visit to a lovely old church in Hughtown. Its overflowing cemetery is populated with gnarled trees and other vegetation amongst the gravestones. The church building is very small and quite basic with hard primitive benches and no stained glass. In contrast, the baptismal font was adorned with colourful fragrant carnations. I also visited a pottery, the sixteenth century ruins of a fort, and had a quick Cornish pasty lunch on a terrace where birds hopped brazenly around on the tables seeking crumbs.

It was an interesting trip but nothing different enough from the mainland to justify the fare. My sartorially challenged fellow passenger was the highlight. He re-claimed his outside seat for the return and removed his hat, revealing patches of wispy, white hair. His brown trousers were badly creased and their zip crudely re-stitched. His shirt collar was frayed, dirty and undone. He did not interact with anyone, so I assumed that he was not anyone's guest. If his clothing was any guide, the £24 fare would have been a lot for him, although there may have been a seniors' discount. Experiences like this are a big part of the attraction of cycle touring. They may not all be pleasant or desirable but they are memorable!

Lost Railway Ticket

Having completed my End to End objective, I was ready for a change of pace and planned to visit Ann, a friend from Oakville who moved back to England a couple of years ago to look after an aged aunt. She lived near Winchester, a considerable distance and expensive train journey from Penzance. But, I had to travel in that direction anyway to get back to Gatwick Airport. So, I bought a ticket for the following day and went to visit St. Michael's Mount.

This is one of those spots in England, like Lindisfarne, that is accessible by land only when the tide is out. Here the cobbled path revealed by the exiting tide leads to a castle-like building set on a hill with the sea providing a huge moat except at low tide. Originally, St Michael's had been a monastery but was taken over during Cromwell's time and given to one of his aides. Descendants of that family still live here with the financial assistance of the National Trust. Once at the hill, access is up a very steep, cobble stone path through lovely varied, almost jungle-like, vegetation emitting a faintly sweet odour. There are also very tall, wind-swept evergreens, bare apart from the needles and cones clinging tightly to their very tops. Battlements and small cannons hug the base of the castle whose entrance is at least thirty metres above sea level.

Much of the building was refurbished in the late nineteenth century but there is an interesting mix of styles. Most impressive for me was the Monk's refectory that houses a long, oak table with a shimmering patina standing stoutly under arched, timbered ceilings and tiny mullioned windows overlooking the sea.

An interesting exhibition called 'Trail of the Dons' in the former kitchen describes the history of the late sixteenth century war between Spain and England. This is the war that many of us know primarily (if at all) as the one in which Sir Francis Drake defeated the Spanish Armada in 1588. It began well before that and continued for years afterward. Parts of the southwest English coast were invaded and burned by the Spanish. The war's catalyst, as best I recall, was an attack by the Spanish against a renegade English trading ship off the coast of Mexico. The ship was transporting African slaves to the Spanish West Indies against Spanish regulations.

One of the villages burned by the Spanish in 1592 was Mousehole (pronounced Mouzel), where I headed next to find a B&B and some nourishment. In just over an hour, I had settled in an inexpensive B&B and was relaxing in the garden of a nearby cafe with a cream tea and the *Times*. The cafe courtyard overlooks a small semicircular harbour dotted with sailboats and colourful fishing boats bobbing on their ropes. Squawking seagulls stood guard on the surrounding chimney pots. Watery sunshine bathed the entire scene.

Later, after a dinner of smoked mackerel and salad at the Ship Inn, I watched the Queen Mother's 90th birthday celebrations on television with my landlady, Mrs Reynolds. We chatted until midnight about all sorts of things but primarily her anger at the injustice of the EC. Her son is skipper of a fishing vessel that is typically at sea for a week at a time. Every trip requires a visit to the authorities for area assignment and rules that can later be countermanded on radio bulletins that forbid them to take fish from certain areas. 'The other countries don't obey the rules', said Mrs. Reynolds 'and the Cornish dairy farmers have been ruined by an EC quota system that forces them to produce below capacity, thus lowering farm values. There hasn't been any compensation', she complained.

Next morning, back at Penzance, about an hour before I was to board the train for Winchester, I couldn't find my previously purchased ticket. The railway people made sympathetic noises but even my charge card receipt didn't persuade them to issue a replacement ticket as I could have sold my ticket or anyone finding it could use it.

Racking my brain for what did I do, where did I go after buying that ticket, I remembered negotiating some traveller's cheques at the bank. So, I rushed there to explain my problem—this time getting a sympathetic, helpful teller. Yes, they recalled finding the ticket and setting it aside—but where? The young man, Julian, searched drawers, checked all the counter's nooks and crannies and ran upstairs to Accounts to no avail. It was now just 25 minutes to train time and Julian was about as frantic as I was. Fortunately, it was early enough in the day that yesterday's rubbish was still waiting collection and after about eight more minutes Julian emerged from the cellar proudly brandishing the now badly rumpled ticket.

Britain isn't known for good customer service. When my family lived in Hertfordshire, it was as if 'the customer is always wrong.' It took us years after moving back to North America to overcome the automatic thought that returning anything or making any kind of a complaint to a retail shop or a service provider would be unpleasant. Today, Julian proved that service is definitely improving but as the next part of my story clearly shows, the improvement is spotty.

I got back to the station with about 10 minutes to spare and asked if it was necessary to have a cycle reservation. 'Donnow—please see enquiries.' With time evaporating, I joined another queue only to be told that they did not know either. At least this clerk provided a useful suggestion, 'why don't you take the following train –that definitely doesn't need a reservation so you can save the three pound reservation fee.' This appealed to my Scots heritage and as time allowed no alternative, I went back into town and used my new found hour to book a B&B ahead for Winchester.

On the way back to the station I spied three cycles set up for touring. Their owners, a Swedish man, his daughter and son, emerged from an ice cream shop as I was examining their bikes. They were on a father's holiday with the kids. He told me that he completed the End to End in 9 ½ days after his wife threw him out! Maybe she was chasing him but I did not press for details nor admit to taking ten days longer.

Winchester

My pre-booked B&B was very close to the station in an elite residential area as the last house on a dead-end street. The proprietors were definitely upscale from my experiences to date but being British, they provided a welcoming pot of tea.

The next morning, a Friday, breakfast is to be early so that Mrs Simms can get her daughters off to school. They are a very active family with four girls—all blondes—involved in tennis, swimming, horses, music and ballet. The mother is run ragged.

She left with the girls before I was ready to go. I needed time to organize myself and sort out my 'best clothes' for meeting with Ann later. Mrs Simms lent me her iron for my trousers, gave me a key to the house and left a camera and other valuables lying about--amazing trust. She knew virtually nothing about me and had not yet asked for payment!

My objective for the first part of the day was to find the lovely villages where Mari and I cycled four years ago. As ever, my directional memory was faulty and those specific villages proved elusive but beauty in this part of England is so prolific it didn't matter. It was a great day anyway. At Alresford's Globe pub, I had a Paté Ploughman in a garden that slopes down to a lake and marsh studded with ducks and swans. The sun was shining, it was warm—probably the best weather of the trip so far. The ducks were very bold—begging like dogs at your feet. A large sign advised that if Duncan the swan takes your food, please complain to Phil and Betty at Buck House. (All swans in Britain belong to the Queen.)

Later, Ann collected me from my B&B for dinner at her caravan home in Alresford and then treated me to an old time music hall performance--a new experience that I enjoyed very much. The compere provided articulate, skilful commentary and abuse for a variety of singers, actors and other performers engaging the enthusiastic audience at every turn. The costumes, acts and smoky atmosphere seemed historically authentic. I was recognized as the member of the audience who had travelled the farthest to be there.

On Saturday morning, I felt rough. Friday's pint of ale, two gin and tonics at dinner and smoke inhalation combined to create a stuffy nose and throbbing sinus headache. Nevertheless, I went down for breakfast at 7.45 since no different time for Saturday was set. Mrs Simms was all ready for me despite a dinner party that lasted until 2 am! The girls are off to tennis lessons this morning.

My old faithful, Sinutab, came to the rescue, restoring me to near normality. So, I roamed Winchester, revisiting the lovely riverbank walk, Winchester College and the Cathedral. An Evensong is scheduled tonight that I think Ann might enjoy. So I rang her at the home of a man, Bert, that she 'does for' as a housekeeper on Saturdays, to see if she could join me. She could and invited to share lunch with them at his home.

Bert proved to be a likeable chap, a professional architect, and currently single but with obvious hopes to instal Ann in his home on a more intimate basis. (I am pleased to report that Ann resisted his blandishments, returned to Canada and remains a close friend.) Bert's home, at least 300 years old, sits on a slope down to the river. He gave me a tour of the house and property, pointing out restored and added bits while Ann worked on lunch. Our conversation was easy, interesting and fun. We did not finish until 3.30!

Later, Ann and I attended Evensong. This is an Anglican service that I enjoy very much and try to attend whenever I am in England, although I am not particularly religious. It is rare to find Evensong in North America. The service consists primarily of hymns sung by the choir, interspersed with a few readings from scripture. It is an opportunity to close your eyes and simply absorb the soul enriching sounds in an atmosphere of peace and inspiring architecture. English choirs are generally very good and those at the main cathedrals are superb.

Afterwards, a short walk from the Cathedral took us to the pedestrian precinct and the Tudor façade restaurant God Bagot where we had an excellent light meal of Welsh rarebit washed down with a celebratory Scotch and ginger. Afterwards we rushed to the nearby but nearly hidden tiny St. Lawrence Church. This is just off the pedestrian precinct close to the statue and arch on the precinct that functions as the gathering place for dissidents, sort of a Speakers' Corner in Winchester. Earlier in the day as I passed by, people were collecting signatures against the poll tax. This tax was an interesting but ultimately unsuccessful Margaret Thatcher idea. It taxed every citizen over 18 equally for the municipal services on the premise that everyone had equal access and benefit. This tax replaced property rates (taxes) and had to be paid to retain the right to vote. I thought the plan made considerable sense but it was wildly unpopular and did not last long. (The rich should pay more for everything!)

I digress; Ann and I were headed for a piano recital at the St. Lawrence Church. The 17 year-old pianist, thin as a rake with wiry, long and totally undisciplined hair, played very well despite having only taken up piano two years ago! Unfortunately he had yet to develop any stage presence and showed no sign of enjoying the playing or the audience's appreciation. We finished our evening at 'Waffle On', a newish bright café specializing in waffles.

Blue Idol

The trip to Gatwick, after Winchester, for the homeward journey, included an overnight at a Quaker B&B, the Blue Idol, which I found purely by good luck. No one was at home when I stopped at the first B&B, the second, although set in lovely grounds, reeked of pig manure and only had a double room. Nevertheless, the landlady rang round finding a single at the Blue Idol, so named because the late 16th century building had been idle for many years and was painted blue.

There, the proprietors accepted me reluctantly; they had hoped for a quiet night without guests, to the point of putting out their 'no vacancy' sign. Hoping to make my presence less objectionable, I did not ask my host to change the television channel from his football match to my preferred programme. Instead I sat down and fell heavily through one of their lounge chairs, disrupting his match anyway. You could see he struggled mightily to avoid being rude.

My room was called the George Fox after the famous Quaker pioneer. A wing of the building houses a small Quaker meeting room where

William Penn worshipped. His home, where he drafted the Pennsylvania constitution, is only about seven kilometres away. Like the other Quaker B&B I experienced, breakfast included my favourite grapefruit segments. I had a healthy helping of them and of the muesli before consuming an egg, perhaps a quarter pound of bacon together with brown toast and four cups of tea.

The new day was beautifully sunny as I set off eastward towards Haywards Heath. This is a much more prosperous part of England. I saw a number of Elizabethan homes and some fantastic gardens. At Worthy, several new homes were under construction in small estates. These were all detached but probably less than 1600 square feet in size with perhaps an eighth of an acre lots. Compared with similar homes in estate agents' listings, their prices would be about £160,000.

About five kilometres from Horley, I began thinking that it was a shame that so far there had been no opportunity to test the cycle repair skills that Thomas, one of my son's friends, had patiently imparted before my departure. A puncture would just round out this adventure. Almost immediately, the back wheel felt odd but the road surface was pocked so I assumed that was the cause.

Not so. I got my puncture! Eagerly pulling off the road onto a convenient open bit of parkland, I unloaded everything, removed the rear wheel, and replaced the tube quite competently only to discover that my pump was broken!

Tucking the remains of the bike and other gear under some handy bushes, I set off, rear wheel in hand, in search of a petrol station with an air pump. Half an hour later, I found one and inflated the tyre to the proper pressure. The station's washroom was equipped with a supply of grease removing compound that worked very well and made me feel like a real mechanic--another star for my competency collection!

This sense was eroded a bit by some difficulty in refitting the wheel and properly engaging the chain and gears but I was still pleased that this final bit of the process took only fifteen minutes. So, I made it to the Parson's Pig Pub with two minutes to spare before they stopped taking lunch orders. The cook probably swore at this last minute order but if so, I didn't hear and enjoyed a beef and horseradish sandwich and a lager in the garden.

This pub's ambiance matches the elevated status of its residential neighbours housing an airy, big room off the bar. I would have loved to spend a prolonged session with lager and book but was eager to get to Horley where I might get a train to possibly see some friends on my next to last night.

This side trip worked. My friends were 'happy' to feed me and put me up for the night. We sat up until almost midnight, showing pictures and exchanging family stories. Next morning I returned to Horley, the closest village to Gatwick Airport.

A Long Night

The tour is at an end. It is the afternoon before my flight home tomorrow morning. The airline advised me to remove the pedals, deflate the tyres and turn the handlebars sideways—no carton was necessary. That was good news, as my carton was discarded over three weeks ago in Inverness. Having established that, I searched for a B&B. The cheapest single available was more than I paid anywhere on the trip and included only a continental breakfast not a full English! The south of Britain has many more facilities than the North and Midlands but the prices are significantly higher and the service is often offhand and uninterested.

With such bleak prospects, I decided to sit up in the airport overnight. I stored my bike and bags at the railway station left luggage and toured the village. Before leaving, I sent the Cycle Touring Club (CTC) my page of postmarks collected at post offices along the route proving I had made the journey. This had been embarrassing to explain to each of the post offices. Many were suspicious and acquiesced only grudgingly.

Returning to the railway station to claim my bike, I caught the left luggage attendant sneaking away a full 25 minutes early--a minute or two later could have spelt disaster for me. After bringing my journal up to date I cycled over to the Curry Garden for a nostalgic meal.

Mari and I dined here twice in 1986. Just recently it was reported that many Indian restaurants in Britain use up to four times the healthy level of food colourings in their meals. This is because the British consumer apparently considers that the brighter the colour, the spicier the food. My Tandoori chicken was fiery red.

Later, at the airport, the wisdom of my decision to sit up all night paled. Time dragged, the cycle has been long prepared, I was bored with my book and could nap only briefly. Finally a queue was formed for the flight but there was another long wait to actually board. Airline travel has certainly lost any glamour it ever had. This was a charter flight with cramped seating and indifferent service but I have had a memorable trip, achieved a long held dream, and become fitter. It is an experience well worth repeating.

Haven from rainstorm near Christmas Common, Oxford

Breton Bike Cycle at canalside cafe, Bon Repos, Brittany

PEAKS, LAKES & DALES TOUR

BRITAIN

PEAKS, LAKES & DALES TOUR

It seems ages since my End to End tour five years ago. Two years later Mari and I discovered the allure of York and fell in love with the Dales of James Herriot fame. Ever since, I longed to explore them in greater detail. Thus the Yorkshire Dales became the foundation of my second solo journey. Adding the nearby Peak District of Derbyshire and the Lake District in memory of long-ago family holidays, both real and aborted—achieved a combination of challenge and nostalgia.

The Route

The route moves south from Manchester into Derbyshire, west into Cumbria, crunching up through much of the rugged Lake District countryside to enter Yorkshire at its south west corner to explore the Dales, York and the North York Moors.

Upgrading My Transport

Taking advantage of a promotion, I upgraded from a charter flight to British Airways. The flight service and accommodation were welcome improvements but choosing BA meant flying first to Heathrow and transferring to Manchester. My bike missed the luggage transfer from the first flight to Manchester, delaying my start by two hours.

This was a new, better, bike, twice the cost of my ten-year old $500 Sakai, but custom sized for me. I had wrapped all the tubes, forks and chain stays with sponge-like pipe lagging but that and the airline provided thick flexible vinyl sack was inadequate protection. The handling had obviously been rough--the brakes were out of alignment and I had a puncture! (Six weeks later, back at home, the repair shop replacing a wheel bent on the return flight found that the frame itself was badly torqued. British Airways, having earlier agreed to pay for the bent wheel, considered its liability honoured.)

Choosing a vacant, private corner of the airport, I re-assembled the bike and was packed, ready to go by 2.45 pm. Airport and residential areas disappeared quickly; the countryside became pastoral as it moved into a small finger of Cheshire where it touches the western edge of the Peak District National Park. The now challenging terrain has climbs so steep that it was all I could do to continue pedalling.

The descents almost overpowered my brakes.   At the junction of Penny and Bull Hill Lanes, I found that the front wheel was bent so that the brake pads did not grab the wheel rim evenly—nothing to do but be more cautious.

This tough terrain continued past the Cat and Fiddle pub then dropped sharply down to Buxton. Relying mainly on the rear brakes, I safely reached Buxton at the bottom but still one of the highest English towns at 307 metres. It is a spa town that owes its fame to the fifth Duke of Devonshire who built the town's beautiful Georgian Crescent to rival fashionable Bath.

On the way down, one pannier fell off and the computer stopped registering speed or distance. Even with all these problems, the 40 km run to Buxton only took three hours. B&B's were plentiful and I was soon installed.

Ilam--My First Hostel

Next morning, I breakfasted alone at a separate table earwigging a group of middle-aged British tourists travelling together.   Their conversation was a hushed tone of trivia that one often comes across in Britain.   You strain to hear the secrets being discussed only to learn what the chiropodist said about Aunt Edith's big toe.

After breakfast, a Buxton cycle shop mended the inflight damage and had me back on the road within half an hour. The repair was a simple (to write, not to do) matter of tightening and loosening some of the spokes so that the front wheel ran true again, making the brakes more effective. Heading south on the B5053 towards Ilam Hostel, the road ran through Peak Park, along rocky outcroppings, sheep, cattle and stone fences bordering lovely green nibble-mown pastures.

At the hostel, thanks to a last minute cancelation, I got the final male bed. Ilam is an impressive place set amidst green peaks and alongside a small river. The hostel building had been a private home but was given by its flour magnate owner to the National Trust on the condition that it be maintained as a Youth Hostel. At the time of his gift in 1934, Ilam was the largest hostel in Britain. The bunk beds look out of place amongst elegant wainscoting, a fireplace and paintings in gilded frames.

Leaving the panniers behind, I set off for lunch and some leisurely riding. The Dog and Pheasant, a moor-top pub, provided a tuna stuffed jacket potato and a lager, producing severe lethargy about an hour later. I just had no energy and had to walk a bit to recover. Back on the bike I was rewarded with a super 5 km stretch of downhill back to the hostel. Brave or foolhardy sheep wandered across the road adding an obstacle course to the thrilling descent. Their wise or cowardly brethren surveyed my dodging manoeuvres from the overlooking hills. It is a rugged, green landscape that perfectly matches my rural British stereotype.

Young people swarmed all over the hostel under the lax supervision of a few adult handlers. There was also a group of about 15 black women from a cosmetics firm on a treasure hunt and training course to build morale and firm loyalty. It would be surprising if their course was any less effective than those I used to attend run by expensive consultants at four-star hotels.

Muted bedlam now reigned in the hostel's 'quiet' room. I moved away from my seat to allow a new arrival to sit with his young friends but he protested, 'no, stay—I insist.' Perhaps as old as eight, there was no doubt about his class background!

California in Derbyshire

Next morning I walked along the river at nearby Dovedale, an acclaimed beauty spot where craggy hills rise directly from the riverbed, somewhat reminiscent of Switzerland. Cycling south, I stopped at Sudbury to get a postcard for our daughter Allison, then newsreader for the local television station in Sudbury, Ontario. Earlier in the year I was proud to witness her evening broadcast from the studio. Her jacketed professional appearance belied the jeans below the news desk. She selects the news to be reported from the various wire service releases, determines what and how much to say about each story and establishes the story order. The few minutes behind the scene before broadcast were hectic, making last minute changes and loading the monitor that she would read from. She told me that the papers that sit on newsreaders' desks are primarily for show and in case of monitor failure.

My somewhat circular route brought me north into Ashbourne where I booked in at the Old Vault pub, a black and white Elizabethan, on the market square. The pub had a warmer ambience than many and wasn't smoky so I stayed there for dinner. This proved to be an excellent choice and breakfast was equally pleasant--good quality and quantity. Later I learned that the proprietors have been in business only ten weeks. Previously they took care of an 18,000 square foot home in California. I am certain that their time in California raised the quality of food and service.

Bakewell Tarts and Well Dressing

Today, I am booked in at a B&B in Bakewell and hope to reacquaint myself with Bakewell tarts (the pastry variety—having no experience with any other!) Bakewell is only 29 km north of Ashbourne, so I took advantage of the light cycling day to explore the town. My first find was a shop that specializes in tools for real artisans, such as elegant wooden planes. It is good to know that the old skills and their tools still survive.

At Bakewell I was disappointed with my tart from the shop advertising 'the original Bakewell pudding'—possibly because they focused on tourists rather than purists. According to the story (again, perhaps, modified for the benefit of tourists) the pudding (tart) was the result of an accident in the Rutland Arms at Bakewell when a junior cook poured the egg mixture over the strawberry jam instead of in the pastry batter—creating its unusual appearance and the distinctive short pastry.

Next stop was Ashford in the Water where well dressings were on display. These dressings are rooted in pagan well worship but are now a Christian custom. The dressing is a design sculpted in clay into which flower petals are pressed to provide colour. The first well was set in a garden wall; others were spotted round the town. I found four of the advertised nine: two of war remembrance, one of working dogs, and the biggest and most impressive dedicated to the 'land girls' that worked the farms during wartime.

My B&B wasn't really in Bakewell but at nearby Monsal Head, across the road from a magnificent river valley view. My landlady recommended a pub in Little Longstone for dinner. I arrived early, waiting on a nearby bench until opening time. By then there was a queue to get in! A group of six at the pub recognized having seen me earlier at one of the dressed wells and invited me to join them. The food was good and we had a pleasant conversation.

Revisiting Ken Mills

After a train journey to visit friends in Wigan, near Manchester, I continued north to Penrith by train, hoping to see Ken Mills at Page Hall. I had stayed there on the End-to-End tour but the Tourist Information Centre people told me that he had since closed the B&B. I booked with another B&B but decided to drop in and see if Ken was home. He was and invited me to stay for dinner! Ken's politics and mine conflict so the dinner conversation was spirited but respectful. That is a rare experience for me; I generally find that when people disagree with you they also think less of you for your contrary opinions. Ken travelled to Canada last year by freighter, carrying only a rucksack and a book by the Canadian author and naturalist, Farley Mowat. Ken is now overseeing a reforestation project for a Buddhist group on an island in the Clyde--trying to ensure real reforestation—replacing the types of trees that populated the forests 1000 years ago. Ken selects and grows the seeds himself.

Appleby Horse Fair

Sequencing for this year's trip and my return to Penrith is, in large part, based on the timing of the Appleby Horse Fair in mid-June that one of Ken's guests told me about in 1990. Appleby is an easy hour's ride away from Penrith on the A66.

What a mess! The road leading into Appleby was an overflowing rubbish bin with the litter continuing on the hill where the travellers' (gypsies') caravans were parked. In the town, even the river was littered. Earlier in the week a horse was driven into the river for the traditional buggy wash ceremony only to be dragged under and drowned when its buggy fell into deep water.

Back at the hill, I wandered round the stalls, many typical of any other sort of fair catering to the mass tourist trade and with no particular connection to travellers. It was obvious where British television drama finds their rural and period characters--people like that were everywhere; ruddy-faced farm folk and some really villainous looking types. Others tried to look the part of the wealthy horsey set. However, very little evoked any kind of a gypsy atmosphere. Traditional clothing and music were missing and the colourful horse drawn wagons were scarce.

While watching a farrier shoeing a horse, I talked with a traveller who claimed that the British government treats travellers much as North Americans treated their indigenous peoples by forcing them on to reservations (caravan parks). He encouraged me to go see the last of the horse selling.

This was staged on a narrow, straight stretch of tarmac at the edge of the hill where the horses, drawing their buggies, were driven at top speed back and forth, racing each other to impress potential buyers. A light rain wet the pavement. Once or twice a horse slipped and nearly fell. Watching from the corner of a traveller's wagon, I observed a sales transaction conducted by a complex series of hand slaps to negotiate the price; the agreed price had a special slap. Judging from the wad of notes pulled out of a shirt pocket, the price was at least £1500 (C$3600)! I also overheard part of a conversation about someone being cheated of twice that amount.

Dufton Hostel-Something Different

Despite providing some interesting experiences, my anticipated gypsy music, dancing and colourful wagons didn't materialize, The fair started earlier this June than usual; so perhaps I came too late. I left at about four to book in at the nearby Dufton hostel along the Sea-to-Sea hiking track. It was a short but lovely ride—the perfectly pastoral scenery blended rugged rock outcroppings with lush, green, manicured-looking paddocks ringed by distant rising hills.

Dufton hostel attracted a different clientele than Ilam. Here, most of the members, apart from a photographer/artist travelling by motorbike were male adults walking the Pennine Way. Most interesting of the lot, he was a former sailor with tattoos over his entire upper body (the intimacy of hostel living offers aspects other accommodation rarely provides).

Our discussion was philosophical, much like mine with Ken at Page Hall. He had a definite antiestablishment bias and didn't believe that profit should be a component of any essential service such as water, gas or education (Margaret Thatcher had privatized the utilities). I was impressed; he is a gentle man whose intelligence, behaviour and interests totally contradicted my generally negative stereotype of tattooed motorbike riders.

The other hostel members were friendly enough but a bit rough round the edges. Here, members are responsible for tidying up before departure. One of the dimmer lights displayed his general unfamiliarity with housekeeping by standing on the dining tables in his hiking boots to sweep off the crumbs with a full size broom.

Next morning while packing up and lubricating the bike, I met two mountain cyclists doing the Sea-to-Sea route that cuts west to east across the country using bridle paths. One of them was concerned that my tyres were about to give out. He has never seen 'slicks' –a tyre that has a totally smooth centre surface bordered by a rugged tread. This tyre almost looks as if the centre tread has been worn off but this design reduces friction on regular roads while providing grip on rougher terrain.

Keswick and Beatrix Potter

Heading west from Dufton for the Lake District, I reached Pooley Bridge, at the head of beautiful Ullswater and just inside the District, about two hours ride from Dufton. There, at a bend in the road, was a perfect-looking tearoom with waterside tables. The prices and food quality shouted tourist trap, but I couldn't resist taking advantage of the setting and glorious sunshine to enjoy a leisurely lunch with my book.

A few kilometres beyond Pooley Bridge, was Aira Force, a National Trust waterfall property, force being the local term for waterfall. Because the car park did not seem secure, I picked my way up the hill, lugging my loaded bike over tree roots, through ferns, past jutting rocks in the rushing brook beds along the narrow, Hobbit-like forest trail until suddenly, Aira Force roared forth from beneath an arched stone bridge. Hikers on the bridge revealed that there was an easier way to see the waterfall.

Back on the road again, huge rhododendrons created a forest of flowers along some stretches east of Keswick. Other stretches expanded the sensory delights with birdcalls, sheep, and stonewalls, overlaid with a pungent aroma of maturing manure. This was reality at its best! Keswick, ringed with soft green mountains, was immediately impressive.

Despite my general aversion to being part of the tourist crowd, I chose to visit the Beatrix Potter exhibit there. This includes a 16-minute film about her life with Dame Judi Dench playing the part of Beatrix. In that short space of time we learned how she started writing, got published and used the proceeds to buy and keep land from development. The man who eventually founded the National Trust introduced Beatrix, then aged 16, to land conservation.

She ran Herdwick sheep, a small but sturdy breed that has been in Cumbria for about 400 years, on her property, no doubt contributing to their survival as a species. The rest of the exhibit was mainly devoted to storyboards that elaborated on various aspects of the film.

Keswick was so appealing that I entertained the idea of proposing it to Mari as our retirement home. Later that morning in one of my regular bookshop prowls, I learned that Keswick's summer time average temperature of 15 degrees Celsius accompanies an annual rainfall average of 145 centimetres. This will never sell to a woman brought up in the dry heat of Oklahoma! The book that reveals this disappointing information is Hunter Davies' *A Walk Around the Lakes*, an otherwise delightful saga of a year he spent doing just that.

Cockermouth Hostel

My walking tour of Keswick complete, I began a B road clockwise route to Cockermouth via the Honister Pass between Borrowdale and Buttermere. This runs alongside the eastern shore of Derwentwater on the B 5289 and is benign until the Honister Pass -- the most severe climb yet. Cycling was impossible; each turn of the crank was agony--the odometer did not even register! Walking was faster.

Despite this, the scenery was perfect with gurgling, rushing brooks, rocks, mountain sheep and a glorious, almost total, absence of man's presence. A car, pulled off the road, its occupants quietly soaking up nature's beauty, was the only example of human habitation.

Honister peaks at 754 metres then falls away about 300 metres to Buttermere where I stopped for a couple mugs of tea and a cheese sandwich at an outside picnic table. Soon the scene was like our bird feeder at home. Without invitation or fear, several birds hopped about on the table hoping for a titbit.

Reaching Cockermouth too early to quit for the day, I continued cycling in the area for another couple of hours delaying my arrival at the hostel until 6.45. This hostel is a 300-year-old former corn mill that sits right on the river at the bottom of a steep, rough track.

It was almost too late to book for the evening meal but since only two people were staying tonight, the warden agreed to serve me as well. The other man and I talked about politics and the comparative beauty of the Peaks, the Dales and Lakeland. He had just completed a week of walking in those areas. Last month he did the same in Crete and claimed that a swim in the Mediterranean is the perfect way to finish off a day's walk. He considered that Margaret Thatcher has changed the country's ideas about work for the better and that this will have lasting benefit. He also believes that she has greatly improved the professionalism of the police and the army. It was refreshing to hear something positive about her after my decidedly left of centre recent conversations.

Experiences like this dinner and the peaceful isolation are the real joys of solitary travel. I find that conversational opportunities are greater for a person on their own and all the choices can be totally your own, not a compromise with others' wishes. The downside is that solitary travel can also be lonely and limiting if you aren't naturally adventurous or curious.

As I was the only person at breakfast, I talked to Martin, the warden, about his job. He gets his afternoons and two full days off plus his board and room and a net £100 per week. During the four months of winter that the hostel is closed he has no home or pay but is free to do as he wishes. Last year, he and his girlfriend spent three months in Nepal financed by his savings.

Joss Naylor--Fell Runner

On Martin's recommendation, I headed south for Wast Water, one of the least visited lakes because there is only one-way in. Isolated and empty, dramatic and mysterious, Wast Water is consequently a bit unsettling. The sole road runs along the west side of the lake eventually ending at a hotel. Two peaks stand guard on opposite sides of the lake: Seatallan at 688 metres and Scafell Pike at 977 metres. Wast Water is perhaps best known for one of its inhabitants, Joss Naylor, a sheep farmer who holds many world records as a fell runner. Hunter Davies, whose book on Lakeland was mentioned earlier, has this to say about Naylor:

'Joss Naylor is known for doing something which requires that much admired quality, hard graft. He runs hard and he works even harder, combining a tough life as a sheep farmer on the high fells where it's surprising anything can live, with running up and down peaks or combinations of peaks, sometimes all day and all night, depending on the particular madness of the race he is running. Fell running is a sport so easy to admire. You can see the peaks. You know how hard it is to walk up them. So imagine tearing up—and down—seventy-two of them in twenty-four hours, just for the fun of it. World-class marathon runners have failed to beat Joss, not aware of the variety of terrain which has to be covered, the complexity of pacing yourself, of knowing how to run over swamp and rocks, how to avoid hidden peaty holes and leap over bracken, what sorts of grass and moss to trust. It's not just long-distance running—it's long-distance, obstacle running.' (1)

Walking the Tough Passes

My hostel for the night is south east of Wast Water at Boot, east of Eskdale and close to the famous Hard Knott and Wrynose Passes.

Hard Knott appeared quickly the next morning and proved even tougher than Honister. Climbs like this with grades of 1 in 4 are not uncommon in Lakeland. My four full panniers were an anchor. When they dragged my speed down to 6 km an hour, I got off and pushed as the lack of momentum made me wobble. Coping with the slope of the road stretched me out at roughly a 45 degree angle resulting in an even slower speed.

The strain of this uphill climb was endurable because I had anticipated and accepted it, counting on the exhilarating downhill to come. The weather was cool and breezy but I was sweating and pausing every so often to cool off, look back and marvel at the climb from the valley and the sheer magnificence of this scenery.

This particular Sunday afternoon, the hills roared with a rally of colourful, darting Minis buzzing up, down and round the hairpin bends like angry wasps. Then, at the peak, one of the Minis went off the road. No one was hurt but I was suddenly alert to the risk of missing a bend on the downhill run. This risk became immediately clear as even on the straight bits, both brakes had to be on full strength to have any effect on my speed. Going round sharp bends at speed caused the heavily weighted rear of the cycle to swing out dangerously close to the edge of this very narrow road; I grudgingly gave up on an exciting downhill experience, dismounted and walked down. At the bottom, a flat stretch with impressive brooks and rocks surrounded by majestic hills permitted a short ride to looming Wrynose. Soon I was pushing again. This climb was slightly shorter than the 1.5 km of Hard Knott but the descent required walking also.

Later, in Ambleside, I booked in at the hotel-like hostel and went looking for a phone for my weekly call home. We picked 3 p.m. British time to be early enough in the Canadian day to catch Mari before she got away for the day's activities.

These calls usually frustrated me, as I hadn't discovered prepaid phone cards and had to involve both British and Canadian operators to get through. While using the public telephone in the anteroom of the Queen's Head pub, someone kept interrupting by opening the bar door to see if the phone was free. Thinking there might be some emergency, I finally ended our conversation and surrendered the phone. The impatient person's call was very brief. He was a tipsy, old, and somewhat shabby church organist who came to the pub straight from his Sunday duties and now wanted his wife to fetch him home. He explained that 'Being righteous works up a thirst.' It would have been interesting to listen in on the going home conversation.

Consistent with this 'religious' experience, I lunched on the patio of the Priest's Hole, in a spot where I could keep an eye on the cycle while eating. During lunch a passerby asked me about my bar-end shifters, as he was having a cycle built for him. These shifters are positioned at the end of the handlebars and were designed for touring cycles so that the gears can be changed without removing your hands from the bars. Today, the shifters are often incorporated into the brake levers on higher end bikes but adjustments require greater mechanical skill than I possess.

Wordsworth, Kendal and Kirkby Lonsdale
After lunch I went north for Grasmere Village and Dove Cottage, Mecca for Wordsworth devotees. The village was streaming with tourists, particularly Japanese. If you see Japanese, you know that you are on the beaten track. I joined the throng queuing for the Cottage, returning later to the hostel on country lanes west of Grasmere overlooking Lake Windermere.

The cycling was glorious with parts of the lanes virtual tunnels of rhododendrons. Back at Ambleside hostel I was assigned to room 217 and given a key! A hostel room key was a new experience; for a brief moment, I thought the room might be private but no, it was only semi-private–six bunks! Mealtime was surprising also, four main course choices and five sweets.

A brief side trip took me to nearby Hawkshead and a cottage where Wordsworth lived while attending the small school (circa 1585). Outside, a gigantic yellow and pink rose bush emitted a sweet natural fragrance. Whitewashed cottages and tiny alleys grace the village.

Then after a night at Kendal's hostel, near the eastern edge of Lakeland, I moved on to Kirkby Lonsdale, a spot that appealed greatly during the End-to-End. It was close enough to permit a leisurely morning looking round Kendal. I visited some of the shops and bought my lunch from Marks & Spencer's tremendous selection of sandwiches. The variety they offer includes all the old standards but much more that reflects the relatively high proportion of British that are vegetarians. My choice that day was indicative: carrot and hummus on sunflower honey bread. This, together with a litre of freshly squeezed orange juice made a perfect, healthy lunch.

While in Kendal, a butcher passed me in the street carrying an apparently live but very placid pig over his shoulder. The pig's pink tongue hung out prominently. Then I noticed that the pig was longitudinally sliced with the cut facing away from me.

A quick eighteen kilometres along the A65 brought me to the Tourist Information Centre in Kirkby Lonsdale where I found a 40 km cycle circular route map. While on this route, just before reaching Sedbergh, Yorkshire, a gnarled old man driving a small horse cart approached me on the opposite side of the road. I called out a friendly 'Good Afternoon' while passing. My greeting was obviously unexpected and startled him but he tugged his flat cloth cap, fixed his crossed eyes on me croaking out 'How Do.'

Sedbergh, the main western gateway to the Yorkshire Dales, was the turning point of the TIC circular route. The town has strong Quaker associations with the oldest Friends' Meeting House in the north of England just two miles away at Brigflatts. Built in 1675, it retains many original furnishings in an atmosphere of calm, cool tranquillity.

Later, back at Kirkby Lonsdale, Mrs. Green, my Courtyard B&B landlady, offered tea and home-baked pastries in an elegant sitting room. I couldn't refuse her hospitality; after all, I tour for teacakes! Her home is very elegant. It is a solid, spacious home built in 1811 as a temporary accommodation for its owner who was having a mansion built nearby. The main door to the house is on the side behind an impressive person-high gate. The entrance hall features a stone floor and stairs bounded by persimmon walls.

After dinner at the Sun, I walked behind St Mary's Church to see the River Lune view, painted by Turner and described by John Ruskin as one of the finest in the country. However, given Ruskin's horrified reaction to the sight of his naked bride on their wedding night, perhaps his vision should be questioned. The marriage was never consummated!(2) The river makes a horseshoe bend here encircling a cow-studded emerald pasture. A stonewall border and distant mountains complete the scene. It must have been much the same when Ruskin was here.

Next morning, I returned to St. Mary's to see the interior of the church. It is very simple without much decoration. Some ladies were busy installing new seat cushions. A group of touring school children were being guided by a lovely older woman who very warmly and capably told them about the building, its current Norman architecture and its Saxon past. I am sure it was as obvious to the children as it was to me that she loves the church and telling people about it.

On the road out of Kirkby Lonsdale, I passed Devil's Bridge, a popular tourist spot here, already besieged by coach tourists stopping for their early morning buns and mugs of tea. The bridge is thought to be thirteenth century. A huge pool beneath it is full of salmon and a favourite spot for aqualung divers. There is a lovely walk from the bridge along a footpath following the River Lune for about a kilometre leading to stone steps up to St. Mary's.

Heading north east towards Dentdale, the cycling became superb—a narrow road, little traffic, crisp air, bright with sunshine and redolent with country smells. Sun shining on scudding clouds made moving mosaics of various greens on the distant hills.

Farmer Sedgewick and the Japanese Cyclist

Dent, with its cobbled main street, is on the little River Dee. There is a stone block monument to Alan Sedgewick, an early nineteenth century geologist and MP. Once a knitting centre, posted historical information claimed some of the Dent knitters worked so fast that they had to stop from time to time to cool their red-hot needles. Dent's railway station, on the Carlisle to Settle line, is the highest in the country.

Continuing past Dent, I went the wrong way and stopped to ask directions of an alert, old farmer standing by a stone wall, keeping a close eye on his nephew cutting hay with a tractor. The farmer told me that he was 77 and his family (the Sedgewicks) had lived in this area for about 1000 years but recently when some relations sold out to the rest of the family there was no legal evidence of ownership. Nevertheless, he observed bitterly, the local council continue to charge him property rates. He broke off our conversation abruptly after a few minutes saying 'its my turn on the tractor.'

Following farmer Sedgewick's directions, I was soon heading south on the B6255 going downhill amidst broad, magnificent vistas. My speed, at times exceeding 50 km per hour, made a paradise-completing breeze. Looming in front was Helwith Bridge, a huge railway bridge with multiple, elegant arches that took six years to build. This is on the B6479 near Horton in Ribblesdale.

Several cars were parked on the shoulder. Some of their owners were off hiking the famous Three Peaks; others simply watched the hills from their cars or on folding chairs outside. Walkers love the area for its access to the fells. Pen-y-ghent (690 metres) overlooks the valley. Two fine potholes, Hunt Pot and Hull Pot, lie beneath the mountain's slopes. The Pennine Way passes between their mouths before descending to Horton and heading north again for Wensleydale.(3)

On the way to have a look at nearby Settle before going to my hostel at Stainforth, I met a cyclist who started the End-to-End last year but had to stop due to bad weather. He is now in training to do the remainder and aiming for over 100 km today. His day's objective is only half completed and he is already very tired. Having just travelled his route, I sympathized with him that the balance of his day's training is up the hills I have just freewheeled down at high speed.

I 'settle' on a park bench at the edge of Settle to read a newspaper and soon nod off. The sunshine and exercise combined to induce a delicious, marginally awake, state in which both the warmth and refreshing breeze could still be consciously enjoyed. Although on this occasion, not much of the paper got read, careful reading of the Times or Telegraph on a fairly regular basis is an important element of these tours. Both papers are well written and offer interesting and useful information about British issues that provides understanding and conversational fodder as well as insight into the British perspective on North American events.

A disdainful ginger cat gracing the entrance to Stainforth hostel completely ignored my conversational gambits. This now run down old estate was vibrating with the sound of a large party of school children.

After dinner, I retired to the member's kitchen, about the only place where one could read or write in reasonable quiet. A Japanese guest, seated at another table, was working assiduously on a laptop computer. We exchanged friendly nods but no conversation. However, next morning I sat with him at breakfast and learned that he is a cyclist working on his fourth year of a round the world trip that began in Alaska. After breakfast, he showed me his cycle, an eighteen-kilogram monster with specially made luggage racks front and rear and a four-litre water bottle.

He carried the huge camera stereotypical of Japanese tourists and uses his laptop to record the location and date of each picture taken (8500 at this point) as well as for writing articles that he sends to a hometown newspaper. His daily route, distance and average daily distance to date are graphed and recorded. He told me that he had already done a several week diversion in Europe so that his arrival in Africa will avoid some bad seasonal weather and expects to be on the road for another two years. He is anything but a stereotype—Japanese or otherwise.

More Dales and the Grange

Today's journey took me to Ingleton, where I turned north towards Hawes and stopped for lunch at the nearby Station Inn--a terrible choice but the only one. I ate outside despite the heat to avoid the racket inside purporting to be music. The fork was filthy and had to be replaced. Some aspects of British life are so contrary to my admittedly dated and somewhat blinkered love-in that it is sometimes hard to believe that the crudities can coexist with the refined loveliness in the same country. They do or I would not still want to cycle here. Perhaps it is a case of intermittent reinforcement being stronger than continuous.

It was hard slog for the first half of the remaining ride to Hawes but the effort was rewarded by a good run down into the village. Hawes is an attractive place with stone buildings, a small waterfall and a generally higgledy-piggledy nature. Many hikers come during the summer; other tourists do the James Herriot tour. The Dales Country Museum offers an interesting chronology of the major changes in people and their way of life in the Dales. There is also a rope maker's shop and a walking trail up to the Force behind a pub.

Pedalling on and into Asygarth at 5.30, I went first to the famous falls to produce a respectable total distance for the day and, without knowing it, cycled right past my B&B host outside in his garden. When I returned, the Jones received me very graciously. They arranged to store my cycle across the road in a farmer's shed. As I walked the bike over, the farmer, an elderly gent with one long white whisker protruding from his chin, was applying a layer of gilt to the top of an iron fence imbedded in stone round his garden.

The day concluded pleasantly with an expensive dinner at the George and Dragon. James, the publican, was a car buff who answered my questions about the Montego, an attractive British Leyland car, which seems to have disappeared. It had. Now the company itself is history.

Next morning, I went back to Asygarth Falls. There are three of them: broad, limestone over shale, stepped falls, not the sheer drops that North Americans tend to associate with the term. The upper falls is visible from the road, the others are reached by a woodland walk on which I saw a scampering squirrel and several strutting grouse.

Later I lunched at the Wheatsheaf Inn (where the Herriots spent their honeymoon in 1941) in Caperby. Caperby is a natural village with animal enclosures mingled between the houses. Remove the cars and a few road signs and you are back in the eighteenth century. The farms fronting the narrow twisty lanes on to Kettlewell maintained Caperby's sense of a distant, simpler past. From Kettlewell it is a clear, gentle slope down towards Skipton.

Dales scenery, a pleasant tea at Threshfield and arrival at Skipton by 5 made it seem a successful day. Then I began to look for my B&B. Its address was Eshton Grange, Gargreave, Skipton. Although this methodology of ordering an address from the most particular to the least particular is also used in North America, Skipton would have probably been left off the address in North America. If it had, I might have gone directly to Gargreave avoiding the six uphill kilometres returning from Skipton. At Gargreave, it took three different stops to get definitive directions to Eshton Grange. Then it was back to Eshton village where I found Eshton House, Eshton Hall, Eshton Lodge and finally the Grange. From my point of view, the address should read The Grange, Eshton, Yorkshire--Gargreave and Skipton simply give an idea of approximately where Eshton is.

Despite the effort to get here, the Grange was worth it; a large farm with lovely views and a big open area in front creating a square between the barn and house. My well-fitted out room overlooked the garden and had a private bath with gold plated fixtures. Getting an evening meal, however, required a 3 km ride back into Gargreave where the Woods Bistro proved to be popular and pleasant restaurant with mediocre cuisine. Tonight it was largely taken over by a big, noisy cricket club party.

Back up the hill at the Grange, the sun, now low in the sky, cast serene shadows that changed shape and colour as the clouds scudded by. I stood at the pasture fence for several silent minutes, soaking up the serenity and the bracing, country-fragrant air before returning to my room.

In the morning, my hostess, Mrs Shelmerdine, said 'Not to worry! I made representations to the authorities for better weather.' She wasn't heard! My breakfast companions arrived late last night from London after a gruelling seven and a half hour, 350 km journey in heavy traffic. They were to spend the weekend at Appleby for a jazz festival and suggested that the terrible litter I saw during the horse fair might be due to a bomb scare. There certainly was a dearth of litter bins to hide bombs. Those that you did see were heavy cast metal with very small cut outs to push the rubbish through. Today, we would almost automatically associate a bomb scare or alert with Muslim terrorists. Then, our immediate reaction was to blame the IRA.

During the day I met a Glaswegian cyclist on the way home from a cycle festival in York. He lived for sixteen years in New Zealand building logging roads. Since returning, he was doing a seven and a half month cycle trip round the country. Shortly after talking with him, I was waved down by a very cheerful cycling postie who wanted to chat. He and his wife would be off to Shropshire the next day for a week's cycle tour. They put the bikes in the postal van and use hostels in a circular tour. Just about the same time a group of cyclists on top class racing cycles and clad in the latest of tight, colourful lycra passed by on a Saturday run. An elderly full white-bearded gentleman riding a three-wheeler completed this sudden concentration of cyclist variety. He gave me one of those peculiarly British nods where the head tilts sideways with a distinctive flip of the chin out to the left. I try to respond in kind but cannot duplicate this motion; I automatically dip my head in greeting. This cluster of cyclists made a cheerful start to the day—other people are just as crazy as I am!

I continued on through appealing country and pleasant villages to Grassington, a popular spot bulging with Saturday shoppers and tourists in the cobble-stoned village centre. A large group of leather-clad, mature motorcyclists milled about, acquiring and consuming intoxicating refreshment while a young woman intoxicated and attracted nearby males in her own way with her very transparent skirt and knickers!

My Fair Lady

The next stop was Pateley Bridge. Its name conjured up comforting images of downhill runs or at least flat river valleys. Initially, the reality was a strong, constant north wind, accompanied by sheets of mist, striking me broadside as it swept across the road. The temperature plunged, robbing my energy. It took all my strength and a severe lean to the left to avoid being blown right--right into any following traffic. This was scary but energizing ----pitting one's strength against the elements in a desolate moorland.

At Pateley Bridge, the Tourist Information Office again came to the rescue, arranging a B&B for me in Harrowgate where there was to be a live performance of My Fair Lady tonight. Theatre is one of my interests so I decided to try to see it. My new landlady, Mrs. Bell, advised the TIC that she had to go out this evening, so could I please arrive by seven. As Harrowgate is just 18 km further, there was time for lunch and a quick look round this pleasant old town on the River Nidd.

After climbing back out of the river valley, it was a downhill run to Harrowgate. I headed straight for the theatre and got a ticket to tonight's performance. Later, at the B&B, Mrs. Bell told me that her engagement for this evening is, most appropriately, bell-ringing practice. During conversation over a pot of tea, she said that, like me, her entire family was on Hardknott Pass last Sunday near the spot where the Mini crashed.

The theatre was a luxurious treat--a marvellous Victorian, lavishly gilded and boasting colourful boxes and balconies. The cast was amateur but several were quite talented and obviously enjoyed themselves. I had forgotten how good the music is. Compared to many modern musicals that are largely group shouts with perhaps one memorable song, all of My Fair Lady's songs linger pleasantly long after the performance is over. I was reminded of a teenage infatuation with Inga, an exotic girl of mixed ethnic origin. Too shy to make a direct approach, I used to cycle by Inga's house while singing 'On the Street where you Live' under my breath, hoping she would be on the porch. This courting strategy was totally unsuccessful.

The next day was so bleak I chose to remain inside at the nearby laundrette. After taking the laundry back to the B&B, I set off on a listless walk round the streets and to the 'Stray', a 200-acre park and sports ground that houses the first well (1527) in Harrowgate. Being Sunday, most places were closed but I did find an open appliance shop. I have no secret passion for appliances but, like the laundrette, the shop offered a temporary warm and dry refuge. Inside, I discovered that while the fridges, washers, tumble dryers, and cookers are narrower than a typical North American equivalent, the British prices are equal or higher.

A proper comparison requires one to adjust for the Value Added Tax (VAT) buried in British prices. I collect these mundane details of British life, regardless of what they are because it helps me better understand Brits, behave accordingly and appear less of a foreigner. However, I must admit that an appropriate application for this knowledge of comparative appliance statistics has yet to appear!

Cold and having exhausted everything of potential interest, I returned to my B&B and read until the weather brightened enough to venture out on the bike. My chosen southbound road (B6162/1) led to a pleasant spot at a wide section on the Wharfe River where people were enjoying paddle-boats and walking along a river path. I bought a chocolate bar and took my book down to a bench by the river. The clouds dissipated suddenly at about 5 p.m. revealing the sun, a bright blue sky and some warmth, justifying another half hour on the bench.

The journey back was on an unmarked north road that runs quite a bit west of Harrowgate to a place called Blubberhouses on the A59. It was uphill most of the way but pretty country and the day was so much improved from earlier that I really did not mind being lost. By the time I found my way to Betty's teahouse in Harrowgate's centre, my planned 30 km had become 48 km. Betty's remaining three takeaway sandwiches became my dinner.

After consuming these in my room, I went down to the sitting room to see the third of a five-part television drama I have been following called Oliver's Travels. Alan Bates plays the main character. It combines a murder mystery with a sort of travelogue. New clues with directional hints were provided by the daily newspaper crossword, a concept now used very successfully by two US crime writers using the name Nero Blanc. Despite the drama's unlikely plot, I enjoyed the intelligent, playful dialogue and interesting scenery. Tonight's episode had some good views of Hadrian's Wall and Lindisfarne (Holy Island on the English north east coast).

Bill Bryson and York

On Monday I visited the crescent of fine Georgian homes for which Harrogate is known and found them basking in brilliant sunshine. I also discovered an intriguing bookshop with a travel book about the US by Bill Bryson, an American then living in North Yorkshire. This was hilarious and very sympathetic to my views about the US. Since then, I have read all but two of Bryson's travel books as well as those about the English language.

A few years ago, Bryson returned to the US and wrote at least four more books. In 2004, he moved back to Britain where he continues to work with the English Heritage Society. I feel him to be a kindred spirit in many ways—a North American that loves Britain for many of the same reasons as I do and has a strong interest in the English language. The main difference is his skill in using it!

York, England's second most popular tourist city, was my next stop. I prefer it to London because of its more human scale and the lower volumes of traffic and noise. York is the former Roman city of Eboracvm that was the capital of the Roman province of Lower Britain. During the later occupation of this part of England by the Danes the city became Jorvik, from which the present name derives. In turn, the Normans sacked the Danish town, establishing their own stronghold. Clifford's Tower is the sole remnant of the Normans' 11th-century castle, but the medieval city walls remain largely intact.

The maze of lanes and alleys that formed the medieval street pattern also survives. The great Minster (cathedral) was built during the years 1220 to 1470. York has a strong cycling tradition, with one of the largest everyday cycle usages in Britain.(4)

For nostalgic reasons, I chose an indirect route to York, in hopes of revisiting a section of road that Mari and I travelled in 1992. We were cycling from Beningbrough along a country road on the way to our B&B when suddenly we became depositories for manure-encrusted straw blowing off a farm wagon in front of us. At the time, it was not at all pleasant but later we took considerable perverse pleasure in relating the story as an adventure to certain friends and neighbours who satisfyingly reacted in horror at our experience. Their idea of travel excludes exertion and demands first-class for everything.

I was not successful in finding this road. Working from an increasingly faulty memory caused a number of false starts and changes of direction. I finally ran out of road at a river and gave up. My journey to York could have been a direct 45 km but this diversionary quest made it 75 km!

The hostel notice board advertised 'Travels with My Aunt' currently playing at the Theatre Royal. Tonight would be my only opportunity for live theatre in York so I quickly went to see if any tickets were available. As this would be my second theatre outing in less than a week, something had to be sacrificed. Not having stopped for afternoon tea today, perhaps a late snack at the nearby Reed's teahouse could double as dinner.

The gorgeous weather demanded something summery and cool--a fruit crumble pastry with ice cream sounded perfect. It was, apart from being totally inadequate for my appetite. Cycling back to the hostel along the Clifton Road amidst gracious homes and pleasant looking small hotels, I realized there would be time to walk back to the theatre, leaving the bike securely at the hostel.

My theatre seat, on the very first row, provided an excellent view of this most unusual play. Three actors played at least six characters. The minimalist scenery and props consisted of just three straight white chairs and a table. The chairs in a line served as a cab. One man was a taxi driver one minute, the nephew the next and then the Aunt all without any change in costume. It was very well done and amazingly did not confuse because the voices were so distinct. Nevertheless, the combination of the day's sun together with the soothing darkness of the theatre had me nodding off from time to time.

Back at the hostel, which is supposed to be open 24 hours, I had to ring the buzzer and wait for several minutes to get my room key. A fog of overpowering body odour swept over me on entering the room. Its source, the other three guests, were just getting into bed and did not bother to acknowledge my presence.

The odour hung heavily in the air until I fell asleep but wasn't noticeable in the morning. Since I can't smell much of anything anymore, perhaps my olfactory senses became totally numbed overnight. But the night's sleep did not improve the level or extent of the conversation. One managed to say 'Good Morning' but that was it. It could have been the full limit of his English.

The Shambles

Today I will stroll York's famous Shambles, fulfil a commission for Mari in the morning and then to go to Scarborough by train. She needs a replacement for a superior back brace that we had bought in York in 1992. Our source then was the 'Able Living Centre' in Walmgate. Walmgate was familiar and very near the Shambles and the Cockatoo Creperie, our favourite restaurant. We ate there twice in 1992 and doing so again this trip was on my 'must' list.

Having acquired the brace, I set off for the Shambles--a cobble-stoned, multi-laned pedestrian mall of historic timber frame buildings sharing common walls or leaning on each other. Today, these buildings primarily house tourist oriented shops and restaurants. In earlier times, butchers largely inhabited the site and today's name comes from 'shamel', the Old English word for slaughterhouse.

This area is contiguous with a broader, still cobble-stoned, pedestrian square bordered by larger, more general interest shops, the famous Betty's teashop, and outside benches. In summer, buskers, Punch and Judy shows, mime artists and jugglers create a lively holiday atmosphere. Today, a group of violins and bass were performing those international stalwarts of the busker repertoire, Mozart's *Eine Kleine Nacht Musik* and Pachobel's *Canon* to extract funds from the tourists.

Scarborough and the North

My knowledge of Scarborough was limited to the Beatles song 'Scarborough Fair' that conjures up visions of warm sunshine and light-hearted activity. Reality was a cold North Sea breeze that cut right through my cycling jacket as I left the railway station but I was determined to see something of the town.

The sea front reverberated to the sounds of ten visiting Scandinavian, mainly Norwegian, bands, some in native costumes. Despite being hopelessly unmusical, even I could tell that they were not very good musically or in marching precision. Perhaps they should be forgiven; it was bitterly cold.

The front is a typically British, somewhat seedy, seaside populated with amusement arcades, fish and chip shops, donkey rides on the beach, fresh mussels and people sunbathing fully clothed behind wind blinds. I walked up and down the front pushing the cycle while absorbing the atmosphere but within an hour headed off to find the hostel and hopefully some warmth.

The hostel is about six kilometres north of the city on a dirt track off the main road. At the top of the track, I was greeted by a group of Pakistani youth asking directions to the hostel. They were part of a school group from Peterborough on a biology field trip. During the day, these students collect things from the seashore, woods and river and make observations. After dinner, they worked until late plotting their findings, making drawings and notes.

The males in the school party were also my roommates. One of the male teachers took me aside whispering 'don't be concerned if there is a little noise early in the morning as the boys are Muslim and will be getting up at four to pray.' I slept right through their devotions. Today, given all our concerns with terrorists and the hatred of 'infidels' held by some fundamental Muslims, I might well have stayed awake and 'on guard' all night.

The new day was warm, making the North Sea breeze welcome instead of the curse it was yesterday. I went north along the A 171 towards Whitby. The hills were manageable and so by eleven; I was more than half way, just opposite Robin Hood's Bay. The downhill run into the village from the main road thrilled despite knowing that an uphill on the way back would be the price for my pleasure. Robin Hood's Bay is a narrow-streeted, cliffhanging coastal village somewhat larger but very reminiscent of Clovelly on the Devon coast. Cliff walking appears to be the principal activity for most tourists with nearby Whitby and Scarborough as diversions.

Later, nine uphill kilometres from Robin Hood's Bay, I arrived at the crest of a hill providing a panoramic view of a river flowing down to the sea and the Whitby harbour. The tide was out, leaving the marooned boats perched dissolute and dishevelled in the mud. The Whitby seafront is much the same as in Scarborough but with a fishier, more workaday ambience. The sunshine attracted many more people than Scarborough had yesterday. Many of these were in wheelchairs or otherwise disabled. I wondered if the seaside attracts them particularly or if Britain has more of such disadvantaged people per capita than North America. A gypsy fortune-teller claiming to be known round the world added to the usual attractions.

Regretfully now, I recall that I did not stay to enjoy the other aspects of Whitby--the old Abbey, the 199 steps up to St. Mary's Church and Captain Cook's house in Grape Lane. Instead, I went on to Sandsend, a village further up the coast with a lovely bay, and then westward across the top of the empty North York moor with its patchy, dark landscape. A Wuthering Heights worthy mist blew across the road limiting visibility and producing a sense of total isolation for perhaps two hours.

The ICI Connection

The British penchant for naming their houses and using that name as an address, sometimes, in small villages, without further definition, complicated the search for my B&B. I had to call on a friendly butcher in Great Broughton to find 'Ingleside.' Once there, a small flat board lying on the door step directed me to 'go round back.' At the back, the doors to the house were wide open. A small table laid with all the tea things sat invitingly in the garden. Uncertain whether to go into the house, I stood outside, looking untidy, when Len, my host, appeared round a shed corner.

Len was a kindly, cultured and white-haired 75 year-old. He quickly produced a pot of tea with delicious buttered scones, delivering them to the garden table. It was perfect; the sun was still warm, my chair faced a low hedge framing a vista of the Cleveland Hills bordering a rich green pasture populated with plump Jerseys. Dave, a Scottish guest, joined me. Dave was retiring from Imperial Chemical Industries (ICI) the next day. His company affiliation provided a common interest as ICI's headquarters were in Welwyn Garden City, Hertfordshire where Mari and I lived for nearly six years. We agreed to go to dinner together and were joined there by Richard, another ICI man who knew one of our friends in Welwyn Garden City. At the pub, to their surprise, I declined the vile looking mushy peas. After dinner, Richard and Dave still had ground to cover and needed several more pints to do so. I returned to the B&B.

There I meet Len's wife, Margaret, for the first time. Margaret is a very pleasant and friendly woman whose daughter has run the New York Marathon three times for charity, once in stocking feet it was so hot! The daughter now looks after Mick Jagger's children on weekends including this one when Mick will be in Paris. The evening concluded (happily for me) with more tea and shortbread.

Apart from reaching Thwaites House by teatime, my new day was unstructured. Thwaites House is the home of more ICI friends of ours, Gillian and John, from Welwyn Garden City days. As so often happens, we met through the children at the nursery school. Gillian is perhaps the only woman I know that lives and breathes feminism-- it is in her DNA.

We maintained contact with them on a sporadic basis after Mari and I left England and spent a weekend with them in the late 70's while they were temporarily based in the US. Other postings took them to Brazil and Pakistan but John is now based at ICI's Middlesbrough operation, a convenient commute from Thwaites House.

Consequently, I had a large part of the day to explore the area without time pressure. Nearby Stokesley is a very pleasant and bustling market town with a village green ringed by mainly Georgian houses. The Leven River running behind the High Street was filled with ducks including three brand new ones already preening themselves as if they had been doing it for years.

Next, I rode over to see Great Ayton, where other ICI connected friends from Welwyn Garden City lived for a while and searched for an ice cream shop selling a famous brand called Sugget. The throng of cyclists there attested to its popularity but there was just one flavour- vanilla and I wasn't impressed. Captain Cook's 1736 schoolhouse is next door to Sugget but wasn't open yet for visitors.

Mari is much more curious than I am; always wanting to see round the bend or over the crest of the next hill. My strong preference is to I choose to get from A to B on familiar routes and to resist roads unless I know where they go. Today, she would have been surprised; I set out on a road without having any idea of where it went!

The terrain was gently rolling, attractively pastoral and perfect for cycling with minimal traffic. Shortly after noon, another cyclist overtook me and rode alongside. He was an anaesthesiologist on his lunch break from Middlesbrough specialist hospital. After about twenty minutes at a good pace, we stopped for a pint outside the pub at Hutton Rudby and discussed the dramatic changes he has witnessed in the National Health Service. He claimed that the paper work has increased tremendously and that rationing of health services is now policy.

As an example, he told of a young woman denied an expensive operation because the chances of success were so small. This caused a great national outcry that persuaded some rich person to buy the operation for her at a private hospital. My companion had to return to work before I could learn whether the young woman survived.

I stayed on for lunch and a second lager. Another chap approached to join me and began a a monologue about his cycle holiday in France last year. Overweight and stereotypically 'Old School' British in appearance and manner he said his holiday was 'To get away from the Brits.' Although I wanted to contradict many times, I bit my tongue and let him carry on thinking I was accepting it all. It was an entertaining monologue despite his self-centred, patronizing, manner.

Now it was time to make a move towards Thwaites House. I went to Carlton in Cleveland, a small picturesque old village and my friends' official address.   No one had heard of 'Thwaites House.' The small shop that also served as the post office had the electoral rolls but my friends weren't on it.   The postmistress said the house must be over the hill, just beyond the Lord Stones café.   Three people have now mentioned this café, as it is unique.   Planning permission required building it into the side of a hill so as not to spoil the natural views. Its name comes from three stones of a nearby ancient monument.

The hill is as steep and long as the Hardknott Pass but without the bends; the climb was monotonously slow.   Keeping track of the distance and elapsed time as a mental exercise on the way up, I calculated that the one in four grade meant a 200-metre vertical climb. The cafe is at the crest.   Sweating like the proverbial pig, I took advantage of the café's washroom to cool off and clean up. Then, not knowing how much further there was to go, I treated myself to a rhubarb crumble with ice cream-it might have been Sugget.

Just two hundred horizontal metres further on, a big gate across a dirt lane sported the sign Thwaites House.   It was a struggle, but I got through that and yet another gate before the house came into view. It is old, smooth grey stucco, sitting at the very edge of the lane. On the other side, the sharply sloping rocky ground hosts sheep and cattle with the Cleveland Hills in the background.

A beer in the garden loosened our tongues and memories after eighteen years, Then John and I walked a bit of the famous Cleveland Way that runs very close to their property, helping to work off a bit of the crumble.   We spent the evening bringing each other up to date on our now adult children and enjoying an excellent late dinner of quiche, fresh cauliflower with cheese sauce, superb tomatoes and new potatoes from their garden, finishing off with a heavenly summer pudding--my capacity had returned.

Gillian and John were off to Wimbledon to see the tennis next morning. An early departure was necessary and I overslept! This left no time for shaving or other early morning functions before breakfast. Despite their timetable, John produced a fabulous and healthy breakfast.

They needed to get away right after breakfast. I wanted to take care of my morning functions at leisure after they left but they clearly preferred to lock up before leaving as they have experienced frequent burglaries due to their isolation and the Cleveland Way hiking traffic that regularly passes their door. So I gathered up my things quickly, forgoing a shave and another pressingly urgent activity.

This would be my earliest start of the entire trip. At 7.30, the morning was cool with bright sunshine. Apart from me, only rabbits were on the road—they were everywhere. It was a marvellous morning that has stayed in my memory as about the best experience of this or any tour. Magnificent scenery, a gentle, downhill slope, warm sunshine and crisp air combined to make it 'perfick.'

The road runs down to intersect with the main Stokesley/Helmsley road at Chopgate. At the front edge of the village, my eye caught a car park and toilets sign alongside me. Twenty minutes later, I emerged a new man--clean shaven and emptied. The air was still cool but the warm sunshine rendered a feeling reminiscent of swimming in a mountain lake—that special sort of cleanliness and contentment one feels being air dried.

Heading Home

Helmsley, little more than an hour away, is a prosperous town that attracts tourists because of nearby Rievaulx Abbey and gardens. Founded in the twelfth century, Rievaulx was the first Cistercian house in the north of England and is considered one of the most magnificent monastic ruins in the country.(5)

It was market day; the square was filled with people surveying a wide variety of stalls selling fruits, vegetables and other foodstuffs. The square is surrounded on two sides with more permanent establishments including The Police Station, my chosen tea stop café. Across the square, All Saints Church offered a blissful cool escape from the now boiling temperature outside. Its ceiling is half painted wood and half arched stone. Adorning one wall is a list of all the vicars back to 1127!

Given York's importance, the choice of routes from Helmsley is extensive. I kept to the B roads and passed through Sutton on Forest where, in 1992, a Shetland pony tried to remove Mari's ankle, getting in a good nip! The pony was otherwise occupied so I called in at the Rose and Crown, an upscale pub that provided free bar snacks of nuts and pickled onions. A white linen cloth on the tables defined this pub's social standing, suggesting an uncertain welcome. Nevertheless, I stayed and ordered the least expensive selection on the menu, a tuna fish and cucumber sandwich which arrived garnished with a salad and pickled onions--definitely a cut above typical pub food. I was good and was not asked to leave for improper attire or behaviour.

Back in York but before heading off to the hostel, I stopped at the Assembly Rooms. This is a grand open place with huge marble columns supporting a ceiling perhaps 30 feet high. Massive paintings, many of the Minster, hang on perimeter walls. An elegant afternoon tea being served in the centre completed the 1920s Palm Court atmosphere-a grand spot for a special anniversary occasion. A shock was waiting at the hostel; my reservation had been cancelled and the hostel was full. After some ineffectual dithering around, I got a refund and they very kindly booked me into a nearby B&B. Staying in York was crucial to my plan to conclude my tour with a fine dinner at the Cockatoo Crêperie.

A new proprietor had taken over the restaurant shortly after Mari and my visit in 1992. Andre, the former owner, returned to Paris. Fortunately, Andre's brother Robert was still chef and most of the menu was unchanged. I had a great meal that fully lived up to my expectations--a fitting finish for the Peaks, Lakes and Dales tour.

CIRCLE TOUR

BRITAIN

BETTER WAY HOLIDAYS

- TIRED OF 'LUXURY' HOLIDAYS THAT LEAVE YOUR BODY BLOATED WITH RICH FOOD, YOUR PURSE RAVAGED BY EXCESSIVE PRICES AND YOUR SOUL EMPTY?

- FED UP WITH THE INSINCERE ATTENTIONS OF SERVICE PEOPLE INTERESTED ONLY IN THE SIZE OF YOUR TIP?

- THIS IS A 3-WEEK CYCLING ADVENTURE COMPLETE WITH FANTASTIC SCENERY, ALL WEATHER EXERCISE, A DRESS CODE AS CASUAL AS YOU WANT TO MAKE IT, ALCOHOL-FREE CUISINE AND NO FUSS, MINIMALIST ACCOMMODATION.

- SHARE THE CHEERY CONVIVIALITY OF HOSTEL DORMITORIES WITH STRANGERS, SECURE IN THE KNOWLEDGE THAT THERE IS A FRESHLY LAUNDERED SHEET BAG FOR EVERY GUEST.

- SAVOUR TRADITIONAL ENGLISH COUNTRY DISHES LIKE 'TOAD IN A HOLE' AND 'BANGERS AND MASH'!

- DISCOVER MUSCLES YOU NEVER KNEW YOU HAD AFTER AN EXHILARATING 75 KM DAILY CYCLE RIDE.

- FORGET RIGID TOUR SCHEDULES WITH EXTENDED HOSTEL CAFETERIA HOURS TO 8 PM.

- GLORY IN THE SELF SUFFICIENCY OF TRAVELLING WITH THE ABSOLUTE MINIMUM OF CREATURE COMFORTS.

- ALL OF THIS FOR AS LITTLE AS $85 PER DAY. TOTAL LAND COSTS ONLY $2100. DEPARTING 15 JUNE 1999.

DON'T WAIT—THIS TOUR WILL FILL UP FAST—GET YOUR RESERVATION IN TODAY.

CIRCLE TOUR

This tour was cobbled together with extracts of routes recommended by cycling guide books. The result really wasn't a circle so much as an oval but that doesn't quite work as a tour name. The preceding page was created for a bit of fun with some neighbours whose idea of a holiday requires five-star hotels, elegant dining and power shopping. It was designed as a flyer announcing an upcoming group tour that portrayed the parts they would find appalling as benefits. My fun never happened as their maid, knowing her clients, tossed out the flyer while they were away.

The Route

From Gatwick Airport, south of London, my route went west to Bath, then north west to skirt Wales' eastern border and onto Chester. From Chester, it continued north to Kendal in Cumbria and east into the Yorkshire Dales and York. The trip's final leg was south from York to Lincoln, Cambridge and back to Gatwick. For me, it was a mix of familiar territory like Yorkshire and unexplored Lincolnshire and Cambridgeshire.

Boxing the Bike

After the damage my bike suffered in the previous tour, I decided to use a bicycle box. Deirdre, a neighbour's adult daughter, kindly lent hers to me. Mari and I met Deirdre at an Oakville restaurant where she was our waitress for a meal on our first house-hunting trip in Canada. Then she was a pleasant teenager who coincidentally lived diagonally across the street from where we chose the house that is still our home. Deirdre's personality strengths continued into adulthood and she and her husband developed a love for hiking and biking the British countryside.

Her box is hard vinyl with three layers of thick foam inside which cushion the bike like a triple-decker or club sandwich. This approach requires more disassembly than using an old cardboard cycle box or an airline supplied plastic bag but provides much better protection. With such boxes, you need to remove the wheels, pedals, saddle and handlebar stem.

The bike is safer but the box isn't disposable, it is expensive and has to be stored somewhere during the tour. Previous experiences proved that the airport left luggage areas are horribly dear and many railway stations have closed theirs down due to potential IRA bomb activity.

My solution to the storage problem was finding a B&B near Gatwick airport that would allow me to unload and leave the box there until I returned from the tour for a final night with them. My taxi to the B&B was an impressive brand new Renault Espace (a highly regarded French minivan) with plenty of space but the driver (not English) was very concerned that his car will be marred by the box and treated me rudely. Consequently, he did not get a tip.

The warm day made hot work of reassembling the bike. It took far longer to put it back together than it had to take it apart and the wheels refused to run straight. Sweat was pouring down my face and attempts to wipe it off just left greasy streaks. It was past two when I finished; I'd not eaten since the puny airline breakfast but was eager to achieve some distance before the day ended. So, I decided to get going and stop for tea at about four. But, when the panniers were loaded on, the bike's weight was almost overwhelming.

Again, work pressures made it impossible to train properly and I was truly unfit. I had done no loaded training at all and now could barely maintain enough momentum to avoid falling. A few kilometres on, climbing a narrow road on the rougher, potholed surface at the road edge, I hit a hole hard, causing the rear wheel to jar loose and slam against the chain stay, stopping me dead. I fell off the saddle but remained upright narrowly avoiding crushing the family jewels on the top tube. Positioning the rear wheel more to the back where the chain stays are further apart seemed a solution--but it wasn't permanent.

Shortly afterwards, on a steeper hill, climbing in semidarkness due to a canopy of trees, I was going so slowly that I couldn't keep the bike balanced. Then the front wheel hit another hole twisting sharply to the left. This and my automatic, still North American, reactions caused me to fall to the right—directly in front of the traffic. Two cars swerved, narrowly missing me.

Unlike a Bond martini, I was both shaken and stirred, but struggled on toward Horsham, Surrey arriving about 4.30, nerves and stomach screaming for a soothing teacake stop. Jet lag, heat and events had taken a toll, physically and mentally. Sadly, there was no tearoom; grumpily, I settled for a cheese and pickle sandwich and a Coke bought from a newsagent. To make things worse, consuming my snack on a roadside bench, I was denied a tearoom's tranquillity.

Heading west towards the real starting point of the first of the guide book tours, I needed some help getting to that point. The newsagent irritatingly told me 'I've only lived here eight years and don't know the area yet.' Given the context, I thought of him as one sandwich short of a picnic but political correctness might demand 'intellectually challenged.' By now, my main objective was to find a B&B and put my weary, untrained, battered and bruised body to bed.

Naturally, no B&B appeared. Finally, reaching Storrington, after 52 km on the B2139, I called in at the White Horse pub to ask about B&B's and wound up staying there. Superficially the room seemed all right but after dinner and a bath, I discovered that neither the teakettle nor the bedside lamp worked. Then I found a thoughtful gift Mari hid in my luggage—a battery operated light that attaches to your book. She is looking after me even 5000 kilometres away.

The White Horse wasn't a good choice. It should have been obvious when they suggested I leave my cycle behind the pub next to the car park footpath. My tiredness had made me less discriminating but not brain-dead enough to leave the bike outside--it bunked with me.

Not wanting to give the White Horse any more of my business, I dined at the rival Anchor pub across the road. That revived me enough to delay bedtime a bit for a look at house prices in estate agent's windows and go for a wander through some lovely residential areas. There was no visible nightlife other than the pubs but the streets roared with a constant stream of traffic.

The White Horse continued its shabby behaviour. They had no marmalade or jam for breakfast and all I got when I mentioned the non-functioning items in the room was 'oh dear, I'll have to tell the manager.' There was no apology or apparent concern that I was inconvenienced. My opinion of this establishment's quality and its clientele was confirmed by finding that someone had peed all over the seat in the toilet reserved for overnight guests.

Galsworthy, a Corgi and Bush House

Now, I've reached the start of my mix of cycle guide book tours and have an adequate map. Chosen to be off the beaten track, the route was marvellous for lack of traffic but also short of facilities.

Before lunch I passed by a manor house at Bury, Sussex where author John Galsworthy lived for seven years. Then, my route became a footpath, erupting in gnarly roots and crossing a narrow bridge over a marsh, ending in a very steep set of steps. At the top, the footpath went in two directions without any indication of where either led. I went to get some advice from some nearby houses.

At the first house, after a vigorous and unfriendly interrogation by an aged Corgi, his mistress emerged from her garden. She was a no-nonsense, white-haired woman with a healthy amount of dirt under her nails but a lovely garden. Looking me square in the face with an amused expression she said 'My Corgi doesn't like your helmet!'

She directed me towards Liphook (west of Haslemere) where I found a more promising road off my route. Getting any accommodation before Overton, some 50 km away, seemed unlikely. If this was right, it would be a 100+ km day but nevertheless, I was unable to resist the temptation of afternoon tea at Bush House in Selborne, Hampshire.

This was a proper place—very old, low ceilings, a beam and vine covered back garden, long open porch and locals as customers, no tourists, apart from me and I am British by sentiment. Quality, however, has its price. My two teacakes, jam and five cups of tea (one pot with extra hot water) came to over C$10! It was after four before I could tear myself away.

An overcast sky threatened rain but within an hour the threat was gone, the sun reappeared and the riding was perfect. The conditions were so pleasant that I unconsciously slowed to an average speed of only 15 km/h. So it was nearly eight p.m. when I arrived in Overton(west of Basingstoke), achieving 107 kilometres for the first full day. Now, pain was the price, everything ached, particularly my neck and shoulders.

Changing animals tonight, I took a room at the White Hart pub, settling for an indifferent meal with my book in their dining room before a soothing hot shower and bed. Sleep became almost impossible after about 3.30 a.m. as my room overlooked the street just above the corner traffic lights. A steady stream of Friday night traffic gunned its engines in anticipation of the light changing and then roared off into the night. Only intermittent pauses punctuated the din, allowing me to doze on and off.

Young People –Bah!

Heading north and west brought me to the 'Grand Avenue' through the Savernake Forest near Marlborough, Wiltshire. The Savernake is a privately owned wood with a magnificent avenue of trees along a restricted speed, narrow public road running through it. Marlborough claims one of the widest high streets in England and is home to a famous public (i.e. private) school. This area is also a centre for English racehorse breeding. After lunch at a Marlborough pub I continued along the A4 towards Calne to be able to visit Long Barrow and Silbury Hill at West Kennet.

'For prehistoric interest, this part of Wiltshire offers serious competition to the more famous stone circles of Stonehenge further south. The ancient track known as the Ridge Way runs along the crest of the Marlborough Downs.

Silbury Hill, the largest earthen mound in Europe, surpasses all other prehistoric monuments in Britain not only in size but also in the degree of utter puzzlement it has created among those who have studied it. The site bears a superficial resemblance to the many smaller round barrows found near Avebury, and local tradition suggested that a great leader lays buried somewhere in its depths— encased in golden armour, according to one legend. A series of extensive excavations, however, has failed to reveal any trace of a burial or other objects entombed within. So, the massive mound's purpose remains a complete mystery.

However, the excavations revealed a surprisingly sophisticated method of construction. The mound's turf façade hides a series of partitioned circular chalk enclosures, packed with earth and stacked one atop another to create a stepped shape like a wedding cake. The smooth finished appearance was achieved by filling in the steps with additional chalk and dirt. In all, it took about 6.5 million cubic feet of material to create.'(1)

Another pub overnight and another interrupted sleep. This time, it wasn't the traffic but noisy, vulgar kids, some sounding almost preteen despite it being two in the morning. I gave up and got out of bed early, forgetting that weekend breakfasts start later. Roughly at 8.30, when I started breakfast, a very well-upholstered young woman in skin-tight clothes breezed through the front door on the way to her room, promising to be back in time for her work shift. The landlady said the girl had been partying all night and wasn't yet 16!

The other person in the room, obviously single and quite possibly gay, started a conversation. Just finishing a week's walking holiday from the Cotswolds through Bath to Avebury, he complained of a dull and poorly paid office job in Yorkshire. Nevertheless, he was interesting to talk with and persuaded me to backtrack the 26 km to Avebury.

Avebury, New Agers and Bikers
Returning to Avebury meant climbing the hill called 'Labour in Vain' that I felt so smug about going down yesterday on the way into Calne. Going back up provided a good view, and more time, to enjoy the Cherhill Chalk Horse carved on the hillside. This horse is a relatively modern imitation of the more famous Uffington Horse in south west Oxfordshire. Cherhill has recently been dated as at least 2,500 years old and is thought originally to have been a symbol of the victory of good over evil.(2)

On the way to Avebury, I saw again and exchanged 'good mornings' with a traveller outside his Romany caravan across the road in a small lay by. A little further on, three beautiful brown and white gypsy ponies grazed beside a sandwich board type folding sign offering Romany Fortune Telling. On my return, later in the morning, the fortune teller was outside brewing tea, apparently for personal consumption, but perhaps also to replenish her stock of leaves to read.

Three beat up vans filled with dogs and dirty, ring-pierced young people sullied the Avebury parking area. Their guru, in full kit of long flowing white hair, beard, beads and headband, distanced himself, as if embarrassed. It took a while to the 'penny to drop' for me and realize the connection between these new agers, Avebury's stone circles, and the summer solstice. The following day at Stonehenge, some of these types broke down the protective fence and 'celebrated' on top of the stones.

Avebury is a one street, seventeenth or eighteenth century village, not particularly notable in itself but round its perimeter there is a deep, dry moat-like structure surrounding rough circles of huge stones.

'The Avebury stone circles are the largest in Britain, and considered by many to surpass even Stonehenge in grandeur. ...The first thing to strike visitors to Avebury is not the stones, but the surrounding bank and ditch. Originally, the ditch reached a depth of nine metres and the adjoining mound stood over five metres. While erosion has taken its toll, the henge still dwarfs the nearly vanished earthworks at Stonehenge. At about 1 mile in circumference, the Avebury henge completely encircles a small village, and even the smallest of the three stone circles within is still larger than Stonehenge.... Of the two inner circles, only four and five stones still stand, respectively. The third circle remains only marginally more complete, with 27 of the original 98 stones still in place.'(3)

Later, returning to the car park area, I passed over a hundred motorcyclists, most attired in stereotypical black leather--probably the perfect antithesis of the new age group suggesting that the situation could become violent quite easily. I was glad to be leaving.

Back through Calne and turning south west to the Somerset border, I was surprised by a sudden steep descent into Bradford on Avon. A sharp bend at the city entrance stacked up the heavy traffic just out of sight and I had to brake hard to avoid hitting a car. Bradford on Avon is very old but looks to be largely ignored by tourists and so was more appealing to me.

Unfortunately, my time to explore the town was very limited, as I wanted to be in time for evening meal at the hostel in Bath. This objective wasn't realized as there were no hostel signs in Bath and most people had no idea where it was. Finally, an hour late for the meal, I found the hostel at the top of a very long hill. After checking in, I walked back into the city, seeking a recommended pub. 'The Greentree' had stopped serving food by that time; the minimum price for a main course at 'The Moon and Sixpence' was C$ 31 and so it went. Finally, I found a French bistro where, by eating lightly, I could eat well and have a glass of wine. My smoked duck breast salad with bacon and walnut dressing with warm celery and Roquefort pate accompanied by a glass of Cabernet Sauvignon was superb. Chewing slowly, I savoured every bite.

On the long hike back up the hill to the hostel, I met my roommates, two university students, one from Wisconsin, and one from Salamanca, Spain. We spoke a little Spanish combined with English and seemed to understand each other. Now, thinking back on that experience, I remember that my Spanish professor, at Edinburgh University, had been trained at Salamanca!

Sulis Minerva

Next morning along the canal, I saw colourful barges moored alongside and one coming through the locks. There wasn't much visible activity so it wasn't clear whether these were holiday barges or permanent homes. In later years, living on the water like this became fairly common, as the mooring fees were often cheaper than rent or property rates (now 'council charge').

Robert Adam's Pultney Bridge over the River Avon and the picturesque weir are together the iconic postcard image of Bath. Buildings filled with shops form the sidewall of the bridge. My birth town in the Finger Lakes district of New York State features a Pultney Park and like many North American towns was named after Bath, England.

I went up the Grand Parade and over to the Roman Baths, meaning only to survey the exterior, not visit. An interior argument raged however, chastising me for letting my aversion to being considered a tourist and my parsimony deny me one of the principal reasons for coming to Bath. An exterior sign, noting that the Baths are a World Heritage Site clinched the argument in favour of going in.

Once inside, I was pleased at my decision; an excellent audio guide was provided and the tour was well arranged. The 'Sacred Spring' continues to overflow and spill its 46.5 degree Celsius water. This entire complex of baths has only been a tourist attraction since the late nineteenth century when it was discovered –some 1500 years after the Romans built it. Much of Bath today is about two metres higher than it was originally as newer civilizations built on top of the older ones.

In Roman times, this facility was known as Sulis Minerva, a combination of the Roman god of healing waters, Sulis, with the Celtic god Minerva. The lead walls of the Great Pool are still watertight from the days of original construction. Then, in an early version of Three Coins in the Fountain, people threw gifts to the gods into the water. According to the tour information, people also sometimes wrote out curses and threw them into the water requesting the gods to intervene in petty crimes. There were no testimonials to the effectiveness of this practice.

After lunch, I exited Bath up a long hard hill along a difficult route to the Severn Bridge at the Bristol Channel. Built in 1966, it was at the time one of the world's largest single-span suspension bridges.(4) Fortunately, there is a guard-railed cycle path across as the winds that roar down the channel could easily slam you right into traffic.

Coach and Horses Redeems Pubs' Reputation
My destination, Chepstow, is only a few kilometres beyond the bridge. Pub beds seem to be my destiny this tour; tonight I'm at the Coach and Horses. I was greeted by a very friendly gnome who gave me a well-appointed double for the price of a single. The only drawback was that the window inside my room served as the fire

escape for the entire floor! In the case of fire, the emergency key to my room was conveniently taped to the wall outside my door.

I enjoyed an excellent sirloin steak dinner in the pub's very friendly atmosphere. After dinner, Neil, the cook, gathered everyone interested for a trivia quiz. Given Chepstow's location, it wasn't surprising that most of his questions were on Welsh subjects. Neil made it very entertaining, informative and reminiscent of an old time music hall. The participants paid a pound to play and the one with the most correct answers went home with the bulk of the takings.

Tonight my room did not face the street, there were no noisy teenagers or cars and there was no fire—so I slept through the entire night. At 7.30, a bright and cheery Neil provided a massive breakfast, including what must have been a half-pound of bacon.

Breakfast time, particularly British style, is one of my favourites. Despite good intentions, I linger longer than intended and eat more than necessary. Playing toss with Sam, the pub's friendly Labrador retriever, further delayed departure. My cost for this most pleasant stop was £26.50, including dinner--40% less than my terrible first stop in Storrington.

Hay on Wye-Book Town

Compounding my late start, progress was very slow this morning: the guidebook route was confusing, including one very blatant error listing the wrong town. I came across a four way crossroads, with two separate signs for my destination, each pointing a different direction. The choice was made by compass but the way that these lanes run, either choice probably would have worked. From a surfeit of signs to none at all, I arrived in a village at lunchtime with no idea of its name and the church that was meant to indicate a right turn was hidden behind dense roadside hedges.

Calling in at a very old (1459) pub for directions and lunch, I found a perfect pub atmosphere with a resident alert, affectionate Doberman. The only other customer during much of my stay was a thin man with terrible teeth and long stringy, dirty blond hair. When not performing product quality tests, he served as the backup barman.

The publican, a man several social stations above his backup, discussed the proposed new lower allowable alcohol content rules for drivers. He is afraid that people will choose to buy from the off-licence and drink at home rather than go to a country pub. City pubs won't be so badly affected because people there have access to public transit and taxis. We also talked about the heavy tax on beer and other business aspects of running a country pub. I try to be a good listener believing that people open up a lot more when the focus is on them and your questions show genuine interest. Asking questions neutrally, without revealing any bias of my own or expressing an opinion on their information provides no clues from me of praise or censure and gives me a more accurate indication of their true feelings. Mari believes however, that my face betrays me. I apparently cannot stop it showing disapproval or disbelief.

I took the publican's advice to follow the A465. This led to the turnoff towards Llanthony where a real climb began. Now I had to push the bike and was soon dripping with sweat although the temperature could not have been more than 17 or 18 degrees Celsius. At Capel y ffin, five and a half kilometres beyond Llanthony, there is a lovely cemetery and a church that provided an excuse to rest. The church is very small, simple and peaceful with a balcony running round two inside walls and ten or so dark oak pews populating the ground floor. Outside, a single house suggested some life in the village. Later I learned that this is the smallest church in Wales and the smallest constituency in the entire United Kingdom!

Beyond Capel y ffin the narrow road runs through wooded, very beautiful country before climbing out onto bare grassy hillside. It's uphill all the way with an average 10-12% grade to the pass at the top--the Bwlch-yr-Efengyl or 'Gospel Pass.' In the days when those who wished to practise nonconformist(i.e. not Anglican) worship were harassed, people would gather at this windswept spot to the hear the gospel--hence its name. The top of the pass is one of the highest roads in Wales at 542 metres and as you broach the top a tremendous view opens over the middle Wye Valley and the hills beyond.(5) My spirits soared at the broad vista, grazed by sheep and apparently wild horses. Golden shafts of sunshine in the western sky pierced the fresh, bracing air. The only negative was the weight of the panniers.

Then, I experienced one of the better runs of my entire cycling career that was probably made more enjoyable by its contrast with the rest of the day's uphill ordeal. The road became a narrow black ribbon unfurling its way downhill through sheep-manicured moorland for what must have been seven kilometres to Hay-on-Wye.

Hay was immediately appealing. It sits high above one of Britain's most enchanting rivers, the Wye, and has the Black Mountains, at their steepest and grandest, looming near. Hay is an old, clean and moderately sized market town that claims to be the second hand book centre of Britain. My first stop to find a room was successful at Skynlas House, an attractive and well-maintained B&B on the main road. Ann, my friendly and competent landlady, gave me a yellow en suite double room for twenty pounds providing another favourable comparison with the White Horse pub in Storrington.

Ann also lets a housekeeping cottage that sleeps four or five for £200-275 a week. The higher price applies during an annual Book Festival week--Ann claims that the festival is the largest of its kind in the world. This year's has just finished, attracting 42,000 for readings, talks and concerts. Hay is also a centre for hiking in the Black Mountains, on nearby Offa's Dyke and along the Wye where canoeing and kayaking are also popular.

In the town, I discovered a ruined castle and a full complement of necessary, everyday shops but about every third one is a bookshop! One of these, an open-air establishment situated in the grounds of the castle, is called the Honesty Shop. It operates primarily on an exchange basis and was totally unattended.

In the morning, Ann provided a massive pile of strong yellow scrambled eggs served on granary bread with grilled tomatoes and mushrooms-excellent quality and delicious. I have had a warm regard for Hay–on-Wye ever since.

Walking Tour Guides at Bridges Hostel

Tonight's destination is Bridges, chosen only because it had a hostel. Both town and hostel proved to be extremely well hidden. There was virtually no signage on the road directing anyone to Bridges, nor any sign to announce that you have arrived and only a tiny sign for the hostel.

Arriving early, despite having covered 81 km today, I found the hostel closed. I rested on an outside bench until the warden and her daughter arrived. They took pity on me and made, guess what, that British cure for every malady known to man, a pot of tea.

Despite its small size, this former schoolhouse hostel serves meals. Tonight's meal was simple and of the 'old British school' style with French onion soup, a meat pie with overdone carrots and broccoli, followed by coconut tart and ice cream. Breakfast was also poorly cooked and presented—my sausage went into the dustbin. Penny, the cook, is just a second year medical student at St. Bartholomew's in London but has already perfected hospital-quality cuisine! Her younger, cheerier, and slimmer sister took over mid-breakfast redeeming the situation somewhat with a five-cup pot of tea!

Over last night's dinner, I talked with the only two other guests, a couple in their sixties doing a scouting trip for a series of walks they are to lead individually next week from Long Mynd. Long Mynd is a 16 km long ridge of bleak heath and moorland that provides some of the finest walking in Shropshire. The Port Way track runs the entire length of the Mynd's crest and commands superb views across the surrounding country.(6) My dinner companions talked primarily about these upcoming walks and the skills necessary to lead them, primarily map reading and first aid.

I was the sole occupant of a room called Ashes Hollow and took the opportunity of unfettered access to the washbasin to do a hand laundry and hung it in the special drying room. Drying rooms are one of the useful facilities that most country hostels provide. Many hostellers arrive with muddy boots and wet clothes or just need to dry out some hand washed clothing, as Britain's generally moisture-laden air is rarely conducive to quick drying. These drying rooms are usually just overheated spaces with clothes lines and racks to lay things on but when you need something dry, the lack of one can seem total deprivation. Larger, more urban hostels may have washers and tumble dryers but the queues can be daunting.

My walking tour couple acquaintances from yesterday joined me for breakfast and she 'entertained' me with tales of her daughter (job transfer to Geneva), their plans for a round-the-world backpacking tour and the posh roll-up dress she bought so they can go to the opera in Sydney. 'Graham, of course, will have to take a tie to go with his non-iron seersucker shirts', she confided. All through this conversation, I reflected on Mari's travelling preferences. She relies on a personal version of the old American Express slogan—'Don't leave home without it'--the home that is!

Exploring Chester

Arriving in Chester at about 6.30, I set out looking for a room, finding Duke's Cottage in a mean street just down from the railway station. This turned out to be just a B—no breakfast was provided but the small room had everything I needed at a small fraction of a hotel's price but none of its privacy and convenience. My German hosts' bedroom was their access and mine to the car park where I had to store the bike. They lived in three rooms, one of which housed a big screen television that ran all day.

Walking into the city centre through a very unappealing set of subways(underground tunnels), I found a wealth of pedestrian walkways, shops, and restaurants making Chester much more attractive than it appeared at first. It is, after all, a walled city with Roman origins. On the walk back to Duke's Cottage from dinner, I stopped at the railway station to check whether the recent Manchester train crash would disrupt journeys to Preston. I wanted to avoid having to cycle through an industrial area and found it was possible to do so, freeing up some time to explore Chester tomorrow.

Despite a late breakfast at the railway station, the walk into town made me hungry again. So, armed with a copy of the *Times* I climbed the stairs to a coffee house on the second tier of one of the Rows. Dating from the thirteenth century onward, these are raised covered galleries with two tiers of shops, unique in Britain,—forming, a sort of medieval covered shopping mall.(7)

I spent a leisurely hour there reading about British life and the interesting parallels with life at home—e.g. the debate about the high proportion of total education spending involving administration and the programming and financing problems facing the national broadcaster. The BBC decided to take the high road concentrating on quality rather than ratings but then they aren't dependent on advertising revenues like the CBC.

After this, I explored the Church of St John the Baptist and its twelfth century ruins, the Roman Amphitheatre and walked along the River Dee. The church's origins go back to the seventh century and the Saxons. A guide to its history introduced me to the term Dissolution--shorthand for the break-up of the monasteries that followed Henry the VIII's split with Rome.

My historical interest piqued; I bought a walking tour pamphlet from Tourist Information and strolled Chester for another couple of hours, climbing walls, studying building architectural styles and trying to absorb the commentary provided by the pamphlet. Remains of the Roman walls from AD79 are still visible. Later the Saxons and Normans added to the walls girdling the city. Chester had been a great port but by about 700, the river silted up and ships could no longer get in. Now the river is largely a canal. There are more than 50 points of interest on the walking tour and with museums along the way, more than a full day would be necessary to do it justice. My two plus hours wasn't nearly enough but I had reached the saturation point and made one of those well-intentioned self-promises that, like New Years' resolutions, never come to fruition, to study the pamphlet and Saxon and Norman history more in the future.

Trains and Cattle

Next morning at the railway station I found that the two-car train had capacity for only two cycles—just enough in this case. My fellow cyclist was a commuter. He cycles thirteen kilometres from home to the station, and then pays Northwest Trains six pounds daily for the round trip into work. He considered Northwest to be the worst operator. Since Margaret Thatcher's privatization program, the railway stations and tracks are owned and operated by one company while several different companies operate the trains. This car was clean and attractive inside but the guy selling snacks was a disgrace. His rumpled suit and spotty tie did not excuse   scruffy hair, dirty nails, unclean, untidy linen and an indifferent manner.

Before noon, I was outside the Preston station ready to roll, with Kirkby Lonsdale as my goal and hoping to stay again at 'The Courtyard' B&B, operated by the nurse that did part of her training in Oakville.

Preston is large, heavily trafficked and poorly signposted. It took careful reading of the map to plot the nearest likely escape route. This led me through a broad residential and commercial section and eventually to my selected turnoff to the east. At Longridge, I stopped for lunch at a pub. At the edge of the car park where I left the bike, a young scummy couple were having a meal while fondling each other and smoking--multi-taskers extraordinaire. Love was definitely blind in this case. I took extra time securing the bike in hope that they would leave–they did.

After lunch, the road undulated, climbing consistently. The pleasant countryside induced a sense of soothing but energizing contentment. Farm fragrant breezes brushed the sheep-spotted basket of eggs topography, adding authenticity. Just before Whitewell, in Forest Bowland, I stopped to admire a magnificent multitiered garden with a stone patio and humped bridges over a stream. I asked the two people wandering round if I might take a picture. Gardeners generally love others to take an interest but this lady, the housekeeper, was especially gracious, particularly so to someone attired in black latex.

She invited me into the garden to take my pictures and provided a very welcome huge glass of cold barley water. I drank this gratefully while absorbing the bucolic ambiance of this converted barn home with its beautiful stone and brown stained wood exterior. A playful brood of black Labrador puppies mingled with the sheep in the paddock enhancing the visual atmosphere. The housekeeper explained that this property is one of the few freeholds in the district.

Stone fences, bubbling streams and tree-canopied tunnels graced the next several kilometres—just ideal! A little while later, I overtook my first touring cyclist—an American on a solo camping tour. We talked for a while but his appearance, odour and conversational style were off-putting. His response to everything, I said was 'gotcha' which I interpreted as 'I understand' but it also suggested a total lack of interest. He claimed to be in theatre arts in Chicago and West Palm Beach and said that if he started smelling too bad, he would stay over in a hostel. The prospect of sharing a hostel room with him prevented me from assuring him that he was already 'overripe.'

From Dunsop Bridge, the road climbed steadily and my hopes of reaching Kirkby Lonsdale at a reasonable time faded. A herd of cattle was crossing the road just ahead at close to what looked to be the summit. As I approached, so did the resident bull. It seemed prudent to give him a wide berth and wait until he and the herd were at a safe distance.

The bull led the cattle astray--beyond where they should be. This caught the attention of a red-haired, massively freckled boy of about 9 or 10 who roared over on a motorbike to guide them back. I complained about the hills and asked about the rest of my day's route. His only response was 'you're in trouble!'

His assessment proved accurate. The climb was tough requiring plenty of walking but this was rewarded by a run-down of about 4 to 5 kilometres into High Bentham at just six p.m.. I quickly chose High Bentham for my overnight, giving up, temporarily, on Kirkby Lonsdale.

Kendal, the Dales and York

Kendal, Cumbria is one of the major destinations planned for this trip because my newest niece now bears that name. Her Australian father's maternal family, surname Ireland, was once prominent in Kendal. Her older sister is called Ireland. So, I thought a visit and perhaps a souvenir from Kendal for Kendal was justified.

First, though, I had to spend some time in one of my favourite places, Kirkby Lonsdale. The new day started out beautifully with lovely countryside and acceptable weather. In less than an hour I was in the Kirkby Lonsdale stone pavilion in the market place writing notes in my journal. At eleven I succumbed to the perpetual call for tea and cakes.

Refreshed, I revisited some of the beauty spots round the town including Ruskin's favourite River Lune view from behind St. Mary's church, discussed in a previous chapter. Then it was off to Kendal.

The difficult terrain restricted my average speed to about 16 kilometres per hour so it took almost two hours to reach Kendal. At the town's edge, I couldn't resist stopping at a Renault dealership. European cars are much more interesting to me than those available at home as function and economy seem to play a much bigger role in their design. Yet their designs are attractive, creative, often elegant, and space utilization is excellent. No salesman bothered me during my inspection tour; perhaps they don't accept cycles as trade-ins!

The hostel didn't open until five so I strolled round the town visiting shops in search of an appropriate souvenir. Kendal's High Street is very long so that my search and general exploration consumed a generally pleasant three hours. Learning in that time, that Kendal has a very long history, a twelfth century castle and a house where Bonny Prince Charlie stayed during the war with England. There weren't any references to the Ireland family but I chose a guidebook that described the town and its history as the souvenir. It is far too old for my niece now but perhaps will be healthier and have more lasting interest than a Kendal ashtray.

My hostel roommates tonight were four walkers from Preston up for the weekend and a sour-faced chap. He never uttered a word, slept under my berth and was still there next morning after the rest of us had breakfasted and were leaving!

Leaving Kendal for the Yorkshire Dales, my run to Dentdale looked easy but the cold rain and steady climb to Sedbergh made it difficult. There the road flattens following the river through idyllic countryside.

Now, rather than spoiling things, the light rain enhanced the atmosphere, providing a more authentic character than a sunshiny day would have. So I wasn't entirely unhappy with the weather at this point.

I reached Dent at 1.30 and quickly chose the King George Pub instead of the Sun for lunch, as it offered Roast Beef and Yorkshire pudding. A very traditional Sunday lunch was exactly what was needed to warm up. Inclusion of a sweet in the price cinched the decision and given that the remainder of the day's journey was short, I also persuaded myself that a half pint of lager was permissible. Being Sunday, the pub was very busy and I got there only half an hour before they stopped taking orders.

Despite the meal, it felt even colder once outside again, so I nipped back into the pub's washroom to put on my long cycling tights. Walking round the cobble stone streets of Dent I met a middle-aged man who took an interest in my cycle. He bought his first frame (a famous Claude Butler) at age 16 but it was stolen last year. He has just found a replacement frame and is going to fit it out with quality components.

Unfortunately, all this rain had stopped my computer and I was unable to track my progress. It was only another ten kilometres to the hostel but I depend on that computer to monitor distance and speed as well as to anticipate the turns on my route that are specified by distance. Although cold and wet, my discomfort was overcome by the perfect countryside, especially the last five kilometres that tracked a rushing brook with glen like topography—its huge rocks worn smooth by centuries of water. I met a man and his wife on the last day of a cycling trip. They were upset at the prospect of returning home tonight because he has to be at work tomorrow. (Sometimes, we destroy the joy of the now with bad thoughts of the past or future, ensuring that much of our lives are spent in mild misery.)

I arrived at the hostel about 4.30 and met an English walking couple from Stockport, Cheshire waiting for the opening at 5. The place was thick with midges—the first real insect problem of my tour. I quickly unloaded the panniers into the entranceway and found an open shed to store the bike. The common room and drying rooms were also open so I put my sopping panniers and shoes in there. By this time, the hostel was ready to register its guests.

Inglebrough, my eight-bedded room also housed two Englishmen and a Yank from Kansas who now works in Toronto in the organic vegetable business. All the facilities were down the hall--two each of sinks, showers and toilets.

Three other Canadians from the Okanogan Valley in British Columbia, an English couple in their thirties and a woman of about sixty were some of the other residents. We four Canadians had dinner together with the English couple and chatted amiably until about nine.

The English couple was very pleasant, refined and educated. He is a semiretired economics and statistics lecturer and is pursuing an Open University course in philosophy. 'The course is good value', he said, 'because you have to write seven or eight essays and take a final examination.' Next morning, I breakfasted with a shy Englishman who nevertheless proved to be an interesting person who knew a lot about canals, geography and transportation history.

Stopping the next day to explore the 350 metre high Dent Railway station, I discovered a waterfall at the end of the platform which would provide perfect architecture for a period drama. The road beyond continued climbing for probably six kilometres to the Garsdale Head junction with the Kirkby Stephen Road. There, perched conveniently, is the tempting Moorcock Inn--one of two historic moorland inns that were essential staging posts for horse-drawn traffic in the bleak trek over the moors—and are still very welcome to cyclists as hungry and thirsty as I was.

Back on the road again, I overtook an elderly gentleman cyclist studying the landscape. He warned me about flooding on the road at Black Boar Fell but it wasn't dangerous. I had to walk a fair bit, particularly one climb with a 20% grade. At my turn on the B6270 to Keld, the prospect of a tea break justified a three kilometre detour into Kirkby Stephen.

Kirkby Stephen caters a lot to the tourist trade but is still an honest, natural, busy and pleasant market town. I stopped at The Mulberry Tree for tea, to be greeted as 'Another Canadian!' by a female university student from British Columbia, travelling for most of the summer. After the usual exchange of superficial information about our travels, I studied a newspaper adding to my knowledge about the latest in British life. Apparently the pound sign is missing from some newly issued notes making the Conservatives nervous that the Labour Party is surreptitiously preparing for adoption of the Euro!

Lying behind the market entrance is a square of green lawn, manicured to be as smooth as a bowling green and broken with footpaths bordered by expertly pruned trees. The Saxon church of St Stephen sits peacefully in the green. Its lovely wooden ceiling features coats of arms where the beams intersect. The rector stopped to say a pleasant hello. A permanent poster advising fourteenth century charges for stalls and hawkers hangs at the market entrance. One felt immediately welcome here.

About four, I started the southeast run to Keld Hostel with better weather and a computer sufficiently dried out to register. The route was tough but included perfect waterfalls, bubbling brooks and sheep-mown moors, sightings of heron, rabbits, cattle and sheep,making this segment another competitor for best of tour.

The sheep responded to my conversational enquiries and the cattle looked up from their grazing, at least acknowledging that I spoke to them. Sometimes, if both sets of animals appear in rapid succession, my languages confused and wind up speaking to cattle in sheep tongue! (This talking to the animals is a harmless foible in my makeup – nothing to do with Dr. Doolittle and I can't speak horse.)

The hostel at Keld was immediately likeable. I was in time for evening meal and there was only one person in my room. He worked on the Aberdeenshire oil rigs and was walking the Pennine Way. We had a pleasant meal served by a bright, open-faced cheerful woman, matching my stereotypical image of a happy country wife—attractive in a fresh, wholesome way. We speculated on her accent so I finally asked. She replied 'I'm from Buxton in North Derbyshire. Our accents are totally different from people just twelve miles south.'

Next morning I spent an unproductive hour trying to improve the power of my brakes by moving the rear pads closer to the rims. Brakes have been my nemesis for years especially for this bike's rear wheel.

En route to Thwaite and Muker, the road runs flat alongside a river and over stone bridges. Again, I considered that the day's ride was the best yet—particularly around Keld. The terrain was gentler than yesterday and carpeted in various shades of green. There are deep valleys, streams, stonewalls--all components of my idyllic vision of rural England. Swaledale and Dentdale are perfect examples of this.

Just beyond Reeth, I decided to go further east along a more level road to Richmond rather than climb out of the valley as planned. There I requested a Baba ('book a bed ahead') booking for Thirsk at the Tourist Information Centre. This would take about an hour to arrange as Thirsk is outside the Richmond TIC district. Waiting for the response on an adjacent park bench, I got into conversation with a retired horticulturist. He told me that he joined the Richmond Cycle Club in 1947 and used to participate in their 160-kilometre Sunday runs over the dales on fixed wheel (only one gear) bikes!

After the specified hour, I had a booking at Long Acre in Thirsk that was offering an evening meal. Being a little leery of the sanitary conditions in private homes, I declined. Long Acre specified that they would hold the reservation only until 6 p.m. It was now 1.30 and the TIC ladies were concerned that four and a half hours wouldn't be enough to cycle the 46 kilometres.

Doing so wasn't a problem. By five I was opposite the former Thirsk home and surgery of veterinarian, Alf Wight (James Herriot of All Creatures Great and Small) regretting having turned down the meal. There was no place in the town for one.

Long Acre's address is 86A Topcliffe Road. After number 84, the name of the road and the numerical sequence changed! At number 84 they told me that Topcliffe Road continued half a block away. Once at 86A, Rose Dawson greeted me warmly and later brought a full pot of tea and buttered scones to me even though I had tea-making facilities in the room. It was obvious that this is a clean and generous household so I asked Rose if it was too late to change my mind about the evening meal. It wasn't!

A necessary decision and a great one! Rose served a massive meal with a large variety of fresh vegetables including parsnips, one of my favourites. A little later her other five guests arrived for similar large meals. After dinner she asked if I had any washing. When I gratefully brought her my laundry, Rose offered me maps and books to suggest pleasant back roads to York where I am going next.

Next morning, the table was laid with grapefruit segments, strawberries, bananas, cantaloupe and orange juice as starters, followed by scrambled eggs on toast and grilled tomatoes. While I was enjoying all of this, my laundry was delivered to my room fresh and folded from the tumble dryer and my cycle was brought out from the shed. She even filled my water bottle and offered to make sandwiches. I have never had such service in a B&B. She definitely deserved a gratuity and I am embarrassed not to have thought of it at the time.

Rose recommended that I visit the Herriot museum in his old surgery. Alf Wight's son, James, took over the practice but now lives outside the village. The museum opened this April and already had 20,000 admissions. Unfortunately, it did not open until ten, so I deferred my visit to another trip and went up the street to St. Mary's, the church where Alf was married in 1941. It is a very old church with a castellated tower, wooden ceilings and pews. Two people were worshiping together in a small chapel. (I am happy to report that the museum is very worthwhile, encompassing the living quarters and surgery as well as the studio sets used for the television series. In addition there is a complete veterinary museum on the first floor. I did indeed visit again.)

Next was Sowerby, which consisted largely of one long, tree-lined pleasant and genteel residential street. After Sowerby came Kilburn, another lovely small village, famous for being the location of Robert Thompson's Mouseman shop, known for traditional oak furniture.

This furniture is made special by a small mouse carved into every piece. Thompson was born in 1876 and apprenticed for five years before becoming an independent craftsman. These five-year apprenticeships are still the career path for furniture artisans, at least at this establishment. Each one has their own version of the mouse so you can tell who made your piece of furniture. I talked to one making a latticework (involving four hours of labour) for a chair back. A small gift shop and museum is housed in Thompson's original home.

Across the road is a modern, upscale furniture showroom where I priced a dining room set very similar to that owned by friends of ours in Hertfordshire. The table and six chairs would have been over C $12,000—out of our league!

Next-door was the Singing Bird, a tea and gift shop. This time my teacakes were spread with a superb lemon cheese instead of my usual black currant jam. However, the proprietor was unfriendly and she overcharged—perhaps she is a recent transplant from the urban south of England. So it wasn't entirely surprising three years later on my 2002 tour to find that this particular 'Bird' no longer sings.

I continued south into York and decided to lunch late at an all-day fish and chip place. Just as I was locking the bike, a yahoo walking along the pavement shouting into his mobile, 'f...this' and 'f...that' and calling the woman he was shouting at, 'a cow.' This was a very upsetting welcome to my favourite city but unfortunately this sort of behaviour is a frequent hazard in the larger centres.

After lunch, I strolled round the Shambles and Newgate Market absorbing the atmosphere. It was impossible to keep all the architectural styles and historical information straight. After very little time, I couldn't distinguish Norman from Saxon or Viking. So at about four, I packed it in, heading towards the Dairy, a vegetarian B&B that Mari and I had stayed in during our 1992 visit.

Amazingly, for directionally challenged me, without benefit of city map, street name or number, I was able to go directly to the B&B location from memory or would have done if a cycle shop hadn't diverted me en route. Inside, the owner, Andy, introduced me to the Gazelle, a Dutch make that he praised highly over Japanese, US and British makes for its quality. He sells other brands as well so his enthusiasm seemed genuine.

Gazelles are primarily urban or commuter type cycles with chain guards, dynamos for the lights, luggage carriers and built in locks. They are heavy but their purpose-built functionality strongly appeals--I would love to have one. Leaving my cycle behind to see if Andy could fix my rear brakes, I continued on foot to the Dairy.

Stopping there only long enough to get more presentable, I went out again towards the Theatre Royal where I have a ticket for 'Iolanthe' at the Theatre Royal and hope to get a meal at their Café Royal.

It took twenty minutes to walk to the café and with time at a premium, my luck was to get a determined idiot as a server. First, she said that the dish I ordered wasn't on the menu--how else could I know they offered it? Then, after a long delay, I asked her to check on my order which she agreed to do but never reported back. I gave up and was just rising from my seat to leave when the meal arrived, nearly an hour after ordering, leaving me 25 minutes before playtime!

It was excellent but had to be wolfed down, not savoured. My Parmesan cheese and leek flan came with a plate of perfectly cooked new potatoes, snow peas and broccoli. Thus, hastily fortified, I rushed across the lobby to the theatre.

The Theatre Royal is very grand in a plush, Victorian style but this production paled in comparison to what I am used to at the Stratford and the Shaw Festivals at home. The sets and costumes were amateurish and I couldn't hear much of the dialogue (this latter complaint may be a personal issue not a production fault). However, the actor playing the part of the Lord Chancellor was outstanding—Stratford, Ontario quality.

The next day was devoted to pedestrian activities—revisiting the Shambles to explore and shop and to find the Cockatoo Crêperie restaurant that Mari and I had enjoyed so much back in 1992. Our Cockatoo is now The Blue Bicycle complete with an elderly blue cycle casually chained to one corner and glowing newspaper reviews displayed prominently outside.

I returned to the B&B, stopping at the cycle shop to collect my bike. Andy reported that my wheel was out of alignment and that the frame's rear brake mounting was set at the wrong level. He trued the wheel but I lived with the other issue until 2007 when Chad, Canada's Olympic cycling mechanic, reminded me while working on some other modifications to my bike. Later, I had a custom builder weld the seat stay bosses holding those brakes lower, solving the problem and justifying a new paint job--in British Racing Green.

Leaving the bike and my purchases at the B&B, I gave in to the lure of The Blue Bicycle and was their first lunch customer. Soon they were packed with prosperous appearing professionals. My goat cheese flan with salad and a glass of wine had to be savoured slowly, giving each bite maximum attention. It was thoroughly enjoyable although more would have been better.

My pedestrian forays continued at a small but elegantly restored Georgian house in Copperfields, called Fairfax House. The house, then a cinema, was bought in 1982 for £30,000. Two years plus £750,000 were spent restoring its former glory. Fairfax had used the house as a coming out residence for his daughter. Ineffectively, apparently, as Miss Fairfax never met anyone suitable and died a spinster at 68.

During the Civil War, Fairfax prevented the soldiers from looting the Cathedral (such activities provided the primary compensation for the common soldier). Consequently, York Minster contributed generously to the Fairfax House restoration fund. Mr. Terry, of chocolate fame, gave all the furnishings. Apart from these historical connections, the house provides an interesting perspective on refined domestic life at the time.

I next visited the Railway Museum—the largest in the world, but had only a couple of hours—not nearly enough. Stephenson's original Rocket, engines back to 1848, Royal Mail trains past and present are all here. Most interesting to me were the Royal carriages, complete with bathtubs.

My day's timetable was dictated by wanting to attend Evensong at York Minster. It is a service I've always enjoyed but is typically only available in the larger cathedrals like Winchester, Salisbury and York. There is very little involvement for the congregation so one can sit peaceably and simply let the glorious music and majesty of the surroundings soothe and refresh your soul. Even an atheist would be moved. Evensong is held in the choir area with visitor seating right behind the choir. This evening's congregation included many foreigners suggesting that many other tourists feel the same way.

The service ended too early to go for an evening meal, so I meandered through Shambles until the clock struck 6.30, then headed directly to the Olde Starre in Stonegate, listed in a pub guidebook my sister, Guila, gave me. This is an extremely old pub but they have caved in to modern pressures, installing games and television and thus spoiling what obviously had been a traditionally authentic atmosphere.

Lincoln and the Old German
Next morning at breakfast in the Dairy, a couple, already at my table, proudly pronounced themselves as the 'X's' from Philadelphia, but immediately lost interest in me when they learned I was from Canada. When Mrs X was presented a poached egg on toast with a sprinkle of sesame seed, she became upset with the egg's colour. She ignored the server's pleasant explanation that that the egg's colour was due to it being organic and free-range, demanding a replacement! Seeing this as another example of US insularity and arrogance, I was embarrassed to be sharing the same table.

The unfamiliar segment of this tour--south into Lincolnshire-begins today. Access to my route was very convenient from the Dairy and I was soon in the countryside travelling on the B1228.

Tomorrow I am booked in at the Lincoln hostel but tonight, I need a B&B somewhere. My route took me south to the port town of Goole, one of Britain's furthest inland seaports, situated nearly 70 kilometres from the North Sea, where the Don and Ouse rivers meet. The rapid growth of Goole as a port dates from 1826 when docks were built and a canal was cut east from Knottingley. Cargo was drawn down the canal in square containers, called 'Tom Puddings' that were like floating railway trucks.(8)

Like so many English towns, Goole's principal shopping area, the High Street, is a pedestrian mall. These are generally very successful, making shopping a much more pleasant activity and creating a stronger sense of community with benches and other amenities scattered throughout.

This is market gardening country with few animals and generally uninteresting homes and villages. This lack of visual stimulation was due in part to the flat terrain which allowed me to make very good time; so good that it seemed possible to get as far as Lincoln tonight. Doing so would allow me to explore Lincoln for part of tomorrow and take some pressure off the rest of my schedule.

Excited children's voices interrupted these thoughts and calculations. A school games day was in progress across the road in a small paddock. I watched the eight to ten year olds compete, girls against girls and boys against boys, at three-legged races and other traditional games. Parents and teachers observed with pride from folding chairs. Childish joy brightened the warm sunny day. Natural and cheerful, the children helped the teachers set up each event and seemed delighted with everything. This sort of scene fits my idealized vision of England and how it should be. Alas, the vision doesn't have much reality anymore, anywhere.

Despite this diversion, by 5 p.m., I was certain that I could reach Lincoln tonight so I rang the hostel to bring my reservation forward and optimistically ordered dinner which is served at seven. I was in luck with the reservation but my estimate of the remaining distance to Lincoln was 13 km short and once there it took twenty minutes to find the hostel. Arrival at 7.30 meant that my dinner, still warming in the cooker was now desiccated.

Arriving on time would not have improved the meal very much. The gourmet touch has yet to reach hostel land and probably never will; although, given the high proportion of vegetarians in Britain, there generally is a choice. The dining room was very hot, so I sat in the conservatory where a breeze blew in from the adjacent and lovely South Park Common.

During my dinner an old German, sitting at an adjacent table with a map, was trying to determine how far he cycled that day. He talked to himself in a manner strongly suggesting that he wanted an audience, so I obliged. Given that he was older and heavier, it was a bit ego-shattering to hear his boast that his day's distance was 93 km when I had been feeling particularly superior with my 134!

Heaven crashed during the night—the loudest thunderstorm I've ever heard—it was particularly potent in my lonely basement room with the windows open. At breakfast, the old German found someone else to impress with his tale. He was very self-centred—never showing any interest in the other person except to bridge into an opportunity to tell more about himself.

Getting into Lincoln proper was easy after last night's navigational activity. Then Lincoln had looked particularly intriguing. Now with Saturday morning shoppers and traffic, it was less so, seemingly indistinguishable from many other similar sized English cities.   I wanted to find out about the cycle museum and locate a tourist information office to do a 'Baba' booking. Inquiring about the TIC in a bookshop in the first floor of Jews House (a 12th century home at the foot of Steephill), I was asked whether I wanted a TIC up the hill or down. Replying, 'It doesn't matter', so she gave me the UP and was it ever!

The cobbled street has an ascent of at least 1 in 3 and is delightfully lined with small quality shops leading to the castle, more cobbled streets, shops and Roman remains. At the TIC, I requested a B&B somewhere in the Grantham area and went along to the Wig and

Mitre, a highly recommended nearby pub, while waiting for the TIC to make the arrangements.

The pub is an elegant place in a solid, middle-class sort of way. Their first-floor coffee room is panelled and has a fireplace. I had my first coffee of the trip with plum bread and jam. The coffee was first rate, improving the already very acceptable ambiance. On the way out, I read posted newspaper reviews highly praising the Wig and Mitre as one of those 'surprisingly good little places'. It was a shame not to have time for a more substantial meal there.

The Flying Scotsman and the San Francisco Connection

I briefly explored the rest of the cobble-stoned area, collected my B&B reservation, cleaned the accumulated mud off the bike, lubricated it and set off on the 60 km run to Grantham, the home of Isaac Newton and Margaret Thatcher. It was probably less than 5 km off my original route and the terrain was still flat, permitting good speed and an early arrival.

There is an attractive market square, some fine old coaching inns and a lovely riverside walk, part of which is maintained by the National Trust. Other points of interest are the 14th century spire of St. Wulfram's Church, a fifteenth century grammar school north of the church, Grantham House and the Angel and Royal Hotel in the High Street. Generally though, Grantham appears a bit worn.

The Crown and Anchor hotel attracted me with an irresistible offer of refreshments in their lounge. I used their washroom to tidy up, and then enjoyed a languid hour on the sofa reading their *Times* and savouring a pot of filter coffee with a single scone. The incongruity of the experience appeals to my memory even now, the scruffy cyclist wearing questionable gear pretending to be a toff in genteel surroundings!

It took some time to find the B&B because its landmark, the crematorium, was poorly signposted. This B&B is called Robert's Roost and this Robert was assigned to the top of the roost in a tiny room whose only window is in the roof. Nevertheless, the room was clean, nicely decorated and equipped with all the comforts, tea fixings and television.   The *Times* guide suggested an interesting murder story on ITV later tonight that I plan to watch.

Next morning the landlady gave me a table by myself.   I had barely cracked my book when another man walked in saying, 'my name is David Y. I'm a professor of physics in San Francisco; may I join you?' pulling out his business card and handing it to me while speaking. The card said Lecturer but I didn't challenge his overstatement. Learning that I was from the Toronto area, he claimed that a University of Toronto professor has helped organize his current tour of ten universities lecturing on 'The Physics of Magic and the Magic of Physics'. Most of the breakfast was devoted to his story, which was very interesting, so I didn't mind doing the bulk of the listening (but, if asked, he probably would remember me as a brilliant conversationalist).

There was an astounding coincidence.   His daughter, Eleanor, is the same age as my son Cameron and like him, a graduate of the San Francisco Conservatory of Music.   According to her father, Eleanor is a 'real looker.' I wondered if he was acting as matchmaker.   Later in the day during my weekly call home, Cameron claimed no recollection of her.

I got away again at 9.30 but as the day's objective—Ramsay, Cambridgeshire, was only 70 km, spent my first half hour enjoying the small riverside park, now being used by a few fishermen and walkers.

Later on in the countryside, I suddenly came across row upon row of cars alongside the road with scores of people staring at the distant railway tracks. One of the spectators told me that the Flying Scotsman, now 76 years old and recently restored at a cost of £1 million, was on its first trip since restoration and would soon pass this spot. People have paid up to £300 for a seat for this run from London. When the train approached, I got an excellent shot of the engine and could see passengers enjoying champagne and nibbles.

At the Bull & Swan in Stamford for lunch, I asked directions at the bar to a particular B road on my route. One of the customers at the bar took an interest. He claimed not to know the road but later realized he lived on it! Locally the road is known by the name of the town it leads to, not by its official number, which isn't even posted. This is a very common phenomenon.

We discussed my afternoon route. He was concerned that I would not be able to find a place to stay in Ramsay and gave me the name and telephone number of a 'woman friend who could help in a pinch'; leaving the impression that they have shared more than a pinch.

Reaching Ramsay before six, I quickly realized that my pub acquaintance was right about accommodation here. Thinking it was too complicated to explain, I choose not to contact his friend and booked in at the George-a big mistake. The George was expensive, dirty and obviously not well patronized—or maintained-- there were cobwebs in the bath!

Next day, however, was warm and bright, mellowing my mood but melting my sunscreen. It streamed down my face and my arms became coated with black insects stuck in the goo. There were compensations; with only 64 km to go today, I could pedal more leisurely through the now rolling countryside, talk to the occasional animals and enjoy the abundant and attractive villages.

St. Ives and Cambridge
St. Ives wasn't on the guide route but it was so close that a detour was a must. I'm still not sure whether this is the St. Ives of the famous children's poem—'I met a man with seven wives' ----or whether it is the Cornish one. Now having seen them both, I prefer this one. The Cornish one is too dependent on tourism and does not have the feel of a natural town functioning normally.

Today was market day; the place throbbed with people, giving it a holiday air. The beautifully sunny day made the riverside location even more attractive. There are handsome homes on one side of the river and outdoor cafes on the other with a fifteenth century bridge between the two sides. The bridge is graced with one of only four medieval bridge chapels surviving in England. This one was converted to a house in the nineteenth century.

House construction and design interests me and I am intrigued by the breeze block exterior and interior wall construction used in Britain, wondering if it is more expensive than the wood skeleton structures used in North America and what the relative merits might be. Consequently, I am always on the lookout for model homes that one can visit. Today, my travels took me past a construction site consisting of a former farm where the barn had been converted to a home with dark brown stained weatherboard on the upper storey and an attractive brick below. The other homes were new and smaller but built in a similar style. I walked round looking in the windows. The layouts were appealing with a comfortable, airy look even though the rooms were generally smaller than we are used to in North America. The ground floor construction features were visible on a few uncompleted homes--solid concrete floors (meaning no basement), breeze block interior walls and plastic plumbing. Despite its reputation for a poor climate, Britain is not so cold that it needs to build basements to get below the frost line.

Despite this diversion and the detour to St. Ives, I arrived in Cambridge by 3.30. Cambridge obviously has a much stronger attraction for tourists than Lincoln; it is more famous and the proximity to London probably adds to its appeal. Strange then that Lincoln had five tourist information offices but I could find only one in Cambridge.

Cambridge is one of Europe's ancient university cities. Dissidents who found that the slightly older Oxford inhibited their freedom of expression established Peterhouse, the oldest Cambridge college, in 1285. The compact college area in Cambridge's centre is fascinating, well worth a day's exploration of its architectural treasures, ranging from the thirteenth century to the late twentieth. Despite a recent city-centre ban, Cambridge is a city where everybody bikes, with the highest level of cycle commuting in Britain.(9)

I enjoy English drama but this was a poor time for live theatre. Shakespeare's "Measure for Measure" at Emmanuel College was the only play on offer but I don't know Shakespeare well enough to appreciate it. Two days later I could have seen Wilde's "The

Importance of Being Earnest" but that night was earmarked for a visit to old friends in Welwyn Garden City, Hertfordshire.

Slovenian tourists packed the pavement outside the hostel and held a religious service in the games room later that night. Their strong and pleasant singing was a soothing accompaniment for completing my journal in the adjacent dining room. Afterwards, I attempted to take advantage of the hostel's laundry facilities but was thwarted by a female Californian dither head. She monopolized the tumble dryer, delaying the completion of my laundry until 11.30.

Unfortunately, you really need to stay put while the laundry is in process so that you don't hold up others or can grab a machine as soon as it becomes available. One washer and dryer for perhaps 100 guests is managing a bit tightly. I sat close by and read my book so while the ambience was not inviting or particularly comfortable this wasn't entirely a waste of time. During my wait, Denise, the rather interesting receptionist, came in to collect her smalls from the top of the dryer where another guest dumped them. Somehow, I 'accidentally' saw the tags on all those frilly bits, getting a much better picture of her personal dimensions than her loose clothing provided.

Hostel tradition is lights out at eleven. This is honoured more in the rural locations where they often lock up then. In larger centres with nightlife the rule has either been abandoned or is just ignored. I noticed on my 2004 trip that some hostels now use combination locks on the outside doors (changing the combination daily) giving members the combination for late night returns.

Given the time I finished my laundry, I felt bound to get ready for bed in the dark to avoid disturbing anyone in the room. So, it was particularly upsetting for the lights to come on at 12.30 and then to have the intruder demand my bed! In my years' of hostelling experience, beds have never been assigned, just 'first come, first choice.' That wasn't the case at Cambridge. Here the room key had a number tag designating which bunk you were to use but this system had not been explained to me.

The intruding idiot woke everyone up with his fuss to get my bunk although there was a free bunk ready and waiting. I refused. Someone shouted **'TURN OUT THE LIGHTS'** and he gave in. Continuing to irritate, he came in and out of the room, turning on the small reading light over his bunk at least four times. In the morning, I traded keys with him and then asked the receptionist (not Denise) to record that I would be in Bunk 1, not 4, this evening. She said it couldn't be done, as someone else was booked into 1! I persuaded her that the new person can be booked into 4 with the stroke of a pen which surely she could do. (I don't whether she really was incapable or just bloody minded, because it did not get changed.)

Next morning at breakfast, the Californian dither head asked me to join her and revealed that she has been on a US Social Security disability pension for the past eleven years. Surprisingly, the disability is a bad back not anything mental. Previously, I would not have thought such a pension would permit a two month long holiday in the UK but perhaps she has saved for years.

After breakfast I walked into the city centre to see the Backs, or lawns, that run down to the river behind the colleges. Here, the views are of pasture with cattle, punters on the river, beautiful lawns and the colleges--a setting bound to be conducive to productive thought.

A path behind Kings and Clare Colleges between the Wren Library and Trinity Hall leads back towards the city centre. On the way, I toured Trinity--the largest college with 650 students. Its large courtyard was used for the famous scene in the film 'Chariots of Fire' where the challenge was to run the entire 367 metre courtyard circumference while the clock was striking noon--a period of 43 seconds-faster than a top marathon speed. This 'Great Court Run' has been a long-standing tradition at Trinity.(10) The students' rooms surround this courtyard in blocks of about eight to ten rooms per doorway. It all oozed tradition, exclusiveness and intellect--at least it does in my imagination.

Circling back to the Wren Library, I found it populated more by tourists than academics. The Wren boasts beautiful woodcarvings and ancient collections, including Newton's first letter regarding gravity, his walking stick and an illuminated bible.

After a lunch on a bench in the market square I completed the self-guided walking tour started yesterday, seeing the Round Church (modelled after the Holy Sepulchre in Jerusalem). C.S. Lewis information and his books were in abundance. C.S. Lewis was of particular interest at the moment as I brought one of his books on this trip intent on studying it thoroughly. Surely good intentions count for something but so far, spy and high finance novels have won out.

College dining halls really appeal to me primarily for their style but as you have no doubt noted, I very much enjoy eating. One such hall, at Emmanuel College, is decorated in a restful cool green and white in Georgian style. Usually, these dining halls have an elevated platform for the top table that is perpendicular to the students' bench style tables on the lower level. Another dining hall with heavy oak panelling was set up for a future meal with all the requisite crystal and extensive cutlery for several courses. I found two discarded menus from the previous day that could have come from a four star restaurant. If one has the ability and opportunity to be an English academic, this looks like the place to be!

I finished my tour with evensong at St. Johns. This was a special experience. The general layout was much the same as York Minster but this evening's service involved virtually the entire building integrating the surrounding long, narrow stained glass windows with the service. The choir was very good and I emerged at peace with the world.

I collected some items from the shops having decided to use the hostel members' kitchen tonight. A young Canadian woman was there preparing dinner for herself and two friends that arrived yesterday on a two-month research project for their English professor back home. I never met the others but this young woman was a bit overwhelmed with her situation. She could not describe her research project, had no idea where she and her friends will live during their stay and has nothing arranged to access research facilities. I gave her my Cambridge map and the remainder of my loaf of bread. Pitiful as they were, she seemed cheered somewhat.

About 1.30 in the morning, the hostel fire alarm jarred us awake—all 100 of us trooped out into the street in various states of undress. The fire brigade arrived shortly and after a brief inspection, allowed us to return to our beds. The young Canadian girl looked wretched and bewildered as if she longed for the comfort and familiarity of home.

After breakfast I got to the railway station early enough to acquire a paper and join the train at a leisurely pace. The train stopped frequently but still took only an hour to get to Welwyn Garden City. I had come an hour early to stroll round, assessing changes to our old hometown. The railway station is the biggest change--much larger now and encompassing a well-appointed shopping mall. Otherwise, there is little obvious change—WGC is still a very attractive place if a little less well cared for. An estate agent's window featured a new home for £235,000 in Scholars' Mews. This is built on the grounds of a school my much younger sister, Guila, attended while living with us in the early 70's.

Detouring through Scholars' Mews to see the tight but tasteful transformation, I arrived at our friends' home at the appointed hour. They are very comfortable to be around and gracious as well as interesting hosts. Shortly after lunch, their daughter Sarah arrived with her daughter, Francesca, then my favourite young person. I've since become a grandparent and am biased. Francesca ('Chessie') claimed to remember me from a visit two years ago, which was very gratifying. She was still lovely, lively, impish and well-socialized.

While my hostess was busy preparing another meal, her husband was in the garden with Chessie helping her to write down a rude poem that clearly delighted her.

> 'There was a woman from Leeds
> Who ate a packet of seeds.
> In less than an hour,
> Her face was a flower and
> Her bottom was covered in weeds.'

Her delight was, of course, focused on the last line. Then grandmother spoiled things by correcting her writing. Chessie crawled up into my lap to be read a book and afterwards engaged me in a vigorous game of hide and seek. We enjoyed a salad supper and parted company after strolling down to the railway for my 8.30 train. This has been a very different day with good, intelligent conversation, ample, well-prepared food, shared memories and a lovely child.

South to Gatwick

Next morning, I was gratified to find that my pre-planned route back towards Gatwick began very close to the hostel going over a cycle bridge and on to a cycle path. Uncertainty still reigned at intersections though, requiring frequent map consultations.

I cycled through a district called the Camps stopping at a small teahouse cum green grocer. While there, I overheard a conversation between the proprietress and an older customer. Their genuine neighbourly affection for each other, simple, good natures and an unhurried attitude toward life was both amusing and appealing.

My lunch stop was at a pub called 'The Fox', situated attractively near a windmill, a small green, a pond by the green and a clutch of shops arranged round the perimeter. As pleasant as it was outside, I chose to eat in, both to enjoy the atmosphere and to avoid the North American voices on the park benches outside. They sound gratingly out of place, diminishing the experience of being away. As I left the gents after lunch, a chicken walked into the pub. This prompted me to say to a woman at the entrance 'Bit of a turnaround isn't it, when the chicken comes into the Fox house?' She just stared, uncomprehendingly.

Next came the Rodings, a series of villages reputed to be idyllic, best-kept village prize candidates. I did not see the evidence for that opinion perhaps because now the traffic, congestion and noise of London was seeping into my consciousness. It was five p.m. and I didn't want to struggle through London at rush hour or to pay nearby London B&B prices. So, I started looking for B&B's right away.

There were none in sight nor any pubs offering accommodation. With the help of a pub's telephone directory, we found three B&Bs in Brentwood, 11 km further south. A pub there gave me directions to two of them. Both were full, the second one having let its last room go five minutes before I arrived—had I gone to it first, the room would have been mine.

Wanting to help, this last landlord did some telephoning for me, finding a room at The Brick Hotel some five kilometres further on in Warley for £40—just the sort of price I had dreaded being so close to London. The ride to Warley was pleasant except for the nagging effect of that price. Once at the Brick, I took a smaller room for £35 and, trying to compensate for this still too high cost, limited dinner to a toasted cheese sandwich and a beer at the hotel bar. The sandwich was a pathetic offering served on a pile of torn up, tired lettuce. This hotel would struggle to merit half a star.

My host advised that there was only one route for cyclists across the Thames--from the Tilbury Docks, an almost straight run from Warley. This was a mainly rural ride despite the proximity to London. I made it to Gray, a nearly there spot, in less than an hour and consulted with an elderly, angular cyclist about the rest of the cycle path. Still vital at 86 with a sparkle about him, he grasped my arm, talking right in my face. Half way through his directions, he apologized, saying 'my water doesn't work so well any more -- I'll just go in the bushes.'

His directions didn't help much and I had to ask three more times to find the ferry–there wasn't a single signpost. Rural and urban merged as I passed cattle and horses roaming among cable spools on a construction site for the new rail line to the Chunnel.

The ferry had a capacity of perhaps twenty, running whenever a few people gathered. No cars were allowed. I spent the ten minutes it took to cross talking to the ticket person about the process of laying cables under the Thames. Although he charged me the adult fare, I later discovered that my receipt was for a child's ticket; the difference in price was equivalent only to a cup of tea but repeated several times a day could finance an evening in the pub.

Gravesend, the end of the ferry run, is a large, well-maintained and very busy town. Although there was little evidence of tourists, they do have a TIC which booked a B&B for me in Sevenoaks. This is in easy reach of Horley for the Gatwick airport and offers a wealth of B roads for my final day of cycling.

After lunch, I followed the Wrotham Road for five kilometres through Meopham ('the longest village in England'). Later, a difficult and busy roundabout with inconsiderate drivers just outside Wrotham caused me grief. Roundabouts are good ideas, however, if they have several exits you need to know your exit and select the right roundabout lane for it as you enter and then move to the far left lane when you approach your exit. A busy roundabout makes this a nerve-racking cycling experience. I went round and round several times trying to move to the correct lane, frustrating drivers with my lack of speed and apparent indecision. Safely out, I was very thankful for the relative peace of the village.

Wrotham is a quiet old village on the Pilgrim's path to Canterbury, a much quieter road. The old school opposite the square-towered St. George's church had been converted into cosy cottages. I pictured myself inside with a bread and cheese meal snug in my tattered retirement cardigan contentedly enjoying a good book.

This vision made me hungry (what doesn't) and the nearby Bull Hotel beckoned. This is a sturdy but genteel establishment perfectly suited for this village. I was their only customer for afternoon tea and enjoyed it thoroughly in their comfortable lounge with a newspaper.

Leaving the Bull, I choose Kemsing Road West simply because Kemsing is closer to Sevenoaks than Wrotham. This was a serendipitous choice; a lovely country road, sufficiently curved and rolling to be an interesting ride with attractive countryside and homes along the way. At Kemsing, I spied a church down a treed lane and went to investigate. The church has a lychgate (a small building at the edge of the church boundary formerly used to shelter a coffin before the burial service) and a well-cared for and well-populated cemetery with an unusual curved brick wall surround. The wall is similar, but shorter, than the famous Thomas Jefferson wall round the University of Virginia. Off to the side is a small-unpaved lane with a YHA sign; there had been no other indication anywhere that there was a hostel in this area. Why are they so shy about telling people where they are?

From Kemsing it was an easy run to the B&B. I was their first guest in a month. Their most recent previous booking failed to turn up. Virtually every surface in my room was labelled to identify or instruct--the sugar and tea containers, a safety warning on the kettle and instructions for operating the shower and the window; all had neatly typed labels in two colours encased in plastic.

The husband was retired and obviously has time on his hands to provide all these little assists for their guests. He was pleasantly prissy. I suggested that he had been an engineer. 'Why do you say that', he inquired? Fortunately, my reply of 'the precision I see in your home' was sufficiently gratifying. However, both he and his wife were former opticians. They did everything to make me comfortable from installing a television in the room to providing special high quality jam at breakfast and bringing me cold drinks after my arrival.

From them I learned many of the details of running a B&B that don't immediately come to mind such as special insurance rules and coverage, alarm systems, etc. Clearly, the B&B business wouldn't be an ideal avocation for me. My hosts recommended the Bullfinch for dinner -- a good choice. I ordered the one whisky and ginger that I promised myself for this trip. British ginger ale has more bite than North American which improves the drink for me. This one was very good but not as special as expected—probably anticipated too long.

Next morning, my host suggested a pleasant route for getting to Horley. However, like his other conversations there was so much detail that the main picture got lost. I remembered 'keep Barclays on your left' but that barely got me underway. I missed an important intersection in his instructions and soon faced an unappealing choice between two dual carriageways. The A21 seemed the least nerve-racking because the map showed a minor road intersection three kilometres ahead where I thought I could escape. The roads did cross but by a flyover; so there was no way to exit.

Carrying on, I noticed a low lane running under the A21 with a bridle path perpendicular to it running parallel with the A21. Getting down there meant going over the guardrail, descending a steep hill and climbing a chest high fence along the path but it seemed preferable to the roaring traffic on the A21. I unloaded my bike and walked it carefully down through the wild roses and nettle, collecting cuts and stings along the way. The return trip to fetch my panniers added to the collection. Once down I hefted everything over the fence.

A woman horse rider came along just then and offered to help with directions. Being male and feeling pleased with my resourcefulness, I declined, thinking I knew what I was doing, which is rarely the case. Two kilometres later, virtually back in Sevenoaks—nearly an hour gone with nothing to show for it but an assortment of leg cuts and nettle abrasions.

Thinking hard about what I had been told, I began again, eventually finding the right road. Now it was lovely cycling country, rolling terrain with woods, plenty of shade for cooling down and interesting houses. The influence of Kentish oast house design was evident in some of the churches and houses. An oast house contains a kiln for drying hops which has an unusual shape—somewhat like a silo wearing a tilted dunce's cap. Later, I stopped to admire a very large new country house in a marvellous location sitting high above a broad valley. From this point the road ran downhill at a 16% slope before levelling out somewhat to a 9% grade. Just as this levelling began, I was startled by a great noise and erratic bike behaviour. The right rear pannier had jarred loose, been sucked between the rack and the wheel and was acting as a massive brake. Scary at 30 km/h but no damage apart from my nerves!

East Grinstead presented another diversion with model homes open for viewing. I toured a well-designed model nicely decorated with four bedrooms, two and a half baths and cornices in all rooms. The house felt spacious but the square footage was only 1,312! Bedrooms had no closets, there was no basement or other storage area of any significance and the lot was quite small. The largest home in the development was 1,563 square feet and was priced at C$600,000! East Grinstead is a prime London commuting location.

Five years later, I found that the high house price situation had become worse and spread wider afield. There was pressure on government to do something. Nurses, teachers and similarly paid professions cannot afford homes at these prices. The rich rewards of other professions makes a weekend or holiday home feasible in areas distant from London creating unnatural demand and higher prices. So it is difficult, if not impossible, for natives of those places to afford a home. Property rates charged for second homes are lower than primary homes, putting a strain on local council finances as the proportion of weekend homes increases. The weekend people want to retain the rural, bucolic features of the village that attracted them and so are opposed to most economic development that might improve the material welfare of the locals. It is not a happy situation.

At Crawley, I turned on to the B2036 towards Horley and the Prinstead B&B, where this journey began a month ago.

By the time I finished my preparations for tomorrow, I had no energy to do more than pick up some snacks at a petrol station convenience shop. Doing so maintained budget integrity but it wasn't how my final meal was meant to be and I still have not had a gooseberry tart or any summer pudding. They will have to wait for the next tour.

My lunch site and loaded bike outside Bordeaux Railway Station

Balliol College Dining Hall, Oxford University

NORTHERN ENGLAND /
SCOTLAND TOUR

BRITAIN

NORTHERN ENGLAND & SCOTLAND

Freedom and temporary release from regular responsibilities have always been major components of my enjoyment and anticipation of these cycling tours. However, this trip is to follow my retirement, promising freedom also from worrying about returning to problems left behind in my interesting but demanding job. While living within a budget is always top of mind whatever I do; at least this tour won't be also constrained by the time limits of my annual holiday. I'm entitled to four weeks but have carried a week over from last year allowing me to tour for five weeks on full pay before retiring officially.

The final months at work were intense--my penalty, perhaps, for future freedoms. I managed my firm's employee pension fund investments. It was the time of the IT bubble. Equity markets were eroding daily and my Board was nervous about the fund's large allocation to equities. During our February 2002 meeting, they requested a complete review of our asset allocations for the May meeting. This was to include overall recommendations for the asset mix including researching the potential of alternative asset classes (like hedge funds) that had been so successful for Yale University.

Together with regular day to day management of the fund, this new assignment was more than enough to keep me fully occupied. But, at the same time, we were trying to dispose of our long-term interest in an Alberta real estate joint venture. I was Treasurer of the venture, responsible for all financial aspects. A large balloon payment due on the mortgage set a, just months away, drop-dead date for completing the transaction. One of our partners was extremely difficult, at least in part, because they were the principal tenants and feared a change in ownership.

Documentation for the 25 year old venture was a major problem. During that time one of the partners merged but failed to file any documents changing the name of their ownership. And, for a frantic week, our own crucial files on the original transaction seemed lost.

We sold the entire property to German interests but experienced several closing delays due to the time difference between Germany and Alberta and our difficult partner's delaying tactics. The mortgage lender was amazingly uncooperative about extending the balloon payment deadline even for a couple of weeks, demanding a refinancing fee plus exorbitant interest.

So I had to find an alternative, affordable short-term loan of tens of millions to meet the payment date. Partner approvals were crucial but none of them sensed or cared about the urgency. The tension was overwhelming for weeks.

Shortly after the April closing, my successor arrived for a three-month overlap period. We already knew and respected each other. She has better academic qualifications, similar experience with one of the other large Canadian banks and was then President of our national professional pension fund association. I was pleased to have the firm accept my recommendation of her as my replacement.

We jointly presented our asset mix recommendations to the Board winning their approval. Massive relief--the hurdles had been overcome—my tour was on the horizon and the company's 'bounty' for attracting someone from the outside was an unexpected bonus. Net of tax, this paid my airfare for the trip.

My colleagues organized a moving and memorable retirement party in my last week. I was pleased but humbled by the speeches and grateful for the gift of a significant amount of cash to buy my own bike box. Mari, and a gratifying number of Board members, attended but I will always regret not having invited my daughters, both of whom lived locally.

My final day at work was to be the last Friday in June. My flight was the next day. Being a summer Friday most of the office left early for the weekend before I felt my post could finally be abandoned. Truth be known, I was now a little reluctant to be ending my career and burnishing my reputation for dedication one last time. There was no one there to take notice but it was important to my self-image.

I returned home to an empty house as Mari left earlier in the day for a long weekend of kayaking with our outdoor club. The solitude might otherwise have been welcome, but totally wired with the emotions of retirement and the trip, her absence left me adrift with no outlet for sharing those feelings. We did not own a mobile phone and could not contact each other.

Many Tours Rolled Together

My objective for this tour was to see the under populated, hauntingly beautiful countryside of Northumberland featured in the television dramas of Cathryn Cookson novels. I also wanted to visit the Scottish Isles. Having five weeks to work with meant that I could, with occasional use of trains, assemble five different routes from Lonely Planet's *Cycling Britain* adding the Lake District and Edinburgh to Northumberland.

Lonely Planet provides an individual map for each day of their routes with route directions and mileage indicators for the turns. I enlarged these directions on a photocopier to a size that just fit my handlebar map case for an easy to read while riding custom guide. The theory is great. The reality was just a bit different, as we will see.

Flying into Manchester gave me good train access to York where I'll start a circular tour of James Herriot country and the North York Moors. Next will be a combination of three separate tours all based on Newcastle upon Tyne, in one circuit running north along the east coast to Berwick upon Tweed then south and west skirting the Cheviot Hills. The circuit then crosses the Pennines to the far west of the Lake District before finally turning east to re-cross the Pennines and return to Newcastle.

From Newcastle a train journey will take me to Edinburgh for a short stay before heading west again by train to Ardrossan for a ten-day, ferry-supported, visit to several of the Scottish Isles. A final train journey from Skye is to take me through Glasgow and on to Penrith, in Cumbria, for the return to Manchester and the flight home.

The Countryside

My chosen landscapes offer both challenge and soul restoring beauty. All three areas severely tested my physical stamina and strength especially in the early days of the tour. James Herriot country takes in much of the dales where 'All Creatures Great and Small', the BBC drama, was filmed.

The Lake District is one of my favourite places in the world. Besides the natural beauty of the lakes and hills, the steep, winding and often desolate roads, there are inviting teashops everywhere, excellent bookshop and plentiful hostels. Lakeland was Beatrix Potter's home and now Keswick offers a museum with a very good short film about her, featuring Dame Judi Dench. Near Sawrey is home to Hill Top Farm where Beatrix lived and restored the Herdwick breed of sheep. Hill Top is a National Trust property and one of the most popular tourist attractions in Lakeland.

The Lake District's beauty also inspired and was home to Coleridge, Wordsworth, Southey and other famous English poets. I find it impossible to describe this beauty as eloquently as it deserves; you must experience it for yourself. There are many picture books dedicated to its beauty but I found that Hunter Davies' 'A Walk Around the Lakes' is a better guide to its history and culture, providing interest without pictures.

As mentioned above, from the Lake District, my route went back east towards Newcastle and through the Northumberland National Park. This park, stretching north from Hadrian's Wall towards the Cheviot Hills, is one of the great remaining open spaces of Britain, covering some 600 square kilometres of high hills and open moorland.

Edinburgh is the capital of Scotland, home to a famous university and was one of Europe's leading cultural centres during the latter half of the 18th and the early part of the 19th century. James Boswell, Robert Burns, Sir Walter Scott, David Hume, Adam Smith and Thomas Telford all made their homes here. Scottish intellectual contributions in engineering, literature, philosophy, education, etc. far outweigh the Scottish proportion of the world's population. James Buchan's 'Capital of the Mind' subtitled 'How Edinburgh Changed the World', published by John Murray, explores these contributions.

My tour includes ferry journeys to three of the Scottish Isles. Arran is first; sometimes described as "Scotland in miniature" for its full scenic range of mountains, low hills, streams, glens and loch The finest scenery is in the north where Goat Fell (850 metres) dominates lofty granite ridges.

Next comes Mull. This is a beautiful island of moorland, forest and peaks. Tobermory is the main centre and fishing port. Its pastel homes and shops ringed round the harbour present a lovely scene that is particularly attractive at night as the bobbing boats in the harbour shimmer in reflected light from the street lamps. From Mull, the route returns to the mainland, runs north along the coast to Mallaig for another ferry crossing to the Isle of Skye. Skye is 80 km long but no part is more than 10 km from the sea.

For me, Skye provided one of the most dramatic bits of scenery and the most exhilarating ride of the entire trip. This was in the far north from Uig down to Portree by way of the Quiraing. Initially this was a single-track high moor road with superb vistas but I was unprepared for the view at the top where a massive, rugged set of peaks frames a long sweep of the coast and the steep winding road down to Staffin.

That experience was no doubt improved by the change in weather from a soggy, wet day to late afternoon sun spotlighting the sea, the green, sheep-mown moors and the naked brown cliffs in watery golden shafts. The road back to Portree, along the coast, was easy and peaceful. Now that you know something of the countryside along my route, we can turn to some of the more memorable experiences.

Getting Started

I took a train from Manchester airport into the city, choosing to get off at the closest station to the hostel. Wrestling the 25-kilo plus bike box with one arm, lugging 13 kilos of duffel bag with the other and carrying a rucksack on my back and hiking over the cobblestones and through Saturday night's litter. These disgraceful streets added a disturbing visual effect to the damp cold of that Sunday morning. Manchester doesn't have litter bins on the streets because of the risk of terrorist bombs and it will probably be Monday before any litter is removed.

The hostel sits along side a canal. This morning the canal was filled with colourful barge houses and houseboats where several owners were out polishing and cleaning their boats. It was still too early to get into my room so I had time to reassemble the bike near the bike shed behind the hostel. Raucous noise blasted from various marquees being set up nearby for an evening fair. Continuing my day on a consistent note, my hands got thoroughly impregnated with grease trying to engage the chain on the rear wheel gear cluster. (I've since learned that surgical gloves are a great way to avoid this.)

Life looked better after a decent sleep, although the weather didn't improve. Today, I'm off to York where my tour really starts. A good breakfast, the comfort of secure accommodation for my new bike box, and a tidy, clean railway station at Piccadilly largely erased yesterday's irritations.

Once in York, I walked in the Shambles area but the continuing cold, wet weather blunted its usual appeal. Despite the temperature, bare midriffs were plentiful. Many of the girls wore off shoulder blouses and wide belts, provocatively low to better display the jewellery in their navels. Wearing 'the gear' seems to provide some assurance that they are OK, even when grossly fat. Their posture and behaviour put the lie to that.

As many Canadians do, I wear a 'Maple Leaf' on my cycling jacket to reduce the likelihood of misplaced antipathy. The full weight of Canada's much-vaunted multiculturalism soon became evident as a Pakistani man stopped me in the Shambles calling out to his wife, 'Here's another Canadian.' He was from Hamilton, Ontario.

Earlier, a very apologetic, impoverished and self-effacing Irish cyclist of perhaps 50 stopped me to ask for directions to the Lake District. It was almost as if he thought it was just round the next bend rather than a hard day's ride away but he appeared harmless and poorly equipped so I hauled out my maps to help.

Television and The Triplets

One of my objectives on this trip was to see the Herriot Museum at Thirsk that I missed on an earlier tour. At only 66 km from York,

Thirsk made an excellent first day destination, letting me ease into the tour. I chose to stay at the Lavender Inn next door to the museum, partly because my brother Byron had several years earlier. Although there was nothing wrong with the Lavender, the fabulous meals and welcome of the Long Acre B&B of my previous visit weren't matched.

My route to Thirsk along the River Ouse was more footpath than cycle trail. I was soon covered in insects and had to abandon this off road route. It was still cold and wet but the countryside was lovely and traffic was virtually non-existent.

James Herriot was the fictional name chosen by Alf Wight for his veterinarian stories-*All Creatures Great and Small*. The Royal College of Veterinarians would consider using his own name as advertising, which was banned. The real Herriot was a top footballer.

This museum is well worth a visit as the home has been maintained much as it was in the 1940s. The television programme was filmed here and some of the stage sets have been left in place showing the marks on the floor where the actors stood and where the cameras were placed. The first floor houses a very interesting exhibit of the history of veterinarian medicine. A wooden Holstein, giving birth, bares its backside at the top of the stairs leading to the exhibit. Visitors are challenged to pull on the emerging calf legs to see if they can 'deliver' the calf. Sufficiently vigorous pulls are rewarded by a ringing bell much like the strong man booths at carnivals.

Another television related objective was to see Goathland, the Yorkshire village called Aidensfield in the BBC series 'Heartbeat' about police officers and villagers in the 1960s. Goathland is located about twenty kilometres from Pickering where I am booked in a B&B. After a side trip to visit friends in the North York Moors, I went to Pickering arriving about 2.30 in the afternoon. Dumping my panniers and refreshing with a cup of tea I headed out. The road between Pickering and the junction to Goathland is largely uphill and took well over an hour. When I turned off this main Whitby road the countryside lost modernity, plunging back in time, displaying railway flyovers, humped back bridges over rocky streams and sheep grazing in the open with their lambs—they were more afraid of me than of the cars!   The village looks exactly like it does in the opening credits of each program and there were a number of the buildings that are regularly featured.

Returning to Pickering downhill was much faster but my search for dinner was frustratingly long.   The first pub was full, the second, a Best Western, wasn't British and the third didn't serve evening meals. This left a café where the only other customers were a family with triplet boys of about three and a half. Each of the boys, in turn, had to explore the lavatory. They were fairly well behaved and their parents were gentle disciplinarians. Although my reading was disturbed, it was fun hearing their constant chatter until the boys turned their attention to me and my mint ice cream.   Much to their parents' embarrassment, one of them called out 'Mum, he's got green cream and some hair.' I persuaded myself that the latter comment related to my emerging beard, not my follicle-challenged top of the head.

Gross Girls

On my first visit to Newcastle on this trip I was booked into the hostel but no one could direct me to it. Traffic was heavy and some signs had been moved deliberately to be confusing. After ninety minutes following a variety of tentative directions, I finally found the hostel only to be told that there was no record of my reservation, so they sent me to their 'annex', one of the university residence halls, 'only five minutes away.' Five minutes became half an hour, thanks to some hair-raising roundabout situations when I could not turn where I wanted to or had to turn when I did not want to, to a total lack of hostel related signs, as well as conflicting directions from three different pedestrians.

Dracula's wife manned the annex, friendly but completely in black, including her lipstick. She sent me to the top floor, four storeys up. My room, like most modern university residences, was totally bleak and without character.

My hunger had been kick started by the enticing smells of dinner preparation at the main hostel but the annex provided no food and had no members' kitchen.

So, I had to brave the deteriorating elements for a meal. The city pedestrian mall area was impressively clean but the night scene of young teens larking about depressed me, particularly the girls' ostentatious lack of dress. Midriffs were bared (the temperature was about 12 degrees)—breasts spilled out of tight tops and pelvises strained against skin-tight, low-rise jeans. Some of these girls could be attractive dressed more modestly but now look like cheap tarts; others are just fat and ugly no-hopers. Their heavy make-up and style of dress only emphasized their ugliness.

Mayflower Connection

Now, I'm going to Alnwick, about 80 kilometres north of Newcastle. Along the way I found a dead magpie on the road. The death must have just happened as another magpie was standing on the shoulder, apparently sorrowed and puzzled by its dead partner. I later saw a dead fawn. There have been a number of pheasants and rabbits running across the road--more potential victims.

A live blue heron on the Coquet River was a welcome introduction to Warkworth, a picture postcard perfect village. Warkworth is home to Warkworth Castle, the 14th century birthplace of Hotspur (Sir Henry Percy). Sir Henry was slain at the Battle of Shrewsbury in 1403, when Henry IV defeated the Percys. For more than four centuries Warkworth was one of the most important castles in the north of England.

My exploration of the castle was guided by a hand-held listening device with commentary keyed to numbered positions throughout the castle that correspond to buttons on the hand-held. Now this approach is common but this was my first experience of a guided tour at my own pace and sequence. The commentary can be ignored, or replayed as you wish. It provided interesting details about domestic life then and about the family history.

Two bits of trivia intrigued me. While visiting the buttery, I learnt that contrary to my understanding, the name buttery refers to the butts that liquid was stored in, not to dairy products. The other interesting bit concerned a small, special room called a garderobe, which functioned principally as a lavatory. However, people also stored their clothes in these rooms thinking that the smell would keep the moths away. British homes' ground floor lavatories often double as storage for outdoor coats and hats--a historic tradition?

When I arrived at my Alnwick B&B, my hosts advised me that some long-term clients decided to stay an extra night; consequently they must put me in a very small room. However, to compensate they were going to only charge me half price. They were most apologetic, not realizing the joy this brought my Scottish-inspired soul. I made appropriate grimaces at the inconvenience but 'graciously' accepted their solution.

With this budget boost, I treated myself to an excellent steak pie dinner and then walked round the very active town centre watching the pub-crawlers. The women gathered in flocks –for courage or companionship? Most of them, even the middle-aged ones, looked like tarts. Pathetically, and with forced hilarity, they swooped into and out of several pubs trying to attract male attention. The designated prey males also travelled in packs and dressed in a semi-uniform short-sleeve shirt worn outside their trousers but apparently feigning interest in the women and only tried to impress each other.

From Alnwick, my first stop was to be Berwick–on-Tweed but first I wanted to visit Lindisfarne, or Holy Island. Lindisfarne lies off the east Northumberland coast perhaps 16 kilometres south of Berwick. Missionaries from Iona settled here in the seventh century but were driven out by the Danes in AD 875. The ruins of a Benedictine priory built in the eleventh century and a small sixteenth century castle are on the island. The limestone cliffs and sand dunes of the north shore are a playground for the swarming bird life from the Farne Islands and seals can often be seen offshore.[1]

My route ran close to the coast, passing Bamburgh, its imposing castle standing high on the horizon, and brought me to the Lindisfarne causeway. Access by land to the island is only feasible when the tide goes out uncovering the causeway. Forgetting this, I arrived an hour and a half early. Clumps of people gathered, waiting for the tide to leave while consuming crab sandwiches or chips from the inevitable food wagons. Waiting would make me late for my weekly call to

Mari and there was no phone box anywhere. So, I decided to carry on to Berwick on Tweed and return to Holy Island tomorrow.

Once in Berwick, I couldn't find my hotel reservation confirmation or remember the name of the hotel. Searching was unsuccessful so I choose to stay instead at Miranda's B&B, now run by Angela, a single mum. The interior was a bit worn and bleak but it was half the price the hotel wanted and had all the facilities I needed. While roaming , I had selected a pub called The Leaping Salmon for dinner and went along there after a bath.

There, by coincidence I saw Chris, an American cyclist I had met at the B&B in Thirsk. Chris was a twenties something Bostonian who claimed that his mother had direct lineage back to Priscilla of the Mayflower. He also told me that he had been a software programmer for start-up technical companies and made enough money selling his stock options before the crash to finance a deposit on a house and a year's tour of Europe. The story made for lively conversation but other aspects of his story suggested that the option profits were modest. His Wal-Mart quality cycle was a bit of a giveaway for a start. Still, where else but on a holiday like this would you even meet such a diversity of interesting people?

Old Tom

Four days later, having returned to Lindisfarne, visited Newcastle, and Alnwick, I was travelling south west through a more rolling, greener and less desolate countryside than the North Yorkshire Moors. My next overnight was at a hotel in Wooler—a surprisingly well-equipped place in rural countryside where they gave me a twin-bedded, en suite room with television, tea making facilities and stacks of towels. There, I met James Noon, a cyclist from Musselburgh, near Edinburgh. James travels with a flask of hot water to make tea or soup and carries spare food to save money. Initially he was reticent and dour but became friendly sharing his extensive knowledge of the area while we had some meals together.

James suggested a detour to see a castle and some rare wild cattle at Chillingham. I took his advice but never saw the cattle, as the farm was only open to tourists one day a week--yesterday, and wouldn't have opened for two hours anyway. So, I returned to my main route and, relying on memory, took the posted turn to Eglingham. After two or three kilometres, sensing something wrong, I checked my compass which showed that my route was going east--my destination was west. What a difference a letter makes—I wanted Edlingham, not Eglingham. This error cost me over half an hour.

Nevertheless, this accidental side trip wasn't a total loss. I met someone who filled in my knowledge gaps about Chillingham cattle and the local farm. The cattle are white--somewhat like small Charlois. There were about 70 of them still at the farm and a few more in Scotland where they had been shipped to avoid last year's outbreak of hoof and mouth disease.

Today, I'm en route to the hostel in Bellingham. It is housed in an old red cedar scout hut located just a couple of streets away from the High Street. My welcome was administered gruffly by a grey, gnarled and rheumy-eyed man sitting at one of the picnic style tables inside. He brusquely instructed me to complete the sign-in book but strongly objected to my filling in the date--'Trying to do my job, are you?'--lingering evidence of British union mentality.

Then he demanded that I tour the facilities to be instructed how to use the cooker, the shower and the rubbish bin! A long monologue followed on the difficultly of running a hostel; 'the record keeping is murder.' I was trapped—an audience of one. The only other hostel occupant, a woman from New Zealand, wisely slipped out—perhaps she had the same treatment earlier.

Excusing myself to take a shower(and escape) did not produce much relief. I did not reappear quickly enough to resume my instruction, so he came after me to continue and found me playing truant with some hand wash laundry. Again, I was a captive audience for his stories and complaints. He was proud of the hostel, built in 1936, claiming that its only alterations from scouting days were the new toilets and showers. This wasn't totally true as he took me to another building to demonstrate the hostel's latest acquisition—a small spin dryer. Using my hand laundry, he whizzed the clothes round, squeezing out the water into a compartment that he emptied on the ground. It was a fairly basic appliance but got enough water out that the drying room could finish the job. Tom was pleased to have something else to demonstrate.

Fortunately, Tom's stomach called him home for his tea and I could get on with mine. Knowing this hostel did not serve meals, I had bought a wedge of steak pie, a wedge of ham and egg pie and two yoghurts at a butcher' shop before arriving at Bellingham.

Despite managing to burn the pies slightly (no doubt, due to inadequate attention to Old Tom's instructions earlier) they were still good and the yoghurts, mango and orange, were superb—my wife would say that meant they were sweet, not proper yoghurt.

The New Zealand woman had a degree in English from the University of Otago. She was the first Otago person I have met since leaving my lecturer's post there twenty-six years ago! Tiring of her journalist job she came to Britain for a cycling holiday. Now, having completed nearly 1800 kilometres in six weeks, she is heading for the Lake District to look for work.

After my meal, I made instant coffee from a nearly empty jar left behind by a previous visitor and sat at the picnic table writing in my journal while she leafed through a six-year-old magazine in one of the ancient easy chairs. The room was warm and comfortable providing a nice sort of quiet domesticity until about ten when Tom came back.

My New Zealand companion quickly said 'goodnight', leaving me stuck. Tom launched back into his complaints about the administrative burden—but in greater detail. In the process, he told me that his wife, Allison, is the official warden of the hostel but that he helps out in the evenings and with the lawn mowing and other manly tasks.

He claimed to be 79 but boasted that his wife was quite a bit younger; 'she keeps me young!' This was the springboard for what must be his favourite story. Before coming to Bellingham, he lived with his adult son in another village with a live-in housekeeper. Tom's son and the housekeeper became engaged but the son later got cold feet and moved out of the house. The housekeeper, feeling her reputation compromised with only one man in the house, moved to Bellingham where she got a cleaning job at the pub. Tom followed to persuade her to return to her housekeeping job with him. She did; Tom deciding to make the arrangement permanent (and perhaps eliminate having to pay her wages) replaced his son and married Allison.

I have severely condensed Tom's story but when he finished, he asked, 'How old do you think she is then?' I knew I had to come in low—his ego demanded it. Thinking that with Tom being 79, his son must at least be in his mid-forties and so Allison must be about the same, so I replied 'about 45.' In glee and almost shouting he roared out 'NO, she's 35!' My face must have registered disbelief because he jumped up from the table to say, 'you don't believe me, let's just call her!' He immediately did so and told her that there was a guy at the hostel who didn't believe how young she is--would she speak to him? I picked up the phone and, without prompting, Allison proudly confirmed that she indeed was 35. That story seemed to be the foundation of their marriage and probably has been told hundreds of times to trapped hostellers.

Next morning, Allison appeared at the hostel about 7.30, on her way to her pub job. After the pub is clean she moves on to yet another job--the school where she serves lunch. She not only keeps Tom young--she keeps him solvent. Allison might be 35 chronologically but 50+ would better describe her appearance. Although she can't smoke in the hostel, like her husband, she reeked of cigarettes. School lunches are bad enough without servers like her!

Dave the Warden
Now early July, it was finally warm enough to wear shorts. I had a fast food breakfast in the pedestrian mall nearby the Carlisle hostel-- another no meals university residence. The restaurant radio was tuned to a talk programme promoting a contest in which the prize was a pack of condoms for the weekend. The female DJ employed every possible double entendre about the prize and its use but principally talked rubbish–failing to complete sentences because there was no thought or purpose behind them—she just filled the airwaves

with noise that she thought clever and trendy--clearly an, 'on-air' airhead.

My destination today was Cockermouth, about 80 kilometres west from Carlisle in the Lake District. Midmorning, at a news agent, I observed another example of Britain's multifaceted personality. The shop, run by two middle-aged and apparently respectable women, openly displayed copies of the gutter press featuring virtually naked women on the front pages in lewd poses. This doesn't seem to bother anyone.

I took my respectable *Times* newspaper to a seedy little café for tea and teacakes and later added a cheese pie because the paper proved so interesting. There were articles on revenue inflation in financial statements and one on US vice-president Cheney being sued for accounting fraud at his former company, Halliburton.

For some reason, these articles stimulated my thinking about statistics. My mind wrestled with fat tails and normal distributions while I pedalled and rehearsed arguments out loud trying to test and reinforce my conclusions. Historical asset class return statistics had been a major aspect of my final asset mix project at work and statistics fascinates me generally. I vowed seriously to study the subject upon returning home. Like earlier vows to study calculus and French this latest one still awaits sustained action!

The hostel at Cockermouth had been a stone-built mill. It sits on a riverbank at the foot of a rocky path off the main road. When here in 1995 they had a full time warden and served meals. Now it is run entirely by volunteers and provides no meals.

After settling in I walked back into town for an excellent steak and ale pie at the Bitter End pub. It claims to be the best pub in Cockermouth for several years running. For a town of 5000, Cockermouth is well supplied with places to eat. There are seventeen of them.

Dave, the acting hostel warden, told me that most of the people that make their money from the tourist trade in Keswick live in Cockermouth. Dave, retired from teaching for ten years, said 'Now, my worldly mobile possessions fit into two cases.' He bought a farmhouse in France following retirement and stayed there for four years. Then he spent three years with the Arts Council in Whitehaven on the Lake District coast and he has been with the Hostel Association for the past two years. He loves the nomadic life and is moving on again at the end of this year, either to Cornwall or Spain. I never meet people like this at home!

My day's agenda included visiting Wordsworth's cottage and exploring at random before going on to the hostel at Keswick. The cottage was Wordsworth's birthplace. His successful and prosperous father provided a large, comfortable home with a formal garden, a separate section for vegetables and a raised terrace overlooking the river at the bottom of the garden.

The father's journals in the library were particularly intriguing. The dates (mid-eighteenth century) were written in the current North American style showing the month before the day and words like favourable and colour were written without the 'u.'

One of the letters was not very legible and someone had later written it out to be readable. They weren't faithful to the original, altering both the way the date order was written and the spellings to conform to current British usage. I also found a late eighteenth century original document in which the dates and the spellings were in the current British fashion. It seems possible that the practice changed sometime in the latter part of that century. Perhaps current US practice reflects the earlier English that settlers brought with them as much as Noah Webster's revolutionary-tinged simplification efforts.

A Wayward Cow

I combined two day's routes for today's run from Keswick to Allenheads. The distance and climbs involved persuaded me to brave some A roads to save time and my legs. Being a Sunday, I planned a proper roast and veggies lunch at a pub but was diverted midmorning by a teashop with the intriguing name of Brief Encounters. The name reminded me of the play and the shop was aptly situated in a working railway station for the Carlisle and Settle Line that evoked a perfect ambiance. Imagining the play's characters' stolen minutes between trains made this stop a very pleasant, nostalgic sort of interlude but killed the budget and time for lunch.

Now, the road began to climb and there were ominous notices that the road rose to 570 metres and winter conditions could be treacherous. I struggled away, stubbornly refusing to get off and walk but just kept my head down pedalling steadily while noisy gnat-like groupings of motorbikes roared past. Shortly before the summit, I ran into four guys pushing their unladen bikes up a side road. The last one, very much overweight, stared at my fully loaded bike, gasping, 'you must be insane.'

From this point the road ran downhill to the Allenheads intersection. I'm staying at the Allenheads Inn at the far end of the village. The current owners, Steve and Sue, were very pleasant and welcoming. They acquired the inn last year just in time to suffer the double-barrelled effects of the foot and mouth outbreak and the drop in overseas tourism due to the Twin Towers attack in New York. The village shop and post office were both out of business.

Allenheads Inn was most unusual; collectibles of all sorts covered every available wall, floor and ceiling surface. Banknotes from every corner of the globe were on display. My room, a good-sized en suite, was a pleasant change after several days in hostel dormitory rooms.

Next morning, as I was just stirring, there was a knock on the door and a voice announced 'Here is your water.' That made no sense but a large flask of water sat outside my door. Later at breakfast, Steve explained that Allenheads is supplied by a spring continuously feeding into a reservoir through an exposed pipe. During the night a cow knocked the pipe sideways so that the water spilled on to the ground instead of into the reservoir. The source of my morning flask and the tea water was never explained--I thought it better not to ask.

Edinburgh Crystal

After Allenheads, I returned to Newcastle for a train to Edinburgh. Arriving at the railway station about two, I bought my ticket, got a sandwich lunch and ate it on a station bench. Although there was plenty of activity to witness, my attention was riveted on a couple passionately kissing on an opposite bench. It wasn't a turn on—quite the reverse. The woman was just so ugly! Then I realized they were both women! As I walked past to join the train, one was fondling and flipping the other's breasts. I suspect a large part of their display was intended to draw attention and disgust. Worked for me!

'Edinburgh, Scotland's capital city, lay originally in the English kingdom of Northumbria and only finally became Scots in 1341. The old part of the city lays south of the castle, now visible in the cobbled streets of the Royal Mile and Grassmarket. The modern city layout is Georgian, the architects leaving the view from the main street, Princes Street, open toward the castle, perched high on its volcanic rock. The oldest part of the castle, St. Margaret's Chapel, dates from the 12th century, though most is much more recent. One of the more fanciful names for elegant and neo-classical Edinburgh is "the Athens of the North," and it has been an academic centre since 1582, when the university was founded. The annual Edinburgh Festival of arts and performance in August attracts tens of thousands of visitors.'(2)

My city map eased the task of finding the hostel but it was still difficult, as the YHA seems loath to provide more than the barest of directional signs. Unfortunately, this is one of those big city hostels that have little character and less warmth. Filled with undisciplined kids on some school outing that travelled in packs through a combination door lock two or three times every minute. Each opening rang a chime. Constant chimes combined with the kids' noise created bedlam in the lobby. It was a relief to learn that I had to go out for meals.

For my first breakfast in Edinburgh, I tried a convenient pub next door to the Edinburgh Bike Cooperative near the hostel. I ate dinner there last night and noted that they offered breakfast all day at £3.95. When I came to pay--breakfast at breakfast time was £5--the tea, while essential for me, was an optional extra. While there, a postman interrupted his morning deliveries for a couple of sustaining pints. He described his recent Western Canada holiday to the barman—'the natives were friendly but the place was far too quiet.'

Former university haunts claimed me for much of the day, such as the 'Old Quad' where I had spent many evenings in the library swotting previous exam papers. The 1959 Jules Verne film 'Twenty-Thousand Leagues Under the Sea' was filmed here featuring my closest friend and fellow digs mate, Norman, as an extra. The building is now almost totally devoted to Law and was essentially closed down for the summer. Consistent with the cool, wet day, I also visited the very austere Church of Scotland (Presbyterian) St. Giles Cathedral.

For breakfast next morning I went to the Doctors pub, on the edge of the big Edinburgh park known as the Meadows. In my days at the university this spot had been 'The Barbecue', a popular student café. It conjured up special images for me of my brief romance with Kathy, one of their waitresses. Head over heels at this relationship with a 'mature' woman, I was unaware of the facts of her life as well as, to be honest, of the 'facts of life.' Some months later, only slightly more aware, I learned just how mature Kathy was--six years my senior, a mother of several children and already divorced! (Strangely enough, my parents did not consider a divorced woman an appropriate companion for their son. They had written asking for her address to thank her for a Christmas gift and I foolishly wrote back--Mrs. K......).

The next day I headed for Melrose, a fairly easy run alongside the Tweed River for much of the way. The countryside differs noticeably from Northern England; subtler with rolling but lower hills. Much was through a pine forest with disturbing evidence of clear cutting.

In the early afternoon, I came across the location of Edinburgh Crystal. Apart from my university association, Edinburgh crystal is meaningful since my parents gave my wife and me a set of Thistle pattern goblets shortly after we moved to Britain.

I visited the showroom and took the works tour. My guide had been one of their designers and a number of his pieces were on display including a special wine decanter made for Prince William's birth with a stopper in the shape of a small liqueur glass. The rest of the tour involved various stages of manufacture. Most interesting for me was a personal (I was the only observer) demonstration of cutting by George, a veteran of 42 years. He showed me the several different cuts that form the Star design, completing a water goblet while I watched. This goblet would be recycled after the demonstration so I asked him for it as a souvenir. He agreed on the condition that the people in the showroom not be told. What a treasure – a very personal and special reminder of this trip! Wrapped carefully and stored it in my handlebar bag for the rest of the journey, my goblet survived but tragically fell out onto a hard surface while unpacking at home, breaking the foot. I was devastated.

No Room/Food at the Inn

After a final breakfast at the Doctors Pub, I cycled off to Waverley Station for a Scottish Rail train west to Glasgow on the first leg of the journey to the Scottish Isles. On these trains, the cycles go in the cars for the disabled, labelled 'facilities'. The system is quite good providing places for up to three bikes per car. The train was clean, modern and comfortable.

The Arran ferry departs from Ardrossan. At Glasgow, there was a three hour wait for the Ardrossan Harbour train, leaving me only six minutes after arrival to buy my ticket and get on the ferry. Any delay in this part of the journey could cost me a full day and mess up all my accommodation arrangements! Further study of the timetable revealed three different stations in Ardrossan--all close to each other. The next train to any of those stations would leave within the hour. I was quickly on it dealing with yet another system for carrying bikes.

In less than an hour, I was cycling along the Ardrossan sea front, energized by the change in atmosphere, a sudden, welcome foreignness that I had yet to experience on this trip. Globalization, particularly in large population centres, has produced increasing similarities across the world, making many foreign places seem somewhat familiar. Not so here! At the ferry terminal I bought a special, several trip, book of tickets called 'Hopscotch' that represented a considerable discount on the single fares. Bikes travelled free--a sensible arrangement in my opinion.

Since there were nearly two hours to departure, I explored Ardrossan, stopping first for lunch in a café whose ambiance and clientele were very reminiscent of a similar café in a similarly poor town in Saskatchewan that Mari and I visited last year. The patrons were smokers and primarily at the lower end of the socio-economic scale, reflecting the general feel of Ardrossan, but the service and atmosphere were friendly and apparently sincere.

Back at the terminal, cars and some huge lorries were already queuing. After boarding, as the journey is very short, I immediately went up to the top deck and was soon engaged in conversation with a man who noticed the Maple Leaf on my jacket.

This man was raised in my town of Oakville, Ontario but now lives in Japan running a food import advisory firm. His entire family lives on Arran and he is back for a visit. We chatted briefly until his mother arrived. They had been into Glasgow for the day.

My hostel was at Whiting Bay, a difficult but short 13 km ride from the terminal. When I arrived, a swarm of 32 teenage girls and their counsellors buzzed round the hostel. Including me, there were only two males. Lockable rooms and priority for all the toilets and showers had been given to the females but the male room door had no lock. We apparently were not considered to be at risk from the women.

Had we been, one of the counsellors would have been an ideal candidate but I contented myself chatting with her about the very rigorous and demanding Duke of Edinburgh awards. The girls just completed a four-day camping expedition as part of their gold award requirements.

My sole roommate was Hailey, yet another cycling Otago graduate! Hailey was following the same Lonely Planet tour of Western Scotland but making a diversion to see the island of Harris. He earned his degree in History but was then working in a local council planning office in London.

Lochranza, my next destination, was only about 45 km away. There were some hard climbs at first but little of historic note. Just about lunchtime, I reached Machrie Bay, site of a coastal golf course and tearoom. The golf course operated an honour system for paying course fees. You simply put your money in a wooden box. There were a few cars pulled off the road but since it wasn't a 'pay and display' system there was no way to tell whether these golfers were honourable. Anyway, it was the tearoom that attracted me.

Initially the only customer, my order for tomato and lentil soup with a cheese scone arrived quickly. But, just as I was ready for something sweet, a horde of mature cyclists from a triathlon club streamed in. Seating was very limited and inadequate to seat all of us in comfort so I left without satisfying my sweet tooth.

Arran's bracing sea air, emphasized by a strong head wind, together with sea, rocks and mountain views stirred my soul, reminding me of the Otago peninsula on the South Island of New Zealand. Although recently meeting two Otago graduates probably contributed to my thought processes.

At this latitude, this summer scene survives beyond 10 p.m extending the beauty of a sea inlet alongside the hostel. The sunset produced a gorgeous golden blend of autumnal and seawater colours at sunset. Lochranza is a self-catering hostel, so I visited the local shop to get food supplies. The grocer boasted that he swam in the sea almost every night despite a maximum temperature of only 12 degrees Celsius.

Next morning, after breakfast, Hailey and I headed for the ferry to Claonaig on the Kintyre Peninsula. The ship was at anchor in the harbour but didn't move to the loading dock until after the scheduled departure time. Once in position, it was very efficient; we were barely boarded before the ferry was underway. As Arran's profile receded in the distance, its dominant high hills presented a magnificent view from the stern. Ferry trips add a special dimension for me, altering and improving my tour's character.

By 10.20 we were ashore again in bright sunshine and cycled together for 16 km when Hailey branched off for a ferry to Bute. Just at the crossroads where we parted, there was a tempting place to stop for coffee but I hadn't yet earned a rest! Kilberry was only another hour away--a stop then would be much more justifiable. This was a minor road on the west shore of Loch Tarbert without any road signs and it looked as if I was retracing our 16 km journey on the opposite shore—and that was exactly the case. I had to stop a passing car to confirm that this was the way to Kilberry.

Precisely at one p.m., I arrived there facing a white, cottage style country inn advertising Sunday lunches. This was a great find as Sunday service can be very spotty, particularly in the west and Highlands of Scotland. This must be the prolonged reward! Alas it wasn't to be. A small notice posted on the door announced 'Closed today for family visit.'

That inn is virtually the whole of Kilberry—I had no snack food and my water bottle was half empty. The guidebook showed that the next possible stop was 25 km away with several 'moderate' climbs. Fortunately, there were also some good down hills. One of these must have been nearly 4 km.

This next leg of the journey took two hours, ending at an open café at Ardrishaig where I had two big mugs of tea and two cheese and pickle toasties. These are a Scottish version of a grilled sandwich and absolutely delicious but then anything would have been by that time.

Moving on to Lochgilphead, I stopped at the TIC to find out my hostel's location. 'But, there is no hostel here', replied the agent. Another senior moment! Sure enough, my itinerary says that I am booked in at Mrs. Sinclair's B&B--about 3 km outside town.

My arrival really surprised the Sinclairs because they had no record of me and no vacancies. They were very apologetic and rang round finding me an alternative spot at the Victoria Hotel back in Lochgilphead. The Sinclairs call their B&B 'Corbiere' after a spot on the island of Jersey where they spend their holidays. The name was an interesting coincidence for me as the land conservation charity of which I was then treasurer had bought a large tract of land on Manitoulin Island in Lake Huron from a native Canadian named Corbiere. I was making monthly mortgage payments to him from the charity but had never heard that surname before.

The Victoria was a dump! My room's carpet lay frayed in great lumps in the middle of the floor; two of the three lamps did not work and the shower was nearly inoperable. However, food, not complaints, was the priority. The Sinclairs had also recommended the Vic as a place to eat. It wasn't clear whether this was based on an absolute standard or one relating to the alternatives in Lochgilphead. Either way, it had to be the Vic--there were other diners but the food was just satisfactory.

Lochgilphead is poor and down at the heels. This was reflected in people's attitudes and their interaction. Young boys were loud, rude, foul-mouthed and disrespectful of females. The odd thing was that the girls seemed not to mind, apparently so starved for male attention that they almost courted abuse.

Finding no one around when I came down for breakfast at 7.35, I rang the bell, read yesterday's paper and rang the bell some more. About eight, the cook entered the front door with the shopping! So much for my planned early start--perhaps just as well; it was raining.

A side trip a short distance north west of Lochgilphead took me to the historic fort at Dunadd, considered the capital of the first settlement by Scotti (from Ireland) in Scotland. A natural rock feature that rises high above the surrounding countryside, it functioned between 500 and 1000 AD. On top, where the timber dwellings used to be, are an ancient footprint, a basin and a carving of a boar (that I never found). Allegedly, this is also the location of the Stone of Destiny, upon which Scottish royalty was crowned.(3)

North beyond Dunadd on the A816 is Kilmartin, an area archeologically rich in cairns and standing stones. The museum features a time map showing what was happening in Argyll throughout history including the animals that were in existence but are now extinct. I also took advantage of their very pleasant but pricey tearoom for a scone and lemon curd (superb).

Joining the official guidebook route along the B840 on the eastern border of Loch Awe, I cycled another couple of hours and then south on the A819 to my hostel at Inveraray, a larger, more touristy place than Lochgilphead. Inveraray has a castle (headquarters of the

Campbells), a gaol, a Bell Tower and a very tired ship museum. There is also a Scottish Episcopalian church. Although Canada uses the term Anglican, both the US and Scotland eschew that term probably because it suggests Church of England.

In the grounds outside the hostel, three English cyclists on an End-to-End tour for a men's cancer charity were trying, without success, to fix a broken spoke. The other occupants were two Slavic girls, five French people, a couple of Germans and a Scottish man with his three children. It is a small, intimate hostel and I enjoyed the domesticity and self-reliant activity of preparing my own meals.

In the morning, I was first up and eating my breakfast of beans, sausage and stewed tomatoes on crusty bread before anyone else stirred. One of the English cyclists came in searching for the phone book to find a place to have his cycle mended. He fumed about the poor service provided by the Cycle Touring Club (CTC) which doesn't do repairs and wanted over £0.50 per kilometre just to transport his bike to the repair shop! Fortunately, I had passed a nearby cycle shop and was pleased to be able to tell him the location and distance as it made me feel like a local.

I ended my stay in Inveraray with a trip to the Bell Tower's interesting display about bell ringing. The music notation is written in numbers from one to eight indicating the sequence of play for the different bells. All bells are suspended upside down—the first pull takes them anticlockwise and the second clockwise, etc. There were records of concerts lasting three to four hours on special occasions.

The Ceilidh

My next stop was Oban, on the coast of the north east corner of the long finger of land that juts southward ending in the Kintyre Peninsula just west of Arran. Oban was a fairly short ride from Inveraray continuing along Loch Awe, then River Awe and through Glen Lonan. Oban's active, boat-filled harbour is ringed with rolling hills.

On my way to dinner along the sea front, a pair of small gull-sized birds was making raucous comments on life, exposing the bright red insides of their mouths that matched their red legs and feet. These contrasted sharply with black bodies and white-splashed wings; they may have been cliff dwellers, as their home was a hole in the wall under the pavement.

After dinner, I lingered to enjoy a pipe band open-air concert. Several of the band members epitomized the strong, silent, dour Scottish stereotype with serious beards and full Highland kit. All their pieces were well performed. 'Green Hills' was especially moving.

In the morning, I experienced behaviour that while fairly common in Britain is incomprehensible to me. The hostel offered a cold breakfast that I had paid for when I booked in. This gave me a choice of cereals. The young chap at reception laid out his display of individual serving sized boxes of available cereals and I chose my favourite, Alpen. 'Oh, sorry sir, that isnae available, we are out of Alpen.'   'Well, in that case, I'll have this Alpen from the display', I responded.   'No, I couldnae give you that one,' he replied, 'then I couldnae display it.' Logic and customer satisfaction were strangers to him!

Today's ferry took me to the Isle of Mull. While waiting for the ferry, I met a Dutch woman cyclist travelling solo on a 1500 km camping tour. Self-contained and assured but not particularly gregarious, she surprised me by suggesting we stop for a coffee at our landing spot. We spent a companionable half an hour together, allowing the ferry traffic to dissipate before heading out on our separate itineraries.

I'm headed for Tobermory along the A849 on the eastern coast of the Sound of Mull. At Salen, where the route turns south west on the B8035, I stopped at a silver shop. The artisan's work wasn't attractive or inspired but he claimed to be the world's largest maker of Celtic Crosses, exporting to the US, Spain and Germany.   He didn't like that aspect of the business because the pricing was too fine producing only about £25 profit per week. Most of his profit depends on coach tour traffic.   We discussed tourism, taxation, UK economics and the meaning of the curved arrows on the road for about an hour.   I felt guilty at taking up so much of his time without buying anything and was relieved when a few others arrived allowing me to leave with no purchases but some grace.

From Salen, the route skirts the coast of Loch na Keal, Loch Tuath and Calgary Bay on the B8073 before veering east. Twenty kilometres beyond Calgary, Tobermory appeared suddenly at the bottom of a very steep hill past the distillery. This first view was broad, encompassing almost a full sweep of this candy shop village of bright or pastel coloured houses and shops ringed round its semicircular harbour.

My interest in silver work, ignited by the earlier visit, caused me to stop at a jeweller displaying more beautiful, quality pieces than I had ever seen anywhere. After much deliberation, I chose an amber necklace in an oval sterling silver setting as an anniversary gift for Mari. I thought it was tastefully elegant and would suit her very well. I was so eager to give it to her that a day after my return, we went to dinner at the 'Twisted Fork', a new restaurant on our Lake Ontario harbour. It was a lovely, relaxed meal that provided an appropriate atmosphere to give her the necklace a month early. She did like it and continues to wear it often, but most husbands will recognize that this was not prudent behaviour. Early anniversary celebrations do not remove the necessity of appropriate recognition on the day.

The hostel, housed in a faded pink building, is just round the next corner from the jewellery store. No one was about so I left my panniers in the lounge and put the cycle under cover. Unencumbered, I went out again to check on tomorrow's ferry north to the Ardnamurchan Peninsula. Departure was scheduled for 7.20 am!

An advertised £6 cut attracted me to a barber's shop on the High Street. A gorgeous, dusky brunette with a superb figure greeted me at the door. My spirits rose at the thought of her hovering close and immediately thought to extend the experience with a shampoo, but it was not to be. She was leaving for the day. My male barber had been a ice hockey player, which is unusual in Scotland and mildly interesting but hardly compensation for the alternative! The shampoo became unnecessary.

After a stop at the grocer to collect the components for my next two meals, I returned to the now open hostel. A very efficient, no-nonsense, slender blonde conducted the sign-in process reminding me very much of Erin, a young woman that guided a week-long kayak trip Mari and I took in the Georgian Bay of Lake Huron. Erin's principal leadership experience was with teenagers for whom a command style may have been necessary but it did not sit well with our 50+ group. A few days into the trip, after a series of arbitrary decisions, her order to visit the woods in pairs for nature's call because of the risk of bears was the last straw. I rebelled. I wasn't going to wake Mari up in the middle of the night to accompany me to the 'toilet.'

However, this woman at the Tobermory hostel was invisible apart from her reception duties. So the hostel retained its homey feel with free cups of tea and a friendly atmosphere. The facilities were very good, particularly the toilets and showers although from my room you had to go downstairs and outside to reach them.

On my way after dinner to attend a ceilidh advertised for tonight, I paused to watch a class of about seven children on windsurfing type boats running races in the harbour, apparently oblivious to the frigid water. A Dutch woman cyclist whom I met in the Lochranza hostel walked by and suggested she come to the ceilidh also. Her travels alternate between solo cycle tours and jaunts to Africa! She said she couldn't come right away but might later.

So, I paid my fee and went into the upstairs hall where the ceilidh was to be held. This was an obviously authentic local function, not designed for tourists. As I entered, the first customer of the evening, white-haired ladies and elderly men were managing the ticket table and dispensing complimentary cups of tea. I chose one of the tables round the room's perimeter to read until the performance started.

The entertainment consisted of two accordionists, one acting as compere, and a piper. Fathers danced with their young daughters and very old couples shuffled, lost in pleasant reminisces. Teenagers stumbled trying to negotiate a waltz. My Dutch acquaintance joined me about an hour later. Although neither one of us took part, we both felt that we had experienced something both natural and special.

Tobermory, by night, enhanced this feeling. The village was truly magical with its ring of lights round the harbour, small vessels bobbing on the waves and the pastel buildings. The illuminated face of the tall village clock, standing at the centre of the harbour curve, created one of those nostalgic Christmas card type pictures. We walked to the far end of the harbour and back to prolong the spell.

Early to Bed/Early to Rise

Given the evening's entertainment and the walk afterwards the first part of this subtitle is definitely not accurate. The second part was; I had to be up very early to catch the first ferry as today's cycle route is one of the longest on this part of the tour.

The window in the dormitory room was at the back of the building facing the hills and thus let in very little light. My roommates closed the window curtains so it was impossible to see my watch. I stumbled out of bed at 2 a.m. to drain and to check the time. Apparently this made others suspicious of my intentions, particularly when I parted the curtains to see a little better--someone grumpily called out 'what the hell are you doing?'

So it was a bad night, waking every little while to avoid oversleeping. Finally, when my watch read 5.30, I got up, packed quietly, dressed in the dark and moved my gear out to the reception room--then washed up and went to check the bike. My bike lock key wasn't in its regular place making me worry that I left it in its lock–an invitation to theft. I hadn't but now feared I had a locked bike and no key.

The key might have fallen out in the dormitory room but searching there would require turning on the light. Rather than invite an immediate lynching, I did a calm, unhurried search of all the other possible locations for the key. As usual, this worked far better than the frenetic, hurried approach, and the key was soon found. Then I discovered that it was just 5!

This gave me plenty of time to prepare and enjoy a leisurely breakfast but by 7 am, with breakfast over, the bike packed, and the book finished, I couldn't delay leaving for the ferry any longer. With some trepidation, I buzzed the receptionist to return the room key and reclaim my YHA membership card that she was holding as security. Tobermory's ice lady was still in bed and decidedly frigid at my interruption. She couldn't complain vocally as reception officially opened at seven but her body language was very articulate!

At that hour, there certainly was no crush of passengers on the ferry. One car, two people and a dog were the only other travellers. This was definitely the low end of the ferry fleet--no cafeteria, observation lounge or bar, just a wooden bench along two walls of a very narrow enclosure but the trip took only half an hour.

Good Samaritan Stan

This ferry goes across the Sound of Mull to the mainland at Kilchoan. From there, my generally northern route of nearly 100 kilometres led to Mallaig. Given that distance, I chose not to stop at any of the historical spots along the way; missing the natural history centre, Glenborrodale Castle (formerly owned by Jesse Boot, pharmacist and founder of the chemist chain), and the Seven Men of Moidart Memorial (they joined Bonnie Prince Charlie's 1745 uprising).

Overnight was at the Moorings B&B. This was a welcome luxury with privacy, a television and although not an en suite, I had exclusive use of the adjacent WC because there were no other guests in my section. The landlady even offered to dry my wet clothes.

Following a pleasant fish and chip dinner with a very refreshing sweet cider, I returned to the Moorings room to watch an interesting sounding film on television. Making myself comfortable in the bed to read until time for the film to start was my downfall. Two and a half hours later I woke just as the film credits were rolling.

Three women from Glasgow 'graced' my breakfast table next morning. The youngest one was wearing an Arkansas sweatshirt--giving it a fair old stretch. Arkansas was my mother's birthplace and where I completed my first university degree but there never was the right opportunity during our conversation to find out how she got the shirt.

Today's ferry ride from Mallaig to Armadale Bay on the Isle of Skye was very short giving me time to take a side trip to the Kyle of Lochalsh and Plockton, sites of a very popular British television drama in which Robert Carlyle plays 'Hamish MacBeth', the local policeman, who, with great difficulty, was adapting normal police routine to a very independent fishing folk.

This side trip provided an opportunity to see and cross the new bridge that now connects Skye to the mainland. The little village of Kyleakin sits on the near side of the bridge. There I briefly visited a village centre designed to teach children a bit of local history and something about animals. The centre is run by a charity that partners with the Born Free Foundation in maintaining the island's former lighthouse as an animal refuge. Gavin Maxwell, the author of 'Ring of Bright Water', lived there and his favourite otter is buried there.

The Skye Bridge is the most expensive toll bridge in the UK but thankfully its officials don't charge cyclists--we're considered pedestrians.   As I was crossing, an approaching car stopped suddenly. Its driver and passengers jumped out yelling, 'A Canuck' (having seen my jacket flag). They were from Vancouver and wanted a picture of themselves on the bridge. Fortunately, traffic was light as they left the car right in the roadway while I took their picture.

Plockton, a very picturesque string of joined up buildings round the bay, was a very tough 10 kilometres further on.   Well-maintained, sometimes lush, gardens lie opposite their houses on the sea side of the road. The tide was out, allowing a number of unattended cows to roam about the pebbly beach. Although I couldn't recognise any of the scenes from the TV series, I was glad to have come, as it was one of the prettiest spots yet (being temporarily dry may have affected my judgement).

It was 4.30 and there were another 26 km to go to the hostel at Broadford but I couldn't resist stopping at a lovely restored railway station that is now the 'Off the Rails' café. I enjoyed tea and scones on the former platform. Including a stop at the Broadford CO-OP for provisions, this delayed my hostel arrival until seven.

Tonight I benefited from a YHA promotion making the sixth night of hostel stay free! Another cyclist from Norwich provided some instant coffee and I chatted with him for a bit and with a Las Vegas woman who was on a 'do it yourself' tour using local buses.

From Broadford, I moved on towards Portree. The direct route was by the A87 but after about 13 km, I turned off on the Moll Road, a narrow, low track following the coast of Loch Ainort, thus avoiding the hill looming just ahead. This is a peaceful and beautiful area dotted with an occasional farm in a landscape painted with sheep, gulls, orange brown seaweed, grass and water. Suddenly, this bliss was shattered by the sharp twang of a broken spoke. Now, the rear wheel was out of true and rubbing badly against the chain stay, making progress very slow.

Thinking I would have to walk, I chose to return to Broadford for help as it was nearer than Portree. Although the wheel still rubbed back on the main road, I could cycle slowly and thus got back to Broadford before noon.

A pipe band was playing near the Fig Tree Café as I limped into town. At the adjacent post office and shop the postmistress suggested that Stan Donaldson at the Fair Winds B&B and Bike Hire could handle my repair. Literally just round the corner, Stan answered my knock at the door, on his way out to take his wife to a local gala but agreed to help later. 'Just leave the bike, go off and have a cuppa and I will have it ready when you get back.'

What luck! He could not have said anything that suited me better. I walked back to the Fig Tree and did as instructed, accompanying the cuppa with a slice of carrot cake and my book. Back at Fair Winds, Stan was just getting started. He didn't have a stock of new spokes— just old ones—all but one of which were too short. While fitting this one and truing the wheel, he discovered another broken spoke but said I could get to Portree with this repair and there was a good cycle shop there that could help. A triangular cycle banner tacked on the wall and sporting the words Mississauga, Ontario, caught my eye as we chatted. What a surprise-- Mississauga is next door to Oakville. Stan couldn't recall how he acquired the banner.

Stan refused to take any payment for his help. I felt so fortunate to have found him, have an excuse to stop for coffee and cake and to be back on the road again by two. I was musing on how much goodwill he generated when the heavens opened up delivering a downpour that lasted the full three hours it took to get to Portree. My Presbyterian upbringing made me ponder whether this punishment was my payment for getting free help.

Drowned Rat living in Style

My last overnight on Skye was at the Armadale hostel near the ferry dock. From there I am to travel by rail down to Penrith in Cumbria and cycle the rest of the way to Manchester for the return flight home.

In the morning while waiting for the 9.20 ferry to Mallaig, I met a couple of young German cyclists on their way home after twelve days of camping. All the visible flesh on one of them was covered in fresh midge bites. Scotland is infamous for midges in the summer. Thank goodness I haven't been camping! The Germans were also travelling south by train through Fort William and Glasgow--a journey considered by some to be one of the ten finest in the world for scenery. My personal experience ranks it tops.

By chance, my seat was on the north side of the train, which had the best views. They were absolutely marvellous with almost continuous gorges, surging water, deep green mountains and glistening lochs. I doubt any other journey could pack in so much beauty over such a short distance. Even after leaving Fort William, heading south, the views continued with an impressive gorge featuring sheer, steep cliffs and rushing water at the bottom, again on my side of the train.

Mimicking the scenery, the sky opened up sending down streams. Shortly before Glasgow, as the train pulled into a station, an announcement requested all passengers to leave the train as the Glasgow platform that we were headed for was flooded. The

Germans and I manhandled our bikes and gear off the train getting soaked in the process. The less laden passengers got out faster and took all the available cover. Another already partially full train arrived in about ten minutes so, sardine-like, we sloshed our way onto it.

At Glasgow, even the alternative platform was flooded, making the lift inaccessible and forcing us to haul our bikes and gear up the steep stairway. Trains headed further south depart from the other station, Glasgow Central, providing more soaking getting there. The Germans had already booked their journey through to London with bike reservations but I had no ticket or reservation. So, we parted company while I went to buy a ticket.

The ticket agent claimed that it was too late to access the bike reservation information on her computer; so she couldn't tell if there were any spaces remaining on that train. She suggested that I not buy a ticket, but just check for a bike space on the train's goods van. If there was one, a ticket could be bought on the train, after departure. I suspected she was just about to clock off and could not be bothered.

I found a space for the bike and, by coincidence, chose the same passenger car as my German travelling companions. About twenty minutes after the scheduled departure time, an official entered our car to announce that now the tracks were flooded, making the train journey impossible. Virgin Rail was arranging transportation for us by coach.

After another hour, the official reappeared to advise us that journey by road was now also impossible-calling out 'Scotland is cut off!' Any of us who lived in the Glasgow area should go home-tickets would be honoured the next day. He promised Virgin Rail would find accommodation for the rest and circulated among us to determine how many single and double rooms were needed.

Another hour passed while others departed to claim their rooms. I was offered a taxi to Penrith (which did not make any sense given the road conditions) and I had no accommodation there either. Just after eight, the last remaining passenger, I was sent to the four star George

Hotel, a few blocks away in one of Glasgow's most prestigious locations.

The rain continued so that I showed up looking like a drowned rat. Even dry, I would not normally venture into such a hotel in cycling gear. Despite this, the reception clerk was very gracious, telling me to just give my dripping cycle to the concierge who took it respectfully. She continued with the booking-in process, advising me regretfully, 'we have no more single rooms; would you mind a suite?'

Bearing up manfully, I replied, 'yes, I can accept that.' As I started to leave the reception desk, she inquired, 'Will you be dining with us this evening? Virgin Rail is providing twenty pounds each for their passengers' evening meals.' Twenty pounds was my food budget for an entire day! 'Yes, I might just do so' was my unsurprising reply.

The suite was massive--a totally separate sitting room with television, huge bedroom with another television and a luxurious bath. Unfortunately, I couldn't savour the shower and thick towels too long as the dining room closed at ten.

My best clothes were decidedly downmarket for this place but what could I do? Despite my appearance, the service was impeccable, if a little slow given the number of other late arrivals like myself. Thank goodness, Virgin provided twenty pounds. The cheapest salad and entrée on the menu absorbed almost the entire allowance. Very interestingly, Virgin stipulated that none of the £20 could be spent on alcohol. No reason was given.

Next morning, I had a fabulous breakfast in the hotel's conservatory overlooking George Square, watching people on their way to work – the rain had stopped momentarily. There was the most extensive buffet selection of cold meats, cheeses, fruit and cold cereals that I have ever seen. The George also provided hot breakfasts so after enjoying a plateful of items from the buffet I ordered scrambled eggs and bacon as well. Complimentary newspapers were available—pure luxury--I could not have been happier.

While checking out, I casually asked the clerk how much they generally charged for my room. Her reply was 'The room is £235, but that includes breakfast.' Virgin surely got a discount but I had yet to buy a ticket!

I felt honour bound to do so right away and went straight to Glasgow Central but the trains still were not running and the buses would not take cycles. There was nothing to do but cycle south. Naturally, once that decision was made, the rain restarted.

It was a long way to Manchester but a planned visit with an old friend near Wigan and my scheduled flight home left no time to stay in Glasgow. I just put my head down and pedalled, heading on A roads towards Dumfries, braving the lightning, thunder and drenching sprays from the lorries roaring past.

This lasted for about two hours before I saw a welcome fast food restaurant at Kilmarnock. Here, at least, was an opportunity to dry off and have a quick meal.

The dirty water I've cycled through had drenched my shoes and left a black decorative edge round the tops of my once white socks. I looked worse than when entering the hotel last night but was not as much out of place.

After that rest and refuelling, I cycled another three hours, promising myself that if I could average 18 kilometres an hour and find a teashop about four p.m.—I would maintain tradition and stop. At 4.01, a petrol station with an attached teashop appeared at Burnside! I wanted desperately to spend a few minutes with my book but the only other customer, also 62 and retired early due to a leg injury, was lonely and talkative. I felt sympathetic so we talked.

Shortly after leaving, the rain stopped and a faint glimmer of blue emerged on the western horizon. The road became a gentle downhill tracking the River Nith. It is wooded, gentle country and was now wreathed in sunshine rewarding this part of the day. Like the rain, the 43 remaining kilometres to Dumfries quickly evaporated.

Graced by a large statute of Robbie Burns in the centre, Dumfries is larger and more prosperous than I remembered. A circular flowerbed and attractive river scenes complemented the statue. A kindly barmaid at my second pub stop for accommodation recommendations rang round to find a vacancy that I could afford.

She booked me in the Waverley Hotel, conveniently close to the railway station as I plan to complete my journey by train. The unshaven, greasy-haired and emaciated check–in clerk advised me not to leave the cycle outside even for a few minutes. So it spent the night locked in the lobby. What a contrast to my Glasgow hotel!

The Canal and Parbold

Given this introduction to the Waverley, I was surprised that my room, while tiny compared with the George suite, was clean and had the necessary facilities, apart from a shower. Advancing age makes it harder and harder to take a regular bath, particularly kneeling under the tap to rinse my hair! Breakfast next morning was another pleasant surprise with a well appointed dining room, uniformed waitress and a full cooked breakfast.

I'm going by train today to Wigan near my friends Colin and Connie's home in Parbold. There was over an hour's wait for the train so I cycled back to explore the River Nith section of town, crossing a suspension bridge to a footpath on which I rode in each direction for some minutes before re-crossing the river on an arched stone bridge.

Returning to the station just before train time I found the platform packed with women and retired people; it appears that many people make day trips down to England for shopping as it is only a 30 minute run. The train was over five minutes late and again I was at the wrong end for the cycle car forcing a run to board.

This short delay at Dumfries caused me to miss my connection at Carlisle and to wait a further two hours for the next train to Wigan. Take advantage of the situation, I told myself—use the time to see a bit of Carlisle. Walking round the pedestrian precinct, everything seemed vaguely familiar, the hanging baskets of flowers, the brickwork of the walkway and even the shops. Suddenly, I realized that it had only been three weeks since I was last here! The only difference was my point of entry. Only just retired and already my mind is gone!

The journey between Carlisle and Wigan ran through some beautiful Lakeland-like country near Penrith and beyond. Once at Wigan, despite the steady drizzle, I wandered, dodging under any available awning or overhang to stay dry and eventually sought refuge in a large modern mall.

The rain just would not quit so I decided to return to the railway station to take a room in a Pub type B&B just opposite. They were fully booked but the publican recommended the Charles Dickens and gave me directions. Either the directions were inadequate or I was. The Charles Dickens just wasn't visible. Neither people on the street or in another pub had ever heard of the place. Finally, my persistence paid off and I found a person with precise knowledge of it.

I shouldn't have bothered. The state of repair was abysmal and their rock bottom meal prices screamed--no star' restaurant. At least the Charles Dickens was dry. My dripping and none too clean cycle was stored in the dining room. I remember thinking that perhaps the intent was to maintain the hotel in a condition that would feel like home to Fagin's band of thieves.

Breakfast itself next morning was acceptable but the dismal atmosphere of the dining room, now doubling as cycle store, and an insipid and imbecilic breakfast television programme marred the experience. I couldn't find a remote control and short of climbing on a table to reach the overhead set, couldn't turn off the programme.

The Wigan TIC found me a B&B in Parbold and provided directions to the canal towpath to get there. The TIC was located right on the canal or a junction off it which complicated getting on the path. Three separate sets of instructions proved at least partially faulty. When I finally found the path, it ended abruptly at a steep set of stairs. I lugged the bike up, crossed a bridge and returned to the path down more steep stairs. Now, surely it would be smooth pedalling.

A few minutes later, I met an elderly couple negotiating a canal lock with their barge. The woman was opening the gates. I watched the process and after her husband guided the barge through, helped her to close the gates again. She showed me how to secure them against vandals with a special tool that they carry on the barge.

Ducks and swans replaced the barge and delicate pink and white-blossomed plants liberally cloaked the canal banks as I continued. A number of men, apparently unconcerned with the murky water, fished on the opposite bank.

After about two kilometres, the path deteriorated from macadam to mud-puddled dirt and was barred with daunting gates every few kilometres. These gates had to be designed to keep cycles out. I worked out a way round the first gate only to find a different design at the next, making it necessary to lift the entire laden cycle over a metre high!

Parbold appeared shortly after my lunch at a pub along the canal and far too soon to stop for the day. So I explored the countryside surrounding Parbold finding well-to-do villages and very expensive homes. After a couple of hours just wandering around with no particular destination, I returned to Parbold to scout out Colin's house so I would know how much time it would take to walk from my B&B this evening.

The B&B was private and conveniently located -- my room was totally self-contained with coffeemaker, en suite, soft armchair and separate entrance--a perfect place to enjoy a quiet hour with the paper. But again, there was no shower. After another session of bathtub contortions to make myself presentable. I set out to walk to Colin's.

Within less than a block, he passed by in his car looking for me. Although nothing had been said about it, Colin and Connie assumed that I would stay overnight with them and were concerned when I had not arrived. We spent the first few minutes apologizing to each other for the failure to communicate clearly.

This was a new home for them. Like my friends' place in North Yorkshire, this home was stacked with books. Colin reminded me that I recommended William Manchester's *A World Lit Only by Fire*, which he thoroughly enjoyed. It had been seven years since we last saw each other but there was instant rapport. Colin is a very natural, likeable guy with no evident ego or air of entitlement—despite being managing director and major owner of his company.

We enjoyed drinks and an excellent meal at a nearby restaurant and talked families. Their son Mark is a freelance focus puller currently under contract to the BBC and John is a surveyor/engineer. Neither is married. Colin and his partners did a management buyout of their company and now operate as a finance company funded by the big banks. They had an IPO in the works last year and printed the prospectus on the 11 of September 2001. The financial markets were in no shape after 9/11 to launch an IPO--so the deal was pulled. If it is re-offered, Colin will be very wealthy.

Given my interest in British home construction methods, we talked about the timber frame houses that are starting to show up in various pockets of the country. Colin's firm finances one such developer that imports pre-cut homes from Sweden. He told me that the big issues in this business are getting the building regulations changed to make this style of construction acceptable officially and to locate workers with the necessary building skills. As one would expect, timber frame construction, particularly pre-cut, is much cheaper than the traditional British double wall brick and breeze block method. However, timber frame homes sell for much the same price so there is more profit.

After a nightcap at their home, Colin walked back to the B&B with me. On the way, we passed a branch of the Royal Bank of Scotland that had been a Williams & Glyn branch years and years ago. Colin was proud to tell me that he was made manager of that branch at age 19. I can't imagine a person that age today that would have the maturity for such responsibility or that any company would offer it to them.

As we parted, Colin challenged me to climb Parbold Hill en route into Manchester tomorrow but said it is a killer and doubted my ability with a loaded bike to get up it. His doubt of course, just intensified my desire to meet his challenge. It was a struggle, but using my lowest gear, I managed the hill without getting out of the saddle. The rest of Colin's suggested route severely tested my navigating abilities and took much longer than it should but these were directional not stamina problems.

Going Home

Back at Manchester hostel, I repacked the bike in its case and walked to the railway station to check on departure times for the airport and to check how long it will take to walk from the hostel in the morning. Twenty minutes seemed enough but that didn't adequately allow for the rain that developed or the extreme weight and clumsiness of all my gear. In the morning, distracted by the rain and effort of this short journey, another bout of directional dysfunction caused me to turn left instead of right, adding about eight minutes to the trip. This delay was extended because the main road I had to cross happened to be the route of the cycle segment of the final triathlon event of the Commonwealth Games then in progress. Colourful, damp female cyclists flashed by as two Bobbies on crowd control checked round the bend until the way was clear and waved me across. If I had to wait for something, nothing could have been more appropriate than a cycling event, particularly one involving athletic young women in latex.

The train was five minutes late, partially offsetting my other delays, but was packed with people on their way to various Games events round the city. It was standing room only in the entry/exit zone. Needing both hands for my bike case and other gear, I could not hold the pole to balance as the train rocked. Every stop required shifting position and gear to let people on or off. Once at the airport, check-in was a kilometre walk.

There was a huge queue due to a totally inadequate number of check-in staff. It took about ninety minutes to reach the desk. Then I was told to rush as the plane was already being loaded. The bike case still had to be checked in at the oversize baggage station. Abandoning all pretence of courtesy, I jumped the security queue making it to the boarding gate fifteen minutes before scheduled takeoff to learn that the flight was now delayed for 'technical difficulties'. These turned out to be that day's euphemism for 'we are still loading the luggage.'

In the end, all today's delays have been worthwhile. Economy class was oversold and being one of the last to check in, I was assigned to first class with its wider seats, more legroom, better food and service, a choice of films and free drinks. My seat mates, a 28-year-old policeman and a 45-year-old Austrian based in Scotland, had the same good luck. These two were getting more attention than other first class passengers and taking full advantage of the free whisky. As the trip progressed, they become very friendly and loquacious. The reason for superior service became clear when I learned that the policeman's girlfriend was one of the first class stewardesses. The other man's mellow mood was due to the whisky and the fact that he is going to see his Canadian girlfriend--all through the journey he kept saying, 'I'm so happy!' to the point where his whisky slurred speech accurately rolled out 'I'm sappy' instead.

The now relaxed policeman pulled up his trouser leg to show me an injury caused by a criminal on a motorcycle. Although now healed, his lower leg was as red and raw-looking as if gnawed by a bear. This accident was responsible for his premature retirement. He expressed frustration and dismay at the state of criminal justice in England resulting from political correctness and too strict rules on admissible evidence.

As the flight continued, my two increasingly inebriated companions paid me some rare compliments on my friendliness and appearance. They proposed getting together in Toronto the next evening with girlfriends and spouse. Sobriety must have changed their minds and opinions, as I never received a call to say when and where this get together would be.

So ended a very interesting, rewarding, frustrating and wet trip.

Derwent Water , Keswick, Cumbria

Hostel at St Brieuc, Brittany

CELTIC TOUR

BRITAIN

FRANCE

CELTIC TOUR

I'm familiar with Britain, its great cycling countryside, numerous hostels, inviting tea shops and I understand most of the dialects. So, there are many advantages touring here but this familiarity reduces the opportunities to test my mettle with new challenges, to experience new cultures, architectures and to observe alternative methods of organizing life. My last tour was the wettest ever; so, longing for better weather, the continent would be my choice for the next trip.

Eighteen months later, however, when starting to plan the new trip, I realized that there were still parts of Britain that I wanted to see, the rugged west coast of Cornwall in particular. As my thinking progressed, Cornwall's Celtic character suggested a continental link with Brittany.

Cycling Britain, the Lonely Planet's guidebook, offers a seven-day Southwest England route, incorporating the coast of Devon and Cornwall that seemed a good foundation. Searching the net for Brittany ideas led me to Breton Bikes, a cycle touring company. Most of the season, they provide the bike and all the gear for self-guided tours on several proprietary routes but twice a year they offer a camping tour led by the owner. As most of their customers are Brits, this seemed an ideal way to explore France in the company of English speakers with a knowledgeable, bilingual guide. The first of these led tours in 2004 was timed perfectly to follow my intended time in Cornwall.

So that combination became the plan. Let's take a quick look at the route.

The Routes - England and France

The tour began at Windsor, Berkshire; went south west into Winchester, Hampshire, continuing generally west to Salisbury in Wiltshire. From there the route tracked north west to Street, iSomerset, then across to the coast at Minehead, Somerset. From there I cycled generally south through Devon into Cornwall, touching at Padstow, Perranporth, Penzance, Land's End, and St. Ives.

Brittany Ferries was to take me from Plymouth, Devon to Roscoff where I'll remount the bike to cycle over two days to Gouarec in central Brittany where the group tour begins. This tour, known as 'The Blavet and Two Chateaus', centred on the Nantes-Brest Canal, visiting Josselin and Pontivy before returning to Gouarec a week later. On my own again, I will head north to Val Andre, Dinan, Cap Frehel and St. Malo for a ferry back to England.

Departure and Arrival

Mari dropped me and my gear at the Toronto airport just after six p.m. on the 27th of May. There was the cycle case, of course, plus a medium sized duffel bag absolutely stuffed with clothing, panniers, helmet, extra shoes, maps, daily route cards, tools, spares and rear rack bag. My carry on rucksack held camera, book, tickets, passport, and handlebar bag. With the cycle and case weighing in at 25 kg, the total must have been over 40. While unloading the car, the hard edge of the cycle case lock hasp fell against my hand. I took no notice but Mari immediately saw blood spurting from the top of my hand and was certain that her old man couldn't cope with all of this! But, I was determined. A plaster from my first-aid kit stemmed the flow and check in was a breeze. I delivered the cycle case to the section for large luggage and in less than fifteen minutes, my load was reduced to the rucksack, now comfortably on my back.

We arrived at Heathrow on time, landing smoothly; the luggage and cycle case were delivered quickly. The promised estate car taxi awaited and its seriously overweight and unfit driver at least feigned an interest in my upcoming adventure. At the B&B, I spent the next few hours unpacking and reassembling the bike and organizing the panniers for balance and ease of finding things. Mounting the handlebar bag bracket took twice the usual time as a crucial tool was missing and the brakes wouldn't function properly. There always seems to be some aspect of reassembly that defeats me.

My host, an amiable Italian with a strong interest in cycling but limited English, advised me that there was a cycle shop just 500 metres away. Three thousand metres involving roundabouts and subways would be more accurate. He wasn't alone in inaccuracy. While attempting to find the shop, I was told once that there was no cycle shop in Windsor and once that it was just another 400 metres further when it was 1500. Being Britain, however, they spoke in yards.

Without brakes, this was a walking expedition. Along the way, I dismissed the thought that if found, the shop might not be open. The gods were smiling; the shop existed, was open and they cheerfully mended the brakes. It was embarrassingly simple. The brake cable had become disengaged from a support when the handlebars and stem were removed for packing and I hadn't noticed. The mechanic also replaced my rear axle and lock nut with sturdier ones to stop the rear wheel from slipping out of position when heavily loaded.

By now it was too late for my planned afternoon tour round the picturesque Thames villages. So I cycled into the city to scout out a place for dinner and as an alternative to my villages tour picked up a map of the Great Park that the taxi driver had told me about.

The Great Park is a fabulous public amenity of Crown land near the Castle. Huge and with an immediately rural feel, the park has ponds, swans, statutes, a polo ground and large estate-like buildings involved in various activities for the Crown. The lattice-like, sporadically signposted, network of lanes disoriented me as many of the lanes go to the same place. The map only added to the confusion-- was it jet lag, hunger or just my normal poor sense of direction?

After a couple of hours, I was starving, having eaten nothing since the dry bit of banana bread and cup of coffee that Air Canada had the nerve to call breakfast. Somewhat later, clad in my formal attire of dark blue sweat shirt and khaki cargo style trousers, I headed for one of the bistros discovered this afternoon but got no further than a brand new Indian restaurant just three minutes away. One of my absolute favourite meals is Dopiaza, a lamb and onion curry, with Nan bread and a lager. So, finding this place seemed a propitious start to the gastronomic experiences for this trip. It didn't disappoint. I had my favourite meal masquerading under a new name but with a sweet coconut flavoured Nan and an excellent salad that improved the experience. The cool Mediterranean ambiance with fresh white linen and brushed stainless cutlery was a refreshing break from the stereotypical heavy red décor of Indian restaurants in Britain.

Continuing the delights of British cuisine, my B&B breakfast next morning included grapefruit segments (that I can never get enough of), kadota figs, prunes, muesli, eggs, tomatoes, beans, sausage, bacon, mushrooms, toast and tea.

Why Don't They Signpost the Hostel?

Then, heading for the hostel at Winchester, I stopped at the Watercress Line station in Alton for directions. This preserved steam railway runs to New Alresford, a watercress-growing centre near Winchester. Watercress is very sensitive to water pollution and can be grown successfully only in broad lagoons or 'beds' fed by the clear waters of chalk streams, such as the River Itchen here. (1)

The ticket agent there told me to 'turn right; I did but he meant his right, not mine. I went some distance feeling increasingly certain that something was wrong then stopped a man on the street and was amused to find myself asking directions from another North American. Alton is home to a Coors Brewery so he probably was one of their imported employees. Anyway, his detailed and accurate directions got me out of town headed towards Winchester.

Once there I had to ask for directions to the hostel. Every other place that might interest a tourist was signposted but not the hostel. So, I inquired at a pub. They didn't even know that a hostel existed but offered me their telephone directory.

After trying every possible permutation: Youth Hostel; International Hostel; Hostel, and Winchester Hostel, I finally found the address just as the publican reappeared saying 'follow the path behind the pub, cross the river, turn right and Bob's your uncle.' (Even though I am Bob and my uncles were called Malcolm, Fred and Fount, the barman wasn't wrong—see glossary.)

I got to the end of the indicated street without seeing anything remotely like a hostel. This was becoming more than irritating so I asked again only to be told it was right in front of me! There were no signs in the street and only one on the front, inconspicuously flush with the wall and high above my line of sight.

Once in, I complained about the situation. Lawrence, the somewhat pedantic warden, explained that the hostel was leased on a year-to-year basis from the National Trust, making any permanent type arrangements such as expensive signs a non-starter. The hostel had been in this location for over thirty years but now signs would be superfluous as the hostel is no more.

Now that frustration was out of my system, I could enjoy this most unusual hostel. It shared the building of a former eighteenth century mill on the River Itchen with a National Trust museum. The dining room, one end of which also served as another museum, was directly over the roaring millrace; outside its backdoor is a small island park crammed with roses and bluebells. Ceilings are low and timbered. The male sleeping area was reached by stairs up, then down, and over a little humped bridge into the bunks area. The showers and toilets were in the basement, possibly below river level.

Entering the nearby cathedral's extensive grounds before dinner, I sensed an almost instant and palpable hush. This and the tree-canopied walks created a sense of peace entirely appropriate for a cathedral providing a welcome contrast to the noisy, secular and materialistic world close by. I wondered how many young residents value this serenely beautiful oasis or were even aware of it.

Continental breakfast at the hostel was a curious mix of formal and casual styles. We all sat together on long picnic type tables and the food was served boarding house fashion but with each member's place marked by a place card! 'No names', that is, the members using the kitchen to make their own breakfast, had to sit together at the end of one of these tables--without place cards. It is a bit of a stretch but you could say they were 'below the salt.'

Magna Carta-Democracy's Birth

Today's route to Salisbury was short, allowing time for side trips. The best of these was Crawley, an upscale bedroom village without shops or post office, just expensive homes and the Fox and Hounds pub. Entrance to the village is on a narrow road alongside a lovely pond surrounded by wildflowers and home then to some black and white ducks and a lone rich brown one. Many of the homes had thatched roofs.

Like Winchester, Salisbury has a great cathedral and lovely river walks. At the cathedral, I quietly attached myself to the last tour group of the day allowed in to see the Magna Carta that is housed in a special Chapel. The display is of one of the forty Magna Carta copies that were distributed round the country in 1215. The writing is so neat and the lines so straight that it could have been run off on a press had Gutenberg's invention been available over 200 years earlier but this work was hand done.

The Carta was forced on King John by English barons fed up with his appropriation of their lands, the failed war with France and heavy taxation to support it. 'The Carta's articles cover every conceivable aspect of feudal dues and rights down to those of widows, hostages, and dispossessed Welshmen. Some of the articles, such as the ban on trials without witnesses or the condemnation of the arrest of freemen "save by the judgement of their peers", were fundamental to the subsequent growth of the rule of law. Indeed, the basic idea underlying the charter, that good government depends on agreed rules of conduct observed by all, is the cornerstone of constitutionalism.'(2) A year later King John tried to break the Carta, starting a civil war during which he died. It is not known whether his death was natural or assisted.

Steven's Girl

Other aspects of the Salisbury hostel have been blotted out by my morning experience there. As I emerged from the men's bedroom going to the washroom, an attractive, young Swedish woman stopped me. She was a major distraction in her nearly transparent, baby doll pyjamas but I feigned no unseemly interest as she asked, 'Is Steven up; may I go in and see him?'

I told her that the men weren't up or were dressing so it was best that she not go in but I could do it for her. She told me which bunk was his and said 'tell him that Vicky wants to see him.' I did so somewhat hesitantly; half expecting to be attacked for waking him, and quickly returned to tell Vicky that he was now awake. She waited outside in the corridor keeping up a conversation, apparently unconcerned at her state of undress. Regardless of my pressing need, I felt obliged to do my bit for Canadian/Swedish relations and stoically remained chatting with her until Steven appeared several minutes later.

Somerton and Street

The route from Salisbury to Street runs westward through rolling, slightly climbing country. A manicured sweep of pastures bordered by a soft sculpted ridge crowned with clumps of canopy trees stretched along the southside of the road. This unusual landscape continued almost the entire 34 km to Shaftesbury. At Shaftesbury, I headed north for an exhilarating eight kilometres downhill run to Gillingham. There, my reading of the map showed another 64 km for the afternoon run to Street with no likely spots for lunch before Somerton, 50 km away. So I settled for a quick sandwich on a bench outside the Gillingham supermarket.

Later in the afternoon, it became clear that my poor map reading exaggerated the distance by about 16 km, making tea at Somerton a definite possibility! At the entrance to the village a development of homes at an old Red Lion coach house looked worth investigating and round the bend was a little market area, benches and a teashop.

After my tea break, the day's intermittent rain returned adding a practical reason for visiting the Red Lion development. Given my soggy and impecunious appearance, it probably wasn't necessary but, I declared that I was not a potential buyer. Nevertheless, I was cordially invited to view the seven homes of varying sizes--some inside the original inn and others in a townhouse arrangement in what had been the stabling area at the back of the inn. All featured fully fitted kitchens, huge original fireplaces, and solid wood barn-like doors that slid open on rails. There were interesting differences from a standard North American design: the electrical points in the wall were much higher than we are used to; the refrigerator and the freezer were two separate units in different kitchen locations; and none of the bedrooms had built-in closets. There were no gardens or garages but the development offered character and convenience. A small two bedroom unit was priced at the equivalent of C$550,000.

Chilling rain continued for the remaining ten kilometres into Street. Sally, my landlady, welcomed me with a warming pot of tea and biscuits that I could not (i.e. did not want to) refuse. She served this in their guests' lounge that also served as her husband's library. You would never believe that I lose weight on these tours.

Next morning the owner of a one-man cycle shop was able to mend my loose luggage rack. While he worked he told me that most of British cycle frame manufacturing is now out-sourced and that he wore surgical gloves to keep his hands free of grease and to protect against the carcinogens in cycle lubricants. He also replaced my front pannier braces with stainless steel bolts that screw into braze-ons built into the forks--a much tidier and more secure arrangement. This stop made a pleasant and reassuring diversion. And now, I could avoid the unnerving experience of having to lean down, while in motion, to reattach the front panniers jarred off by hitting a road bump.

Families and Economics

Today my route and the guidebook's merged so I set my odometer back to zero to achieve consistency with the book's distance indicators. Initially this worked well; the turns appeared just when the odometer indicated they should. Then minor differences began to develop. At first, the difference was only .16 km and could be mentally adjusted for as a constant discrepancy but the differences grew and were followed by a specified right turn that should have been left. I, of course, blamed these differences on the book, not my transcription. Later in the trip, a cyclist told me that he had a full page of mistakes found in the same guidebook. (However, it could be that my odometer is mis-calibrated. If my odometer isn't set up correctly, the difference between a 700 mm wheel and a 27-inch wheel could easily account for the accumulating variances in distance.)

So, from this point on, I relied mainly on my map. From my lunch stop at Bridgewater, I used the A39 most of the way to Minehead, breaking a personal rule not to use A roads—but their traffic is lighter in the West Country. At one point, the road entered a forest of trees whose canopy created a dark tunnel with lace-like light patterns on the tarmac. Outside the tunnel, the landscape was a tidy set of jigsaw puzzle pieces in multi-shades of green and yellow.

On a whim, at Nether Sowerby, I went south into the lanes of the Quantock Forest towards Crowcombe. Here the landscape was quiet and more rural. Canopied, cool tunnels and plentiful livestock added to the appeal. But the hilly terrain was so tough that the six kilometres to Crowcombe took an hour. Turning west again on the A358 to rejoin the A39 into Minehead, I freewheeled much of way down to the coast.

The YHA at Minehead, sitting high above the town at the end of a forest trail, is a pleasant place--largely due to the warden. His guests today were several young British families and a group of young foreigners. He encouraged a sense of community by changing the table you sat at for meals, creating an opportunity to meet several different people. He asked your permission so pleasantly you just couldn't refuse. My first table mates were a teacher father with two pre-school age children. They were spending a few days together on a cycle built for three. Mum will join them later in the week but for now, Dad was managing very well, patient and kind, yet firm when necessary--the sort of father I wished I could have been. Despite the attention the children required, the two of us had an interesting discussion about British economic life over dinner.

This is a topic that I introduce to many of my conversations, as I can't understand how, with incomes no better than the North American average, the British manage a cost of living structure that is nearly twice as high. He said that most people are heavily in debt, living beyond their incomes, but of course that is also true in North America. As an example of one of his own economies, he told me that their one family car, a Toyota Corolla, was bought used at auction for about one-sixth of the cost new in Britain. Holidaying at a hostel would be another example but my understanding increased only marginally. It would need a comparison of budget category amounts in detail to appreciate the differences. Property and income taxes could be significantly different. In the morning, my new family was complete: Mum, Dad and two children, one just ten months, but they had no interest in conversation, economics or politics or conversation. So, I read.

Revising my Will

An hour and a half along from Minehead on the A39, I climbed the steep hill up to Selworthy, a National Trust village within the Trust's 12,000 acre holding of the Holnicote estate. Sir Thomas Acland of Killerton rebuilt the village in 1828 to provide housing for the aged and infirm of the estate. Set on wooded slopes of Selworthy Combe, the village is laid out round a green and climbs the hill to the fifteenth century church of All Saints. At the top, the church and a number of thatched, creamy yellow cottages overlook a broad sweep of valley at the edge of Exmoor.

After visiting the church and spending a few moments on a bench absorbing the valley view, I returned down the hill, passing by a hillside track off to the side. Deciding to investigate I was rewarded with a small green ringed with more creamy yellow cottages. One of these was a famous teashop!

Its fame is justified. The teacakes were huge and stuffed with juicy currants. I sat out in the garden, overlooking the valley and observed the interactions of other guests. A mother chastised her unrepentant son for kicking her. A multi-generation family arrived, complete with matriarch in a pushchair. Two burley family members manoeuvred her up the hill, the flagstone path and finally to the table. Despite being worn out with their exertions, each, in turn, asked about her comfort, perhaps competing for her estate. The men looked as if missing this meal and many more would do no harm.

This village, the best example I have seen of the work the Trust does to preserve British history, confirmed my decision a few days ago to leave a bequest to the National Trust in my will. This decision was strengthened when the young woman attendant in the information centre told me that Selworthy is doubly protected from British housing development pressures by being both National Trust and part of the Exmoor National Forest.

Stand and Stare

The next place of interest was Porlock, a pleasant small village, famous for the 30% grade hill that begins just east of it on the A39. This hill is so steep that two toll roads have been built to the sides to reduce the strain of climbing it. I chose to use one of them and quickly realised how tough Porlock Hill must be if this toll road is easier. A sign at the entrance specified a charge for cycles, but no tollbooth was visible.

This heavily forested road is nearly 7 kilometres long with occasional glimpses of the sea off to the right; bird song added a happy note. After about 5 km, I came upon a little, apparently empty, brown tollbooth. Just as I drew abreast of it, a man appeared at the doorway and waved me on without charge. Pleased but humbled and cross with myself for thinking that I might slip by unnoticed avoiding having to pay when the operators were gracious enough to waive the toll. My sense of well-being is very dependent on behaving according to my conscience yet financial considerations are a powerful influence on that behaviour. A constant battle between my conscience and my wallet--is that a civil war? If so, I'm fighting myself and can never win!

Pausing at a cattle grate to admire the now broad view of the sea across a steep valley full of grazing sheep, I chatted for a while with a bird watching, hiking couple at the same point. She quoted a line she attributed to Walter de la Mare—'what value is this life of care, if we cannot stop and stare.' She repeated it so I could record the quotation in my notes. It has more meaning for me than the hackneyed 'stop and smell the roses' but perhaps that is because it is just less familiar. Subsequently, I traced the poem to its true author, the Welsh poet William Henry Davies (1871-1940). The full poem reads:

> 'A poor life this, if full of care,
> We have no time to stand and stare
>
> No time to stand beneath the boughs
> And stare as long as sheep or cows
>
> No time to see, when woods we pass,
> Where squirrels hide their nuts in grass
>
> No time to see, in broad daylight
> Streams full of stars, like skies at night

No time to turn at Beauty's glance
And watch her feet, how they can dance

Not time to wait till her mouth can
Enrich that smile her eyes began

A poor life this, if full of care,
We have no time to stand and stare.'

The remaining run to Lynmouth on the A39 was easy and unexpectedly beautiful. A magnificent rocky river rushes through abruptly rising soft green grazed hills and forests. As always there wasn't any YHA sign.

I had been warned that Lynton hostel was at Lynton Hill, but misinterpreted my directions and wasted a good half an hour round-tripping on the wrong road. The correct road was in the opposite direction from Lynmouth and straight up. There was no opportunity for a flying downhill start and any momentum gained could not have been maintained more than a few seconds. I walked. When the road eventually levelled out, I saw another cyclist ahead, just abreast of the landmark hostel turnoff. Unfortunately, this brought no relief; the access road was so steep that I still had to walk.

Gaining ground on the other cyclist; I saw that he was thin and quite frail looking, perhaps in his seventies. His bike, an old Claude Butler, looked equally worn out. Climbing these hills was hot work but he was wearing two sweaters under a jacket and a reflective shoulder belt on top of all that.

Since we shared the same room, I later observed him undressing and discovered that there were three sweaters, not two, as well as three pairs of underpants. The latter, I imagined, were a a low cost alternative for the chamois pad built into my cycling shorts.

There were also three, 30 something, cyclists at the hostel nearing the end of a north to south End-to-End ride. They have averaged an impressive 120 km daily so far and plan to do the same the next day in this terrain! Despite a late evening at the pub in Lynton, they got away the next morning at 7.30.

Later, at breakfast, I attempted to learn something about my heavily clothed cycling roommate and another man. It was like pulling teeth. Neither of them was pleased with their regular lives.   The cyclist, whom I thought well beyond retirement, was still working and probably no older than I am.   Grudgingly, he told us that he is a quality control inspector at a work uniform firm. For him, the job is boring and unimportant.   The other man repeatedly said that he wished he could cycle but it hurts his shoulders and neck. He was equally dismissive of his work. It was depressing; I had to get away.

Forda Farm

After about twenty minutes on the phone, the Lynton TIC found me a B&B at Forda Farm, some 10 kilometres north of Holsworthy with a convenient nearby pub. The landlady even offered to drive me to and from the pub. The price was higher than I like to pay but I didn't want to spend any more time looking as the farm was nearly 75 km and it was already 10.30. The TIC attendant provided a detailed map for finding the farm and I was on my way.

At Barnstaple, I joined the Tarka Trail (a converted railway bed). This is flat, pleasant and reasonably fast but also a bit boring.   Hills are definitely unwelcome when they have to be climbed but they provide variety and generally there is a bit of a reward on the down slope. However, the trail has some attractive watering holes.   The first, a former station stop turned café, had long queues so I carried on to a café made from a railway car. A chatty, grandmotherly type sold me a lemon mayonnaise chicken sandwich and a ginger beer that I enjoyed with my book at one of the picnic tables arranged on the old station's platform. Grandmother lost most of her charm coming out regularly for a smoke.

Rejoining the main Holsworthy road at this point, my pace has been quick enough to make possible a teatime stop at a country club along the road whose cafe was open for non-members. The day was warm and their beer garden inviting which persuaded me to accept the scones, strawberry jam and clotted cream that comprise a cream tea, de rigueur in Devon, in place of my favoured teacakes.

The TIC provided map showed that I was close to the Holsworthy Beacon landmark for a turn to the east for the farm B&B. However, my detailed road map was so unlike the TIC map that they could be for different countries. The waitress, a local girl, couldn't make them out either.

Trusting to luck, I chose the first lane to the east and stopped at a farm for directions. This interrupted their evening tea but provided an apparently welcome diversion. The farmer came out to the road to speak to me and was soon joined by his wife and son. None of them knew Forda Farm but she rang her uncle and got specific directions for me. Nevertheless, their rural-style ('follow that ridge where you can see the white farmhouse') was still a little vague for someone more comfortable with urban style directions e.g. 'take the first left after Barclay's Bank'. So later I had to flag down a passing vehicle for confirmation and checked again at a farm implement repair shop.

By this time, I was so close that the TIC directions were a seemingly unambiguous 'down the hill, at the dip.' Nevertheless, once at the dip, I still almost missed the farm. There was no B&B sign; the Forda Farm sign was small, very faded and faced the opposite direction.

My friendly, chubby and barefoot hostess Val was also Chair of the Devon Farm B&B's. She made me a welcoming cup of tea with assorted biscuits and joined me for a chat in the sitting room. This was a gracious gesture but I got the impression that her girth was a product of these chats that are as welcome to her as to her guests. I did not point out that her advertising could be upgraded.

As promised, Val drove me to Woody's, the local pub that she recommended. She offered to pick me up after dinner but as it was only about a ten-minute walk I borrowed a torch from her to walk back. My pork roasted in cider with mashed potatoes and peas was massive but very plain.

The meal was neither memorable nor objectionable, but its size caused me to reflect on accepting recommendations without considering the source, in this case a woman for whom the quantity of food appears to be crucial. When I was about half finished, another single man came in, sat at the adjacent table facing me and ordered the identical meal. I was drawn, somewhat reluctantly away from my book, into conversation but, as usually happens, found it interesting.

He was from London but had just bought a retirement home here after years of visiting North Devon. He reacted strongly to my conversational gambit that property values in Devon must be much more affordable than London. He claimed that commercial property prices in London plummeted following the Twin Towers disaster in New York on the risk that a similar terrorist attack might hit London. (In 2005, it did.) He believes he lost £100,000 as a result.

My next faux pas was to praise Ken Livingstone, London's Mayor, for the stiff parking charge levied in Central London that so significantly reduced traffic and grid lock in that section of the city. According to my dinner companion, its other effect was to severely reduce trade for many businesses in Central London, including his. I decided to quit before Canadian/British diplomacy suffered a setback.

Relying on the closing minutes of twilight, I successfully negotiated my way back to Forda Farm to meet Val's husband, Richard, who was just finishing off a huge bowl of strawberry shortcake and reading a very scholarly history of the WW II Normandy invasion. This year is, of course, the sixtieth anniversary of the invasion and celebrations are only a few days away. Our conversation turned to my lack of accommodation tomorrow; Val immediately offered to find me a place with her contacts and booked me into another farm near Wadebridge.

Next morning Val arrived barefoot again, at my bedroom door with a promised cup of coffee. Later, as I tackled the huge farmhouse breakfast, we talked about her university work towards a degree in agriculture. She hadn't been able to complete the degree because at the time she could not drive (a medical condition) a tractor. The degree required a period working on a farm and she could not find a farmer willing to take on a non-driver. She isn't unhappy as she feels very satisfied with what she has accomplished with her B&B business and becoming Chair of the Devon Farmhouse group.

Cycling Museum

Leaving Forda Farm I negotiated through a morning mist, making my way along the lanes to Holsworthy Beacon. Turning south to rejoin the A39, I could see no more than 50 metres ahead and nearly missed the turn going west towards Bude on the A3072.

It was about 100 kilometres to Wadebridge. Fed up with climbing hills, I studied the map for shorter, alternative routes and found one that could cut perhaps 15 km off freeing up an hour to see the cycle museum near Camelford.

Amazingly, there was a sign to the museum. In a few minutes, I found it, housed in an old railway building, surrounded by odd metal sculptures and looking somewhat desolate. The parking lot was empty and the building door was locked. I had just decided that the museum was closed when a voice called out 'hello.'

The woman curator had taken advantage of a lull in visitors to walk to her nearby home for a cup of tea. She delivered her opening spiel, collected my entrance fee and left. The place is chock-a-block with memorabilia: old advertisements, product boxes, posters, parts and accessories, books, magazines and of course, cycles. They are arranged essentially in chronological order of development starting with the mid to late nineteenth century. Most of the exhibits are of British origin but both France and the US are represented. Accompanying this display was a constantly repeating four-part set of period cycling songs of the *Bicycle Built for Two* ilk. Initially, the songs set an appropriate, nostalgic mood but became irritating as the set took only about ten minutes before immediately starting over. By the end of my 45-minute stay, I could take no more.

There were samples of military use, of postal cycles, and of exotic developments such as the 'Zero.' This is a chain-less, shaft driven cycle recently marketed in Britain but with late nineteenth century French origins. Various styles of tables and chairs made from cycle chain wheels and painted bright colours were for sale at reduced prices. The husband produces these in an adjacent workshop and is probably also responsible for the sculptures outside.

Although the displays were poorly lit and provided no history other than a date, it is an interesting museum that shows the progression of cycle design from the huge front-wheel, tiny rear wheel 'ordinary' to the equal sized wheel 'safety' that modern road cycles so closely resemble. The museum represents this couple's collection over about two decades. So much more could be done. The cycle powerfully affected social class mobility and improved gender equality. Exhibits illustrating this and the history of cycling dress would be interesting. Technical exhibits dealing with the effects of frame and wheel weight, with gearing and a comparison of the relative energy efficiency of the cycle with other forms of transport would be fascinating. (See appendix for details.)

The couple's resources don't run to that. Entrance fees are obviously barely adequate to keep the museum open. Manufacturers have been unwilling to do more than provide a single sample of their products, sometimes not even that.

Val had told me to go to 'Greenfields', a bungalow at a particular intersection. It was there but no one else was. The bungalow is part of a farm catering to caravans and campers so I cycled down the farm road to the main farmhouse and spoke to the family matriarch. She pleasantly passed me on to Richard, her son, in the barn working on his tractor.

Richard, a fine-looking young man in rude good health, welcomed me, saying 'My girlfriend Kelly is returning to the bungalow in a few minutes and she will show you the room.' Just then, Kelly, a large friendly blonde, arrived.

Kelly got me settled and said that the Cornish Arms, just a half mile away, would be a great place for dinner. My room had a television and tea making facilities as well as being next to an almost private sitting room but the washroom was nearly at the other side of the house and was shared with all the other guests as well as Richard and Kelly. I passed their room on the way for a shower and as their door was slightly ajar could see that the tidy housekeeping stopped at their door.

The distance to the pub was only double Kelly's estimate. I arrived by 7.30 but seating was already very limited and I was relegated to the billiards room, tucked away in a corner just barely out of harm's way from protruding cues, elbows and bums. Access to the ladies' loo was off to my left so I was treated to a constant stream of round-trip female traffic. All ages and shapes were represented; most of the middle-aged ones had squeezed into something meant, but failed, to make them look younger.

It was a Friday night; the men playing billiards had come straight from work, not bothering to change or clean up. They were noisy, smoking, drinking and taunting each other. It was interesting to watch but not conducive to a peaceful meal with my book. The meal was just acceptable; maybe Kelly's 'great' referred to the happy atmosphere, not the food.

On my return to the bungalow, Richard kindly offered the use of their washing machine, thereby saving me both time and money. I read the Telegraph in 'my' sitting room while the machine was working and later hung the laundry on a large wooden multi-slatted rack suspended from the kitchen ceiling over the Aga cooker. The rack was raised and lowered by a rope pulley. Agas burn continuously generating perfect drying conditions. Next morning, the clothes were dry and pleasantly warm just as if they had been taken from a tumble drier.

A Bug, Dicey Directions and Scotch Eggs

Somehow a bug got me; that night I coughed up phlegm and stumbled across the dark house to the toilet several times. Despite the lack of sleep, I climbed out finally at 6.45 to make a cup of coffee and work on my notes. At least the coffee kept my throat lubricated. Kelly appeared at 8 with my breakfast, took pity on me and produced a box of throat lozenges that helped a lot. For the first time ever, I could not finish my breakfast—the fat, bursting sausage looked particularly loathsome, rationalizing the waste by thinking that this heavy, fat laden meal wasn't healthy anyway.

I cycled from Wadebridge towards Padstow on the Camel Trail, another cycling and hiking track made from a disused railway line. The Camel Trail is popular and attracts enough cyclists to support two cycle hire shops. Not feeling very robust, I was grateful for the flat, lovely riverside scenery, narrow cuttings through steep rocks, and the colour and scent of wildflowers.

Padstow, is an old Cornish fishing town. Like many similar towns, the main road circles the harbour and is itself ringed with commercial buildings and homes. Other streets running in spoke like fashion from the ring road hub are full of shops touting postcards and other tourist oriented items. This is standard stuff but the narrowness of the streets and the period architecture was worthy of a picture postcard.

Attractive as it is, Padstow is a touristy place that doesn't feel natural or representative of regular British life--so I became disenchanted and left at noon heading for Newquay on the B3276. The distance indicators disagreed. After several minutes, Newquay was no closer. Five minutes on, another sign indicated that, based on the distance remaining, my speed was 38 kilometres an hour! Another five minutes more and yet another sign suggested negative speed! My computer told a different story. In fact, I averaged a positive 11 kilometres an hour today, not a blistering speed, but not too shabby considering the terrain. Richard's claim that the road to Newquay was flat, rang hollow.

From Newquay to Perranporth, the road hugged the coastline, rising and dropping with regularity and passing a number of public beaches. These typically had cafes and shops selling beach gear. The day was very warm, sunny and buzzing with surf-boarders, swimmers and sunbathers. Some of the latter faced away from the sea and read newspapers while protected by canvas windbreaks. I stopped at a cafe but was put off by its hoarding promoting a stereotypically British range of choice. It offered eggs and chips, sausage and chips, beans and chips, etc.; the only combination not listed was chips and chips! I chose another place.

My day's journey finished at Perranporth. It isn't the sleepy, small out of the way coastal village that I assumed but a very busy beach town, renowned for its perfect surfing waves. The hostel perches high above the beach but by the time I arrived a thick mist rolled in, obscuring the view of the beach and quickly swallowing one barely visible surfer paddling out from shore.

This is a very small hostel, consisting of a common lounge with perimeter benches and long all purpose tables that serve for eating, conversation, games and reading. Most of the sleeping rooms open on to this lounge. There is also a members' kitchen and outside storage for surfboards and cycles.

I was drawn to John, an English, fiftyish, former dustman who described himself as having been in 'waste management.' John is hiking, using local buses to get between hostels and the hiking trails. He sold his home to an investor, leasing it back at a market rate. This action freed up enough cash to make him feel independent so he quit his job and decided to travel until he gets bored.

One of John's most important possessions is an MP3 player loaded with his favourite music. We met while he was hunting round the hostel for a place to recharge it. John claims to do a lot for charity, taking part in various fund-raising marathons and giving to many others. He complained constantly about the inconvenience of the buses. John was an initially likeable, uncomplicated guy but his constant, repetitive chatter soon wore me out.

My breakfast consisted of two scotch eggs (a hard-boiled egg cooked in batter), steamed tomatoes, tea and orange juice acquired last night from the village convenience store. In the middle of my transaction, a middle-aged, bottle-blond 'surfer guy' with earrings breezed in for cigarettes and tried to persuade me to go elsewhere for the scotch eggs. This 'persuasion' was overbearing, loud and directly in front of the shopkeeper. I think he was just full of himself, but it was a strange, unpleasant experience. Later, I saw him outside a pub, surrounded by apparently adoring teen-aged girls.

Land's End

I spent the next night at the upscale and more expensive Penzance hostel stopping along the way to climb the dramatic coastal cliff at Hell's Mouth and staying several minutes simply soaking up the vista of waves crashing over rugged rock outcroppings.

St. Just, a hostel location near Land's End, came after Penzance. The day's undemanding plans allowed plenty of time to first scout the coastal roads and absorb the scenery. A heavy early mist cleared rapidly making the day warm and humid, so I abandoned the helmet.

A few kilometres west of Mousehole, I slipped off the B3315 down to Lamorna Cove. The last kilometre or so of this is a lovely, leafy lane bordered by a bubbling creek. Cosy cottage roofs just at or slightly below the lane level overlook the creek through dense vegetation. I was almost joyfully content, warmed by the sunny day and unconcerned with distance or time pressures.

This gently sloping lane ends at the cove. Going out as close to the sea as possible, I met a young Vancouver woman hiking the coastal path to Land's End, supremely confident of her ability to manage the round trip before nightfall. Later that evening at the hostel, a New Zealand couple who had gone to Land's End for the sunset told me of meeting a Canadian woman just arriving at Land's End after 10 p.m. She had lost her way on alternative paths because directions on the main coastal path were not clear. I believe the couple gave her a lift back to Penzance.

I took the B3315 from Lamorna towards Land's End deviating for another side trip to the Minack Theatre, one of the world's most remarkable open-air theatres, on the cliff top near Porthcurno.

Once at Land's End I spent several silent minutes entranced by the action of the waves on the rocks before checking out the 'attractions'. A group of Yorkshire tourists was posing in front of the famous Land's End signpost showing the direction and distance to New York, Paris and other famous cities. For this group, there was an extra arm showing those details for Settle, Yorkshire. I was skeptical that the photos would ever arrive. There might not even be film in this pre-digital camera.

Land's End is very popular with British and foreign visitors. There is a hotel, a variety of places to eat, film shows of sea rescues, beached fishing boats to explore and tacky souvenirs to buy. A line painted on the tarmac of the parking lot indicates the 'official' starting point for the End-to-End cycle ride that wasn't there when I completed my tour in 1990. There is also a small brass plaque dedicated to a man that was killed in a road accident during his twelfth End-to-End ride.

The End-to-End seems to be the definitive indicator of serious British cycling. There are many other, more difficult rides but this is the one that stands out. Completion appears to be the crucial factor; it doesn't seem to matter very much how long you take, although many try to finish in the shortest possible time. So, knowing that some manage it in a week or less, I usually don't volunteer that my trip took 19 days.

By four, I had my fill of Land's End, and set off towards St Just, 10 kilometres away. En route, I noticed a small aerodrome boasting a café and couldn't resist. Inside a couple was treating their grandson to the close-up views of arriving and departing small propeller planes.

Despite being in Cornwall, cream teas weren't even on the menu but teacakes were--good for me but a clear sign that this aerodrome isn't high on the list of tourist spots. I made a mistake asking for black currant instead of the strawberry jam that is so ubiquitous in Devon and Cornwall. The waitress sniffed dismissively 'You are the first person that has asked me for something other than strawberry in my thirteen years. Sorry, we don't have black currant.'

The café and waiting area were well stocked with United Kingdom Independence Party (UKIP) pamphlets. The party's signs, primarily concerned with the upcoming European Parliament elections, have been dotted around the roads in this part of the country. As best I can understand it, UKIP wants to undo Britain's membership in the EU or, failing that, to defeat the newly drafted EU constitution that would significantly weaken Britain's sovereignty. Member countries of the

EU must hold referendums by 2006 on this constitution. (Voters in France and the Netherlands both rejected the constitution in 2005, which effectively killed it, as then drafted.)

St Just hostel is really out in the country but is very active because of its proximity to Land's End. It was at least half full despite this being early in the season. Katie, the warden and cook, an extremely large lady, squeezed into the very narrow reception area to sign me in. Busy and committed, she works seven days a week in the season from 7.30 in the morning to past 10 at night.

Being a remote hostel, Katie offers both breakfast and evening meal and clearly takes pride in being adventurous with the menus. Given her workday, shopping has to be done very early—as early as 4.30. We talked about the national hostel organization generally and its financial health. She told me that hostels are being closed where heavy maintenance is required and where the real estate values are high or performance is poor. Katie is very proud of her own performance –turning a profit close to target. New hostels are being opened in other locations.

John, my waste management guy from the Perranporth hostel, was here also, still concerned about recharging his MP3 player and the buses. An Irish guy breezed in after dinner while I was reading in the common room. Discovering that I am Canadian, he declared, 'I love Canadians' and disappeared, reappearing a few minutes later wearing a CANADA shirt on his way to the nearest pub-a walk of a few kilometres.

Sometime, during the night, the Irish guy and someone else crashed into the sleeping room, turned on the light, ignoring the complaints. I was still suffering from the bad cough and muting the sound with my pillow. Despite my problem, I must have slept part of the night as I was rapped on the shoulder at one point and asked to stop snoring. All things considered, it was a bad night.

Saint Piran and St. Ives

Another day began with a relaxed plan; track the coast north on the B3306 to St. Ives, back down on B3311 to Penzance, and west to return to St. Just. My first stop was at the Geevor tin mine in Pendeen where a group of schoolchildren wearing construction helmets was assembled for a tour. Current mine activity is limited to these tours and a gift shop as operations ceased in 1990. The nearly C$16 charge and an hour wait for the next tour put me off. Instead I wandered round the shop, learning that the flag I have seen so much of is St Piran's, the patron saint of Cornwall. It looks a lot like the St. George's cross flag of England but with a black background. Piran was a 6th Century abbot. The choice of colours is thought to represent the white metal of tin against black earth or possibly a link to Brittany's colours. There are 3 St. Piran's churches in Perranporth.

Further on, I stopped briefly at Zennor, a tiny village off the side of the road. A small stone basin along the entry road was used by strangers to put their money during the plague. The basin then contained a vinegar solution to cleanse the money before it was spent in the village.

My vision of St. Ives was of an idyllic, unspoilt fishing village whose harbour would be dotted with colourful artists clad in smocks and berets amidst garrulous, bearded fishermen hauling in nets bursting with fish. OK, that is a bit over the top; but St Ives did not come close.

The place was full of art galleries but I saw no one that looked remotely artistic or was even engaged in producing art. The village is more upscale (due to the galleries) than other seaside resorts, the harbour is attractive and there is a lovely sweep of sandy beach off to the north. St. Ives' popularity showed as its narrow, single car width lanes were jammed with people and cars.

Despite exploring all the lanes, I could find no place to leave the bike during lunch without blocking the narrow pedestrian passages. Effectively barred from any of the interesting pubs and cafes, I settled for a bakery selection on a harbour bench, with gulls and pigeons fighting over every crumb.

The weather turned cool and overcast again, encouraging me to head up the long climb out of St. Ives towards Penzance. A sign at the top showed a distance of about ten kilometres. Two kilometres further on, the next sign showed no change in the distance, 25 metres further and the distance increased! This is very frustrating on a loaded bike.

Once in Penzance, on the way back to St Just, I started building mental totals of the accumulating distance in two categories–uphill and down, on the theory that these statistics could be applied in reverse to determine the time I need tomorrow to return for my train to Plymouth where the ferry leaves for France. This engaging mental exercise made the ride back seem very quick.

Rather than go directly to the hostel I went into the village to buy a newspaper and some things for breakfast since my departure will be too early for the hostel breakfast. Despite this side trip, I still had a good hour at the hostel before dinner and chose to spend it devouring the paper and a steaming cuppa.

There always seem to be interesting stories about life in Britain. Today's paper was no exception. I read about the problems caused for small, beautiful villages by the influx of weekenders and second home buyers that have pushed home prices above the ability of villagers to buy. This has forced many villagers to move to be able to afford a first home. These exits have reduced school enrolments forcing some closures. In addition, current British law offers a discount on the council charge for second homes, squeezing village finances.

Another story dealt with the huge gap in life expectancy between the classes that still exists despite eight years of government efforts to close it. The article referred to a recent book that attributes long life to the ability to control it. More moneyed classes are generally better educated and consequently have healthier life styles. As a result, they have a broader range of occupational choices offering jobs that are more interesting and flexible.

Off to France

My continuing cough and the need to be up early made for another bad night. The upstairs dormitory room was still hot from the day and, unable to check the time in the dark room without disturbing others, my sleep was fitful. At 5.45, when enough light penetrated the room to see my watch, I finally got up and made preparations for departure.

First I discovered that last night's efficiency in packing for a quick getaway resulted in my razor and blood pressure medication being buried in one of the panniers. These were loaded on the bike, now locked in the shed and inaccessible until Katie comes on duty at 7.30, my planned departure time.

So, I cleaned up to the extent possible, dressing warmly in anticipation of rain and/or cold and had a satisfying breakfast of pork pie, tomatoes and tea in the members' kitchen with my book. I was eagerly anticipating a new adventure, a feeling intensified by the morning's cool, misty stillness and solitude. The simple tasks of breakfast preparation and yesterday's timing run produced an empowering sense of control and self-sufficiency, no doubt increasing my life expectancy!

Katie was only five minutes late opening the bike shed so I left virtually on time. The run to Penzance was special at this cool, quiet time of day and faster than yesterday's calculation. This provided time to restock my supply of throat lozenges, supplement my breakfast at the station café and to shave.

The early arrival also ensured that I got one of the two cycle spaces. The train was ten minutes late but quite empty. Despite the considerable number of seats available, I was drawn to a seat opposite a well-formed young woman who complemented the external scenery. Unfortunately, my human scenery left the train about half way through the two-hour trip.

Ferry passengers are warned to arrive at least 45 minutes early or risk not being able to board, so pausing only to have a quick sandwich I left Plymouth railway station for the harbour. The route to the terminal is very well marked but involved heavy lunchtime traffic and a couple of major roundabouts. In each case, the required roundabout turn meant moving across two lanes of traffic on the approach. I made very obvious hand signals well before starting the move and the traffic was kind to me, making the trip smooth, efficient and left me feeling pleased at my traffic skills.

Queues were building in each of the several entrance lanes. I sat in one for a while wondering whether cyclists were considered vehicles or foot passengers since foot passengers waited inside and boarded the ship at a different point. A light rain started, adding a sense of urgency to finding out my classification, so I cycled up to the distant passenger lounge to learn that I was a vehicle.

Returning now to a further back position in the wet queue, I and the other 'vehicles' fumed as the just now arriving officials were in no hurry to start checking passports and tickets. Once they did, we moved at a snail's pace. The yellow van at the head of the queue was 'of interest' to the authorities.

After this first stage each vehicle was assigned to a lane for boarding the vessel but still had to wait at a point just about 100 metres from the entry ramps. I was the first in my assigned lane alongside the suspect yellow van. Its two occupants, Muslim in appearance, leaned out of the window to apologize profusely for holding everyone else up. 'We very sorry to cause delay, don't understand why they asked us so many questions'.

Soon we were motioned aboard. I was directed all the way to the bow directly in front of a huge lorry. A crew member quickly lashed the bike to the side of the ship, leaving me to escape the exhaust fumes by scurrying between arriving vehicles to a door leading to the upper decks.

The upper decks are spacious and well maintained with a bar lounge and two or three restaurants catering to different budgets. Wait staff were smartly dressed in crisp white shirts, ties and well-ironed black trousers and didn't wear the 'bored out of my mind' expressions that one often finds in tourist oriented restaurants and cafes in Britain.

The cafeteria had a good selection of main courses, interesting looking desserts and wine by the carafe with more acceptable prices than the other restaurants. I choose pork and ginger with vegetables, a fruit tart and a carafe of red wine. The cutlery was good quality and the napkins, although paper, were heavy and didn't fall apart with the first use. Compared to hostel conditions, this was true luxury; I enjoyed the meal and ambience immensely.

Thinking I might get in a nap before the 10 p.m. arrival, I had reserved a reclining chair at the time of booking but should not have bothered. The reclining chair room was overrun by French teenagers that kept coming in and going out, shrieking and generally being modern teenagers which is to say loud, superficial, silly and totally inconsiderate.

To be honest, I probably couldn't have slept anyway. This was such a departure from my usual trips that I was energized by the change and somewhat anxious about being able to find the hotel that had been booked for me in Roscoff. Would it still be open?

Eventually, I abandoned the attempt to nap and went back to the much more sedate lounge. By this time, arrival at Roscoff was imminent. When we were allowed to go to the vehicle level, I headed straight down to the correct deck but chose a companionway on the wrong side of the ship. Correcting this meant climbing all the steps back, fighting and irritating the flow of traffic in the opposite direction, to get on the other side.

Once there, I barely got the bike untied before I was waved off the ship—the very first one to exit and emerging into a welcoming twilight, on French soil, free to go wherever with no customs officials or passport control to contend with. This is still the European Union and officially my journey is no more significant than leaving Ontario to drive into Quebec but it felt so different and special!

My French cycle tour company booked me into the Hotel d'Angleterre. I had no idea where this was but happily rode into the city along streets invitingly lit by Victorian style lamps feeling positive, confident and eager for this new experience.

Roscoff is attractive, well maintained and French. The evening air was soft; the limited light enhanced the feeling of adventure. Deeper into the city, signs appeared for several other hotels but not for mine. I stopped a well-dressed matron to ask for directions. Despite our mutual lack of each other's language, she very pleasantly managed to direct me with hand and arm movements together with a few 'a gauche and tout droits'. Once there, the Hotel d' Angleterre loomed up in the twilight like a small chateau, making me fear that I was booked into an expensive hotel due to some miscommunication. The attractively decorated and antique filled lobby further intensified my concern.

A pleasant woman receptionist confirmed that I did have a reservation and escorted me up to the room. The expensive ambiance disappeared at the stairway; the vibrant colours of the lobby were replaced by drab, dimly lit walls and worn carpets. My room was clean but just adequate with a washbasin but no toilet or shower.

After she left, I went to look for a shower room emerging into a pitch black corridor. Patting down the walls revealed a light button outside my room that restored vision, allowing me to examine each door for signs of a bathroom. My search went the full length of my corridor, round the corner and all the way back to the stairwell. There, an unnumbered door opened to the only bath for this floor. Inside, I assessed what I needed to bring from my room, and returned to a dark corridor! The switch was obviously timed to give you just enough time to find the stairway.

Back in the bath, I stripped off and eagerly jumped into the large shower only to discover that it did not work. I got out, suddenly realizing that I was standing starkers in front of a large window looking out at the homes on the opposite side of the street. A flimsy lace partial side curtain provided the only privacy. An internal voice said, 'what the hell, this is France.' Filling the high-sided narrow ancient tub, I told myself not to be concerned about being overlooked. A tub bath is not, of course, a new experience. But, shampooing your hair and rinsing it without even a hand held spray requires an on-the-knees posture and a bobbing for apples action bound to amuse any observers from across the street.

This situation reminded me of my medical for an overseas assignment early in my career. The examining room door opened onto the full waiting room and for some inexplicable reason, that door was opened just as I, lying on my stomach with my feet facing the door, had been elevated into position for a proctoscopy, truly letting it all hang out!

Next morning, back on the hotel's attractive entrance level, I entered the big breakfast room with its high ceiling and wide board, seemingly original, floors. Wrought iron chandeliers painted French blue, a large assortment of country antique furniture and attractive tablecloths completed the scene. Only two tables were occupied giving the room a feeling of being at peace.

The coffee was excellent and my pot, supplemented with milk, provided nearly three cups. Orange juice, a fresh croissant and some crusty bread with a large quantity of fresh butter replacing the fat content of a 'full English' made a very satisfying first petit déjeuner.

Negotiating French Roads
A light rain fell as I loaded the bike for today's ride to Huelgoat. Huelgoat is east of Roscoff, a little more than half way to the home site of Breton Bikes in Gouarec where the group tour is to begin. Despite the rain, I prolonged the loading routine to watch a small man hauling coal from a large flatbed truck, bag by bag, into the basement of the hotel. The only modern aspects of the scene were the blue nylon bags instead of burlap and the truck in place of a horse-drawn cart. Otherwise, it could have been from over a hundred years ago.

Breton Bikes provided a suggested route that nearly duplicated the one that I designed for myself. The problem was finding the indicated road and making sure I stayed on it. Like the British, the French use roundabouts to good effect. Most of the French roundabouts have attractively landscaped centres with individually designed gardens. At first, negotiating them felt very strange because you go round them anticlockwise instead of clockwise as in Britain.

Often a turning off the roundabout would be signposted for several locations but not necessarily for the town on my directions. Often the route number wasn't shown; I was constantly getting out the map to see if a particular town shown on the sign was somewhere on the same route as the town I wanted.

This frustrated and confused, causing me, at one-point, to wind up on a stretch of dual carriageway which was illegal as a couple of drivers pointed out to me as they passed shaking their fingers at my transgression. Fortunately, an acceptable exit appeared before I was crushed or apprehended.

I made slow progress, not arriving in the attractive and well-maintained river port city, Morlaix, until lunch time. It was only 20 km from Roscoff. Colourful boats in the harbour and gay flowers decorating the streets and bridges made it festive. I found a small, unpretentious café with reasonable prices. The inside had blue-grey stained wainscoting, a seaside motif on the walls and bright yellow tablecloths—much nicer than the exterior suggested. I ordered a croque monsieur and café au lait grande. A small, excellent salad came with the sandwich and the coffee was superb—so good that a refill was necessary. It was a great lunch but a budget disaster. Unlike North America, coffee refills are not free and coffee is très cher. Those two coffees cost more than the sandwich and salad! (For clarity, it should be noted that the term 'grande' for coffee in France means a quantity equal to perhaps half a Starbuck's 16 ounce Grande.)

At about 3 p.m., with the odometer registering 48 km for the day, I saw the first sign for Huelgoat—just 15 km further. The last bit of this was downhill, bringing a beautifully blue lake into view on the right. A wooded grotto of huge rocks overhanging a tumbling stream was on the left. The lake spills down under a bridge, feeding the stream.

The road alongside the lake is lined with shops, my imaginatively named Hotel du Lac and cafes offering lakeside patios. After checking in, I explored the grotto's narrow, winding trail on foot, navigating over trees roots battling the rocks, breaking the trail surface. Then the trail broadened as the huge rocks (more like boulders) gradually ran out robbing the trail of its drama.

I took advantage of a convenient bench and the solitude to update my journal and then returned to the lake to enjoy a waterside pression (draught beer). During dinner later on my hotel's piazza, I chatted briefly with a couple from Wiltshire. It was one of those conversations that don't get much beyond an exchange of generalities but it demonstrated how little people really know about Canada. Often, what they do know is out of date or flat out wrong. This man's knowledge of Canadian theatre seemed to be entirely based on reading some patronizing comments about Christopher Newton and the Stratford, Ontario Festival, over fifty years ago.

I set him straight on that, extolling the high quality of the annual six-month long Stratford and Shaw Festivals. I also pointed out that Toronto's theatre count is second, only to New York City, in North America. But, he will, more than likely, retain the 1950s view rather than the update.

So far, I was very impressed with Brittany. The cleanliness and friendliness, the quality of the food, how reasonable a carafe of wine can be, all contributed to this impression. Huelgoat is beautiful and I certainly like the luxury of a soft, clean bed. Two hotels in succession have dulled my anticipation of the camping experience to come.

Next morning, I stretched my petit déjeuner in the hotel bar out for almost an hour with my latest book, Arthur Hailey's Evening News, packed up and paid my bill. It was a shock to learn that my dinner cost an extra 10% just for the privilege of eating on the piazza.

A light mist while loading the bike made me realize my cycling gloves were still in the room. Since I had surrendered my room key, this would be the first true test of my ability to communicate in French. Back in the bar, somehow the necessary three nouns came tumbling out without thinking,-'gant, chambre et clef'—no connecting articles or verbs but enough to convey my meaning. I was sent to find the chambermaid but my room wasn't locked so I quickly retrieved my gloves without having to test my wobbly French further.

The countryside wasn't as attractive or manicured looking as the UK but was still pleasant. It is very rural and well-populated with cattle but these French cattle don't respond to my greetings. Perhaps it is my pronunciation and accent—but 'moo' sounds much the same in any language doesn't it?

I arrived in Gouarec about four and immediately went to the post office to buy a French phone card and its accompanying several page instruction manual. Returning to my bike, a red Fiat convertible sports car driven by a grey bearded and tousle-haired chap pulled up, its driver calling out 'Are you Bob?' It was Geoff Husband, owner of Breton Bikes and the leader of the tour I am about to take. We have only ever communicated by e-mail but it was a good guess on his part. After a hearty welcome and directions to the campground where 'home site' is located, he roared off on some errand.

The campground nestles between the Brest-Nantes canal and the Blavet River. Its entrance has an office and storeroom in a block of buildings that also house the washrooms and laundry facilities. There were a few caravans nearby, but otherwise the site was almost empty. However, as I cycled through the gate, a man and his daughter from Vancouver came round the corner. They had just completed a self-guided trip with Breton Bikes and pointed out a large white tent at the far end of the campground that is Breton Bikes' storage and maintenance area.

Geoff was there talking with another Vancouverite, who had also just finished a week's solo trip using Breton's equipment. Her tent, sleeping bag and foam-sleeping mat immediately became mine. There wasn't even a pretence of getting me a 'fresh set.' Reflecting back now, this was the first evidence of comfort levels and general standards. Geoff demonstrated how to erect the tent, threatening good-naturedly that I had only this one opportunity to learn.

Then he showed me the bike prepared for me based on my personal measurements. It was new and an appropriate French blue but had a saggy, weather-beaten Brooks saddle that proved to be surprisingly comfortable. The handlebars were 'sit up and beg' style with thumb operated gear changers mounted next to the handgrips. The bike was equipped with very low gears 'capable of climbing the Pyrenees'. Geoff encouraged me to try this bike tomorrow before deciding whether to use it or my own on the tour.

I took it out immediately for a trial and to find a phone box to test my new phone card. Apart from needing to raise the saddle, the bike was comfortable and worked well but I had no success with the phone card.

This minor disappointment added to my growing discomfort about the looming privations of this tour. My comfortable hotel rooms of the last two nights make the tent seem small and unappealing; the site is cool and damp being bordered by two bodies of water and none of my tour companions have arrived yet. Half of the intended group cancelled at the last moment, leaving only five plus Geoff.

Dave, the campsite manager, tried to help with the phone card but had no success. Also British, he left his job as a teacher, came to Brittany a year or so ago and leased this campsite from the town. Dave now lives on site in a small caravan, but his wife Marianne remains working in Cornwall. They have been assessing where they want to live on a permanent basis but appear close to deciding for France.

The story is similar for Geoff and Kate. Geoff was also a teacher but they have been here for twelve years, own an established successful business, have three fully bilingual children in French schools and are well integrated into the community.

For me, a long-time Anglophile, finding two couples that have or are close to abandoning Britain for historical enemy France was intriguing. Both of them answered 'lifestyle' as the primary reason for their decisions. Over the course of the week, I learned that the reasons weren't financial in either case. Geoff discussed enough of the economics of his business for me to know that a British teaching salary would produce more income. Apart from lower housing costs, the French cost of living appears about equal to the British. Dave admitted that he was living on the financial brink.

One of the remaining tour participants, Rawdon O'Connor, arrived about six. He and Geoff are long-time friends and Rawdon often participates in these tours as back-up leader. This time, he tells me, he is definitely not taking any responsibility.

The French Way
After a few days in Brittany's relaxed, more measured pace of life, a sense emerged of what Geoff and Dave must mean by 'lifestyle.' People are regulars in the boulangeries and pâtisseries, in the bars and cafés. Greeted as friends more than customers, with handshakes and sometimes kisses. There is a pleasant routine rhythm to life that is comforting and stress-reducing.

Most of us are familiar with the apparent contradiction between the rich French diet and their relatively low incidence of heart disease. Red wine consumption is often suggested as the rationale but I think that their lifestyle might also be a positive factor.

Some of my observations may be due to Brittany being a relatively poor part of France where, by necessity, sincere interpersonal interaction takes precedence over conspicuous consumption. When you don't have as much material wealth, other factors, like relationships take on more significance. Newfoundland exhibits similar characteristics. It is entirely possible, however, that I was drawing quick, unwarranted conclusions due to my being on holiday in an unfamiliar country. Anyway, I was becoming a nascent Francophile.

Not that first night though, dining alone at Hotel Brevet feeling abandoned and dreading the prospect of a night in a cold damp tent. Stammering in more than normally garbled French, I also stuttered some unintelligible English when I came across Geoff, Kate, Dave and Marianne, celebrating an anniversary in the bar. Rawdon came to my rescue later, joining me for a drink as I finished my solo meal and we walked back to the camp together.

I fashioned a makeshift pillow from a plastic bag stuffed with spare clothing but could not get comfortable. The thin sleeping mat neither insulated nor cushioned and despite staying fully clothed, I was cold and my cough was still a bother. Sometime in the middle of the night, a visit to the washroom became urgent. This meant finding the tent zipper, pivoting my legs out through the opening, searching for my shoes under the flap while assuming a tilted 'Z' shape, half in, half out, of the tent to put the shoes on without getting the interior of the tent dirty.

Bursting with need, I highly resented the seemingly interminable long walk to the washroom at the far end of the campground with only moonlight to guide me. Once there, the washroom was pitch black and I could find no light switches. Standing, exposed, in front of the urinal with my right leg stuck out to prop the door open for moonlight, I became alarmed as suddenly all the lights came on. Was a trigger built into the urinal? Would an armed security guard burst in? No, I obviously read too many espionage novels. Someone else had arrived who knew that the light switch was located near the women's washroom. Dave told me the next day that this was a timed switch that allowed seven minutes to complete your activities. I trudged back to the tent, reversed my 'Z' exercises, popped a cough lozenge and tried to get some sleep.

Next morning, Rawdon introduced me to the tour breakfast routine. First a trip to the pâtisserie for croissants or decadent fruit and chocolate pastries, then on to a bar for coffee or hot chocolate in his case. It could not have been later than 9.30 when we arrived but already there were men at the bar having a Saturday morning beer.

We made an odd looking pair; neither of us giving the appearance of wealth or savoir-faire. Rawdon is large and dressed almost entirely in black and with a two-week growth of beard looks intimidating, more bodyguard than companion. This and his military bearing belied his character. There was no pretence or posturing and as the week wore on, it became increasingly clear that he is well educated, widely travelled, and very considerate.

Later, he introduced me to the bargain that lunchtime can be in France. A large number of French workers receive lunch vouchers as part of their compensation. In 2004, the value of these averaged around eight to nine Euros daily. Consequently, there was tremendous demand for lunches at that price and the competition was fierce.

We went to a café in Gouarec that provided a cold buffet of sausage and salads for starters, followed by a choice of main course, a dessert, cheese and wine for 8.5€. The small rich coffee was another euro. At the end of the week, eight of us had lunch at this cafe and were given six bottles of wine between us. They kept bringing more as we ran out—with no extra charge! In the evening, the story is different; an equivalent amount of food is much more expensive and every glass of wine is extra. I found that red wine is an excellent cycling lubricant so fill up at lunch!

These lunch arrangements are a powerful example of France's different life style. For much of my career, lunchtime was either a quick sandwich at my desk or a brief fast food offering at a nearby mall food court. The three-martini lunch and company cafeterias with subsidized three-course, quality meals were largely history. Drinking at lunchtime was limited to expense account lunches when one was entertaining and even then a single glass of wine generally sufficed. Here in France, employers and employees consider a leisurely lunch, at a restaurant, with 'adequate' quantities of wine to be natural and normal. Vive le difference!

Rawdon and I continued to share personal details and to discuss French life. I asked his opinion of the French work ethic. Half-jokingly he replied, 'Would that there were any.' According to him, some professionals take Mondays off by tradition; most schools are closed, at least partially, on Wednesdays, requiring parents to make special arrangements or close down their shops or businesses. Sundays, particularly in Brittany, all the shops and bars close by midday at the latest. In his view, Tuesdays, Thursdays and Fridays are the only reliable days to get business done.

We also talked about France's move to a 35-hour workweek. The government's objective was to create more jobs, oblivious to the fact that business would try to extract greater productivity from existing employees during the shorter workweek to maintain profit levels rather than hire more people. In France, having a job is crucial to one's social status. However, performing well in that job seems to be a lower order concern. In fact, shortly after I returned from this trip, I read a review of a new French book advocating employees to do whatever they could to frustrate their employers----Dilbert with a French twist!

The Group Gathers

When we returned to the campsite after lunch, the rest of our group had arrived and was in various stages of putting up tents and loading their gear in panniers. We introduced ourselves to Yassmin from England, a married lady, but alone on this trip, and Murray and Cara, a sixties couple from New Zealand. Yassmin lives on a houseboat in Kent, works as a secretary in the legal department of a hospital and is studying towards a degree in Archaeology. Murray is a plumbing and drainage inspector for the county in Oamaru, on the east coast of the South Island.

Since it was about 3 p.m., Mari and my agreed calling time, I decided to have another go with the phone card. Studying the posted instructions inside the booth, I learned that the only problem was using the wrong code for an international call and was able to get through!

Geoff issued what could only be considered command invitations to a 'pig roast' at his children's school this evening but at ten euros each, we weren't likely to find a more economical dinner or a more natural cultural example. We all walked to the school, about 15 minutes away. Tonight's event was the culmination of a full day's activities. They were announcing prizes from a drawing when we arrived. People milled about, patronizing the cash bar, waiting for the pig and chatting. A few children and adults made fairly feeble attempts to dress in the traditional black and white Breton fashion.

There was ample home-prepared food to accompany the pig. Geoff demonstrated his generous nature that was so evident during our tour by buying wine for our group. As a former internal auditor, I observed the internal controls breaking down in the general good nature of this community event. People were to buy a ticket and surrender it for their meal. There were different stations for the roasted pig and vegetables, for the salad and the desserts. Sometimes you were asked for your ticket, sometimes you weren't. Second helpings were allowed. I saw no one refused anything for lack of a ticket.

As I was musing on internal controls, a bagpipe blast from behind shattered the air jolting me alert as a young Breton piper strode in. Having planned this trip as a Celtic excursion to witness similar traditions, it should not have been surprising.

Back at the campsite, twilight became darkness and we gradually retired to our separate tents. It was still cold and damp; my cough persisted making this night as uncomfortable as the night before although I now had a torch to guide me to the washroom and knew where to turn on the lights. I also knew that one of the four stalls contained a modern, instead of a squat toilet.

Next morning, our group gathered at a local bar for breakfast with Geoff, Kate, their children and Dave and Marianne. This was our group send off and one of the best (i.e. largest) breakfasts of the tour. The barman greeted all the males individually with a handshake and the women in the double-kiss French fashion. He poured bowls of coffee considerably larger than even the café grande size. Each of us had a croissant, a couple of baguette rounds and access to a plate stacked with crêpes. The fresh butter and jams were almost unlimited and refills of the coffee automatic.

Boules

This ample, leisurely breakfast made a friendly, communal start to the day. By the time we got back to the campsite for final preparations, an American mother and her two teenage daughters had arrived. Initially they will travel the same route as the rest of us but stay at hotels.

About eleven, everyone's panniers were packed, tents and cooking gear strapped on and their saddle heights adjusted. We set off east along the canal towards a large open-air Sunday market. The market backed on to a pasture and faced a bar with an outdoor terrace that soon claimed several of our number. Apart from providing local colour, the objective of our stop was to buy food for a picnic. There were stalls for bread, for cheese, for meats, for preserves. Some also sold wine or cider.

As Mari will attest, I am not too diligent with hygiene standards in our own home but can become quite squeamish when strangers are involved. So this market was a bit of a cultural cold shock coming so early in the tour; it was like jumping in icy water all at once rather than easing in gradually. The bread was unwrapped until bought; no one wore surgical gloves or hairnets. The same people that took your money handled the food; and there was no refrigeration for the meat. If any one of the sales assistants needed to wash their hands, they would have to go over to the bar's washroom. The communal towel there did not inspire.

Ecstatic with the market ambiance and its 'exotic' wares, there was nary a murmur of discontent from the group about the lack of hygiene. I held my tongue. Laden with our lunches, we cycled off and partially climbed a forested hill before abandoning the cycles to walk further up to the picnic site----a large set of rock outcroppings near an ancient tomb. The weather was warm but we weren't yet comfortable enough with each other for more than awkward and stilted conversation.

This awkwardness broke down considerably that evening when after our campsite meal, we walked over to the nearby hotel where the American women were staying. We ordered beers and played boules outside the hotel as they enjoyed their dinner in the hotel. Soon, they were beckoning us to the window to pass food out for us. It was a five-course meal and they became full on the appetizer. The 70+ proprietress of this small, unrated hotel was a lovely, warm grandmotherly type and the cook. She took great pride in treating her guests well. The Americans did not want to offend her by not eating everything.

Boules, a game similar to curling without the sweeps, is played in a long rectangular space; ours was slightly more than a metre wide and enclosed by low wooden walls like a long sandbox. Someone throws out a small ball towards the far end. Different coloured larger balls identify the separate teams. Each team member attempts to roll these larger balls from the near end as close to the small ball as possible, sometimes intentionally knocking the other team's balls away. Only the team with the most balls closest to the small ball wins any points.

We split into two teams of three with Geoff and Rawdon as captains because they were the only ones that had ever played before. The hotel proprietor offered a constant stream of advice, pointing out the lay of the pitch and suggesting how the ball should be thrown. We listened politely but ignored the advice realizing that it was worthless. Lubricated with beer, playing this game was reasonably diverting for me despite being on the losing side. Fortunately, the skill required was minimal and I managed enough close balls to contribute to our team's score, preserving some self-respect.

As the light faded, Geoff became agitated showing signs of wanting to end play. He did not say what was the matter but soon disappeared into the hotel. We later found him in the kitchen watching the World Cup football match between France and England that had started at eight. Some time later, remembering his duties as group leader, he came back out to invite us to join him for the last ten minutes of the game. I did, unconsciously justifying him staying until the bitter end.

The promised ten minutes became at least twenty but England was close to winning, pleasing both Geoff and myself, when France scored twice in the last two minutes to turn the tables. It was indeed a bitter end! We walked back to the campsite, deflated by the loss and mainly silent except for Geoff's periodic muttering 'I don't even like football! How could they lose the game like that?'

Around the Campfire

The Americans restored their appetites and shamed us by jogging before joining us for breakfast at the hotel. We then separated permanently from them as their hotel-based route ended the day at Rohan where we will be by lunchtime. Initially, our route was downhill but then ran flat through very pastoral scenery on quiet roads spotted with some beautiful Breton homes and cattle.

I was definitely in a better mood now than during than the last two days. A decent night's sleep away from the cold damp of the Gouarec campsite was a major factor and the warm sunshine with light breezes off the canal added to the sense of contentment. I even concluded tentatively that I enjoyed cycling in France more than Britain. That was close to heresy for me!

We lunched heavily at the Rohan Hotel, starting with an aperitif, followed by the full luncheon voucher special of appetizer, main course, dessert, wine and coffee. The total price was 11.50€ or C $18.40, including taxes and the incorporated gratuity.

We weren't legless but it was fortunate that the rest of the day's route was along the canal path, requiring little exertion. All the lock stations and operators' homes along the way were individual and attractive, with flowers in every imaginable place, showing the operators' considerable pride.

Towards four, we arrived in Josselin, the first of our two chateau city stops. Geoff conducted a prolonged search over the campsite for the location offering the best combination of proximity to the facilities, to the rising sun (for drying the tents and any laundry) and reasonably flat surfaces. Most of the sites were OK but Rawdon quietly advised us 'site selection is Geoff's special concern; just let him do his thing.'

Tents erected and showered, we gathered for a very relaxed dinner. Some bought wine and cider that they shared along with some pre-dinner nibbles. We sat and talked while the individual methanol-fired camp stoves boiled pasta or fried sausages. All the others bought far more than they could eat, so my somewhat meagre dinner was supplemented. Although I never asked to share, this pattern tended to repeat itself over the week, giving me a scrounger's reputation.

Around the campfire that evening, the group began to open up and share personal information starting with our respective ages. Murray claimed to be 64, relieving me of the responsibility of being the senior member. It was only at the end of the week that he added the detail, 'next birthday in December', making me oldest by a month!

During this evening of revelations, we discovered some of those astounding coincidences that so often occur in group settings. Yassmin, the product of a Yemeni father and a Welsh mother, speaks Arabic, as does Rawdon. Murray and Cara's daughter, a nurse, married an American and moved recently to Albuquerque, New Mexico, where my oldest daughter has just moved. Their daughter earned her US qualifications working in the same hospital in Little Rock, Arkansas where a cousin of mine is a pharmacologist.

We discussed a full range of subjects from music, to books, to Ireland and Palestine. Yassmin admitted that she had been a masseuse and was persuaded to try to ease Rawdon's lumbago. He removed his shirt and laid face down on the grass at the edge of our campfire circle while she administered the massage kneeling beside him. Geoff quickly whipped out his camera to get pictures for the Breton Bike website as evidence of the wide range of available options. We had a good time, the conversation was both serious and humorous and carried on until we could barely see to crawl into our tents.

Bistromatics

The tour continued much along this placid, pleasant pattern for the balance of the week interlaced with interesting experiences. Geoff's leadership was relaxed and intermittent but crucial in selecting the routes, finding restaurants and booking campsites. I was disappointed though that he did not try to inform us of the history and culture of the area. Our tour's name was 'Two Chateaus and the Blavet' yet we did not visit either chateau. The little that I learned about Brittany came from observation and asking questions.

At the lovely canal-side village of St. Nicolas de Eaux, an elderly English woman, her tongue significantly loosened with beer, invited herself to join our outdoor bar table where we tarried after dinner. She claimed to have lived in the village for the past two years after her husband abruptly abandoned her. She was starved for an audience but we quickly became satiated and parted company when we could do so without giving offence.

Our dinner that evening had been at a round table in the corner of a crêperie. This was our second dinner at a crêperie making me feel experienced and comfortable. In an attempt to dispel my unwelcome scrounge image, I bought a bottle of Muscatel as a table apéritif while we waited for our meals.

Yassmin introduced the multi-syllable French word, embrouiller, which intrigued Murray. As his wine consumption increased, his attempts at this word progressively mangled it beyond recognition. Little did I realise at the time how appropriate this was as the word's English meaning is 'to muddle'. His failures were comic, fuelling our good mood and generating more humour. We gradually evolved into a state where every comment, no matter how mundane or inane, was witty and hilarious.

'Bistromatics', a term coined years ago by Geoff and Rawdon, describes the mathematics of working out each person's share of the total bistro bill. Now a Breton Bike ritual, the various charges on the bill are allocated to the appropriate individual in separate columns on a table napkin. At our previous crêperie meal, the individual amounts did not equal the bill's total, even though the exercise is easy because sales taxes and gratuities are built into menu prices.

This evening, I volunteered to do the math and successfully matched the totals. Our good mood continued and we had more fun in the process as I announced the damage to each in turn, collected their cash and made change at the table. The proprietress, hovered, looking a little agitated, concerned perhaps that our meal would be underfunded. The green calculation napkin came home with me as a souvenir!

Bicycle Physics

Our route left the canal towpaths on the way back to Gouarec, becoming hilly and providing opportunities for freewheeling at speed around downhill bends. Rawdon explained the physics of doing so and helped improve my technique. He also taught me how to determine the proper tyre pressure. This is so dead simple that I could not believe I had not worked it out myself. It is just a question of the weight of the rider divided by two (half for each tyre). This determines the required PSI (pounds per square inch) since the fore to aft portion of the tyre supporting the cycle at any moment is about one inch.   Tyres narrower or wider than one inch require proportionally more or less pressure. I think the weight of the gear should also be part of the calculation but Rawdon claimed it wasn't necessary.

We returned to the Gouarec campsite about 3.30. The others left to buy food for the evening but I stayed to get my tent up before the threatened rain became a reality. I still had a few leftovers and did not feel particularly hungry anyway. It was also a good opportunity for me to launder my week's accumulation of dirty clothes. Marianne, sold me the necessary token for the machine and provided the soap.

The group returned with more than enough food for everyone. I was again invited to share and did so having recovered some appetite but this time, made a financial contribution to each of them to cover my consumption. We ate at the picnic tables, somewhat subdued by the realization that our week together was over. Conversation turned to what each of us was to do next. Yassmin and Rawdon were headed home, back to work. Murray and Cara were going off by themselves for another week of cycling with Geoff's equipment and I was destined for the Emerald Coast en route to St. Malo and the ferry back to Britain.

Final Parting

We breakfasted and lunched together as a group on Saturday. Yassmin and a British couple, that had just completed a solo week, left afterward for the St. Brieux railway station by minibus. Geoff had arranged for the minibus to collect their cases from the campsite and them from the restaurant. In a clear demonstration of the Breton pace of life, the minibus driver sat patiently for fifteen minutes while his passengers finished their meals and goodbyes.

After lunch I recovered my own bike from Geoff and was grateful for his quick check over and chain lubrication. The remainder of our group was adrift--all going our separate ways tomorrow and feeling somewhat distant already. Rawdon came to the rescue, suggesting that we go in his car to Kumquat, a Rostrenan crêperie.

After a particularly chilly night (5 degrees Celsius), we repeated our initial joint breakfast at the generous local bar with all of Geoff's family, Dave and Marianne from the campsite, Murray and Cara and Bill and Melissa, an American father and daughter from St. Louis. This last couple had arrived late on Saturday and chose to do the same self-guided route as Murray and Cara.

My route initially ran in the same direction as the others, so the five of us rode together for about 40 minutes until our routes deviated. I felt strangely liberated; despite having enjoyed the group week, there was an immediate sensation of empowerment and a release from group constraints.

The bike ran well, chewing up the countryside at a pace that exceeded the group's best full day. Lunching on my before Sunday noon supermarket acquisitions alongside a lovely river park in Quintin while reading my latest book—a John le Carre that Geoff gave me, I was still envious of the happy people wining and dining on the patios of three cafes overlooking the river.

On reaching Val Andre, a coastal town and my objective for the day, I went in search of a hotel. French hotels post their number of stars on their signs providing a helpful guide to quality. My experiences in Roscoff and Heulgoat, confirmed that two stars were good enough. So, I ignored three star and better hotels. Hotels also post their rates outside for each level of room offered. After a bit of looking round, I found the creatively named, two star Hotel de la Mer, booking a single room. My cycle spent the night in a narrow corridor next to the lobster tank and kitchen.

Despite this inauspicious beginning, I decided to dine here. The hotel's restaurant is bright, colourful and claims gourmet status. My slight budget surplus would only accommodate the cheapest selection but that was excellent as was the service. I managed a half carafe of wine myself and finished off with the tart sweetness of my favourite sorbet--blackcurrant. All in all, it was a successful day, good distance, pleasant scenery, excellent meal, a stroll along the adjacent seafront, and after eight days, a real bed!

Medieval Splendours

The medieval city of Dinan beckoned--a relatively easy 60 kilometres away. The direct route was on a major highway, so I diverted to the minor or 'white roads' adding about 10 kilometres to the distance and some confusion as there were several T junctions, some without directional signs.

Riding into Dinan, a mustard-yellow Hotel de Marmite appeared on my right. If possible, I had to stay here to honour my Australian brother-in-law's morning passion for vegemite, marmite's close cousin. That is really a stretch as the hotel's name translates to Hotel Cooking Pot but it is the thought that counts. I took a picture to prove my thoughtfulness and checked in as Hotel de Marmite was a two star and had a vacancy.

Dinan has delightful old houses and streets; it is surrounded by thirteenth to fifteenth century ramparts and guarded by a castle. All this is in a spectacularly attractive setting 75 metres above a charming stretch of the lovely Rance River with a busy little port. The port side streets feature interesting shops and restaurants overlooking a variety of colourful river craft. I found this area at the end of a steep, cobbled stone street that began at an impressive stone archway and meandered down to the water between ancient buildings.

Coastal Scenery Again

After an enjoyable breakfast I set out en route to Cap Frehel on the northern coast of Brittany. The Cap or cape is sort of a national reserve or park that is on the 'must' list of many Brittany guidebooks. The ride through Dinan's centre tested my skill at judging traffic, the lights, and negotiating roundabouts. I've become the leader of my group of one! Yesterday's on foot scouting of the best route out of the city helped a lot. Today's first objective is Ploubalay -- an easy run at an average speed of just over 19 km an hour.

Ploubalay offered a sorely needed comfort stop. Their public facility was unisex with the urinals in full view of anyone walking in the door. I thought I had developed a French indifference to such situations but still caught myself grateful to be zipped up and leaving when a woman walked in.

Cap Frehel was an easy hour and a half further on. The volume of approaching cars and buses testified to its popularity. Numerous paths crisscross through a dense covering of low-level gorse. Many visitors parked outside the tollbooth and simply walked in on the paths, avoiding the charge. Cyclists weren't charged, so I rode right in. The cliffs aren't nearly as dramatic as I had hoped but met my need for coastal scenery. I sat on the cliff edge with my eyes closed, soaking up today's first sunshine, appreciating a gentle breeze and the hum of bees in the yellow gorse flowers. Moving then to another spot to sit some more was so relaxing that I was afraid of dozing off and falling over the edge. After a few more minutes the sun disappeared and a strong misty wind broke my rêverie.

I cycled into the nearby village of Plevenon to find something for tonight's meal at the hostel. Fortunately, the grocery was open, but being a Monday, the pâtisserie was not. The hostel's access road was about half way back towards Cap Frehel. I was apprehensive about French hostels due to a dim but bad memory of my first hostel experience at a brand-new French one with my younger brother, Byron, in 1957. That was our introduction to the squat style toilet.

This hostel building is reminiscent of the Bates motel in Hitchcock's *Psycho*. Three picnic type tables sat outside together with some stuffed furniture that wouldn't look amiss in a rubbish tip. No one was around as I was early for opening time.

Half an hour later, the warden emerged from her quarters. Her English was better than my French but we still had quite a struggle communicating. Assuming that the long and narrow tube-like sheet that she gave me was the French equivalent of the British hostel sheet sleeping bag, I protested that I was too big to fit inside. I need not have worried. What she had given me was intended for use as a case for cylindrical French pillows!

She took me upstairs to my room, grabbing what I now understood was the actual sheet sleeping bag from a closet. The room had two single beds, a washbasin and a small open wardrobe. Stacked on top of the short wardrobe were two grubby blankets and long, sausage shaped bags of cut up foam rubber—the pillows for my five foot long pillowcase.

The supposed sheet bag was just a sheet, not a bag at all. Improvising, I folded it lengthwise with the open side away from the wall, thus creating an upper and lower sheet to separate me from the blanket and bare mattress. This worked very well. The hostel was virtually empty so I had the room to myself.

The members' kitchen had a fair amount of left behind food, including a large bottle of wine but given the other conditions in the hostel; I wasn't tempted even though my purchases at the grocery store weren't adequate for my appetite.

I was the only person at breakfast the next morning and was surprised to find a place laid with a stack of small crisp toasts, orange juice, jam and muesli. After a minute or two, a young woman arrived with a full pot of coffee and abject apologies for the lack of baguettes and croissants. No fresh bread was available as the bakery wasn't open today. I could not complain, the quantity of food was far greater than most French breakfasts and elsewhere just the coffee would have cost more.

My only specific destination for the day was the nearby Fort la Latte, after that I will simply explore the peninsula and return to the hostel in the evening. So I am free to go wherever my fancy takes me.

My French skills were sufficiently adequate to understand the fort signs claiming that it is an important historical spot but they weren't up to the detailed history inside the fortress. So, I chose to just explore the views and walks around it, looking across to Cap Frehel, and then set out along the coast road south east of the cape.

Blowing strongly off the sea, the wind fought me all the way. I angled the bike sharply to the right balancing by leaning my body to the left to avoid being blown into the path of the overtaking cars. Magnificent surf crashed onto long, lovely sweeps of almost deserted white sand beaches. Stalwart surf boarders in wet suits courageously fought the waves below but I couldn't enjoy the view properly for concentrating so hard on staying out of the traffic.

Heading for another coastal area brought me to a small village called St. Giran. There, a steep road led down to a small park overlooking a sea filled with colourful fishing and sailboats. I claimed a convenient bench facing the sea and sunbathed a while, enjoying the quiet peace and beauty of this spot. Others arrived and departed, mainly English tourists, including one nursing mother with huge dispensers.

These tourists stayed only briefly but one visitor was a local fisherman clad stereotypically in beret and loose corduroy jacket. He provided some interesting action as he took a small boat from the beach, rowed out to a larger boat anchored in the bay and set off in the larger boat for some evening fishing.

Walking back up the steep road, I met a couple that spoke to me in French. This was the perfect time to use a much-needed response that I had been rehearsing out loud for a day or two: 'Je parlez l'Anglais seulement.' Their response, after some hesitation, was 'So do we.' It wasn't clear whether their delay reflected my poor pronunciation, the phrase or both.

Fortunately, I had just passed a sign leading to the hiking path they were looking for and could help. It was only much later that I realized that my verb was wrong because my phrase was constructed using what I thought were the relevant bits of 'Do you speak English?' It should have been 'parle', not 'parlez.'

Continuing with my aimless cycling, I came across a picturesque looking crêperie called La Clepsydre in Pleherel-Plage that claimed to be open tonight from 7 p.m. Since it was only a few kilometres from the hostel there was time to go back for a shower, return to the crêperie for dinner and still possibly have time to see a sunset at Cap Frehel.

A family of three cyclists from Montreal spending most of their summer in France had just arrived at the hostel. The father, a computer sciences professor, pulled a specially built trailer filled with all their cooking and camping gear. He is considering early retirement to set up a cycle touring company concentrating on France and is already acquainted (by email) with Geoff Husband of Breton Bikes. I did not learn much about the mother as her English, although better than my French by far, was not adequate for real conversation. Their son, now eleven, has been making these trips with his parents for the past three years.

La Clepsydre was an excellent choice, boasting a fireplace, red-painted wooden ceiling beams, a black and white tile floor and red checked tablecloths. The pleasant and attractive waitress complemented her husband, a cheerful and competent chef. I enjoyed a Montangarde gallette, citron crêpe, vin rouge and café.

An hour and a half later, I emerged, at peace with the world, to a still bright evening for my sunset quest ride to Cap Frehel. Traffic was light, enhancing the very pleasant five-kilometre ride. The coast was cooler and windy but being nearly at the end of my trip, I wanted to savour every moment and wait for the sunset. However, it was getting colder by the minute. Realizing that there could be an hour's wait and that it could be dangerous without cycle lights to negotiate in the dark after sunset. So, I regretfully returned to the hostel at about 9.30.

St. Malo and the Restored City of Intra Muros
Today's trip to St. Malo promised to be long and complex as most of the bridges over the Rance River are major highways, not open to cycles. Much of my earlier route from Dinan to Cap Frehel had to be retraced to find a suitable river crossing. Careful map reading was required to discover the right combination of white roads to get across the Rance. This navigational challenge added a sense of achievement improving the day's enjoyment.

My hotel search began near to the port in the fortress-like walled city known as Intra Muros. The city was left in utter ruins in July 1944 when the Americans fought to dislodge the Germans. The French rebuilt much of the city as it had been, re-creating history for future generations. Entering through one of the formidable entry gates I saw a red and white sign listing dozens of hotels. Inside, the cobbled streets and fifteenth century architecture contrasted dramatically with the modern broad boulevards, busy traffic and port activity outside the gates. Intra Muros attracts thousands of tourists with its myriad cafes, restaurants, hotels and high-end international brand shops. I immediately wanted to explore and was frustrated with the need to first find lodging.

Signs posted at relevant intersections pointed the direction to various hotels and helpfully showed each hotel's star rating. I looked for two stars but found the prices excessive; some were full and three stars offered rooms at double my expected rate. Then out of the corner of my eye, I saw Auberge des Chiens du Guet, a colourfully picturesque inn with its own outdoor café tucked into a corner of the wall at a sea-facing gate, Port St. Pierre. Les Guets were fierce mastiff dogs that for five hundred years were let out at nightfall to discourage any Englishmen from sneaking up and taking the town by stealth. The dogs were recalled at dawn by a trumpet blast. (3)

The inn had no rating but it did have a vacancy for 34€. Success! As the manageress escorted me up to the room, she mentioned a shower on the ground floor. I took little notice but later returning from dinner, wanted to take a shower and could not find any on my floor. Remembering her comment, I gathered towel, shampoo, etc. and went into the public washroom on the ground floor. No shower was evident. An entrance to the kitchen was opposite the washroom and the cook just happened to be standing in the doorway, taking a break. With my vast knowledge of French, I blurted out 'Douche?' nonchalantly, trying not to think of the word's common English meaning. The cook took me back into the washroom and pointed to an internal locked door. Drawing again on my considerable vocabulary, I managed 'Clef?' He said 'see the manageress' or something like it. She was dealing with her customers in the restaurant. Putting both words together 'Clef de douche?' proved successful but perhaps my towel, shampoo and soap did the communicating. She came out into the hall, marched over to the kitchen, retrieving a large ball attached to a key from the top of the refrigerator. Voila! I showered quickly, concerned by possible interruptions by women diners coming in to powder their nose.

Next morning I noticed that the hotel's posted tariff showed that a room for one person was 30€ not the 34€ that she told me and decided to challenge the situation with the manageress. Despite our mutual inabilities with each other's language, after several minutes we managed to communicate effectively. For me, effectively means that she reduced the price. In the process, I finally understood that because the room could accommodate more than one person she quoted a price based on its capacity not its actual occupancy.

Despite this delay, I got to the ferry on time and immediately made for the upper deck to stake out a chair in the sunshine. It was probably the best weather of the entire tour. Apart from two meals, most of the crossing was spent there devouring yesterday's Daily Telegraph and soaking up the sun. A carafe of vin rouge accompanied my midday meal but for my late afternoon snack I had my first cup of tea since landing in France a fortnight ago. It was one of the best ever—a great reunion!

Portsmouth, Windsor, Eton and Home
The good weather lasted all the way to the Portsmouth terminal. For me, disembarkation meant quite a delay as this time the bike was moored at the stern and all the cars got off first. While waiting in the increasing fog of carbon monoxide, I discovered that I had misplaced my favourite souvenir, a black and white Breton cycling cap. Trying to find it would have meant fighting my way up the companionways through other passengers on the way down to their cars and possibly being too late to get off. So, I reluctantly gave up on it. (Geoff Husband very kindly bought and sent me a replacement—as a gift!)

Portsmouth is a naval city; one of the sights is the historic naval dockyard which houses several vessels, including H.M.S. Victory, the flagship of Admiral Horatio Nelson at the Battle of Trafalgar against the French in 1805. The vessel has a special place in British heroics because the decisive engagement established Britain as the dominant naval nation in the world. Tragically, but perhaps ensuring his enduring fame, Nelson was killed just as victory was his. (A book, Nelson's Purse, deals with the fairly recent discovery of the still full purse that Nelson carried at the time of his death.) Also housed at Portsmouth is a less fortunate vessel, the ill-fated sixteenth century

Mary Rose, which sank soon after its launch. Portsmouth docks date from the 12th century, and the world's first dry dock was built here as early as 1495.(4)

Getting to the Portsmouth hostel, some distance from the harbour, took me through some poor and depressing residential areas heavy with early evening traffic. The 'one size/style fits all' council houses looked as if they had been built in the early socialist fervour in Britain following WWII. Lack of ambition appeared ubiquitous. The contrast with what I had seen of Brittany was unfavourable to Britain.

The hostel building itself is interesting being a sixteenth century manor house but it was poorly maintained and managed. I loaded up the hostel washing machine with my accumulated laundry and went into the member's kitchen to scrounge a cup of tea. The only other occupant, a man in his sixties, was sitting quietly, fastidiously cutting and eating a meat pie that had been wrapped in wax paper. He was very neat and tidy in his dress and habits but did not look at all out of place in the hostel. I formed the immediate impression that he was trying to live very frugally as a matter of necessity.

Imagine my surprise then when during a long conversation, he told me that he spoke eight languages, had lived in New York, Chicago and Montreal and had visited 150 different countries. He told stories of having met both Sadam Hussein and Gadaffi, lived in Denmark with his Danish, now ex-wife, and travelled all over the world in a technical sales job. His entire story was in sharp contrast to his apparent current circumstances—perhaps I am too gullible—but it all had the ring of truth.

A younger Briton of an entirely different stripe joined us later. This man was grossly overweight and a whiner. He complained bitterly about Britain as a place to live, the monarchy, taxes, etc. On learning that I was a Canadian, he claimed to want to know all about Canada, but never got around to asking any questions. Both these men were in my dormitory room. The fat one complained that he 'was chesty and not too good on his pins' despite being considerably younger than either of us. He had brought both a small television and a heater to the hostel and negotiated a swap of beds to have access to an electric point to use both appliances.   Sometime during the night he disappeared and we never saw him again.

Celebrating my return to England, the heavens bestowed a light drizzle and gloomy atmosphere next morning tempting me not to cycle. My plan had been to do one of the day trips featured in the Ordnance Survey (OS) Cycle Tours series, return to Portsmouth and then take a train to Windsor this evening.

The rain moderated somewhat persuading me to carry on with the original plan.   Now back in England, it was time to resume the tea and teacakes routine and those treats had to be earned. About half past ten, I promised myself, if the opportunity presented itself, to make a ritual stop in Hambledon, the approaching village. Miraculously, a teashop attached to a small grocery appeared at a bend in the road marking the front edge of the village. The tearoom window displayed a closed sign but as there was a couple already inside, I ignored the sign and went in. While there, I studied the map carefully and decided not to return to Portsmouth but carry on northwards, cycling all the way to Windsor. This would be a better accomplishment than the original plan and save the train fare as well, perhaps financing a special dinner tonight.

With more thought this plan deteriorated. It could have been done but would have meant a late arrival at Windsor. Packing up the cycle and cleaning up afterwards could mean that my hopes for a great dinner would have to be forfeited. So, I compromised and cycled as far as Basingstoke and took trains from there. Amazingly, this saved only about two pounds on the fare compared with coming all the way from Portsmouth. I am happy to report that I did dine well, treating myself to a whisky and ginger, lamb dopiaza, sweet nan and a lager, completing this journey with the same meal, in the same restaurant where it began just a month ago.

On departure day, I had a couple spare hours before having to leave for the airport so set off on a walk along some of the river, watching boats, people, swans and ducks and crossed the bridge to Eton. The famous school sits several blocks along the road over the bridge. There was no public access into the quadrangle of the school but there was a fair amount of activity in the archway leading in. Several boys crowded round a notice board that perhaps announced examination results. A few of them came out together on their way to church. Their pinstriped trousers and tailed Edwardian style jackets added sartorial emphasis to their social status. One, sporting a handsome golden brown mane, sharply aquiline face and erect posture looked right through me with total self-assurance of his superiority. Soon the street was teeming with similarly dressed boys moving towards the church. Tomorrow's future leaders and don't they know it!

King Henry VI established Eton as a religious foundation in 1440. Initially it was to include an almshouse, a chantry and a men's choir. Henry expected to generate revenue by attracting pilgrims to see two dubious relics—fragments of the True Cross and of the Crown of Thorns. Henry also funded a school and provided scholarships for 70 poor scholars. Today, Eton College is known as 'the chief nurse of England's statesmen.' Eighteen former Prime Ministers have been Etonians.(5)

On the way to collect me, my taxi driver noticed a motorway traffic accident so took a back road route to the airport. Along the way he pointed out the Windsor Castle gate through the Great Park where Queen Elizabeth exits if she wishes to avoid the crowds and he showed me the home of Jackie Collins the author. According to the driver she is not liked but her sister, Joan, the actress, is very popular.

Overall, this tour successfully combined solo and group, Britain and Brittany, inside and out accommodation. Camping improved with experience and I'll definitely want to continue building variety in my tours.

Breton Festival at Roscoff, Brittany

Author(left) and Geoff, Breton Bikes owner and tour leader

WALES & WYE VALLEY TOUR

BRITAIN

WALES & THE WYE VALLEY TOUR

The Celtic tour ignited my interest in seeking variety beyond Britain leading me initially to plan combining another Breton Bikes group tour with a solo trip through German fairyland villages along the Moselle River. This plan lost some of its appeal when I learned that Breton Bikes' only group tour in 2006 would be in early September–still in the airlines' high season fare period that I wanted to avoid.

By chance, I learned about the Gower Peninsula in south western Wales, Britain's first designated area of outstanding natural beauty (AONB). Remembering fondly the spiritual quality of the remote Black Mountain countryside on the Welsh border from a previous trip, the nearby book town, Hay on Wye, and the cathedral city of Hereford suggested the nucleus of a tour centred on Wales. Such a tour would also permit visiting Oxford and the golden Cotswold villages. So, I decided, again, to spend the entire tour in Britain.

I roughed out a general itinerary and explored the potential for a cheap flight. This search uncovered a Canadian airline operating under the somewhat dubious name of Zoom. Now bankrupt, Zoom then flew to several destinations in the UK and to Paris. Return flights were sold separately from different locations, providing greater flexibility and Zoom had no high fare season. This meant that my original destination and plan was financially possible but by that time I was mentally committed to Wales and to a late May start.

My timing overlooked the late May British Bank Holiday when many school groups arrange field trips. Their accommodations are usually in hostels which are then often reluctant to accept adult males. As a consequence, some hostels claim to be fully booked even if they aren't. So, virtually all hostels I needed were full. I booked those few hostels with a vacancy, reworking my itinerary to fit and found acceptably priced B&B's and farm stays to fill in the gaps. The farms proved to be excellent choices for their very welcoming hospitality and generous tables.

In early May, after everything was booked, Zoom Airlines rang to say that my flight into Gatwick would now be landing at Stansted--did I want to accept that, cancel, or take a two day earlier departure into

Gatwick. I immediately chose to go earlier and scrambling a bit, found a nearby hostel vacancy and was able to organize a visit with a friend who lives in Kent.

Determined to take care of at least some of my domestic duties before leaving, I decided to attack the accumulated leaves and twigs in our gutters. Pulling myself up onto the roof, the ladder slipped, crashing backward on to the deck. Under the ladder and briefly stunned, I did not realise what had happened. Standing was possible only on one leg; the ankle on the other had been twisted by the ladder rung. My lower back ached from being slammed on the deck and my aluminium ladder was a bent out of shape write-off.

At first, Mari thought I was doing my sympathy limp, but once convinced that the limp was genuine, she enlisted her chiropractor to mitigate the damage. He treated me five times over the ten days remaining before departure, taping my ankle in the final treatment.

Where I Went

My extra two-day portion of the tour went east from Gatwick across the North Downs to Kemsing hostel near Wrotham, Kent then reversed direction to Oxford. The map opening this chapter doesn't show this brief foray into Kent but does show going through Sussex on the way to the main tour. This went north from Oxford to Shropshire, then west and south in Wales. The return from Wales took me into the Forest of Dean in Gloucestershire, to the renowned Symonds Yat viewpoint of the Wye, and north through the Roman city, Cirencester, to the Cotswold villages. Finally, I took a train to Paddington station in west London, cycled across the city to Kings Cross railway station and joined another train to my former home in Welwyn Garden City, Hertfordshire for a brief visit with friends.

Kemsing Hostel and Dinner at the Bull

Zoom Airlines was a good choice. The seats were comfortable soft leather; legroom was adequate, the food acceptable and the attendants polite. It provided my first experience with the regular screen updates on speed, altitude and time to arrival. I appreciated these and marvelled that the outside temperature was –56C.

This particular flight landed first at Cardiff. While waiting there, I removed the tape from my ankle and found that it was a brilliant red right up to the top of the sock. The tape had been applied too tightly and left on too long.

I had again arranged to leave my cycle box at a B&B close to Gatwick Airport until my return in a month's time. The B&B doesn't charge for this and provides a free run back to the airport so the £36 overnight charge (full English breakfast included) is almost a bargain.

However, my welcome there on arrival was cool and uninterested. I was not invited inside to change into my cycling gear or to wash up after reassembling the cycle. All the unpacking, packing, assembly and changing clothes had to be done on the forecourt of the B&B. The whole process took about 90 minutes so it was mid-afternoon by the time I got on the road.

My portion of the North Downs was up. Despite having done close to 700 km of training, it was tough going. The terrain sloped resolutely upward; distances felt grossly understated. They were probably accurate but I could not monitor progress as my odometer computer was either misplaced or totally forgotten.

Kemsing hostel sat at the end of a long, sodden and muddy track with the cycle storage shed conveniently situated directly opposite the muddiest part of the whole track. During the checking in process, I discovered that my membership card had been left behind risking having to pay a premium for all my hostel stays. Fortunately, my bookings had been done by e-mail and none of the hostels gave me any grief over the lack of membership proof. My most immediate concern though was the time. It was already after seven and I needed to find a pub that stayed open long enough for me to have an evening meal.

Fortunately, perhaps just ten minutes' walk away, I found 'The Bell' which served until nine. My dinner, vegetarian lasagne with garlic bread and a lager, was a perfect companion for my hunger and my current book.

Choosing a window-side table for better light, I found myself facing a family at the adjacent table. Tattoos covered every visible part of the father's body (he had only a string vest on top). His hair was dyed a very patriotic English red and white. None of the other patrons appeared to find this unusual. I had arrived in the midst of football fever over the World Cup and saw every possible variety of St. George's Cross over the next couple of weeks. Probably three-quarters of the cars flew the flag from a side window.

It was only after dinner, when it was too late, that I realized the need to buy some food for breakfast. Fortunately, my sole roommate that evening, a Water Board engineer from Glasgow, was returning home the next day after a week in the field and offered me his spare food. This consisted of one tea bag, a small bowl's worth of muesli and just enough milk to dampen it. So, I did not have to start my day totally hungry--close but not totally.

I did, however, have to wait quite a while to start cycling, as the rain that had been falling all week continued until about eleven. Despite all that rain, south eastern England was still officially suffering drought conditions and was under a hosepipe ban.

While waiting, I chatted with two stocky Dutch women of about 50 who holiday together in England at this time every year. One was clearly dominant but as a smoker had to keep leaving the building for a puff. In between smoke breaks they told me about the seventeenth century Dutch naval success at Medway in the Thames. I wasn't aware that there had been any hostility between the Netherlands and Britain. However, there were three Dutch wars, 1652-4, 1665-7, and 1672-4. Medway occurred during the middle period when the Dutch blockaded the Thames, captured two warships in the Medway and burned five more. At the time, the Dutch had a superior navy.[1] Later on in the century, an invasion in 1688 at Torbay, South Devon led to William of Orange becoming King of England. At the time, although King James II was a Catholic, much of his Parliament was Protestant. Parliament took comfort in the fact that Mary, James' daughter, and next in line for the throne was Protestant. Then James' wife finally (after ten failures) produced a son and alternative heir causing the Protestants to fear a perpetuation of Catholic monarchs.[2] Historians disagree whether William invaded by invitation or of his own volition. It hardly matters as invasion suited William's objective of strengthening his hand against Louis XIV and Parliament's desire for Protestant succession. King James was allowed to move to France but never officially abdicated. Nevertheless, William became King and his wife Mary (King James' daughter) became Queen. From that point forward, the throne has been denied to Catholics.(3) In 2011, the British government initiated action which required approval of all the Commonwealth to eliminate this restriction.

My destination tonight is the 'Barn Cottage', a B&B in the village of Wrotham Heath, where I had arranged to meet Yassmin, my cycling friend from the 2004 Brittany trip, and her husband, Ian, for dinner. It was reasonably close, giving me time to explore the area and its somewhat unique architecture. Oast house buildings with their dunce's cap style silo were abundant as well as a few clapperboard house exteriors that are not typically seen in other parts of Britain. The countryside was lovely with sweeping, quintessentially English views and many impressive homes. There was also a sense of a worn out, tired landscape, particularly in the towns—perhaps the day's gloomy weather contributed to this sense and to people's attitudes—they weren't friendly. At the same time there were many examples of people making spectacles of themselves in outlandish costumes, hair colours or modes of dress inappropriate for their age and physical condition. The road traffic was heavy and fast and many of the drivers were impatient and rude. There are just too many people in this part of the country.

Yassmin and Ian collected me that evening from the 'Barn Cottage' for the short but round about drive to 'The Bull', a hotel in nearby Wrotham that I remembered fondly as a tea stop from an earlier tour. We were quickly conversing as if the intervening two years had been only a fortnight. Ian was not at all what I had expected of a PhD candidate in science and we both took some time to adjust to our very different natures. He is very much an outdoor, can-do type of man, not a stereotypical academic. Cycling is too tame for him. Nevertheless, we had a pleasant, relaxed meal together, reminiscing and getting to know each other better. I have since come to like and respect him. Ian has overcome many early disadvantages.

Back at the 'Barn Cottage', I appreciated its lovely setting well back from the road with a garden of beautiful flowers including a giant yellow azalea. Amber, the resident ginger female cat, warmed up to me the next morning and came running to join me for a stroll through the back rooms of the garden—part of the path was like a private wood. Pine needles carpeted the earth and massive tree roots broke the velvety green moss.

Oxford Fantasies and Television Dramas

The English public (i.e. private) schools and Oxford and Cambridge universities have always stirred a part of me that fantasizes a scholarly, stoic sort of life rooted in 1940s and 50s Britain. It is totally unrealistic, even if I had the necessary intellect. Nevertheless, the mental images continue to have strong appeal and are influential in my choice of films and books.

So spending a few days in Oxford was a main objective of this trip. I left the B&B about nine, intending to go back to Horley for a train to Oxford. First stop for the train was north to Redhill. Realizing that my cycling route was already north of Horley, I decided to save time and money by going directly to Redhill and arrived just in time to get my ticket before the train departed.

Oxford's modern, very large hostel is conveniently located behind the railway station. Today it was staffed by some cheerful Australian girls. The hostel's décor added to the Aussies' warm welcome with interesting posters and information about famous Oxford writers, scientists, and film locations lining the hallways. Rowan Atkinson (Mr Bean), Hugh Grant and Oscar Wilde were among them. Scenes from two of my favourite television series, 'Inspector Morse' and 'Midsomer Murders' were prominently featured. A large map of the surrounding countryside on the wall identified the different locations for several of the 'Midsomer Murders' episodes. I took notes of the closest ones as the basis for a tour in a day or so.

My first day was dedicated to exploring Oxford, rejoicing in the solid oak doors, the stone floors, the grandeur and dignity of the college buildings and tranquil quadrangles. Nearby, flowed the bucolic Cherwell River tributary with contented, grazing cattle in the adjacent pasture. All these sights and sounds evoked my scholarly fantasies. My tour included Christ Church Meadow by the river, a walk round tiny St Edmund's 13th century College where Mari attended a week's music course twenty years ago, and a walk over the Magdalen Bridge.

In the meadow, I shared a park bench with Zoe Pettersen, an eccentric botanical artist labouring over a huge rendition of one of the majestic trees bordering the pathway. She showed me numerous examples of her published poems that accompany her drawings. She has these produced with silk covers and ribbons for wedding gifts. Zoe worked hard to sell me one of her greeting cards but when I declined, she abruptly ended the sales pitch, dismissing me by saying tersely 'let me get on with my work.'

Later, I attended Evensong at Christ College Cathedral and felt the full majesty of the music by sitting immediately next to the choir. Even so, the service wasn't as absorbing and meaningful as the ones in previous years at Winchester and Salisbury. My spiritual receptivity may have been diminished by the proximity of a well-upholstered blonde.

There, for the first time, I became aware of the current British approach to charitable giving. The donation envelope required that you supply your name and address and pledge that you had paid tax on the amount of the donation. The envelope also informed that the church would claim back, for itself, the tax (at the base rate) that you had paid. This seemed to me an eminently sensible approach that is much more efficient than what I am used to at home where each donation requires the charity to complete a tax receipt that must be saved to file with your income tax return. This British approach magnifies the cash donated to the charity and probably reduces the tax cost to the Exchequer, but provides no benefit to the donor other than a sense of altruism.

During my day's meanderings, I discovered William Morris' first garage. Morris was famous for MG (Morris Garage) and the original Mini. He started out, as did many famous mechanics (Peugeot, Glenn Curtiss, the Wright Brothers, etc.), with cycles.

Next day, en route to my selected Midsomer villages, I passed the Cowley plant where the latest version of the Mini is manufactured by BMW. The first village on my tour was Brightwell Baldwin (site of 'Destroying Angel'). It is a pleasant, unspoilt village but I could see nothing that I remembered from that episode. The next village, Watlington, was having a festival day. A parade of Scouts was led by one character on stilts and others holding sticks to support the gigantic arms. The street was shut off to traffic and lined with local charity stalls selling plants, baked goods, old books or raffle tickets. Some carnival-like games of chance, a tiny ride and novelty balloons completed the picture. Several provocatively dressed teenagers promenaded up and down the fairly short street conversing loudly on their mobiles and otherwise seeking attention.

I went on to the lovely small village of Ewelme ('Beyond the Grave') that has a great pastoral setting. Its St Mary's Church (associated with the Chaucer family) has a wooden ceiling, old carved pews and high side windows that make the interior very bright. Back outside, hail pelted down.

I gave up on the weather and returned to Oxford, enduring rain most of the way but promising myself a compensating cup of tea and a pastry. It was not to be; I had to be content with hostel tea without pastry as the teashops were closed when I arrived.

Ironbridge and Coalport

This phase of the tour started in Telford, Shropshire which I reached by train from Oxford. After lunching in Marks and Spencer's café in the Telford Mall, I followed a bike path for perhaps eight kilometres alongside the main road to Ironbridge.

The village takes its name from the first totally iron bridge ever made. It was completed in 1779 with financing primarily from Abraham Darby III, the grandson of the Quaker, Abraham Darby who was the first to use coke to produce iron, making it a much cheaper process. The younger Darby was financially ruined when the bridge's costs rose to £6,400, double the original estimate. Despite these men's importance in British history there are no portraits of them as their Quaker faith forbids images.

Tolls were charged on the bridge until 1950. One of the original signs still on display indicates the several different charges depending on the number of horses, donkeys or asses involved. The bridge is now a National Trust property and Prince Charles is its current patron.

Although quite cool and very windy, the day was bright, complementing the Severn River scene, its rising hills and the Victorian buildings along the bank. The attractive village clusters alongside the road following the river and caters primarily to the tourist trade. I was particularly drawn to a small close of renovated brick commercial buildings that are being turned into 'The Wharfage', a development of compact homes and flats facing each other across a brick courtyard. The homes were gracious and gentile but you'd need really considerate neighbours as every home faced each other over a courtyard rectangle of perhaps 100 square feet.

My destination tonight was Coalport hostel, just a couple of kilometres further along the river on a winding road where speed is restricted. The hostel was created less than ten years ago in part of the old Coalport China factory. After checking in, I toured the china museum behind the hostel in the remaining factory buildings. Here, all the special moulds and moulding machines were displayed, described in the particular jargon of the china making trade—e.g. slipware, throwing, jigger, jolley, and staggers. I learnt that each colour must be applied and fired separately in a specific sequence determined by the level of heat required for each colour. Blues require the most heat and so are fired first.

These firings were done in a huge, fat-bottom, bottle-shaped kiln. The process took as much as a week for each colour. Part of this time involved just getting the kiln to the right temperature for the particular colour and re-bricking up the kiln entrance after the pottery had been moved in. Some of the exhibits dealt with health issues— dust, potter's rot (lead absorbed in hands), and paint taken in the mouth by licking the brushes. Overall, it was a very informative visit.

Nearby are the remains of the 'Hay Incline', a sort of two-way escalator for boats that could move two boats with their cargoes of raw materials in four minutes between the river and the Shropshire and Union Canal some 60 metres above. Without it, a single boat would require three hours and 27 locks to cover the same distance.

My hostel 'roommates' were all cyclists; one was about my age and well along on an 'End to End' tour. He was impressively fit and dedicated, having done nearly 140 km that day. After breakfast with one of the younger cyclists, I set off for the nearby 'Blists Hill' Victorian village museum.

Blists Hill occupies a large area set on a plateau above the river with Hays Incline tucked into a distant corner. A large banner across the entrance proclaims 'Happy Birthday' to Queen Victoria, regardless of which day it is. Lloyd's Bank, the first establishment in the village, had a great long queue waiting to be served by the very severely dressed tellers. Having been a banker for part of my career and aware of the public's generally low opinion of bankers, I was surprised at this apparent popularity but decided to avoid the queue and return later. The queue never shortened but I did find out why it was so long. The bank exchanged 'old' money for new so that people could make transactions at old prices in £sd to enhance the experience. The village has a special dispensation from the Crown to mint its own currency in the old form that is legal tender only in the village as it lacks the Queen's head on the coins.

My informant, an appropriately costumed chemist, was a coin collector himself and showed me several items from his collection that he carried in his jacket. One of these was a one-thirteenth shilling coin from the Channel Islands. According to him, nineteen different coins ranging from a one-eighth shilling up to £5, circulated in Victorian times.

A real period drama character hosting at the candle maker shop, explained that the animal tallow for the candles is extracted from butcher's remains and that the residue of this extraction process is fed to pigs so that nothing is wasted. Apparently, some children in poor families at the time went to bed with a bit of candle for their supper (and night light?). The village also features a schoolhouse, Methodist church, squatter's cottage, a baker, a doctor's surgery, a coffin man and a pub. After lunch there, I set out south for Ludlow.

Initially the going was very tough, but after Much Wenlock, I made better time, arriving in Ludlow by 4.30, just in time for last tea orders. The first shop I found was De Grey's, recently chosen the best teashop in Shropshire. A queue waited for tables but I was fortunate not to need a table for three or more and quickly moved to the head of the queue. De Grey's is a superior establishment with friendly, efficient waitresses garbed in smart black and white uniforms. My very proper pot of tea (no bags) held 5 cups; the teacakes, perfectly toasted and generously coated with real butter were served in a silver covered dish.

'The Old Mill', my B&B, was on 'Squirrel Lane', in the nearby village of Lower Ledwyche. No such lane appeared but Squirrel Close did which sounded worth trying. As I rode down the long, narrow road the sudden sound of running water suggested that a mill might be nearby and suddenly, round the next bend, it was.

I was greeted by a long drive (Squirrel Lane, perhaps, but not posted as such), a number of brick buildings, one housing numerous dated vehicles that overflowed into the parking area and a workshop where the landlord grudgingly stored my cycle. Other buildings at the back seemed derelict. My landlady, Jean, was pleasant but her husband was very dour, hardly deigning to speak.

After cleaning up, I cycled back into Ludlow for a very good salmon dinner at the Queen. My waitress was surprised that I didn't want both chips and new potatoes but allowed me to substitute carrots, green beans and baby corn for the chips—a healthy trade. Completing my requisite daily servings of vegetables, the salmon came on a bed of spinach.

Next morning, I breakfasted with two Dutch brothers. One lives in Watford, the other is still in the Netherlands but they get together every year for a long weekend of cycling. Afterwards, I decided to explore Ludlow, known as one of the 'black and white' towns for its Elizabethan/Tudor style buildings. The 'Feathers' Hotel, a seventeenth century inn and perhaps Ludlow's most famous building, is featured on many postcards and attracts wealthy tourists.

Taking a lunch tip from my breakfast companions, I sought out a quiet bench in the cemetery garden of the sandstone St Laurence church with A.E. Housman's remains as company. St. Laurence is Ludlow's patron saint and the church is appropriately grand. I was particularly impressed by the marvellous woodcarvings of animals and plants on the misericords each of which was different. The misericords are a sort of seat that allowed priests to appear standing while supported. My memory recalls that many priests earned their keep by praying for other people's relatives and performed these prayers seated on the misericords.

Ludlow also has a famous sandstone castle built originally in 1085 but destroyed and rebuilt many times since. Edward IV's two sons were sent here for 'safe keeping' until they were removed to the Tower of London and executed.(4) Arthur, Henry the VIII's elder brother, moved to the castle with his wife, Catherine of Aragon, but died a few months later. Henry claimed his brother's throne and his widow.

I wandered the town's alleyways with their little antique and book shops, walked along some of the paths by the River Teme below the castle and learnt that one was called the 'Bread Walk' because the labourers that built it were paid in bread. Late in the afternoon, I had a haircut in a small shop where the barber and his family lived above the shop climbing up to their living quarters by a steep staircase inside the shop. All was not well on the domestic front. A separation or divorce was in progress and the barber muttered that he wished his wife 'something terminal' so that he could keep the children. This was in keeping with the generally sour tone of all his conversation. Crime was rampant, the previous customer had too much hair so he should have paid at least double. On that argument, my thinning pate more than justified my claiming the senior discount rate which I did and left.

Wheels into Wales

A week into the trip, I'm finally heading for Wales. The day was sunny. My Dutch breakfast companions were cheery and Jean, my landlady, memorably described St. Laurence Church as 'one window short of a cathedral' while delivering my clean laundry. She did not charge anything for this kindness.

The countryside is very pastoral and green with cattle, sheep, birdsong, insects and barnyard smells. (I know, appreciating such odours seems odd but for me they are natural and preferable to industrial pollution.) Crossing the nearby Welsh border was seamless, marked no more significantly than crossing between two Canadian provinces. Now, of course, I have to contend with a new language. The welcome sign was in both languages but some of the road markings were only in Welsh.

The address for my lodging for tonight indicates Prestiegne but it is much nearer to New Radnor. Local names in the directions evoked speculation of unknown but likely interesting events: across Offa's Dyke to Beggar's Bush and Kinnerton then up Bache Hill to the farmhouse. Much of the journey was up, making the 53 km an all day job.

My directions for finding the farm were a little vague—'turn right at the telephone box next to a white cottage.' So, I was relieved to find Bache Farm and delighted with the vision it presented--three friendly black Labradors and wisteria over the front door.

With a roaring brook on one side and a pasture of grazing sheep on the other, the long entry road delivered a magnificent view at its end. There, a 600-metre hill of velvety like grass rose dramatically behind the barnyard forming a splendid backdrop to this very active farm. A thousand lambs were born this spring and they also run Welsh black cattle.

My mature, grandmotherly landlady looked totally worn out. Although her son-in-law and daughter now run the farm, they live nearby and often call on her for babysitting. She asked if I wished to join them for dinner but I felt that an extra person for dinner was probably the last thing she needed so chose to cycle to a pub into New Radnor.

Lilting Welsh voices filled the pub. One very rotund short man, apparently the local top shearer, held court on a bar stool, accepting the crowd's respect and happily downing their proffered whiskies and cigarettes. The main topic seemed to be the 80p shearing cost per fleece. Later in the trip, at another farm, I was told that 80p was on the low side and that often the value of the wool does not cover the cost of the shearing!

So far my impression of Wales is positive for much the same reasons that I like Brittany and Newfoundland. Despite being relatively poor, the people are friendlier and more cheerful. The countryside is pastoral and cycle friendly if you can manage the hills.

Llanwyrtd Wells

After a full Welsh breakfast (apart from the black pudding), I packed up leisurely, adjusted the rear brakes that had failed yesterday and ventured forth in shorts for the first time this trip.

The route ran west and continued hilly. At the last possible moment for changing direction, I discovered that my pre-planned route goes to Llandrindod Wells not Llanwyrtd Wells where my new lodgings are. Given the difficult spelling, I abbreviated it to LW in my notes and charted a course to the wrong one.

Realising and correcting that error took me south to Builth Wells on the Wye just before lunch. So, I bought a sandwich and drink and lunched on a rock in a riverside park. Being Saturday, the park was packed with picnickers, dog walkers, sunbathers and fly fishers-- benches were at a premium.

Builth Wells is a former spa town. There has been a settlement here since Norman times, when a castle was constructed to guard a crossing of the River Wye and the entrance to Irfon Valley. Today only the remains of the Norman motte and bailey can be seen. The discovery of mineral water springs made the town popular during Victorian times, when the railway reached Builth.

I cycled round the town exploring some of the shops before continuing south west on the A483 to Llanwyrtd Wells. Although my booked hotel is right at the entrance to the village, the Drover's Arms claiming to serve the largest teacake in Wales claimed me first. I never saw any bigger--15 cm in diameter—filling, but not nearly the quality of those at De Grey's.

Today's countryside has been lovely. The road ran almost entirely up or between rounded hills of mown soft velvet. Hedges rather than fences divided the pastures creating a solid colour patchwork quilt stitched together with hedges of a different shade. Overall it is a very rural landscape whose agricultural health seems poor relative to England.

I dined at 'Basset's Bistro', in reality a pub with a fancy name, eating alone in a room otherwise arranged and decorated for a wedding party coming in later. While eating, I started this trip's study of British newspapers and read a disturbing article claiming that 40% of school leavers can't handle Level 2 (the level of reading and maths necessary for normal life) and another 7% cannot handle the lower Level 1. In short, 47% of them are illiterate.

Another article dealt with a National Health Service database intended to hold patient records, make appointments, allow new doctors to review patient history, etc. The project was over two years behind schedule and way over budget. This was particularly interesting to me because a physician cycling acquaintance of mine has designed such a system and offered it free to the Ontario medical establishment. Years have gone by without interest. In 2009, a minor scandal erupted when reports revealed that the provincial government spent over $1 billion on Ontario's system, much of it paid to consultants selected more for their connections than their expertise. At the beginning of 2014, Ontario still has no functioning system.

There was also a review of errors and fraud in a British government scheme that 'tops up' people's incomes if they don't earn enough for their circumstances—a sort of negative income tax. Billions of pounds have been overpaid and the government believes that it will never be able to reduce the excess payments to less than £1 billion annually.

The extent and nature of concern with government waste, incompetence and wrong headedness was surprising, even for a conservative paper. This particular paper reported that since Labour became the government in the late 90's, an additional 900,000 civil servants have been hired. Finally, the prisons are overcrowded, in part due to drug addicts committing crimes to get the free prison drug treatments. It was a dispiriting way to end the day.

My pre-chosen route for the new day through Llangammarch Wells and Beulah was interrupted by road construction but my detour, along a valley by the River Irfon proved idyllic. This narrow, flat and lightly travelled road led back to Bullith Wells and the Wye where I lunched again riverside.

Back in LW, and thinking my day's distance a bit puny, I struck out north on an unmarked road along the River Irfon. Here it was more babbling brook than river with large rocks, small falls and turbulent water. Parts of the road were forest-like, dark and narrow; others opened up to the surrounding hills of lush green pastures.

The road circled back south to Beulah from Abergywesyn where I turned round. Blessed with birdsong, sheep bleats and water sounds, almost no traffic and mellow sunshine--this early evening excursion was a perfect example of why I love cycling in Britain.

Book Town-Hay on Wye
Returning east towards the border town, Hay on Wye, took me through Builth Wells again. This time, I interrupted a widow returning from shopping for her lunch to ask a question. This morphed into a chat of some 20 minutes, primarily about her family, her history and her will! She produced some adventurous and capable children despite a very pedestrian husband who was anything but adventurous.

As I left Builth Wells, the sky was a mass of feathery cirrus clouds resembling horse manes in the wind together with one wide jet stream that stretched rainbow like across the sky. The 50 km route to Hay on Wye was pleasant but had a number of tough hills that forced me to walk so I was ready to stop for the day once there. My B&B's address was confusing—just a number followed by 'Gypsy Castle.' It took a number of attempts to find anyone that knew the name.

Gypsy Castle is the extraordinary name for an ordinary residential street on the western side of the Wye, so still in Wales. The houses, almost identical, had perhaps been built in the 50s or 60s. My landlady, a very gregarious and active recent widow told me of her travels since bereavement—to Costa Rica, Paraguay, and Venezuela. Her objective now is to see all of South America and she is booked to go to Ecuador and the Galapagos later this year. Tonight she is off to her regular Spanish lesson. A very full bucket list!

I went out for a stroll, stopping for a while in Booth's bookshop that claims to be the largest second hand bookshop in the world and the largest buyer of second hand books from the US. There are two storeys of floor to ceiling, very basic, wooden bookshelves barely separated by narrow aisles. Booth is primarily responsible for Hay on Wye becoming the home of one of the largest annual book fairs in the world; it regularly attracts literary and other celebrities. Al Gore spoke at this year's fair which ended yesterday.

While there, I got a brief glance of Richard Booth, a grey-haired, stooped and bearded gent on crutches. Later, I learnt that my landlady had been his personal assistant for a brief period but was terminated without cause a few months later. Now, she supplements her B&B takings with house or dog-sitting assignments and working at local stalls on market days.

Having been too tired yesterday, I dedicated today to explore Golden Valley, an area where a long-term friend of ours spent some of her summers with relatives during WW II. She wrote me about several features of the landscape and wanted a report on their condition when I visit at the end of this tour.

The valley is east of Hay on Wye at Dorstone and runs south along the River Dore to Pointrilas. My friend's landmarks were at Peterchurch and Vowchurch. Before reaching Dorstone, I meandered through a lovely church cemetery at Hardwicke that houses a beautiful flowering tree and four headstones of women named Agnes. Epitaph creativity had obviously been scarce as the same stone sentiments were used repeatedly.

The road south from Dorstone was through cornfields. Orchards and rich green meadows were bracketed on the west by the Black

Mountains and on the east by the gentle Herefordshire hills. After visiting Peterchurch and its three-celled Norman church now augmented with a plastic steeple, I retraced my route as far as a small lane signposted to Arthur's Stone. That sounded interesting enough to undertake the 25% grade up but once on the lane there were no further signs so I never saw the stone, returning to Hay on Wye on the B4352 near Bredwardine.

Next I ventured north east to the Whitney Toll Bridge across the Wye. The toll tariff posted outside the home-cum-collecting station was last changed in 1990 but, in my case, was waived anyway, saving me all of 5p. The condition of the bridge suggests that the tolls aren't high enough for adequate maintenance or that the toll collector is as kind to everyone. This bridge, built in 1796, was narrow with a none-too-sturdy wooden floor. From Whitney, I took the B438 west to Clyro recrossing the river to Hay on Wye to spend the rest of the afternoon visiting the myriad bookshops.

One of these shops, 'Murder and Mayhem', is devoted to mysteries. Their shop window and the landings between floors display scenes evocative of famous characters such as Sherlock Holmes or mystery story extracts. While there I found and bought an early Dick Francis novel that was unknown to me. Although I've never had any real involvement with horses, Dick Francis books show genuine love for them, generating similar appreciation from his readers. His books are immediately engaging and very enjoyable. This one was so old that its second hand price was more than it originally cost new!

Another gorgeous day! My route to Hertford retraced some of yesterday's beyond Bredwardine to Moccas then followed an unmarked road up to the A438 and into the city. The ride was a superb combination of sunny, dry weather, great farm views augmented with natural sounds and smells. There was virtually no traffic.

Beautiful large homes grace the city's western edge as does a huge complex of barns and sheds devoted at that moment to an agricultural market which promised an interesting bit of local colour. Drawn by the familiar cadence of an auctioneer, I went to a poultry auction whose entrance was partially blocked by roughly dressed, robust farmers having a smoke. Ignoring their smirks at my skinny legs emerging from lycra, I pushed through the crowd inside to see racks and racks of caged birds awaiting sale. In the corner, on a raised platform, the auctioneer was touting Lot No. 212, a brace of roosters.

Other buildings housed auctions of different animals as well as more common market fare such as clothing, books, and DVDs while the space in between buildings offered a variety of food and drink. It was interesting to see this aspect of British life, but I was appalled at the rough treatment of the animals. Perspiring myself, I was particularly upset by the sheep stuffed into huge oven-like lorries.

Moving on to Hereford cathedral, set in a vast park which today was spotted with sunbathing clerks on their lunch break, some having removed more clothing than was modest. As I approached, a batch of youngsters in cricket whites paraded by smartly led by their teacher. Inside, I admired the huge and ornately decorated high ceilings, noted the number of former bishops now lodged in the walls and tried, without success, to absorb the posted bits of history.

History abounds as there has been a church on this site since 626 but I found that cathedral history and architecture terminology merged into such a homogenized glob that I couldn't differentiate the specifics. One unusual feature was a rustic underground chapel.

In the town square, I toured a 'black and white' house filled with period oak furniture. There were two versions of early infant walkers. One of these was very similar in design to today's elevated seat on wheels while the other was a rectangular box that provided a sort of track on either side of the child's square support harness allowing the child to walk forwards about five feet. To start over, of course, the child had to walk backwards five feet, perhaps that is why the design hasn't survived. More adult oriented furniture was very ornately carved.

Hereford has historic homes and a wealth of shopping and restaurants. Its prices are cheaper than Hay on Wye where my landlady says the prices go up each year for the Book Festival but don't come down when its over. Fortunately for me, she doesn't operate on the same principle and charged me £2 per night less than I expected.

I returned there now through Vowchurch where my Welwyn Garden City friend had spent so many summers. She particularly remembered a nearby 'sweet' shop that was also the petrol station and post office. I found the station closed for the day shortly after five p.m. The old petrol pumps remain in place, although it wasn't clear whether they still function.

This year's return to Hay on Wye was motivated in large part by wanting to revisit the Gospel Pass that so impressed me on my Circle Tour. Then, without knowing what was ahead, I freewheeled downhill from the Pass through magnificent scenery for about six kilometres into Hay on Wye. I re-found the Hay on Wye end of that road while walking a day ago and planned to tackle it this morning but got diverted by an urge to walk the town again. So, I returned to Booth's bookshop for a more thorough investigation and to search for another book by the author of my current one. While in the basement pursuing this search, the famous Mr Booth entered a small windowless room in the centre of the shop that appeared to be his office, given the 'private, staff only' notices. Fifteen minutes later the sound of flushing water clarified the situation. He emerged, caned his way up two flights of stairs and into his real office, similarly marked 'private.' I continued my investigations unsuccessfully. Given the volume of books and the condition of many of them, this isn't a place that really invites browsing.

My lunch was at a Christian bookshop café, chosen, I must admit, on the prospect of more reasonable prices. The café was staffed by volunteers with the look of country women doing their bit of good waiting on others while having a day off from doing much the same thing at home. Both women were very shy, sitting together whispering in the corner while waiting for trade.

Afterwards, I strolled the day's outdoor market offerings in the old Butter Market, a roofed but open building. Home-baked goods and meat products wrapped in plastic were for sale but without benefit of refrigeration. I used free Internet access at the library. Then, having exhausted my delaying tactics, began the arduous ascent of Gospel Pass.

It wasn't nearly as tough as I remembered. My destination vista was only about seven kilometres away and while the climb was slow, it was more manageable without panniers. I planned also to go beyond Gospel Pass and on to Llanthony but when the road started its steep and sharply curving drop to Capel y fin, I chose to stop. Going down that hill would be extremely dangerous and re-climbing it would be very difficult. Fully loaded and seven years younger in 1999, there was no alternative but to continue.

So instead of continuing on to Capel y fin, I scrambled up a knoll on foot to overlook the narrow road and sat on a rock gazing contentedly at the magnificent, broad sweep of tightly cropped moorland surrounded by 680 metre peaks. There were a few people about also enjoying the development free solitude.

The ride back to Hay on Wye took 25 minutes, surprisingly slow given the slope but still over three times as fast as the climb had been. Like so many things, the second time's thrill didn't equal the first but then that ride down was in sharp contrast to the earlier extremely tough climb. Compensating for my abbreviated excursion, I explored a stretch of the Wye Valley Trail that runs through a forest along the river.

Leaving Hay the next morning at 8.45 am, my earliest start so far, gave a cool, fresh character to the new day, complementing the lovely countryside. I followed some unmarked roads running south west to join up with the B4560 out of Talgarth and then the B4558 along the River Usk, crossing a narrow bridge into Crickhowell.

The long bridge here presents an optical illusion. From the eastern end all its 13 arches can be seen, but from the west it appears to have only 12. Crickhowell has some fine Georgian houses and fragments of a castle. The village was extremely busy as traffic was concentrated into just a couple of streets.

I continued west beyond Llangynidr on the B4558 to Brecon hostel. The countryside and cool day made for a perfect cycling experience. Along the way, I stopped at a barn conversion property where four homes had been created within the existing walls of an old stone barn. A large stone patio surrounded the rear entrance to the homes. The mistress of the adjacent farm home was on a ladder in her front garden pruning some bushes clinging to a ten foot high wall. Peering over the wall, she told me that all the homes but one were already sold. Her home was next in line for the conversion process as she and her husband have finally been given permission to build in the nearby Brecon Beacons National Park, years after their initial application. She invited me to inspect the development's exterior but her Jack Russell protested vigorously, constantly yapping. He hated cycles. I left after peering into the front window of one that revealed a very spacious open plan studio and sitting room of an artist.

The Brecon hostel at Groesffordd sits up a long wooded drive from the road facing a large meadow with grazing sheep. After getting settled in my room, I contentedly contemplated the joys of nature while enjoying a strong local ale on one of the benches opposite the meadow.

There was a pub within a couple of kilometres, but I was pleased that the hostel served an evening meal. This pleasure moderated considerably when a school party of very young, excited students trooped in at dinner time on their first school overnight outing without parents.

Tonight I had Steve as a dinner companion. He was driving the support van for a group of four cyclists from Hull doing a sea-to-sea route within Wales over four days. His duties were light enough to allow him to train for the upcoming annual 3 Peaks event. In this event, the contestants have to run up Ben Nevis in Scotland, Scafell Pike in the Lake District and Mount Snowdon in Wales in 17 hours or less, including transport between each of these locations!

I also met John Lewis, a Welsh cyclist of 60+ who arrived on a made to order tricycle with three full-sized wheels. At the rear, the space between the wheels enclosed a luggage rack. Given my difficulty with these hills, I marvelled that he could manage such a heavy cycle. He further humbled me with his annual cycling of 20,000 km and lifetime total of over 180,000. Just to make matters worse, he told me of a club, consisting of about 67 members that have each done close to 500,000 km.

After breakfasting with John and finishing Robert Harris' 'Enigma' about British code-breaking activity during WW II at Bletchley Park, I went down to ride alongside the canal into Brecon. The cycle portion of a triathlon was in progress in front of the access to the canal lock and path so I watched that, for a while, lock-side, before continuing.

The path runs between the canal on the right and the River Usk, crashing over rocks on the left, with rolling hills in the distance. The sunny weekend day brought out scores of walkers with their dogs and children on to the path. Dodging them made the three kilometres into Brecon take longer than expected. A 'boot' sale (communal 'garage' sale of items transported in and, in some cases, displayed in the cars' boots) was in progress in a large playing field at the edge of the town. I wandered round that for a while; it was mainly flea market quality but a good opportunity to observe another aspect of British life.

The canal path comes into Brecon beside a very impressive and quite new theatre complex with a busy outdoor café—a Saturday vista of moored riverboats, strolling families, and begging ducks, producing a day of gentle pleasures.

Brecon is an attractive old market town of narrow streets where the Rivers Honddu and Usk come together. It has museums, the ruins of a medieval castle and a fortified cathedral. The cathedral houses a fine Norman font and the largest preserved cresset stone in Wales. The cresset was an ancient stone that had 30 cups containing oil for lighting the cathedral.

As you know by now, visiting tourist attractions isn't my main objective. I moved on to follow the moderate portion of a scenic route rated 'strenuous' by Collins 'Cycling in South Wales and the Wye Valley.' The road rises steadily from 100 metres to 400 metres above sea level at Upper Chapel where I crossed over to a parallel road running downhill back to Brecon.

Returning to the hostel along the canal, I became nervous riding through the very narrow tunnel formed by a flyover and temporarily lost my balance, started to wobble and finally intentionally fell against the tunnel's stonewall to avoid falling in the canal. It was a 'mind over body' situation. The available cycling space was adequate and would not have bothered me if the wall hadn't been there, blocking a possible escape route from the canal.

After dinner and a bit of hand laundry, I retired with my book to an outside bench overlooking the sheep pasture. Tranquillity disappeared when the young school party came out for a game that was a mix of cricket and football. Their joy and the teachers' playful participation erased my initial irritation. The teachers did their utmost to ensure that the children had an enjoyable, meaningful experience and when needed, which was rare, diplomatically provided behavioural corrections. It presented a very positive image of the teaching profession.

The next day, headed for the National Cave Centre, I travelled along the busy A40 west for some while before going south on an unmarked road that had the same sense of vast loneliness as Gospel Pass. Very strong headwinds made the general upgrade even more difficult. So, when a lovely white pub appeared off the road with a riverside picnic table nestled under willows, I easily persuaded myself that it was lunchtime.

Not, however, at this pub. They had decided not to serve until time for the World Cup match-a couple of hours wait. So I carried on to the National Cave Centre café. It, of course, had a typical tourist style menu of largely overpriced fried food with indifferent, unhygienic service. For a national centre, such a café was a disgrace. This and the £10 admission charge put me off visiting the caves--I should have waited for lunch at the pub with a couple of beers.

I did stop at a small ancient burial cave whose rock entrance was barred but an sensor controlled, body-less voice explained that the

hadn't specified a single journey and had been sold a return. When the conductor walked back along the aisle, I asked for a refund and was told that the single fare would have been £8! Railway ticket prices can be very confusing. The fare structures offer seasonal rates, off-peak daily rates, advance purchase rates, and more but the choices are rarely displayed or compared.

A several kilometres long cycling and walking coastal path led from Swansea to Mumbles. There, my 'Coast House' B&B, faces a sea full of water skiers and sailboats. People strolled along a boardwalk beside an outdoor café where I stopped to enjoy the passing scene. It was a showy sort of place where one comes to see and be seen.

The new day was devoted to the Gower Peninsula, the first area of outstanding natural beauty to be named by Britain. My landlady, Janet, in Hay on Wye, spoke highly of the National Trust site, Rhossili, on the Gower and there were a number of other spots I wanted to see.

Cycling west, it began to rain, spoiling my mental image of sunny, sandy, magnificently cliffed Gower. Following country lanes led to the Ship Inn at Port Eynon. It was an 'any ship in a storm' situation. Totally chilled, I thought---'why not have a meal and wait out the rain?' Consistent with the day so far, the service and food were poor but by the time I was finished, the rain had stopped.

Thank goodness, I did not give up at this stage, but carried on to Rhossili. The weather co-operated, drying up and becoming bright. Rhossili is at the southwestern edge of the Gower; its scenery deserves good weather. As a National Trust property it is protected from development. A few white stone cottage type buildings housing the necessary facilities and a gift shop stand at the forward edge. From that point out to the coast is open, close-cropped moorland abundantly flecked with yellow-flowered gorse. A lonely small white cottage, recently an artist's studio, sits back 20 metres from the cliff. There a marvellous circular sweep of cliff overlooked a now brilliantly blue sea banded with a swath of sparkling white sand. What a lift to the spirits for an otherwise dismal day.

Rhossili, in particular, but much of Gower, reminded me of the Otago Peninsula in New Zealand. Apart from the romance and beauty of historical buildings, the Otago Peninsula, which I visited last year, wins the comparison. On the way back to Mumbles, I saw one lovely church and cemetery overlooking pasture and the coast at Nicholaston. A lone palm tree sits dejected in a cemetery corner. Three Cliffs Bay has another excellent view.

A Heritage Centre offering a tour of a still working 13th century corn mill briefly claimed me. Old millstones, recently recovered from a shipwreck off St. David's on the northwestern Pembrokeshire coast, were on display outside. With the improved weather, the country lanes on the way back to Mumbles provided the best riding of the day. They led through villages too small to appear on my map with some very fine homes on narrow lanes that my 1997 Ford Escort would find tight. Like some roads in Scotland, these lanes had 'snake at lunch' bulges ever so often that allow two cars to be abreast.

On my final Swansea morning, people were out enjoying themselves in the now bright weather. One man walking briskly along the beach sporadically kicked a small ball towards the water for his sheepdog to catch. The dog crouched in the water, tensed as if eyeing a wayward sheep, waiting for the ball to come. Once caught he would return it to the beach some distance in front of his master and go back to his position in the water. Occasionally, the dog just could not wait and ran up to steal the ball. It was a joy to watch their companionship and fun together.

Tonight's lodging was at a farmhouse near Usk. As it was more than a day's cycling from Swansea so taking a train east as far as Newport made it manageable. Once in Newport, a busy industrial town and seaport on the Usk estuary, I strolled round its extensive pedestrianized shopping area discovering Newport's famous son, W.H. Davies, the 'tramp poet.' Davies was the author of the lines 'what is this life if, full of care, we have no time to stand and stare?' that I heard in 2004 for the first time on my Celtic tour. After lunch, I went north on unmarked roads into Usk.

The Usk village square is featured on many picture postcards; the care taken to make it appealing is obvious. But some people just do not appreciate such amenities and seem to go out of their way to show disrespect. While there, I saw a young woman deliberately drop rubbish on the ground and leave it there. She was a real role model; falling out of her top while smoking on a bench sharing the second hand smoke with her baby in a nearby pram.

Usk's attractions appeared limited to this square, so I set off for my farmhouse lodgings at Bettws Newydd on an unmarked road just east of the B4598. On the way, I stopped at an interesting looking pub to ask directions but it wasn't open. Serendipitously, a neighbour, just then returning home, told me that the farmhouse road intersected my route at that very spot.

My landlady, Francis Jones, was outside doing some heavy gardening work when I arrived but left that to get me settled. She advised that there were two pubs for dinner, one where the menu is basic pub fare and the 'Black Bear' back at the intersection. Francis told me that Stephen, the Black Bear's chef, is a bit pricey but served lovely fish. With an unusual name like that and the prospect of a good fish dinner, the 'Black Bear' it was.

The pub was quite dark inside and not in particularly good condition. Nor was the aged, emaciated, hippy barman sporting straggly, long grey hair. He recommended one fish dish but seeing the prices, I chose his least expensive, salmon and, explaining my tight budget, ordered a half pint of beer. He refused, pulling me a full pint.

Then he disappeared and I realized this was Stephen, both barman and cook. His only customer, I sipped my pint and read my book enjoying the dusky solitude. After perhaps half an hour, the meal arrived steaming on a silver plate with a generous piece of salmon in a delicious balsamic sauce accompanied by perfectly cooked snow peas and new potatoes.

One other person arrived and left without even having a drink--a very slow night. Perhaps there is another World Cup match on. Anyway, Stephen, having nothing better to do, told me about the pub business and in particular this one. He partnered with another man but the relationship didn't work. Stephen borrowed money at exorbitant rates to buy out the other man and was now scraping the bottom of the barrel just to be able to make the payments. So, he is trying to sell. If a sale can be closed, Stephen will take a year off to write a book of poetry. Now he is frustrated by the lack of time to write. He showed me a book with one of his poems, whose subject and style confirmed my image of him as a former beatnik longing to return to that life. He talked a lot about music and changed the disk on his player to allow me to listen to some of his favourites.

Stephen's business was painfully poor. Being booked elsewhere, I was sorry to have to decline his extremely attractive offer of a room and evening meal tomorrow for £20. He persuaded me to borrow his history of Owain Glyndower overnight and presented his bill, charging only for a half pint. Finally, he asked for a hug—I'm not a hugging person but how could I refuse? Well-fed and in a mellow mood, I walked up the lane in the dusk towards the farm, musing on an unusual and memorable evening.

Francis' generous breakfast hospitality was typically farmhouse. The teapot easily provided five cups to accompany a jug of orange juice, cereal and a full cooked 'Welsh' breakfast--for me, indistinguishable from the English version. Andrew, a Scottish visitor, received an equally substantial breakfast and likely very similar to the Scottish version. He is here working with a neighbouring farmer to learn about computerized milking equipment for his home farm.

Waddling stuffed outside to pack up for the day's ride to Abergavenny and busily attending to this task, I noticed Francis' Border collie eyeing me plaintively. When she saw that she had my attention, she picked up a small rock in her mouth and brought it to me. Obligingly, I tossed the rock several times along the lawn for her to fetch and bring back to me, enjoying the interaction and her endearing expression. I think many farmers don't have the time to be sensitive or sympathetic to their animals' emotional needs but that may simply be my urban mentality. Anyway, for me, it was a heart-warming start to a sunny day.

I rode down to the Black Bear to return Stephen's book on Glyndower. Engaged at the rear by a delivery of some sort, he didn't see me. It was just as well; I feared being quizzed about the book, which would have been embarrassing as it had only claimed about an hour of my time.

Later, savouring my lunch at a street side table in the sunshine outside Raglan's Ship Inn, my bike attracted the attention of an older man. He stayed to chat about his cycling history and achievements. I'd have no bragging rights at all if I lived in Britain permanently as there are so many men of my vintage that cycled almost as a way of life. This general area is particularly good cycling country with a wealth of small, lightly trafficked roads.

From Raglan, I travelled a 'white road' (i.e. Unmarked by number or name) to Abergavenny. Less than fresh and dripping with perspiration, I headed straight for my B&B for a much-needed shower. My hosts had just returned from a holiday in Spain and the wife had rushed out to buy something for my breakfast. Her husband was mowing the lawn. While explaining the idiosyncrasies of the house and taking me to my room, he gave the impression that the B&B business was beneath him. It may just have been the smelly cyclist that was off putting. The house, a former Baptist teaching college, is really two houses joined so that the B&B part has its own private entrance.

That evening, an Indian restaurant, 'The Bay Leaf' provided my first experience of a meat and rice dish known as Biryani. It was fine but not nearly as good as my favourite, Dopiaza, which I would have ordered except that a senior moment denied me its name. Walking back to the B&B, my normally serious face apparently affronted some noisy inebriates outside a pub. They accosted me, shouting 'Smile, England won!' over and over. I was momentarily alarmed, thinking my lack of football enthusiasm might lead to some facial rearrangement, but these guys were simply sloshed--not violent.

I breakfasted in the company of a mother and daughter from Leipzig. The daughter studies cello in Cardiff and her mother had come over for a short walking holiday. Since my son, Cameron, completed a university performance program in cello, we had a basis for conversation. I also met my landlady for the first time and learned that she teaches swimming opening another avenue of conversation about Mari's basement resistance pool. That led to the news that the organic eggs on my plate had been bartered for swimming lessons.

Last Days in Wales

My destination tonight was Ross on Wye. After a hard ride along the B4233 to Monmouth, I lunched and explored there until nearly three. Monmouth is an interesting, apparently prosperous town. Three rivers, the Trothy, Monnow and Wye flow round the town's Tudor and Georgian buildings. There is an 11th century castle, where Henry V was born in 1387. In the town are the Shire Hall, built in 1724, several fine old inns and a Nelson Museum. Monnow Bridge, built in 1260, as one of the four medieval gates into the town, is the only surviving Norman fortified bridge in Britain.(5)

Given the hour, I was concerned about being able to reach Ross on Wye on time, but would not risk the busy A40, choosing the A4136 east towards the Forest of Dean instead. Initially this was a steady climb, forcing me to walk several times, exacerbating the time problem. Approaching the intersection with my needed B4234, signs warned that the road was closed due to flooding. I could see cars turning into and out of that intersection suggesting that the signs might be from a previous day. So, I too turned on the B4234 north. The road went down, down, down through a West Virginia like landscape of mean, poor and dilapidated buildings that had to be a former coal mining area. At the bottom, the village of Lower Lydbrook occupies the banks of the Wye, where flooding is an obvious risk but fortunately was not a present one.

While riding into Ross, in a flash of budget-inspired creativity, I had a brilliant idea to 'have my cake and eat it too.' Saving money is always a goal, but one that conflicts with my love of certain pleasures like tea and teacakes. Rather than spend £2 to £3 in a teashop, why not buy my cakes in a shop and then use the tea making facilities at my lodgings?

I collected a 'Genoa' cake (a rich fruitcake with almonds on top) from the supermarket large enough to provide ample sustenance for at least three interludes at an average cost of £0.60 and went on to the Linden Guest House on Church Street. This is a pleasant, residential street close to the town's 17th century arcaded market hall and just opposite 'The Prospect', a public garden, near St Mary's 14th century church. Laid out by John Kyrle (1637-1724), The Prospect has magnificent views of the river and hills. Kyrle's Walk starts from a stone arch at the southwest side of the garden. Alexander Pope called Kyrle the 'Man of Ross'; he is also remembered as the man who gave Ross-on-Wye its first public water supply. (6)

My gregarious landlord, Patrick O'Reilly greeted me at the door and had me push the cycle through the hall and out the kitchen side door to a small back patio. This serves to dry laundry and to house sundry bits that would look untidy elsewhere. I retired to my room to test my new thrifty approach to tea and cake. This first test confirmed it a winner.

The new morning looked lovely on the way down to breakfast. Patrick cheerfully invited me to help myself from the sideboard housing a selection of cereals and fruits and took my order for the cooked portion. He clearly enjoyed creating a new menu item daily and while recounting the choices, he, like a magician doing a card trick, gently 'forced' his day's special. As an amateur magician in my teens, I realized what he was doing but didn't mind in the least, finding it more adventuresome than anything I would have requested and very good.

After breakfast, I wandered out for a better look at the town, initially exploring the Prospect opposite. Kyrle left a marvellous legacy; the grounds are like a formal park. A stone cross outside St. Mary's church marks a pit where 315 people were buried—victims of the plague in 1646. The church is desperate for donations to support its £2,000 weekly running costs. There are so many churches in a similar plight that it is hard to imagine there being many left in a few decades.

Descending from the Prospect to a street running parallel, I saw a very bold, powerful sculpture of a peregrine falcon outside a small theatre. Theatres always attract me and this was no different. A posted playbill announced that tonight was opening night for 'The Beauty Island', a new play by a local playwright. The box office attendant led me into the 64-seat auditorium to show me the location of each of the six unsold seats. I bought one on the very front row.

The next stop was the Heritage Centre above the Market Hall that featured a number of videos oriented to children about the history of Ross-on-Wye. At the time, it seemed the appropriate intellectual level for me. Clearly it was not, for I can remember none of that history now. My meandering also took me to a cycle shop and then to an antique shop in a fifteenth century building that looked as if it were folding in on itself. Inside I found a beautiful early nineteenth century long case clock. It was relatively small with a brass pendulum and round face--just what Mari has wanted for years. (After returning home, I sent an e-mail to the shop to see if the clock was still available—and learned it had been sold the previous day.)

The man tending the shop was a restorer of nineteenth century paintings. He had visited his Amish relatives in Kitchener, Ontario recently and was very enthusiastic about seeing their nineteenth century lifestyle. Not Amish himself, he was also intrigued by the conflict between his profession and his relatives' abhorrence of images.

I spent my afternoon on a circuit round Ross. First stop was nearby Goodrich Castle, maintained by the Heritage Trust. The castle sits high on a hill overlooking the main road. There is an impressive, empty moat crossed by a massive drawbridge into the castle but I chose to simply walk round the exterior.

Next, I climbed the very steep, narrow and winding road to Symond's Yat, a popular viewing spot, overlooking the Wye just where it forms a giant U through the forest. The river was busy with canoes, kayaks and swans. Some quiet portions were beautifully blanketed with the white water lilies. The site was full of hikers, picnickers, and birdwatchers looking for hawks.

From Symond's Yat, I travelled through Coleford, Berry Hill, and English Bicknor, arriving again at yesterday's Lower Lydbrook, just 13 km from Ross-on-Wye.   A 'Town and Country' trail just at the outskirts of Ross took me through the woods circling the town and eventually led into the centre. The entire afternoon's excursion was just 40 km.

Later, at the theatre, **a** hum of neighbourly conversation filled the lobby as I entered—most of the audience seemed to know each other. 'Beauty Island' was set in a department store with the cosmetics counter as the focus of attention.   Three sales assistants, one brand new to the position, were the principal characters. Customers, managers, janitors, etc., came and went.   It was not especially well written or acted but added variety to my day.   During the interval, I chatted with the woman next to me.   Then, in the lobby, after the end of the play, she brought the playwright over for introductions.   Of course, he asked the inevitable question and of course, I lied.

In the morning, Patrick told me that he had built the set for the play but wouldn't act with that group—'they aren't good enough.' He was particularly dismissive of the troupe for using a prompter. While paying my bill afterwards we talked some more.   This time it was about the standards in schools.   I had read in the Times Educational Supplement that many parents and students were upset that some British universities are now demanding applicants take standardized admission tests because the school records were so variable.   This surprised me because the 'A' level examinations required for university entrance are set by the government, not the schools.

Patrick explained that the universities' concerns relate to a new practice of awarding 'A' level grades based on combining work during the year with examination results rather than relying only on the examination, so there is more subjectivity in the current blended grades. Sounded much like the grade inflation issues in North America.

Headed east today for a Brinscombe, Gloucestershire B&B, I pulled over at a VW dealer on the outskirts of Gloucester to read my map and was surprised to find them open on a Sunday. So, I got a chance to view some VW models not available in Canada and was given directions which got me as far as Stroud on a quiet road.

While doing a quick survey of Stroud, I crossed paths with three other cyclists aged about 45. Two of them were headed to Stonehenge for the Summer Solstice. 'Going to sacrifice a virgin' they told me with obvious pleasure. They had been camping, apparently without access to water and weren't the best advertisement for cyclists in appearance, odour or sentiments.

I did eventually find Brinscombe, south of Stroud. Finding the B&B was another matter. The specific address was Walls Quarry, Brinscombe, Stroud, Gloucestershire. Walls Quarry meant nothing to those I asked so I tried my other information which described the B&B as near the intersection of Brinscombe Hill and the Roundabouts. The latter turned out to be a road name rather than an actual gathering of roundabouts.

The relevant intersection was, of course, at the top of the very steep Brinscombe Hill and once there, the landlady was out. Looking for a telephone to confirm my next day's B&B reservation, I climbed another hill to a four-star hotel near the summit, rolling past guests taking coffee on the terrace while watching a croquet game on the extensive lawns. Viewing me as an uninvited intruder, they were obviously curious what a scruffy cyclist was doing there, as was the staff in the hotel. At first the rather severe matron coolly informed me that there was no telephone for public use, but she relented and offered their office phone. After my call, I asked the young man in the office for dining recommendations. He quickly but tactfully indicated that I wasn't eligible to dine there, but pleasantly provided me with a list of affordable, more accepting alternatives.

Continuing into the countryside along a narrow, horse-dung decorated lane brought me to a T-junction facing a very large, flat plateau of common land. I cycled along this, glorying in a level surface at last, enjoying the distant views of the village and watching animal and human activity on the common. This was the famous

Minchinhampton Common, a 600-acre National Trust property that overlooks the Stroudwater Hills.

About six, I returned to Walls Quarry, approaching the B&B from above this time and nearly burned out my brakes on the way down. The landlady had returned and gave me a tour of her five storey home, a former pub, some parts of which date to 1550. There are circular stone staircases with rope banisters and a storage area built into the old beer vault. Despite its age and solid stone construction, she has managed to modernize the house to include heated towel rails, a complete laundry and top-line showers.

My next two days were spent in Cirencester and vicinity, returning to Walls Quarry the first night and carrying on to Stow-in-the-Wold on the second. Cirencester, the old part of which was called Corinium by the Romans, was, after London, the largest town in Britain in the second century. The site of the old town has been excavated and there are many exciting Roman finds, including coins and mosaics, in the museum. Cirencester has blended old with new so its more modern buildings fit in gracefully with the old houses of Cotswold stone. The fifteenth century church, built when Cirencester was the greatest wool market in England, has a magnificent nave and screen. There are some lovely walks in 3000-acre Cirencester Park, containing woodland, farms and pleasant villages. Its trees include beeches and a 3 km long avenue of chestnuts. (7)

Cirencester was one of the last places that the Romans evacuated when they left Britain to fight the Huns about 400 AD. Their departure largely destroyed the economic base for the city and people gradually moved back to the countryside letting the city deteriorate.

Just outside Cirencester, I stopped at a Waitrose market for lunch, meeting a cycle camping couple. The wife was very distant but her husband engaged me in conversation for some time. They had cycle camped in British Columbia and Alberta as well as in parts of the U.S. According to him, he had then (during the second Bush administration) told a number of 'Yanks' that what Europe wanted from the U.S. was 'leadership, not opting out of everything' (e.g. strategic arms limitation treaties, International Criminal Court).

Apparently they weren't aware of these issues so he disdainfully told them 'you should get out more.'

From Cirencester, I went to Bibury, a lovely town, oriented to home grown tourists interested in idyllic spots. The majestic Swan Hotel sits at the end of the main road facing the narrow Coln River, huge weeping willows; hump bridges, beautiful gardens and Cotswold stone houses. Nearby are Atherton Row and Rack Isle, a National Trust property of ancient row houses. A lane to Northleach provided excellent cycling terrain with a perfect mix of level and up and down. The wind swept across the adjacent field swaying the grasses creating an ever changing, ever moving, mosaic of light.

In Northleach, I visited their fifteenth century church that is considered to be one of the finest left by the old wool merchants in gratitude for their good fortune. A pleasant woman there, reminding me very much, in manner, appearance and voice of a friend in Oakville, gave me a brief tour. She asked that I sign the guest book, which I rarely do but did this time.

My return to Walls Quarry was along much the same route but for some variety and to add some distance, I chose the turnoff to Nailsworth. On the way there, I descended its main attraction, the 'Nailsworth Ladder', a chalky hill with a gradient of one in three in places. The Nailsworth Ladder is frequently used as a motorcycle trials test hill. Fortunately, there was an alternative way back to Walls Quarry that did not require climbing the ladder on the way out.

Next morning, I travelled the Minchinhampton Common road one last time, returning to Cirencester to visit the Corinium Museum where a progressive set of exhibits displayed life in the area during pre-Roman, Roman, Anglo Saxon and Norman times. One of the largest exhibits was dedicated to a nearly complete intricate mosaic floor from the Roman period. My most lasting memory is that the gender of many of the children's' skeletons could not be determined because they were too young (less than seven).

Continuing to duplicate yesterday, I went back to Northleach and the Wool Church in the hopes of finding my sunglasses that had been left somewhere. They were there waiting for me, right next to the church visitors' book where I had put them down to sign. I went on to Bourton on the Water, a beautiful village with the little River Windrush flowing alongside the main street under low bridges beside trees and lawns. Bourton is sometimes referred to as the Venice of the Cotswolds for this reason. The buildings on this street are largely dedicated to the tourist trade and were very busy during my visit. An outside tea break allowed me to observe the constant stream of tourists strolling along the river walkway.

Across the road, I bought one of my favourite country man's style Tattersall check shirts at the Edinburgh Woollen Mill shop where I met and chatted with a couple from Corvallis, Oregon before leaving for Stow-in-the-Wold, about 7 km along the busy A 429.

My Stow B&B room was a comfortable, spacious en-suite. It was convenient to town, so after cleaning up, I set out to see what Stow had to offer. It is a quiet hilltop town that was once a bustling centre of the wool trade partly because it stands at the junction of several main roads. The market square is large, hemmed in by old houses and inns arranged in higgledy-piggledy fashion. The local saying 'Stow-in-the Wold, where the wind blows cold' might explain why the buildings are huddled together.

Today, many of those buildings are home to antique shops and restaurants. One of the antique shops had a very handsome golden walnut bureau much like our oak one at home. The dealer thought his was very rare but would have parted with it for £6,000. He proudly told me that he was a jazz musician and had played trombone with a Toronto jazz band in New Orleans.

Another of these aged buildings is the 'Eagle and Child' pub that claims to be have been born in 947 AD, the oldest in England. The pub is linked physically with the adjoining Royalist Hotel where there is a first class restaurant. Since the pub and hotel shared the same kitchen I chose to eat in the less expensive pub enjoying the ambiance of its original beamed ceilings and large fireplace.

Breakfast at the B&B was served on a long antique communal table next to the kitchen where Michael, my landlord, cooked while keeping up a running conversation with a couple that are frequent guests.   When I asked about the location of a laundrette, he generously offered to do my laundry, freeing me to explore the town more fully.   As well as host and cook, Michael is a devoted gardener and jam maker. He is also an attached bachelor whose girlfriend lives elsewhere but 'visits'. So I was never quite sure who was in residence.

Expanding my frugal teatime approach to lunch, I bought a pasta salad from the Tesco supermarket and ate in my room with today's Telegraph. After collecting my sun-dried laundry from Michael's clothesline, I set off on the bike to explore the Cotswold lanes. This took me to Lower Swell, the Slaughters, back to Bourton on the Water and the Rissingtons, returning to Stow.   Stiff breezes made for an invigorating ride.   The scenery was richly green, manicured, yet natural and made special by the golden stone homes.   Some of these are very grand with gorgeous private gardens.   One house had a hedge on three sides that must have been six metres high, 30 metres long and 75 cm thick--total privacy!

Small villages don't provide a great deal of privacy; everyone is your neighbour and your comings and goings are seen by most. Even so, the couple from Oregon seemed startled when I called out to them as they crossed the road to the Stow bus stop. Continuing my exploration of Stow, I visited St Edward's Church where a group of five in a side chapel was holding a private worship service. Outside, I saw a stone inscribed to the Royalist officer killed in the first Civil War in 1646.   Stow was the site of the last major battle of that war. Parliament's officers (i.e. Cromwell's) won that battle and the war. The main street here runs downhill and the bloodbath from the battle was so great that the ducks were said to be bathed in blood.   The street's current name 'Digbeth' is said to be an evolution of duck bath.

My cycling this afternoon took me through the lanes to Moreton-in-Marsh, which has the most convenient link for my train journey to Oxford and London tomorrow.   Arriving at the station, I saw the Oregon couple again, waiting for a train to Scotland. They seemed to think my constant appearance a bit suspicious even after being assured them that my train was for tomorrow and in the opposite direction. After we said our final goodbyes, I discovered that by taking a 9 a.m. train, I could go directly to London's Paddington Station avoiding having to change at Oxford.

I continued my exploration of the lanes thoroughly enjoying the day and the rolling countryside, its broad views and frequent villages. At Edge Hill, a high ridge that gave its name to the first battle of the Civil War, I visited Rollright Stones, a Bronze Age stone circle and the King Stone. The first was a small circle, perhaps 30 metres in diameter ringed with about 70 stones of various sizes and positions. Visitors are challenged to count the stones to see if they can get the same count twice. I tried several times but never could. The site had been used as a meeting place rather than for burial and its legend is that a witch turned an officer and his men to stones –the rationale is lost to me now. Across the road rests the King Stone, a burial memorial, the shape of which has been altered overtime by drovers chipping bits away for good luck. Now, though protected from further such damage, it looks like a circus seal balancing a ball on its nose.

At Chipping Norton, I visited an attractive conversion project called White Hart Mews just off the High Street. It consisted of several terraced dwellings faced in golden limestone on each side of a cobblestone courtyard. The show home had a tiny kitchen where the washing machine and dishwasher took up most of the cabinet space, three small bedrooms, two baths and a front room the back end of which had to be used for meals. A very narrow stairwell at the rear of the kitchen led to the two upper storeys. Storage space was almost non-existent. The quality of construction and finishing was very high and the overall ambiance was charming. Even so, £295,000 with no garden or garage seemed just a bit dear for such limited accommodation.

Returning through Stow, I stopped to read the menu at Talbots and met the publican just starting a walk with his dog. He seemed a friendly, interesting chap, so I resolved to eat there this evening. When I entered Talbots, there was an immediate sense of a cliquish atmosphere. Obviously a stranger in a pub used to locals, my intrusion seemed almost resented. There was considerable banter between the regulars and my publican acquaintance. He had to have a drink with most and grew increasingly red-faced but took no notice of me. A friendly welcoming nod of recognition would have made all the difference. My Thai Chicken Curry was well prepared and enjoyable but overpriced.

On the way back to the B&B, I saw Michael, my landlord, with his lady friend on their way to Talbots and advised him of my need for an early start in the morning to catch the train. He said, 'no bother, I'll get your breakfast in time.' Obliging, yes, and a tactful way of increasing the probability of collecting the £120 owed him by a complete stranger. B&B operators outside of London and the Southeast are almost unfailingly trusting, providing keys to their guests for access to the house, day and night, often not requiring a deposit or credit card number and waiting for payment until the day of departure. I very much like human relationships, private or business, that operate on the assumption of everyone doing the right thing but such relationships have become increasingly rare. And, relying on such assumptions can be considered foolish.

The second run to Moreton-in-Marsh repeated yesterday's ride through Broadwell and Evenlode but the cool hush of early morning worked its usual magic on me, giving my ride a fresh, more adventurous character. I arrived at the station in plenty of time and was amused by some of the other passengers travelling in top hat and tails or fascinators for the race meeting at Royal Ascot.

During the train journey I worried about having to cycle from Paddington Station, across London and up to my friends in Hertfordshire without getting very lost or injured on the much busier roads. So, I decided to make my way across London to Kings Cross station, taking another train north from there.

Nature called urgently on arrival at Paddington so I immediately went in search of a washroom. Signs everywhere warned against leaving luggage or cycles anywhere but at designated areas. No such area could be found. The male washroom was down a steep set of stairs and I did not want to haul the loaded bike down them or leave it at the top of the stairs for fear of it being removed. In desperation, I explained my problem to an attendant who suggested that using the handicapped toilet at ground level. He said 'just ring the bell; someone will come to unlock the door and you can take the bike inside.' Just as I reached for the bell, an elderly woman stepped in front of me, claiming the bell for herself.

Contrary to what I had been told, no attendant came to open the door. My queue-jumping woman pulled the door open to reveal a stooped, fragile and even more elderly woman beside the lavatory with her knickers round her knees looking perplexed at her audience, mentally incapable of embarrassment. Certain that there would be no relief at Paddington, I left heading east towards the general direction of Kings Cross.

One of the several lanes of traffic was reserved for taxis, buses and cycles. The taxis and buses didn't stay in that lane but darted in and out, creating hazardous conditions. I chose not to be intimidated but to make dramatic turn and lane changing signals and trust they would be seen and respected.   Strangely, the concentration this required shut off the pressure on my waterworks.

Characteristically, I had told my friends that I would arrive at teatime. My actual arrival at Welwyn Garden City was well ahead of that, so there was time to cycle round this town that had been home for nearly six years. I also ventured out to some of the villages that had been my cycling haunts: Digswell, Ayot St. Peter, Welwyn and Shaw's Corner, where George Bernard Shaw lived. One of my neighbours here used to see George at the barbershop.

All of these places were sufficiently close that I was able to time my return to allow for acquiring a couple of bottles of wine as a house gift and arrive as scheduled. We had a very pleasant visit during which their granddaughter Chessie, a great favourite of mine, came over to see me. Next morning, after a leisurely breakfast, Jeff kindly drove me to St. Albans for a through train to Gatwick Airport.

I had to stand most of the way in the railway car's entry area holding on to the bike with one hand and a post with the other but the entire trip was probably no more than an hour. The train's pause for passengers at Blackfriars' Bridge over the Thames provided a great opportunity to see the broad sweep of the river with St. Paul's in the background. Once at the airport, I again took my life in my hands and braved the dual carriageway for the short trip into Horley and the B&B where my cycle box was stored a month ago.

My reception at the B&B was much warmer this time and I was soon dismantling and packing the bike. This time it only took 50 minutes! The B&B's free run to the airport in the morning saved me about £7 and ended one of my better trips. Staying for several days at some locations allowed me to ride unloaded on some of the tougher terrain and gave me an opportunity to explore more on foot. The rural countryside offered tranquillity and friendly people while the weather was the best ever. There is no question ----I'll be back.

French Tricolour waves proudly on Brittany Ferry's night
voyage to St Malo from Portsmouth Harbour with British Naval
vessels in the background.

One of Dordogne's several 'Most Beautiful Villages'

BRITTANY, AUVERGNE & LIMOUSINE TOUR

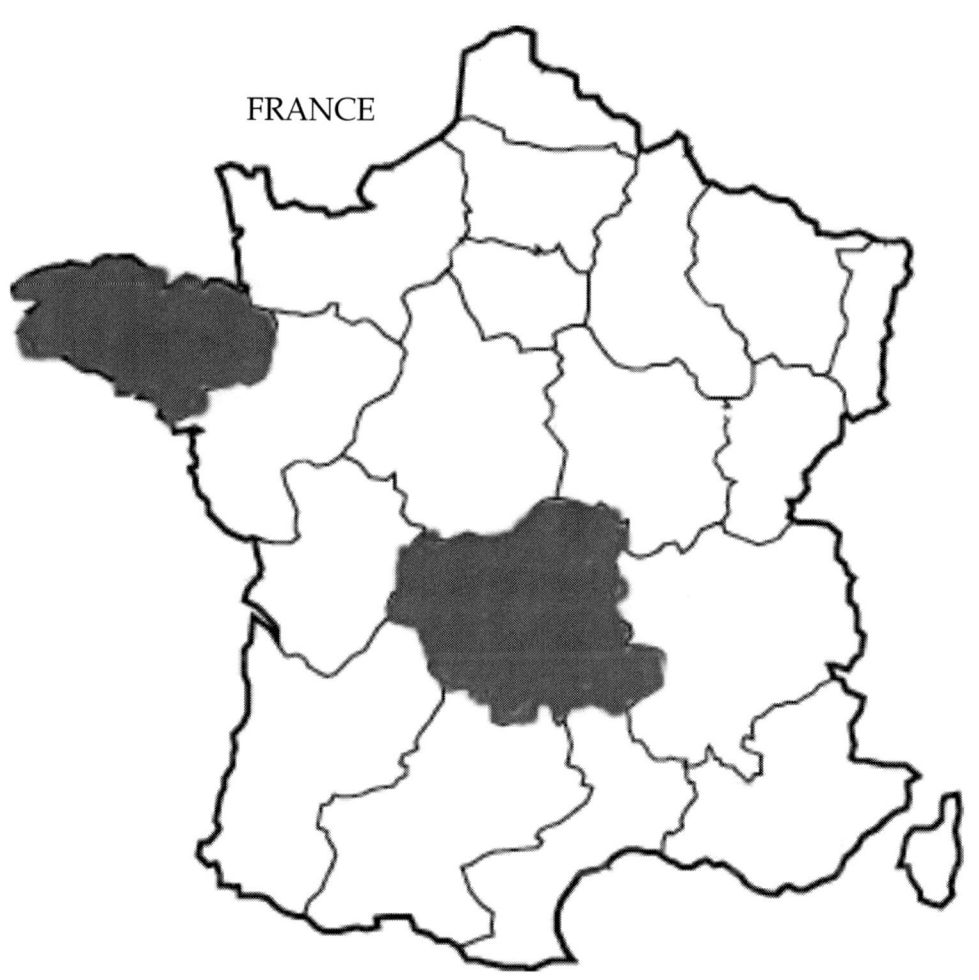

FRANCE

BRITTANY, AUVERGNE & LIMOUSINE
Shattered Plans

'Are you Robert Adams? Here for an angioplasty?' was Dr Watson's terse and perfunctory greeting at the operating theatre door. 'Let me just outline some of the potential complications of this procedure which include possible death.' Pausing for perhaps ten seconds, he thrust his clipboard at me saying 'sign here.'

I had arrived at this juncture because my lack of speed and stamina touring Wales last year concerned me. Blaming these deficiencies on the bike justified a prolonged search for the perfect new bike. However, declining ability on the treadmill made it clear, I was the problem.

My family doctor arranged an August appointment for me with a cardiologist after reading the results of a cardiolite stress test I took in late May 2007. I left the testing centre feeling very confident as the test did not tax my strength at all, my pulse never got to the level they targeted and returned to resting level very quickly. The report, however, told another story indicating a 'severe reversible anterior, anteroseptal and apical defect.' The cardiologist did more tests and immediately prescribed an angioplasty with stent.

This was the worst possible news. I was booked on a flight to Paris in three weeks time. A several day solo cycle tour in Brittany was to be followed by a trip to Limoges for twelve days of group cycle camping. The Breton Bikes group included four people from my Brittany tour in 2004: Geoff, the tour leader, Murray and Cara, a couple from New Zealand and Yassmin from England who I had dinner with at the outset of my tour in 2006. I had looked forward to this tour all year.

Amazingly, my cardiologist is also a cyclist and fully sympathized with my dismay. He wouldn't recommend postponing the operation until after the trip so he immediately set about arranging for it while his assistant performed more tests. Before she finished, he returned, saying that my operation would be the following Wednesday—two weeks before my scheduled departure and would be performed by one of the top men in the country. In Canada, we are used to waits for surgery numbered in months, not days. This was miraculous and held a distinct promise that my trip to France could go ahead.

Dr Watson told me that I would be only mildly sedated and should be able to observe the operation on an adjacent screen. About an hour later, I woke, back in the ward, having seen, heard and felt nothing. During the afternoon, one of the nurses came to talk. She knew about the planned cycle tour and related a few horror stories about foreign medical costs and the intransigence of insurance companies in compensating 'prior conditions'.

Later, another nurse, carefully draping my private bits from view, attempted to redress the area near my groin where the stent was inserted. She couldn't apply enough pressure required to stem the blood flow, yelling out for help. In her urgency to help, the more seasoned second nurse impatiently flung off my modesty sheet, exposing me to all and sundry in the ward, to get the room necessary to apply more pressure. It worked and although shaken and embarrassed, I was still reasonably confident about the trip.

Just before the evening meal, yet another nurse spoke of the financial problems patients of hers had faced when they had medical difficulties outside of Canada. About 8 p.m., Dr Watson stopped by to add his voice to the growing chorus, strongly advising me against going, suggesting I would not be able to get medical insurance for a trip so soon after the operation.

Grudgingly realizing that the trip could result in financial ruin if a medical problem arose, I decided that it would be selfish and immature to go ahead. So, I postponed the tour to 2008. The airfare was lost but Breton Bikes agreed to assign my payments to 2008.

Why France?
Since becoming a Canadian citizen in 2003, I have felt entitled and compelled to extend my cultural connections to France to embrace both of Canada's founding countries. This expansion of my horizons began by splitting my 2004 Celtic tour equally between Britain and France. Prior cycling trips in France with Mari had been very pleasant but weren't motivated by Canadian history. Splitting the

Celtic tour with Britain confirmed that France is excellent cycling country deserving more attention. Hence this trip totally dedicated to France.

Apart from the cycling, I was interested in the history after reading two books on the wars between the French and English in the mid-18th century and visiting the former French fortress at Louisbourg, Cape Breton, Nova Scotia. Louisbourg is a marvellously reconstructed site that deserves a full day visit. Its second defeat in 1758 by the English opened up the sea-lanes, making it safer for Wolfe to approach Quebec and led to his defeat of Montcalm the following year at the Plains of Abraham. I was at Louisbourg in June 2007 on a week's group cycle tour before learning about my heart condition.

A French interpreter there, posing as a soldier guarding the entrance, challenged our group in French, suggesting we might be English spies. Our leader assured him (in French) that we could not be spies as none of us could read or write and explained that our accents were a bit odd because we were from St. Malo, Brittany. That interchange set the tone for a very authentic and interesting day. It also reinforced my decision for a tour devoted to France.

Plans for 2008—Déjà vu

The Breton Bikes led tour was to begin on the 14 of September so I planned a 2 September departure, as I wanted to solo for ten days in Brittany first. Mari and I organized our entire year around those dates--her winter holiday for thermal therapy in southern California, our joint summer holiday; a late August week's stay with my mother to give my caregiving sister a holiday break; an early celebration of our anniversary, and finally a visit from Mari's aunt and uncle just before my departure.

The week with my mother was very difficult. At 89, she was still in her own home. She was physically mobile but had virtually no conversational ability and was unable to deal with most domestic tasks. She often did not understand, chose not to, or was obstinate. All the time she remained a gentle lady. Her nights were disturbed by wild dreams, a total absence of any sense of time, and incontinence.

Changing your Mother's nappy and linens at 2 a.m., three nights out of seven, strains and dramatically changes the relationship. I had no right to complain given how little I faced these problems compared with my sister but it was very difficult. These were long days unrelieved by adult conversation, television, or radio.

Returning home from my mother's the Thursday evening before my Tuesday departure, I discovered an e-mail saying that my airline, ZOOM, had declared bankruptcy---all future flights were cancelled. My nerves weren't recovered sufficiently from visiting my mother to deal calmly with this and was like a zombie at dinner. All I could think about was finding a flight, any flight, to get me to Paris in time.

Air France had a departure for the same day as my original flight arriving in plenty of time for my train booking west to Brittany. Relief! Panic roared back when the Air France website would not accept my booking. Forcing myself to calm down, I tried to book through Expedia and was successful. After receiving my confirmation, I checked some of the fine print in the booking requirements and learnt for the first time that France requires visitors' passports to be valid for three months after their planned departure from France. My passport expired two weeks too early to meet this requirement.

Now, I was in full panic mode. If this passport rule was enforced my new flight booking could potentially double last year's financial loss. Could the French Embassy make an exception for me? What could I do to try to get a refund from ZOOM?

Four days remained to the flight, two of them weekend days when embassies aren't open. The embassy assured me on Friday that there would be no problem as long as the passport was still valid during my whole time in France. ZOOM advised that claims for refunds should be forwarded to credit card companies. MasterCard was ready for my call and while there was absolutely no guarantee of success, the claim procedure was straightforward and could be initiated without delay by fax. By Friday night everything that could be done, was done and we could enjoy our Saturday pre-anniversary celebration----a rail trail cycle ride followed by a late restaurant lunch at the end of the trail.

The weather and cycling were good but we deviated from the trail, took a wrong turn and wound up half an hour late for our reservation. The restaurant was just about to end the lunch period so there was no time for anything more than a hurried face rinse and hair brush. Although the service and food were fine, our remote table location suggested that we might have had an air of 'Eau de Sweat Velo.'

Mari's aunt and uncle arrived on the Sunday and we enjoyed a lunch and theatre outing with them on Monday. Tuesday was departure day. My accumulated anticipation for this trip over two years had nearly been dashed. Mari drove me to the airport and now, checked in, and waiting alone for the flight was like an early morning dream that you realize is unreal but stay in bed anyway to see how it turns out. Travelling without my bike compounded the sensation of unreality. I wasn't taking it because BB strongly encourages clients to use BB cycles so that they can be sure to have the necessary spares to mend and provide maintenance for the bikes on the tour. This policy is also motivated by the uncertain quality of client cycles.

The Journey

Air France was immediately impressive. Boarding was timely enough to make departure at the scheduled time likely rather than hopeless. Standing in the boarding queue, I was surprised to find one of the owners of my local cycle shop with his wife. They were off to do a week's group tour in Provence organized by a travel subsidiary of the TREK cycle company.

Service on the flight was professional and attentive. The meal was way above airline average and included complementary wine. It made the journey much more civilized and helped to blunt the reality that the flight cost some $500 more than ZOOM. I read, dozed and mused about my neighbour's book *'Six Sigma for Dummies'*.

A railway station is conveniently located in the massive Charles de Gaulle Aéroport but due to the change in flight, I had a seven-hour wait for my train to Brittany. I read, tried to doze, paced the floor with my bag trolley for exercise and surveyed the diversity of other passengers.   There were several women in very colourful native African and South Pacific garments and some beautiful brunettes (my personal favourite).   My first attempt at using French, to buy a ballpoint pen, proved successful, cheering me because the necessary word 'stylo' came to mind automatically.   This minor pleasure was offset by my irritation at the cost of having forgotten to bring a pen but now I could stave off boredom by working on my journal.

I also had plenty of time to study the electronic board announcing train departures, understand that it withholds platform information until about 20 minutes before departure and little by little translate its other information.

Although the train journey to Rennes and then on to St Brieuc was uneventful, I was impressed with the fact that my seat reservation, made on-line from Canada, was exactly where it should be. The train was punctual, quiet, comfortable and very efficient.

St Brieuc hostel is about three kilometres from the railway station. Being late afternoon and not knowing how to get there, I splurged on a taxi, rehearsing on the way, the French I would use to claim my reservation. The taxi ventured down a narrow lane, depositing me alongside a stone manor house in a small parkette setting.   The manor's French blue doors and window trim and its open cobble-stoned courtyard created an appropriate introduction to a French holiday.

But, it was just my luck that the two men at reception were both young Germans, doing their national obligatory social service by working at the hostel (why Germany allows this to be done in another country, I don't know).   However, they were new in their jobs and uncertain how to deal with me, as there was no record of my reservation.   French as a second language for all three of us did not contribute to effective communication. The manager overhearing all the confusion was finally unable to take it any longer and intervened to resolve everything satisfactorily.

My room was en suite except for the lavatory and given the time of year, I did not have to share. I walked, perhaps a kilometre, to a commercial district with a family style cafeteria. Uncertain of my French, I simply pointed at what I wanted, including a 25 cl carafe of red wine. My table-side window looked out on a culturally jarring Speedy Muffler outpost.

The hostel breakfast was provided, appropriately, in what may have been the former grand manor house dining room. Now elegance and comfort were very much lacking. It was a buffet affair that apart from the baguettes consisted mainly of packaged products such as apricot jam and peanut butter packets, machine coffee and the like. There was plenty. The worst of it was that all the dining room doors facing the courtyard were open to the outside temperature of perhaps 7 C! I closed the doors and warmed myself with three bowls of coffee.

Getting to Gouarec and Bon Repos
Geoff from Breton Bikes arrived at 10.15, in his red Fiat sports convertible. I was immediately comfortable with Geoff; it was hard to believe that over four years had passed since we were last together.

He is a very competent driver and loves to drive at the car's limits severely testing my jet-lagged nerves, particularly since his Fiat was set up, British style, with right hand drive putting me next to oncoming traffic. Thankfully, we arrived safely at his imposing, dark stone home near Gouarec about an hour later after a quick stop at the local pâtisserie. His wife, Kate, greeted us with a fresh jug of coffee, leaving us to chat at the back of their home in a sort of full width stonewalled conservatory.

I had scolded Geoff by e-mail for not providing more information about the camping tour route and places of cultural interest along the way. I wanted to buy relevant maps and research some of the history and culture that we might be seeing. He chose to answer me in a broadcast e-mail to the entire group. Since much of the group is primarily interested in the cycling, food and wine, They quickly tagged me, somewhat dismissively, as the 'culture guy.' This became a double-edged nickname as I displayed little interest in culture on the tour. Without any information from Geoff for researching cultural opportunities, my poor French would render any explanatory notes in potential museums, cathedrals and chateaus, fairly useless for me.

Now, over coffee, Geoff explained that he purposely chooses not to provide more detail because where we cycle depends so much on how fit the group is, what the weather turns out to be, possible accidents and/or illnesses along the way. He advises the starting point and the general direction but waits to plan each day's route until the night before.

This coffee and pastry interlude so relaxed my drive-shattered nerves that I was in no particular hurry to leave but Geoff needed to get on with his day. So we went to the Breton Bike's home site at the local campground where he got me organized with my cycle and other gear. I still wasn't functioning effectively, taking too much time to fit my gear in Geoff's compact panniers. I brought more than could be accommodated and was having difficulty thinking through what could safely be left leave along with the camping gear that would not be needed for the solo hotel portion of my trip.

This solo bit is to be a combination of two of Geoff's standard tours. It is designed to allow me to visit Belle Ile de Mer (not on his routes) and return to Gouarec in time to travel by van and trailer with Geoff, the bikes and camping gear to Poitiers where the group tour is to start.

My first night was to be at Bon Repos, 5 km along the towpath of the Brent-Nantes canal. Despite having only recently eaten, my stomach clock was suddenly on European time and needed sustenance. However, by the time I got packed up and into Gouarec, the supermarket had closed for their lunch break and the few available restaurants had already stopped serving lunch. So, I set off along the canal towpath.

The lack of food coloured my mood grey, matching the damp, dull atmosphere along the canal. The forest-bordered towpath was spotted with puddles from recent rains and my pace seemed irritatingly slow but without an odometer there was no way to know just how slow. Then suddenly, the vista broadened and brightened, raising my spirits. Off to my left a large expanse of green lawn sloped down from a group of large ancient buildings to the canal. On my right, by a weir and a large humpback bridge, like the pot of gold at the end of rainbow, was a colourful, open café.

I quickly placed an order for 'un croque monsieur et pression.' The somewhat disreputable looking character smoking with clients on the terrace turned out to be the chef who had to be summoned to the kitchen. My beer came first, accompanied by two wasps that repeatedly attempted to drown themselves and finally succeeded. When the meal arrived, the sandwich plate had a narrow ring of salad barely qualifying as one of my required daily servings of vegetables. However, having already repressed the condition of the washroom and the chef's doubtful hygiene, this was a trifling concern.

The ancient pile across the canal from the café was my lodging for the night but the now warm sunshine and full stomach energized me sufficiently to explore a bit more of the countryside. The canal and bordering farmland scenery became more lovely also but after about an hour and a quarter, the combination of jet lag, beer and the load on the bike had me returning to Bon Repos. The former, now ruined, 700-year-old abbey church is now a museum while the adjacent residential wing was is a hotel and restaurant.

My room's walls are at least 50 centimetres thick but they only served to keep the outside warmth outside. I did a bit of hand laundry, showered and napped until the dinner hour at 7 p.m. Rosa, a French born woman, long resident in the US, returned to France and took on this hotel just a couple of months ago. She persuaded me to choose a special meal to celebrate the start of my tour. It may have been the best meal of the entire trip—brie, pear and spinach salad followed by an entrecote with Roquefort sauce, frites maison, rhubarb mousse and a bottle of wine. Rosa knocked over the bottle of wine while serving the main course and immediately offered to replace it. Since less than half had spilt, I suggested that she just charge me for half a bottle instead which she was more than happy to do.

Well-fortified and mellow with wine, I slept for nearly 11 hours, totally unaware of a raging storm outside that was still pelting down at breakfast time. Fortunately, there was a connecting door from the hotel proper into the breakfast room with its welcoming fire. As late as I was, the room was empty. When the others did arrive, they were all British.

Rosa's mother assaulted me after breakfast with a stream of criticism of modern France that seemed largely based on her conviction that a 'communist' mentality dominates the country producing lazy people only interested in government handouts and teachers that perpetuate the situation by indoctrinating the children. After just a few months, she was ready to return to the US. Then the rain stopped, giving me a valid reason to escape.

I returned to Gouarec along the now nearly liquid towpath. A huge tree straddling the canal was further evidence of the storm's violence. Stopping at Breton Bikes' home site to collect my French language book left behind in my duffel bag, I found Geoff and Kate hosing down the tents to be used on the camping tour. After settling up financially with Kate for Geoff's taxi ride and some additional costs, I finally got truly underway.

A Soggy Carnival

Either the terrain became easier or my body was finally ready to work and reached Mael-Carhaix by one p.m. –just in time to take advantage of a lunchtime special—four courses with wine. As I emerged from the restaurant, it began to rain, forcing me to take cover under an awning until it stopped, 15 minutes later. Of course, once back on the road, the rain started again with a vengeance. Now there was no shelter, and no alternative but to continue the remaining 10 km to Carhaix and Noz Vod, my hotel. Cold and soaked on arrival, I dried off, put on all my warmest clothes and buried beneath the bedclothes for an hour. The electric wall heater was still on its summer holidays and refused to work.

Life began dry and more hopeful the next day following a serve yourself breakfast of which I took full advantage –to the benefit of body and budget. Despite lingering with my book over breakfast, I was underway at nine. In less than two kilometres, I faced the steepest hill of my solo tour but managed to climb it without getting out of the saddle.

Midmorning, passing through the village of Corrorec, a crowd of people was just about to cross the road in front of me on their way to a church for a baptism. One of their number shouted out to me 'tout droit, tout droit, tout droit.' It took a while for my brain to sort out that, he was telling me to not to wait for them but just 'go ahead.' As I did, it began to rain----again, but only lasted a few minutes. The roads were quiet. Even the spotless cattle in the bordering pastures were silent, choosing not to respond to my attempts at conversation.

By 15.30, I had found 'Le Chrismas', my hotel in Chateaulin. It was closed. Carrying on into the centre to explore, as there was no other option, familiar carnival sounds blared in the distance. Sure enough, there at the bottom of the hill, stretched alongside the river, was a somewhat dispirited, dripping carnival. Given the cool, rain-sodden weather, patronage was light. The operators' faces reflected discomfort and considerable boredom. One sign advertised 'American frites'. At the time, I interpreted this as a French retaliation to the US Congressional restaurant renaming French fries as 'Freedom Fries' after France declined to participate in the Iraq invasion. I was wrong and should have known that at 8€ there had to be something more substantial than frites. The term, 'American frites', means a sandwich with everything on it, including a side order of frites. It dates back to World War II and the huge GI appetites--perhaps it originally was 'American avec frites.'

The dismal weather strengthened my normal aversion to this tawdry spectacle with its expensive rides and overpriced junk that seems to have special appeal to those who can least afford it. I chose to spend my money on a grand café crème and a couple of chocolate pastries, unconsciously providing support for the expression 'different strokes for different folks'.

When I got back to the hotel, an envelope addressed to 'Breton Bikes' was taped to the door. This must be for me. My first reaction was 'Oh No!, my reservation has been cancelled.' I seem always ready to think the worst--instead, the note inside gave me the combination of the outside lock releasing the front door, my room number, the location of the room key and where to store my cycle! There was no evidence of any other guests.

Shortly after I had settled in the room, the manageress knocked on the door to advise me that the restaurant and bar were closed tonight. She recommended a restaurant that I set out to find but my pathetic navigational skills and sense of direction led me astray.

By the time I arrived at the correct location about 8 p.m., the area was jammed with people watching a foot race through and around the carnival area. Protected from the damp, cold evening air by heavy sweaters or jackets, the spectators contrasted sharply with the runners clad in shorts and thin vests. The restaurants were full of the carnival and race crowd and unable to seat me right away. So, I wound up, some distance away, at Resto, a budget operation, that provided quantity but little else.

I went back to the hotel through the carnival area where the music was still blaring for the few remaining, rather desultory citizens. A gaggle of teen-age boys kicked a soccer ball into a goal to test their strength and some obvious, outlandish prostitutes prowled for patrons.

Le Pouldu, the Alignments and Quiberon

My journal exclaims 'dry morning' as the start of the next day! It also was a bit warmer than the past three days. As it was Sunday, the country roads were particularly quiet, although some of the cattle now responded to my moos—the accent must be improving. The scenery was beautiful, particularly the roadside mossy rock outcroppings and dark overhanging branches through Foret Domaniale.

Geoff had cobbled my custom route together from bits of two regular routes. Unfortunately, his text editing was spotty and some of the landmarks were out of date. My route notes contained a two-day early reference to Sunday closures and indicated that yesterday's 47 km distance would be the longest of the tour. Today's actual distance totalled 78 km because he had eliminated an intermediate overnight and failed to edit thoroughly. Midway through today's route, at Briec, I could not find the Hotel du Midi where I was to turn left. The hotel no longer existed and probably hasn't for a few years. It is now a pizzeria!

Despite today's distance, I was at Le Pouldu, on Brittany's southern coast by 5 p.m. My modern hotel 'Le Panoramique' is set along a beach amidst expensive high rises. A seaside walk along the dune grass and rocks sharpened my appetite for dinner at the hotel's crêperie. Galettes, a savoury sort of crêpe, are quite popular in Brittany and fit in with my budget. Although some crêperies have a few specials, most offer a standard range at nearly identical prices. Tonight, I finished off with a sweet puree of chestnut filled crêpe called marron.

Geoff's route ended here so I crafted my own to get to Quiberon for the ferry to Belle Ile de Mer. This took me past some lovely Blavet River views at Pont Scorff and to a minor outpost of the famous 'alignments' near Carnac. Carnac is considered the most important prehistoric site in Europe. Continuously inhabited longer than any other place in the world; its alignments of two thousand menhirs stretch over four kilometres. The site has been used since 5700 BC, long predating the Knossos, the Pyramids, Stonehenge or the great Egyptian temples of the same name at Karnak.(1)

What little I saw of the alignments wasn't especially impressive and might have been missed them altogether had there not been a few cars parked by the roadside. These stones that I saw stood perhaps 3 metres tall, much smaller than those at Stonehenge but, as their name suggests, in rough straight lines.

Toward the end of today's ride I cycled along the western coast of the Quiberon peninsula known as the 'Côte Sauvage', a long protected stretch of beach and dune grass. It was somewhat like a seacoast version of the Yorkshire Dales moorland, absent the sheep. Bright sunshine attracted many people out on the trails. By 15.30, I was at the ferry ticket office in Port Maria having done almost 70 km.

Je ne parle pas francais

I had resolved to develop a vocabulary for this tour of 1200 French words at the rate of 150 words per month. On par with my previous New Years' resolutions, this goal was progressively whittled down to only 600 words. It wasn't too difficult—just memory work but with no grammar or other language structure to build on, all I achieved was a grab bag of assorted words that could not be combined in any kind of effective communication.

Up to this point in the tour, my kindergarten French made the few conversational opportunities simply embarrassing and often ineffective. Today, poor French nearly became expensive. While buying the return trip ferry ticket for the bike and myself to Belle Île de Mer, I recognized vendredi as a day of the week on the list of choices and requested it instead of the intended jeudi. It was only after leaving the ticket office that I realized my mistake about the return day. I was temporarily distressed at the potential loss but the ticket seller cheerfully reissued the ticket—probably wondering 'how many senior moments does this guy have left?'

Colourful cafes ringed the harbour; people were in a contagious holiday mood. Giving way to irrational budget rationalization, I decided that my ferry senior discount would fund a coffee and pastry quayside to participate in this holiday spirit. I revelled in the strong, bright sunshine, happy with having successfully navigated my way here, the beautiful scenery along the way and the prospect of the ferry excursion.

Belle Île de Mer appealed because it is off the beaten track, involves a ferry ride, and is particularly relevant to Canadian history. The British and the French alternated ownership of the island until the mid-18th century. At the time of the 1763 Treaty of Paris that settled land claims between the two countries following Montcalm's defeat at Quebec in 1759, Belle Ile de Mer was in Britain's possession. They agreed to give it up to get Nova Scotia.(2)

As the ferry approached the main town at Le Palais, brilliant sunshine splashed the small harbour. A cheerful chaos of traffic and pedestrians flowed past hotels and busy cafes along the harbour road. Rising above the water on the harbour's western flank is the Citadelle, an imposing star-shaped fortress. Vauban, the great fortress builder, built the Citadelle in the early eighteenth century after Dutch attacks. It served as a prison until 1961 and housed a number of state enemies and revolutionary heroes—including the son of Toussaint L'Overture of Haiti, Ben Bella of Algeria and even, for a brief period after 1848, Karl Marx. The Citadelle is startlingly large and filled with doorways leading to mysterious cellars, underground passages, dungeons and rooms.

Over the years, Monet, Matisse, Flaubert, Proust, and Sarah Bernhardt spent time on Belle Ile. Sarah Bernhardt built a luxurious mansion near the northern lighthouse of Pointe des Poulins but the Germans destroyed it during World War II. Her lifestyle did not endear her to the local population, which might explain why they named the German fortifications Fort Sarah Bernhardt.(3)

My French was adequate to ask for directions to the hostel at a harbour cycle hire shop and the owner's English allowed me to understand his answer, particularly as it was accompanied by a free map. While settling in my room, pleased that I would have the two-berth room to myself, in walked a handsome young Frenchman. Although it was obvious that his English was worse than my French, I did learn that he was an engineer from Toulouse. Conversation was almost impossible and prone to misunderstanding. With a combination of hand motions and words, I understood that he wanted to get up early in the morning to go on a boat cruise round the island and thought he was being courteous to let me know that he might disturb my sleep.

When morning came, he woke me up—intentionally and tried to persuade me to come outside. I now thought he was inviting me to join him for breakfast in the dining hall but since that would not be served for another hour, I declined to go outside. Why wait out in the cold for an hour just to be companionable?

He returned about 45 minutes later and we did go to breakfast together. Slowly, with our tortured conversation, I realized his invitation wasn't for breakfast, it was to observe sunrise over the harbour! It was awkward, as I could not apologize in either language.

Another communication difficulty surfaced with my attempt to use the hostel's internet but this one had nothing to do with human language. The ancient computer was without the benefit of broadband. It took over half an hour just to bring up my e-mail server. Then, I discovered the joys of a French keyboard. These provide all the necessary keys to make the various French accent marks but put many of them where regular letters and symbols are on a Querty keyboard. With the glacially slow response time and that keyboard, it took over an hour to write a fairly brief note.

Unlike St Brieuc, this hostel's facilities were down the hall. Unlike home or an en suite hotel room, everything you need has to be taken with you. Room key, towel, soap, shampoo, and clothes to change into. The stalls for showers and toilets looked identical and extra decorum was necessary as all the facilities were unisex. At night the hall lights operated on an automatic controlled time switch that barely gave you enough time to get between your room and the washroom.

A big group of mature hikers was here for a few days. Their care was the main concern of hostel staff while my roommate and I were relegated to the end of one of the long dining tables and largely neglected. At breakfast the group arrived to find their table laid with place mats, cutlery, butter, pots of coffee and baskets of baguettes. We had to gather our own cutlery and humbly present ourselves at the kitchen door to receive our trays of a more meagre breakfast.

Afterwards, I was ready to explore the countryside, having seen much of the town centre the night before while searching for an affordable restaurant. So, I set out and given my usual directional sense, went round in circles for a while before discovering the Porte Vauban tunnel leading out of town. Cyclists are diverted to an adjacent special tunnel (built in 1862) and onto a woodland cycle path to yet another tunnel that opens onto a primarily flattish landscape.

There was little evidence of human or animal activity. The roads were so free of traffic that they could serve as cycle routes but a number of other roads are officially designated as such. I chose one that led down to Pointe de Sainte Marc ending at a coastal path. Unfortunately the path was off limits to cycles so I retraced my route pausing to enjoy a colourful cluster of farmhouses along the way. A blue and yellow one had a spirited rooster chasing his harem round the garden; another house was purple and blue and a third, pure flamingo—none particularly agricultural in character.

My al fresco lunch on a low stone wall under a tree was spoilt by rain. I huddled there, only partially sheltered by the tree and envious of a recently arrived group on hired cycles that were now safely ensconced under a large umbrella at an adjacent café.

When the rain subsided I went to see Port Coton and its famous rocks. The roaring sea round these rocks created spectacular sprays but my camera failed. I returned to Le Palais to find a replacement battery but no one stocked any so I bought a disposable camera.

Then parking myself at a quayside café with an iron railing for securing my bike, I settled down to observe the harbour scene. My waiter was a twenty something Brit who came to Belle lle for the surfing six years ago, fell in love with the land, a lass and is now a permanent resident with a baby on the way. He hates going back home to England and has persuaded his parents to buy a home in Brittany! He seemed to fit in perfectly. I ordered a second coffee to observe the cheery hubbub of people and cars exiting the ferry in the late afternoon sunshine.

In little more than an hour, I was back in town, showered and in clean clothes, to try a restaurant offering a special menu dinner. Despite a sudden total shutdown of my poor French, I did get a table for one. Considerable help from the nearly tolerant waitress overcame my ineffective stutters, so I managed to order my steak bien cuit (well done). At home, my order would have specified 'medium' but the French tend to like their meat bloody so you have to order well done to get medium. It was a simple 'steak frites' meal with salad and a glass of wine but so well prepared that every bite was savoured, making the meal last as long as possible, ignoring looks suggesting I was overstaying.

The next day, after drying my hand laundry at the laundrette, I set out north west for Sauzon, the next largest community on the island. The fine weather brought out a crowd of people; brightly sailed boats danced in the sparkling water. I absorbed the ambience for several minutes, then explored a bit of the village, pushing the bike through the crowded streets, concluding my visit on a stone wall overlooking the harbour with un baquette sandwich avec du jambon et fromage.

My next goal was to return to Port Coton for the pictures I had been unable to take yesterday but was diverted by a sign to Pointe des Poulains and went there instead. This was a better choice, as the rock scenery there is more magnificent, perhaps the best I've ever seen. The clear blue sky, a warm sun and the green sea rhythmically crashing between the jagged rocks lulled me to a near trance. Later, I tracked some of the dune grass bordered trails that run to Sarah Bernhardt's former home, a museum and the fort named for her.

The day was so perfect that I decided to carry on to Locmaria, about 15 kilometres away, right at the other end of the island. Locmaria is a poor cousin to Sauzon and Le Palais and does not attract normal tourists. The squat style public toilet there, indicated Locmaria's lack of prosperity. At a small-secluded beach in a sheltered inlet a few waders were testing the water but no one swam. I read for a while resting in the sunshine on a beached tree then returned the 11 km to Le Palais, foolishly ignoring the sensible instructions to dismount on some steep down hills.

It was now 'teatime' but it was Wednesday afternoon, the pâtisseries are closed. I solved this problem with two packaged pain raisin from the supermarket. Yesterday's quayside café table was waiting and faced a lovely young woman with a group of friends. She had a winsome, toothy smile and a way of pursing her lips that was most engaging. Given this outlook and the ferry activity at the harbour, I again extended my viewing time with a second coffee.

Since devoting all my attention to her could have been embarrassing or considered rude, I diverted myself with a survey of the French car models passing in front of the café developing general personal conclusions about the style sense of the various manufacturers. Peugeot won my award for elegant design. Renault is a bit stodgy by comparison apart from its Modus and Vel Satis models while Citroen designs are distinctly quirky.

Bike Fridays, Auberge de Chine and Teenagers

On the return ferry to Port Maria on Quiberon, I met a middle-aged couple from Portland, Oregon touring France on their Bike Fridays. These cycles have small wheels and fold up to fit into a regular size suitcase but supposedly perform like a full size bike. When touring, the suitcase holds your clothes and is pulled behind on a little trailer. I first became aware of these Portland built bikes in New Zealand in 2005 but haven't yet discovered where the clothes go when the bike is in the case.

As these were the first English-speaking people I had met in several days, I immediately become much more gregarious than is normal. It was the chance to talk to someone in English and to fellow cyclists. I was humbled to realize that they were fluent in both languages!

By the time the ferry reached Quiberon, the harbour was bathed in brilliant sunshine. Going north I rode the main road up the peninsula rather than along the west coast but the narrow peninsula still provided sea views and a bracing breeze. Adding visual variety, a group of soldiers walked tight ropes and swung down on the overhead wires of an obstacle course while a number of people raced along the beach in little colourfully sailed wind carts.

Today's destination was Baud, about 50 km from Quiberon, so I wasn't under much time pressure. En route I stopped for lunch at Carnac, just east of the top of the peninsula. The village centre was quite busy given the tourist appeal of the nearby Alignments. I explored the restaurant alternatives, settling on a café that had an open-air terrace.

Suddenly shy about even trying my French, I simply pointed out my choice on the menu to the waitress. My croque monsieur arrived with an egg perched on top. Re-inspection of the menu suggested that my fat finger must have indicated the croque madame listed just above the monsieur on the menu. When it came time to pay, the café was very busy. Inside, the dim lighting at the cash register made it difficult to see my change. Sometime later, I realised she had given me the cost of my meal as change rather what she owed me. Enough for an extra café somewhere!

The Pluvigner village square offered the opportunity to have my bonus café on the pavement facing a car park in the centre of the square. A middle-aged couple that I thought might be Dutch given the wooden clogs he was wearing sat nearby. Suddenly he became very agitated, gesticulating at an arriving Corvette. My 'Dutchman' jumped up, clogging over to see the car. He dragged the driver over to his table, beginning a long discussion about cars. I was amused by his enthusiasm and surprised that he was English. Finally he exclaimed that his favourite car was the 1960 Citroen used in the 'Maigret' detective series on television. It is also my favourite and I wish Citroen would revive it as VW has with the Beetle.

Auberge de Cheval Blanc, my hotel in Baud, was difficult to find and no one seemed to know where it was, even though it was only two streets away from where I was asking. It isn't a very obvious sort of place. There are no protruding signs to indicate its presence—just the name painted on the front. I hesitantly pushed the bike into the semi-dark, seemingly deserted, interior through a dining room and reception area. There an attendant told me to store my cycle in the one of the dining rooms.

This did not encourage me to sample the hotel's cuisine so it wasn't upsetting to see a sign that I translated to say the dining room wasn't open tonight. I showered, spent some time on my journal and walked the town searching for alternative restaurants. This tour brought me full circle to a crêperie diagonally across from my hotel. During dinner there I met a very pleasant English couple from Braintree, Essex that owns a cottage here. They have been restoring it for 18 years, justifying spending their summers in France. Their plan is to live half the year in Brittany and the rest in the UK after her retirement. Although the meal was ample and well prepared, it would not have been a good evening without meeting this couple, as the waitress was unfriendly and too business like.

I returned to find the hotel full of dining customers seemingly enjoying their meals. Re-checking the sign showed that just like the Belle Île ferry ticket incident, I had confused vendredi with jeudi!

Pontivy, the first major city of this trip, was my next stop some 25 km away. The route was a pleasantly rural one with river scenes, a few hills and long views. Donkeys, goats, geese and cows grazed the pastures making the city a bit of shock after my more bucolic explorations. Pontivy is at a central junction of the Nantes-Brest canal, where the canal breaks off from the Blavet River and you can take barges—all the way to the Loire.

The city owes much of its appearance and its size, to the canal. When the waterway opened, the small medieval centre was expanded, redesigned and given broad avenues to fit its new role. It was even renamed Napoleonville for a time to honour the man responsible for its new prosperity. (4)

When I arrived, schools had just emptied for the day, releasing scores of teenagers that swarmed the streets of the shopping district in jabbering packs. The jabbering wasn't with their companions but with a distant someone on a mobile phone. A few smoked and there were some ostentatious displays of 'affection.' Apart from these, it was quite an interesting example of social interaction or perhaps social distance would be more accurate as they walked along or clustered together at shop fronts, all talking to someone who wasn't there. I window shopped the expensive shops a bit then hunted round for my hotel. It was equally as elusive as yesterday's had been. However, I had directions and was determined to find it on my own. My search was eventually successful. The hotel was a large square building that looked like a discreet office building or private mansion. 'Hotel De Europe' is displayed on a small inconspicuous brass plate mounted on the wall.

Without benefit of any introduction, the friendly elderly woman at reception immediately addressed me by name and welcomed me. She directed me back outside to a set of electronically controlled wooden gates at the side of the building. Once there, she buzzed me into their fenced parking area where I left the bike under an overhanging eave, entering the hotel through the back.

Seeking culture, I wandered up to the Chateau de Rohan built in the fifteenth century by the lord of Josselin. My 1992 guidebook indicated that the family still owns it and is slowly restoring the building but it was too near closing time for a visit to learn if the work is finished. The Portland, Oregon couple must have been inside as their Bike Fridays were parked nearby.

On the way back to the hotel, a sudden desire to learn what was going on in the world led me to buy a *Daily Telegraph*. This became my dinner companion at Auberge de Chine, a restaurant recommended by Geoff as the best Chinese restaurant in all of Brittany. Its ambience was certainly more up market than I have been frequenting and it was obvious that they are used to wealthy clientele. The meal was good although not as enjoyable as French cuisine. My service was correct but perfunctory, not nearly as subservient as that received by some of the, mainly English, customers. The adjacent table was full of superior acting Brits. As a strong Anglophile and nascent Francophile, I was embarrassed by their derogatory comments about the French. They blamed the French for everything generally and particularly for the slow speed of rescue after the terrible Chunnel fire yesterday.

Obviously informed by bias rather than facts, they had not read the *Daily Telegraph*'s very complimentary report on the French rescue efforts. There was also an interesting profile of Henry Paulson, then US Secretary of the Treasury, a report on the sensation Sarah Palin was creating in the US election, Lance Armstrong's decision to have another go at the Tour de France in 2009 and one on the British Conservative Party's election prospects. As I have come to expect, there was no coverage of Canadian news despite that, like the US, we were in the middle of a federal election. Perhaps, our 36-day campaign isn't long enough to generate sufficient interest. Despite having started months later, our election results will be known three weeks before the US even votes.

Breakfast in Hotel de Europe's dining room was a delight. Ornate mouldings surrounding the five metre high ceilings complemented two sets of double doors, one on each side of the 50 centimetre thick walls. There was an ample choice of cheeses, bread and meat served buffet style on fine English china--a very refined way to start the day.

Return to Gouarec, the Coypu and Rawdon

I left Pontivy, headed for Gouarec to complete the solo portion of this trip. Major thoroughfares, busy with traffic, run alongside both sides of the broad river. My lasting memory is of the grand sweep of river, adjacent parks and the festive, flower-bedecked bridge crossing it. Once out of the city the road passed the massive 'Foret de Quenecan' that was devastated by a hurricane in 1987. There was no obvious remaining damage. By lunchtime I arrived in St Brigitte where Geoff recommends a 'wonderful' crêperie. Geoff believes that the more disreputable a place looks, the more likely it is to be good. Using that criterion, this place should be superb. The tiny, cramped washroom under the stairs with its common, well-used hand towel certainly confirmed little concern with hygiene. Nevertheless, I stayed, receiving a very tasty meal with quick and friendly service. Standing outside later, studying my map, a friendly old man approached me. He spoke extremely slowly in hopes that I might understand his directions. We parted with that repeated excess of goodwill common to such meetings with strangers. All the while his haggard, suspicious wife kept poking her head round the corner of a nearby alley to check what he was doing.

It was now quite cool and became even more so as the road wound through a dense dark forest. About five kilometres beyond the restaurant, was 'Les Forges des Salles', a restored historical industrial centre that offered tours. I was over an hour early for the afternoon tours and did not feel like waiting in the cold. A few kilometres later, again alongside the canal, I passed Bon Repos to retrace the towpath to Gouarec and the campsite. As it was early afternoon, I hoped to be able to use the campsite laundry but Dave, the manager, reminded me that there was no tumble drier. We had met in 2004 during his first year as manager. At the time, his wife only spent summers in France, as they were uncertain about living permanently there. Since then, they made the move but now are having doubts again. This year has been particularly wet, campers aren't coming and Dave's income is almost non-existent. It was a sad reunion as his usual engagingly unconcerned and irreverent manner rang a bit forced.

Geoff, Kate and their 15-year-old son, Arthur, were at the other end of the campsite preparing the trailer, bikes and gear for tomorrow's run to Poitiers. Geoff told me that Rawdon, one of our 2004 group that I had especially enjoyed, was now living in Gouarec and was interested in getting together with me. Geoff scratched out a scrap paper map to Rawdon's place and Kate directed me to a trail through the campsite to my B&B for the evening.

Linda and Trevor, my B&B hosts were yet more English transplants! Former publicans in Aberdeen, they also had lived in Welwyn Garden City, my home for nearly six years. Their home here is definitely French but is decorated in a way that feels English. My room was pleasant and had a private bathroom. I gladly accepted Linda's offer to do my laundry.

Following Geoff's map, I walked into the village to find Rawdon's place. He wasn't at home so I left a note suggesting that we get together for dinner at seven then went exploring for likely restaurants. The Hotel Blavet, renowned for its food in 2004, was no longer in business and the only viable spot seemed to be a pizzeria.

Back at the B&B, my laundry was now drying on the line in the riverside garden. Linda was tending her extensive flower gardens while keeping an eye on her fishing line dangling in the river. She and Trevor spend a fair amount of time fishing and watching the wild life. One of their favourites is an animal I had never heard of–the Coypu. These are native to South America but are farmed in Europe for their fur and meat. A pair of these vegetarian water creatures (somewhat like a muskrat) lives nearby. The French don't like them because they eat the bank side vegetation causing erosion.

Rawdon arrived at the B&B at 6.50 but seemed a bit stiff at first. It wasn't until after dinner that he said he never received my note. I had put it at a door he does not use. Perhaps, he was miffed thinking that I had not bothered to get in touch with him. Although still formidable because of his height and sturdy build, tonight it was a more prosperous formidableness. He had levered his linguistic abilities in French, English and Arabic to get a position as a translator at the International Criminal Court in The Hague that may have required and provided the means for better clothes.

As I expected, we went to the pizzeria where he knows the owner chef and his wife. He greeted them in typical French fashion with a kiss on both cheeks as we entered. The chef was particularly gregarious and grew increasingly boisterous during the evening. His cooking area was open, facing the dining area so he carried on a running commentary sometimes directed to specific customers. At one point, he yelled at a potential customer, telling him to leave and although my vocabulary did not include the rough French used, it obviously was not a genteel request.

The chef has been drinking beer as he cooked, becoming more vocal and louder. Finally, Rawdon, fed up with his behaviour, suggested we go back to his place for coffee blaming the volume of business as Gouarec's sole restaurant as proving too much for the pizzeria owner. He thought tonight's performance symptomatic of the stress.

Given the sensitive nature of The Hague trials, Rawdon could not say much about his time there. Now he has branched out to what he hopes will be a brand new career in tracking–both man and beast. I was so astounded that I had to ask him to repeat his intentions twice to understand. In the past year he trained with the US military doing patrols along the Mexican border and with trappers in Africa, learning tell–tale signs of different animals. Tonight he is expecting an e-mail confirming a contract for an assignment in the Middle East that would use both his tracking and his Arabic skills.

Sounds of significant human activity in the street below drew us to the window with our coffee. A procession of people carrying lit candles passed in front of his house. Irreverently, Rawdon said it must be 'feast day for Our Lady of the Hedgehogs'. Geoff later told me that it likely was in honour of the Pope's arrival in France.

Next morning, my 'full English' breakfast at the B&B and my first pot of tea on this trip, reinforced the British ambiance. When I was ready to leave, Trevor retrieved my cycle from the barn and held it steady it while I loaded on the panniers. It was a very pleasant stop that took me back to Britain briefly without leaving France.

The Journey to Poitiers

Then it was down the path to Geoff's van and trailer at the campsite. Geoff arrived in his red Fiat sports car shortly after nine and we were soon on the way. Having visited his home, the well-lived in condition of the van wasn't surprising. We made two stops, one for cash and one for diesel before leaving Gouarec. Geoff brought some apples, some buns and a large flask of coffee for the journey, as he did not intend any stops during our five-hour trip. It was a real test of my bladder capacity!

Most of the trip was on excellent roads with very little traffic and I was pleased that pulling the trailer moderated Geoff's driving style to a very smooth and relaxing pace. We arrived at the campsite on the outskirts of Poitiers at about 3.30 to find Allan and Spencer already there.

Allan, a 60ish Brit, is Geoff's longest, continuous client having been on 18 of the 19 September tours run by Breton Bikes. Spencer, a new or 'virgin' client was a 25-year-old, US two-tour Iraq War veteran. Now, I remember Spencer principally for his almost daily repeated statement that 'You're over the hill at 27 and there is no point living beyond age 50.'

We helped Geoff unload the trailer, set about selecting our individual campsites and erecting our tents. Geoff gave me a much-needed refresher course on the tent and set up one for Daniela, a repeat German client who will be arriving after dark. The others arrived by taxi from the airport about six. I was pleased to see Yassmin again, an e-mail correspondent of mine since the 2004 trip when we first met. She and I are to be cooking partners for this tour. All the rest of the group were new to me.

All the latest arrivals were British. In addition to Yassmin, there were Evelyn and Jenny, good friends in their 50s, both employed in scientific positions and also frequent BB clients; Gill, another virgin, is a university lecturer in Marketing at Lancaster in her late forties; Frank, an engineer from Edinburgh whose age I never learned, and Barry, 71, a retired type compositor, security guard and now weekend bus driver from Essex. Both men have toured with BB before.

Once organized, we set off looking for a restaurant winding up at a chain establishment with an extensive menu. Everyone was in a party mood and determined to consume considerable quantities of wine. Given their objective, I foolishly agreed to share in a bottle to be split four ways and ended up sharing in one quarter of the cost of three bottles. It probably would have run to four bottles had I not stopped drinking after two glasses. It took a couple of days of scrimping to recover from that damage to the budget!

We get to know each other a little over dinner. Jenny, formerly from Belfast, or as she said, 'Nr'trn Irl'n', proved to be a caustic wit, very different from her seriously reserved friend Evelyn. Barry, the oldest, was self-disparagingly funny and frank. Allan, slender, athletic and taciturn is also well-mannered and without doubt the neatest and best-dressed person in the group on and off the bike. Frank seemed to be a thoroughly pleasant, contented and unassuming chap. He is engaged to a woman from Chicago and hopes to move there once the US authorities complete all the paperwork.

Toward the end of the meal, Geoff received a phone call from Daniela at the Poitiers railway station, inquiring where to find us. About half an hour later, she arrived by taxi with over 20 kg of rucksack on her back. Daniela, a just turned 40, Doctor of Psychology, is attractive, vibrant and immediately likeable. She got to the restaurant just in time for dessert and then humped that rucksack the long walk back to the campsite. Daniela is petite but she carried the heaviest load on her bike of any of us by a factor of about 6 kg and had no difficulty staying close to the front of the group.

After a four year gap and immediately following several nights of hotel luxury, the first night of camping was an uncomfortable reintroduction. I forgot to bring a pillow and my sleeping bag was definitely under strength for the night-time cold. My normally dependable bladder shrivelled, requiring four trips to the lavatory.

Each of these involved a lot more preparation than you might first imagine. Before emerging from the tent you need to be clothed, you need a torch to avoid tripping over others' tent ropes and you need some easy-on shoes (kayak water shoes work well). I developed a little ritual that can be done in a semi-awake state without forgetting anything crucial such as a supply of paper products.

To avoid dirtying the inside of the tent or waking my neighbours, I unzip the tent flap the minimum necessary to stick my legs through the flap and grab the easy-on shoes stored outside the tent. Then, half inside, half outside the tent, I sit in a jack knife position, put the shoes on and crawl out. Of course, the whole procedure has to be reversed getting back into the tent. Such a routine almost guarantees difficulty in getting back to sleep. Later in the trip, Yassmin taught me to fill my metal water bottle with hot water from the camp laundry to warm the sleeping bag, reducing the frequency of such trips.

Pride dictated that I not be the last person ready to leave camp in the morning. This produced stress, inhibiting sleep and ensured getting up way too early. Packing needed to be properly sequenced as a fuzzy, barely functioning head can easily do things in the wrong order such as closing up the panniers before getting out the clothes for the day. The first morning I forgot that the sleeping bag should simply be stuffed into its sack rather than rolled up first—a mistake that cost me about 15 minutes of fruitless effort. Once all the bits were loaded on the bike, the tent could come down. It and its stakes had to fit into a small bag without much excess room so refolding was often necessary. Condensed moisture, sometimes in icicle form, grass and/or pine needles often made this a messy task--or one that had to be redone entirely when I'd left something crucial inside the tent--like my money belt. Somehow, Geoff was always the last person to crawl out but one of the first to be ready to go.

Now, at 8 am on 15 September, the tour started in earnest as we rode off on our daily search for a pâtisserie and a bar. This morning, the buns came from a small grocery that made its own croissants. Together, we probably bought two dozen, cleaning out their entire stock. Then at the bar with our coffee, most of us took turns recording Geoff's route for the day onto our own maps with a highlighter.

Spencer, who had no maps, couldn't be bothered. He chose instead to find out only the name of the day's intended destination and lunch stop. Spencer tended not to socialize with the ancients and generally rode alone. Daniela did not have any maps either which surprised me as she is an excellent map-reader. She simply recorded the principal route numbers and destinations on scrap bits of paper. The lack of detailed pre-tour information caused me to bring maps that only partially covered our route so I chose to stick close to the group, particularly Jennie and Evelyn, trusting in their maps and skills.

Shortly after starting, while riding east through a patch of forest, we met a man wearing a fluorescent orange safety jacket and carrying a rifle. Just a few metres on, several more similarly dressed men were milling around their vehicles or heading off into the woods with their dogs while blowing on a trumpet. Geoff disdainfully described them as peasants pretending to be on a proper fox hunt.

At lunch, Spencer told us that he managed to save US$ 50,000 on last year's tour in Iraq. The pay is very good, is tax-free and there are virtually no expenses. At times, Spencer sounded very much like a military recruiter. When I pointed this out to him, he said 'why don't you join up?' 'The US government generously allows non-citizens to volunteer for a tour in Iraq!'

This first lunch proved to be the pattern for the whole tour. It was massive. The feast began with a selection of salads and pate followed by confit de canard, vegetables, cheese and a sweet. The wine was dispensed like soft drinks in a North American fast food restaurant-- from an on-demand, serve-yourself refill station. We did not finish until just before three p.m. I pleased myself by ordering my favourite flavour of sorbet without even having to think of the proper French!

We travelled almost due east through gently rolling countryside to a magnificent view of a broad river below a flower-laden bridge at the edge of Angles sur l'Anglin. An abandoned mill wheel sat on the riverbank and the remains of a ninth century fort rose above it. I explored an eleventh century chapel in the fort grounds that housed an exhibition of local art. One of the chapel walls is home to a permanent exhibition of a Lascaux cave-age like drawing of a red horse.

Yesterday, at the Poitiers campsite, there was a perfect example of why Geoff chooses to provide so little tour detail. At about five p.m., Geoff received a telephone call from Lauren, a young Australian woman who was supposed to be on the same flight from England as the others. Her train to Stansted Airport had been cancelled due to a suicide on the line—so she missed the flight and would be 24 hours late in arriving at Poitiers. Plan B had to be crafted even before Plan A got underway! This new plan involved arranging for the Poitiers campsite to store Lauren's bike and gear so that she could collect them the following day and choosing an alternative campsite for our second night close enough for Lauren to taxi to us.

Geoff's choice was at Le Blanc, about 50 kilometres from Poitiers. Once there, I set up my tent in 15 minutes and then attempted to cope with the showers. Camp shower facilities were typically two-part spaces, the front part providing a couple of hooks for your clothes while the back portion was the shower area. The French are either stingy or strong conservationists. Like the time-controlled hall lights in hostels and hotels, the shower water flow was limited to about 30 seconds in all but one or two campsites. Pushing a button restored the flow for another 30 seconds. Sometimes the water temperature felt little different from the outside air and I was happy to minimize my water consumption but when it was warm, standing with my back to the shower and bumping the button repeatedly with my elbow maintained a continuous flow. Curtains were generally non-existent or too short to prevent the water splashing out into the front section. So getting dressed required special care. You could dry off entirely but for your feet that were in puddles. Standing stork-like to dry one elevated foot, I inserted that foot into a trouser leg while holding the other trouser leg high--repeating the process three more times to deal with the second trouser leg and socks and shoes.

As anyone would be under the circumstances, Lauren was very pleased finally to join the group. She was a sturdy young physiotherapist from Perth with plans to do an Iron Man triathlon in the next year or so. Although nearly the same age as Spencer, she did not share, so far as I know, his view that one is over the hill at 27. What her views were on anything was difficult to establish at first, as her responses were largely limited to repeated 'Ryaight, Ryaight' in a strong Australian accent.

Since we had a short first day to accommodate Lauren, the distance shortfall had to be made up the next day. Geoff assured us it was reasonably flat, so 80 or so kilometres would not be difficult. Describing that terrain as flat is accurate only in a relative sense— perhaps to the foothills of the Alps or by smoothing out the ups and downs. We stopped for another long, wine saturated lunch after 42 km and don't leave until after two. Another 46 km further, most of the group stopped for a beer. However, three of us (including me) missed an earlier turn and had to do an extra 6 km to catch up. I joined the beer drinkers and then bought a few munchies to serve as dinner, as Yassmin wasn't interested in cooking tonight and I was still trying save enough to fill the three wine bottle hole in my budget.

In the final run that afternoon towards the campsite at Montgivray (north of La Chatre), we passed a chateau at which point Geoff called out 'Here is today's culture.' I interpreted the comment to be directed at me but was too knackered to bother stopping. My personal total for the day was 100 km.

Later, at the campsite and returning to my tent from the lavatory, I passed Spencer on his way there and told him that there was no toilet paper. He responded, 'My Daddy, used to say, be a man—use your hand.' Knowing this was meant to shock, I did not react.

At an intersection about noon the next day, I was separated from both the front and rear groups and without a map was routeless as well as clueless. Assuming, but not certain, that the rear group would be picnicking; I decided not to wait, consulted my compass and headed east. About 4 km later, Gillian, glass of wine in hand, waved to me from outside a small café. What a relief! Half the group was inside and within 15 minutes the other half arrived!

We camped that night in a lovely riverside spot at Huriel. Tall hedges produced campsite cubicles and a measure of privacy. Geoff later explained that the presence of such hedges adds to campsite star ratings. This was a three star site that offered a washing machine but no toilet paper. Just like the ranking systems for hotels, the system for campsites has serious design flaws. I looked after a load of laundry for Yassmin and myself while she organized our dinner.

Washing clothes is a necessary regular routine as the size of panniers Geoff provides significantly limits carrying capacity. He advocates an involved routine for washing and drying gear that involves bringing only three of anything you wear next to your skin. His method results in one clean dry set to wear, a dirty set and one drying set. For Geoff, drying often involved wearing some of the damp gear to sleep in. Few seemed to follow this particular step so as the tour wore on and we became less inhibited, most of the bikes sported that drying set on the back rack including some bras and knickers flying in the breeze.

Our campsite meals were casually complex concoctions. The women generally did the shopping and cooking while the men washed up. Most of the group were in loose cooking units of two or three for the main course but we all shared appetizers, bread, wine, cheese and sweets. The cooking gear was very basic: a small burner, a couple of handleless pots and a detachable pot handle for each pair. Despite these limitations, I was amazed at what these women achieved. Yassmin is particularly well skilled and equipped. She brought a load of Middle Eastern spices neatly packaged in little laboratory water specimen bottles. Her husband, a marine biologist, supplies the bottles for which she made very neat typed labels. Yassmin also thought to bring washing up liquid, a scrubber and a tea towel— equipment that never occurred to me despite my cleaning up responsibilities!

This particular night, we stayed round the camp table until quite late telling stories and drinking wine. The next morning, I counted six dead wine bottles on the table—only ten of us had been drinking. Following my angioplasty last year, I was advised to take no more than one 30 ml glass per day. My resolve to maintain that discipline quickly eroded on this trip to the point where I probably quadrupled my allowance.

It seems as if we spent virtually the entire next day climbing, sometimes at a very slow pace requiring my lowest gear, but never so bad that I had to get off and walk. We were rewarded for this hard work with an exhilarating seven-kilometre downhill to our next campsite at Chateauneuf des Bains.

The final approach to the campsite passed a couple of village cafes, one of which attracted Daniela and me to stop for coffee and gave us the first real opportunity to get to know each other. The camaraderie established in that coffee break strengthened through the rest of the trip and continues. Daniela is a vegetarian, a state not well served or respected in France. It was often difficult to find a vegetarian option at lunchtime and even when one was available; it created a bit of a stir to have that choice honoured. Today, the restaurant proprietor teased repeatedly, taking every opportunity to offer her beef before finally, after every one else was served, bringing her some salmon.

Tonight's site, also by a river, was a very well hedged place, managed by a particularly helpful woman. Geoff decided that we would take a rest day and spend two nights here so there was no rush next morning to pack up. Despite this, I was, as usual, one of the first up. Needing a new toothbrush, I walked over to the little camp shop in hopes they might stock them. The manager was just setting out a big jug of hot coffee for all of us. Not having to pack up for departure, I enjoyed a quiet interlude, warmed by the fresh coffee, with my book in the crisp sunshine.

Over the past few days my thoughts have alternated between considering this tour to be a marvellous experience and still feeling a bit awkward with the others and uncomfortable with the camping privations. This morning was definitely on the marvellous side.

Later, Allan, Barry and I went into the village pâtisserie and thoroughly confused the little, old redheaded serving woman. It certainly wasn't intentional but the effect of three foreigners all at once without an intelligible French word between them must have been overwhelming.

Since we stayed put, our day was relatively unstructured, but it split along gender lines. After breakfast, the women chose to try the nearby thermal baths while the men strolled together to a religious monument a top a small hill where we met the women returning from their trip to the baths. Group cohesion disintegrated further in the afternoon as people decided to read, do laundry, nap or cycle. I tried each of these, starting with a cycle ride along both sides of the river. An old, but still operating, elegant little bakery hugs the riverbank close to a bridge where I stood for some time watching a fisherman pull trout from the water.

The following morning, we returned to routine, leaving the campsite, fully loaded, by nine. It was quite cool, less than 6 degrees Celsius with a heavy fog. Daniela's brain, working so hard to converse in English, must have got stuck in England, as she headed off cycling on the left side of the road and did not realize the error until at least three cars passed coming straight towards her.

We had a long hard climb out of the valley that continued until lunchtime. By midmorning, the fog had burned off, the day became warm and one by one we paused roadside to shed clothes. This aspect of cycle touring is another example of how one needs to plan, dressing in layers that can be shed progressively without embarrassment.

The morning provided gorgeous views of the river snaking its way below us through deep pine covered gorges while our final 15 km was a narrow, much flatter road that ran beside small farmyards populated with geese and ducks and along lovely pastures. We camped at Merinchal in a small open park near a former stately home that now serves as a conference centre.

While travelling on my own several days ago, I had thoroughly enjoyed a crepe marron. Today, at breakfast, Daniela was spreading marron on her baguette from a jar. It is no wonder that she rides with 6 kg more than anyone else. That extra weight is in part due to her North Pole quality sleeping bag but the rest must be her breakfast gear. She carries coffee, granola, a cereal bowl, the marron, and a variety of other foodstuffs catering to her vegetarian tastes.

Anyway, she let me try some of her marron, which was good but so sugary that I decided to return to the campsite after breakfast to clean my teeth. This delay separated me from the group and after circling the village two or three times trying to find the route out, the group was nowhere in sight. When I gave up and asked directions, the turnoff was just 50 metres away!

Consequently, the day was mainly spent on my own. That could have been upsetting, but it was lovely, rolling countryside, the sunshine was bright and warm and I must have been ready for a bit of solitude. Arriving by five at our campsite in Aubusson to find the group already there and preparing to leave for dinner at six. This gave me less than an hour to erect my tent, shower and get ready. No one seemed concerned that I had been out of the group all day—no search party had been organized—I did not know whether to be upset by their indifference or pleased that they thought me competent enough to find my own way!

Shower and toilet facilities were arranged quite differently here. The path from the tent sites led directly to the women's shower section. A totally open general dressing area with washbasins occupied the area in front of their shower stalls. As I approached, just before the path turned left to the men's area, a number of now dressed women was applying makeup or cleaning their teeth. At that instant, Gil emerged from a shower stall dressed only in her minimalist smalls. Hopefully, my progress betrayed no undue hesitation and I certainly did not call out any greetings!

The adjacent men's shower area had a different design, consisting of individual stall doors flush with the external walls and no general dressing area. As there was no way to determine whether the stalls were occupied, I yanked open the nearest door, exposing Geoff's bare flanks to the world. Muttering an apology, I quickly closed the door and scurried away. Ah, the camaraderie of camping! These events were never mentioned later.

Only one of all the maps I brought has been useful. On our second Monday, my one good map no longer covered our route. I was riding

304

with Barry who brought no maps at all. So, we relied on staying close to Gil. Unfortunately, just before lunch, while he was in front of her and I was behind, she turned up a side street at the edge of town. Thinking it was a comfort stop, I do not follow but just carried on at a slower pace thinking she would catch up. She never did. It was a culture not a comfort stop.

That changed the rest of the day for Barry and me. We circled through the town twice but could not find any one of our group. All I could remember was the name of the town where we were to camp-- Montmorillon. A road sign, pointing towards Montmorillon, made me confident, knowing at least one way to get there. Barry definitely did not share my confidence. He wanted to call Geoff on his mobile right away but I persuaded him that it would not achieve anything.

The road was dull, but flat and fast, at least for me. Barry protested the pace so I eased off. By about one p.m. we stopped at a small grocery in a village as we were hungry. The grocer gave us directions to a pleasant little park where we ate our lunch on a bench while Barry told me about his son, David, then the current lead in the London production of 'Wicked.'

Despite our fairly leisurely lunch, our pace had been so fast that we arrived in Montmorillon by 2.30. It was far too early to go to the campsite, so I went into a large newspaper shop, found the maps I needed, bought a newspaper and another disposable camera. It seemed fitting now that the trip is nearly over, to find out where we have been and to be able to record those details from someone else's maps thus creating a backdated souvenir.

After my purchases, Barry and I had a coffee in the small square near that shop. He was visibly more relaxed now that we had arrived. Then we made our way to the campsite, arriving about 3.30 when (as a matter of courtesy) he did ring Geoff. I did a hand laundry and, with the help of an English woman, found a clothes line and sufficient pegs to hang it out. Despite her helpfulness, it was a bit irritating that she thought Canada consisted of nothing more than snow and pine trees. Given her general friendliness, it was more likely basic ignorance rather than an intentional slur.

Lauren's twenty-fifth birthday was near the end of the tour so the group decided to celebrate with a restaurant meal that evening. Our only choice was a pizzeria café. Even that would have been closed if several of us had not stopped there for an afternoon beer or coffee on the way to the campsite. The café owners, two Englishwomen, sympathetically agreed to stay open and to bake a special cake for the event. We were in a cheerful mood. Lauren basked in everyone's good wishes and was particularly moved by the unexpected surprise of a cake.

As usual, I selected my meal and drink with as much attention to cost as to taste and so was upset that the group chose not to have individual bills. Once more, I was sharing the cost of others' heavy drinking as well as a portion of Lauren's meal. It would have been churlish to complain so I just smouldered away quietly.

Our final day began very cold after a frigid night. I needed three trips to the toilet and two refills of my 'hot water' bottle. It was so miserably uncomfortable packing up that I really felt ready to end the trip then and there but once loaded and underway to breakfast, my mood changed completely. Bright sunshine, the beautiful river and bridge we crossed, the pride of overcoming privations and being part of an adventure made everything seem marvellous again!

Late that morning, Daniela, Spencer and I became sufficiently detached from the group that we missed a turning and a fourth century cemetery featuring several stone coffins lying above ground, lidless and empty. This provided a photo opportunity for some of the shorter members of the group to 'try on' the coffins. None of us could miss the gigantic nuclear plant cooling towers looming on the horizon. They looked rather benign but felt ominous if you thought about Chernobyl or Three Mile Island.

Missing the cemetery further dented my reputation as a person interested in culture. The final blow was delivered when I chose to ride on to the Poitiers campsite with Daniela rather than visit a cathedral after lunch. It was a chivalrous decision for me and if I'm truly honest, motivated by superior architecture.

We got back to the beginning Poitiers campsite about 5.30 and began the final night's routine. Geoff had left the keys to his van with the manager so early arrivers were able to get their suitcases and start organizing for tomorrow's separate departures.

First, we had to have a final evening meal together at a restaurant. Geoff totted up all the bills for our campsites, announcing an amount that would cover everything including one final drink tonight. Since he had been estimating that the cost would be much higher, I was definitely relieved. This lower amount, coupled with a 'bonus' drink, produced a psychologically positive conclusion to the tour. Although it was unintentional, the overestimate was good business. Several of the more cost conscious of us were also worried about the taxi ride into the centre and/or airport tomorrow. Then the camp manager told us we could get as far as the railway station by bus. Buses came at frequent intervals and the bus stop was only 200 metres away.

Despite Geoff's hopes of finding somewhere special for dinner, a cut above, we settled for the same spot as our very first night. People were hungry, tired and just not prepared to continue searching. We even got the same table as before.

I don't remember much about the evening other than declining wine to avoid facing another three-bottle debacle. Everyone had to have a picture of the dining group until the initial bright smiles became weary and thin. Gears had shifted to returning home, being welcomed by family and friends and for many, going back to work.

Departure Day

In the morning, we made our usual trip to a pâtisserie, collected our buns and found a bar for coffee. My pastry choices this morning, a croissant amande and something similar to a sweet pain raisin called a Suisse, were especially good. Back at the campsite, we dismantled and packed our tents, loaded all Geoff's gear into his van and helped him put the bikes on the trailer. More pictures were taken and farewells repeated until time to walk down to the bus stop.

Nine of us chose to take the same bus, creating quite a commotion. The other passengers' initial amusement changed to irritation at the delay as we made our way to the rear of the bus slowed by lugging heavy gear. We were unusually silent on the ride into the centre; I stood, trying to stay upright and keep out of the way of the cases piled round me so I couldn't pay attention to the passing scene. Suddenly, one of our group called out 'here's the railway station.' Grabbing my bag, scrambling out the rear door and waving clumsy final goodbyes with Daniela right on my heels, as we were both travelling on by rail. Her train was scheduled for 1.30 but mine wasn't until tomorrow so I wanted to get rid of my large bag.

There wasn't any railway left-luggage facility. We crossed the road to the two-star Regina Hotel. Before entering, I did not think how the situation might look to the receptionist until she twice asked me if the room was 'pour une personne?'   Daniela remained just inside the door, indicating some level of unease with her body language but she said nothing.

During a coffee and a light lunch at a table outside the station in the bright sunshine we talked about her work as a psychologist, life in Germany and similar topics.   After seeing her off, I wandered aimlessly round Poitiers through some shopping districts, nursed a beer at a main square cafe and watched people. Earlier, perhaps in an attempt to redeem my cultural reputation, at least with myself, I visited a free sculpture exhibition of wooden nudes.

Then, I began a search for an appealing and affordable restaurant. This took an inordinate amount of time, as those two qualities didn't manifest themselves together in a single restaurant. Once finally settling on one, I tried to fix its location and surroundings in my mind and returned to the Regina to clean up.

The dinner was fine, although like my previous experience with the Chinese restaurant, there was a strong sense that my appearance did not measure up to their regular clientele. It was dark when I left the restaurant and my earlier noted landmarks weren't recognizable or visible. Swarms of young people were out boisterously enjoying their Friday evening but making me feel a little uncomfortable. Walking briskly, feigning confidence and purpose, along the streets in what was the general direction of the hotel. Spotting a harmless-looking group of mature people with children I still played it safe by asking for directions to the railway station rather than the hotel. Fittingly, now at the end, my question was understood and I understood the answer—that is progress!

My train the next day took me directly into Charles de Gaulle airport —back to the same lounge where this trip began over three weeks ago. Like then, facing a long wait, as my flight did not leave until 11.30 tomorrow but I've decided to use the airport lounge as my overnight accommodation to avoid the hassle of getting into and out of the city. After the first hour or so, it became incredibly boring. I read, dozed, visited the bookshop repeatedly, pushed my luggage trolley round and round the cavernous airport for exercise but was still bored. Sleep was never a viable possibility as no seated position was comfortable for more than a few minutes and my trolley had to be guarded from the few wandering unsavoury types. I amused myself watching other overnight dwellers attempting repeatedly, without success, to find a sustainable sleeping position. One man used his suitcases as a mattress achieving a simultaneous solution to the sleeping and security problem. It wasn't very effective though as when he relaxed, a leg, arm or his head fell off his perch, waking him. Modifying his technique, I sat on a chair, propping my legs on top of my duffle bag on the trolley to create a comfortable hassock arrangement. It wasn't perfect as the plastic seat back was rigid and my head rolled to the side or fell forward, jolting me awake. Nevertheless, it solved the security problem and permitted perhaps a quarter of an hour snooze at a time.

Sleep would have kept hunger at bay. The lack of sleep intensified the desire to eat brought on by boredom. With a sudden surge of will power, I resisted, limiting my purchases to the remaining supply of coins, thus preserving a small stash of notes for my next tour.

So, as this tour ends, I've covered over 1000 km, had a good mix of solo and group riding, hotel and campsite living with an interesting range of experiences and people. The camping was very uncomfortable and inconvenient at times but braving the elements and sharing the deprivations with others made it more endurable and towards the end I developed a warm sense of satisfaction with my fortitude and new skills.

BRITAIN & BRITTANY TOUR

BRITAIN

FRANCE

BRITAIN & BRITTANY TOUR

This 2009 tour combined familiar and new components that produced a quite different experience. Some objectives went unrealized, unexpected difficulties arose, and old comforts could not be enjoyed to their full extent. Instead, there were offsetting compensations.

I very much wanted to participate in Breton Bike's twentieth anniversary trip around Brittany's Rose Granite Coast with the several members of last year's group that planned to be there. Also on the agenda was The Isle of Wight, which houses many examples of England's varied landscapes in a relatively small space. And, it was convenient for the Portsmouth ferry to Brittany, so with a flight to Gatwick, these two 'anchors' shaped a rough skeleton of the pre-Breton Bikes portion of the tour. Evensong at Canterbury Cathedral and visits to the 1066 battlefield near Hastings, fleshed it out.

My friend, David Chan, on sabbatical leave from his university post in 2009, had asked to join my next tour. Given the rigours of hostelling and camping, I didn't think he would be really interested in my plan but he accepted enthusiastically, even to the point of giving me carte blanche to make all the decisions and arrangements.

David's acceptance increased my interest in the tour but also raised the bar for planning it well. Now, I felt it necessary to prepare, not only the cycling route and directions for each day, but to merge them on to colour maps that would fit into a handlebar map case and to be more discerning in the choice of any necessary B&Bs. I consulted train and ferry schedules and fares, found and booked hostels or B&Bs at achievable distance intervals and researched points of interest along the way.

None of this was a burden; it provided welcome, interesting activity for the winter months. Then, one frosty February day, David sent me an e-mail announcing that he had ordered a custom touring bike that I had coveted ever since seeing a pale green tourer at True North's workshop in Guelph, Ontario. Fitted with a Brooks leather saddle, top of the line racks and stainless steel couplers, it was built for a woman heading for a cycle camping excursion to Vietnam. The couplers allow the bike to be taken apart and packed into a special nylon case that just meets airlines' size limit for a suitcase.

My customary cost-benefit analytical approach clearly proved that there weren't enough trips left in my lifetime for the airlines' excess baggage charges to offset the cost of such a cycle. Nevertheless, I dithered; researching similar bikes from a variety of suppliers and considering having my existing bike severed and fitted with the couplings. Other suppliers' offerings would be 'off the peg', so to speak, they would not be customized to my personal measurements. Hugh Black at True North knew my existing bike and judged that its tubing wouldn't take the strain of fitting couplings. I'd covered all the elements of a rational decision process--a customized bike couldn't be justified--but desire and extreme jealously won the day. By May, Hugh had my order.

I collected the bike in late July, shortly before Mari and I left on a three-week motoring holiday in Newfoundland so the bike was a virtual strangers when David and I boarded our 30 August flight to Gatwick. Travelling with an unfamiliar bike and with a companion, feeling personally responsible for every difficulty or error in the route or quality of accommodations altered the 'feel' of this tour significantly. But, David could not have been a better partner. He was making good use of his sabbatical and had packed and unpacked his new bike on at least five trips before this. So, he was experienced and able to help a lot. David also is an interesting conversationalist and enthusiastic about everything except history. However, from the standpoint of my ego, he had two defects: good navigational skills and strong cycling fitness.

Getting There

Our discount airline, Air Transat, had strict weight limits for both checked and cabin baggage, but allowed cycles to go for $30, regardless of weight. David and I tucked tools and some clothing into the corners of our bike cases to bring down the weight of the other luggage as Transat would not permit any offsets between categories. We sweated the outcome of the weighing in but need not have bothered. The check-in process was fairly casual—the bike and other checked luggage were weighed together.

A beautiful warm day greeted our arrival at Gatwick—20 degrees Celsius at 9.30 in the morning! We travelled in style in a big, black Mercedes estate to my usual B&B in nearby Horley. Fiona had again agreed to store the cycle cases while we were away on the understanding that we would return for a two-night stay.

Once at the B&B, we started the reassembly process on the large forecourt, grateful for the warm, dry day. It was a nearly three-hour struggle. The panniers' capacity seemed to have shrunk during flight and our sleep-starved brains had difficulty deciding what we could did not really need and could leave behind inside our cases. The housekeeper needed to get them locked up before she left at one. It was two p.m. before we finished.

We were starving but it was too late for a proper pub lunch. The Waitrose supermarket café would have to do. As we were parking the bikes there, David could not find his bike lock and assumed it had been left in his bike case, now securely locked away in the B&B and inaccessible for hours! After lunch he discovered the lock in another section of the pannier--such was the quality of our thinking at that point.

On Our Way

Finishing lunch at three, we faced a ride of 40 km to Tonbridge Railway Station for one of the hourly trains to Canterbury. Plan B was to save 10 km going to Royal Tunbridge Wells station instead. The first part of both plans was along the same route with the decision point very close to Royal Tunbridge Wells. Fatigue and heavy traffic made us choose Plan B only to find that no trains were running due to engineering work--originally scheduled for the day before but delayed just for us.

Now, there was no choice but to go on to Tonbridge. David fearlessly headed south, making perhaps his only navigational error of the whole tour. After about two kilometres, I consulted my compass and turned us north. We had now gone about 38 hours without real sleep and were becoming a bit testy with each other. When we found Tonbridge station, David went to hunt down something for us to snack on while I bought the tickets.

The train was comfortable, clean and quiet. Twilight faded the peaceful countryside racing past our window raising fears that we would have problems finding the Canterbury hostel in the dark.

Starting a persisting pattern, I blamed myself for overlooking how quickly it becomes dark in September at this latitude. Nor had I allowed for the difficulty assembling the bikes and the change in trains which had cost us a couple extra hours.

So it was truly dark when we emerged from Canterbury station about 8.20. A helpful railway staff person provided a map and directions to the hostel. David automatically pulled a miner's headlamp out of his pannier and turned on his flashing rear LED lamp demonstrating his experience of winter cycling to and from work. I was totally unprepared for night riding and felt my leadership role slipping away.

Nevertheless, I led the way for a very brief ride in traffic before turning into a long, well lit pedestrian mall area that flowed into the largely residential street on which the hostel was located. Even so, we still stopped twice to ask directions. The last people we asked were out for a stroll from the hostel.

It was far too late for the evening meal but the receptionist offered to make us some tea and beans on toast while we settled in. So, we locked our bikes away in the cycle shed, collected our panniers, bed sheets, duvet covers and pillowcases and climbed the stairs to our room. As this was David's first hostel experience, he was relieved to find that we were the only occupants of an eight-bed room.

Our humble but most welcome meal was served in the cosy members' kitchen. I went to bed still somewhat hungry but pleased that two-thirds of the day's food budget was still available for future tea and teacakes treats.

After breakfast next morning, we each had different agendas but agreed to meet at the hostel in time to attend Evensong at Canterbury Cathedral. A poster on the hostel's information board provided the times for all the services. I set off to find the Cathedral and explore the city. David returned to bed.

As usual, my city explorations took me to a bookshop and after a suitable interval to a teashop. I wandered the streets, found the Cathedral, checked on alternatives for dinner, strolled along the canal and uncharacteristically, took a riverboat historical tour; my spirits were good, it was another warm, dry day.

The tour guide was amusing, irreverent and informative. It was a small boat that could hold perhaps eight passengers. Its gentle motion was pleasantly soporific as he poled us along in the warm sunshine. But the experience was fleeting. Now, I remember none of the history that he related. Perhaps it is just as well, I suspect much of it was invented to impress the tourist trade.

David returned to the hostel having spent much of his waking time shopping.   At Wilkinson's, an upmarket British dollar store equivalent, he found an LED reading light and at a mobile phone shop, he acquired a phone and both British and international SIM cards.

At the Cathedral, we found the most likely entrance to the sanctuary closed. While walking round the back through the cloisters, we came across a young priest striding along.   He had just come from Evensong—it was over.   What a disappointment!   Attending Evensong in a lovely cathedral always produces a strong sense of serenity and is one of my favourite experiences. It was my mistake—I had read the timetable for Sunday instead of for weekdays. There would be no other opportunities on this tour as we would not be in any other English cathedral cities.

We consoled ourselves with an excellent meal at 'Weavers Huguenot' the riverside pub from which the boat ride left earlier. I persuaded David that the golden treacle sponge sweet special was a British tradition that should not be missed, but it was sold out. I considered this meal a success when David declared that the 'English reputation for poor cooking isn't valid.'

In the morning, we loaded up the bikes, checked our maps for the best exit to our route west and set out. My bike would not cooperate. Steering was very tight and a black greasy substance emerged from the headset. It was perplexing, as we had ridden close to 50 km two days ago without apparent difficulty.

I had no idea of what to do, all my experience was with the older quill stem form that is held in place by an expander nut and bolt. We went immediately to a nearby cycle shop that we had passed last night. As luck would have it, their mechanic was off for the day but they directed us to another cycle shop just a few blocks away. True to Murphy's law, this second shop's mechanic was also away. David thought it was a simple matter of adding grease to all the headset bits and pieces. Borrowing some tools and grease, David taught me the importance of proper sequence in reassembling and tightening my thread-less headset components. The repair seemed effective and we were underway again about 11 having lost two hours.

Our agenda included a number of stops en route south west to Portsmouth; for me the most significant was the town of Battle near Hastings. My schoolboy history memory retained the signing of the Magna Carta in 1215, the Battle of Hastings in 1066 and the Jacobite Uprising of 1745 primarily as dates. When history is taught as a chronological list of dates, those dates that stick tend to do so with no particular importance or understanding.

That was the case for me. I knew the 1066 battle took place, knew it was important but not why. This tour was to fill that gap. British history and the English language have been heavily influenced by successive invasions: Romans, Anglo-Saxons, Vikings, and, in this case, the Normans (which had Viking ancestry). The Dutch successfully invaded Devon in 1688, which led to William of Orange replacing James II as King. The Germans invaded and occupied the Channel Islands during WWII but this was very limited in scope and brief. There was also an unsuccessful invasion by the French in 1797. They meant to seize Bristol but were driven north by the wind and landed near Fishguard, in Wales. These invaders mistook a group of red-cloaked women onlookers for redcoats and surrendered!(1) Traces of these early invasions remain in place names, in some architecture and infrastructure and in the language itself. It seemed important to know something more about the Norman legacy given that it had the most lasting effects.

This Norman invasion came on the heels of the last attempt by Vikings. Both invaders saw the death of Edward the Confessor in January 1066 as an opportunity. Harold Godwinson, who has the distinction of being the first English king to be born and die in England, succeeded Edward.

Harold represented residual Danish influence that remained after the death of Knúter the Great in 1035. Knúter had been King of Denmark and England. I have not been able to determine how Edward the Confessor became King or what justified Harold's claim.

Guillaume le Bâtard (William the Bastard, later the Conqueror) disputed Harold's claim to the throne because Guillaume was Edward's cousin while Harold had no blood ties. In addition, it is believed that Harold had taken an oath supporting Guillaume's claim years before while a 'reluctant guest' at Guillaume's pleasure following Harold's ship being wrecked on the Norman coast.

The Vikings attacked England in Yorkshire in September 1066 but were soundly defeated on the twenty-sixth at Stamford Bridge by an army, commanded by Harold, that had marched from southern England on the fifteenth. About a week later, Harold learned of the Norman invasion at Pevensey, just west of the coastal town of Hastings, and began a forced march back south.

Despite battle fatigue, Harold's army covered the 250 miles in 12 days to engage the Normans at Senlac Hill on 14 October. The defence was effective, until the Normans faked a retreat, which the English pursued, weakening their defensive position. The Normans took advantage of this, killed Harold with an arrow and won the battle, changing the course of British history.

William honoured his promise to build an abbey on the battlefield if he won the battle. Although not an ideal site, St Martins Abbey was built on the hill where Harold died and consecrated in 1094, seven years after William's death.(2)

All this history is displayed at Battle in a national park established in 1976 with a significant donation from US citizens in their bicentennial year. Like Evensong, visiting this site was a major objective for me. David's enthusiasms slight the past in favour of the future so he chose to ride on to the hostel at Alfriston while I absorbed my cultural fix.

William's line continued as the English monarchy through Henry VI's reign, over 400 years later. French became the official language of court. Henry VI was also King of France. Both countries formed the foundations of Canada, a connection that provides my historical and academic justification for cycling in both countries--that is, good excuses for doing what I want to do.

Arriving at the hostel, I found David in the parking area talking to another cyclist who had a brand new coupled bike built by the British firm, Roberts. This was interesting because I had contacted Roberts about buying such a bike from them but never got any response.

Next morning, in what was to be the first of several similar encounters, we met a group of mature cyclists just arriving at the hostel. They had crossed from France on an overnight ferry and cycled to the hostel for a long weekend. In just four days' time David and I would be reversing their journey.

Crossing to the Isle of Wight
The island, at 37 km by 21 km, is smaller than Greater London. Having been adopted by the Victorians as a holiday location, it continues to thrive on tourism. The appeal was and remains the relatively high level of sunshine and the scenic attraction of high chalk downs and clefts or chines along the south coast.

Many fine examples of Victorian architecture, built then, are a bonus. My interest was piqued by the idea that the Isle of Wight embodies most of the elements of English landscape and is home to the famous yachting races at Cowes. I also wanted to see The Needles, the tall, narrow chalk stacks at the south-western tip of the island.

By chance, we arrived at the ferry location just before the next departure. There were no savings available by buying a return fare, so we bought a single fare for greater flexibility of a return time. In all my previous experience with ferries, one simply rode or walked the bike onto the boat. So, I was unprepared for the procedure with a hovercraft. Since departure was imminent, we had immediately to unpack our bikes so that the staff could load them. Then, juggling panniers, water bottles, helmets, and sleeping bags, with tickets clenched in our teeth, we bumped our way through ticket collection. Outside in the loading area, I saw David's bike being laid on its side in a luggage compartment but could not see mine and shuddered to think that it might be underneath David's or overlooked.

There was no time to check the status of my bike—the boat's engines fired up, the boarding pace was rapid and we were off. I took comfort in the thought that if my bike had been missed, it was only half an hour before the next ferry. After the safety announcements we got into conversation with a Scotsman who had moved to IOW for the sunshine--that sounded promising until we realized that IOW and Newfoundland are at roughly the same latitude.

Within ten minutes we were in Ryde. My cycle was wheeled out from its storage area on the other side of the boat but again everything was all hustle and bustle for the next departure. Reloading the bikes there would block boarding passengers. So we again struggled out, arms laden with gear, trying to push the bikes out of the gate. A great experience it was not—too hurried and harrying. The staff was very courteous but perhaps too efficient.

Our B&B, 'Fern Cottage' was high above the seafront and required several direction seeking stops. Once found, it was a very convenient location for visiting the town on foot, which we did after a welcoming cup of tea with biscuits and a shower. Our room was described as having en suite facilities but one had to exit the room, pass through a tiny hall way and squeeze through another door to access them. The dollhouse-sized washroom basin could not have been smaller and still contain a drain. It was hard up against the toilet and the paper roll was tucked into a space carved out of the wall cavity. David showered first and warned me to be extremely careful getting in and out as the tub was so narrow that its floor space provided hardly any room to get a foothold.

Over the past several days I had been working on David to try an 'Indian', i.e. a meal in an Indian restaurant. Finally successful, we asked our landlady to recommend a good one in town. After a few wrong turnings, we found it and were convinced by the restaurant being nearly full and their special Sunday night offer of a four-course meal for £9.95.

The only table available was next to a very large unkempt man who made no eye contact or conversation. After a smoke-break outside, he returned, grabbed his huge rucksack and left, refusing to pay. We felt sorry for the waiters who were obviously very distressed but chose not to make a scene. Our meal was excellent; David became an immediate enthusiast for Indian food and especially for the oversized Kingfisher beer that accompanied it.

Afterwards, we strolled contentedly round the well-lit streets, discovered another Indian restaurant in the process, admired architecture, and felt mellow enough to start sharing personal confidences. I think we also got lost temporarily as it took about three times as long to return to the B&B as it had to go to the restaurant.

Our next objective was to see The Needles near Totland Bay where our new B&B is located, visiting Cowes, the famous yachting centre, on the way. Again, the history behind Cowes didn't interest David, so we went directly south west towards Newport.

About noon, somewhere between Newport and Totland Bay, we came across what was billed as the oldest mill on the Isle of Wight. Neither one of us wanted to spend the time to tour the mill but we were definitely interested in patronizing the café. The lady ticket seller, overcome with such manly athletes, allowed us to come in without buying a ticket. We both enjoyed the day's special of tomato basil soup with crunchy bread. I added an Eccles cake (similar to a covered mincemeat tart) for good measure.

Later on the south coast at Freshwater Bay, we paused to enjoy the sea and sand views and for photographs. Some brave souls were swimming, a number of hikers passed on their way to or from Tennyson Down, a cliff walkway to Tennyson's mid-nineteenth century former home at Farringford. David and I cycled by the house, now a hotel, on our way to The Needles.

At the crest of a small hill, just before the road down to The Needles, we met a hiking US couple from Chicago, now permanently resident in Freshwater. They had moved to Britain on a 'retirement visa' which allows you to stay for two years providing you can prove that you are financially secure and have health insurance. This was the couple's third year so they now have full free access to the National Health Service and can stay. Having never heard of such a visa, I was surprised and remain envious as Mari could not stand the lack of sunshine in the British climate. Canada is about the limit!

David and I were surprised and disappointed to find an amusement park atmosphere at the bottom of the hill. We had anticipated a protected and serene National Trust site. Instead it was garish and noisy. The most egregious, yet most indicative of modern life bit, was a ski resort type chair lift down to a viewing platform. Paying £4 for this very popular facility allowed people to avoid a steep but fairly short staircase.

Although aptly named and impressive in their own right, the Needles' potential to produce a sense of wonder or awe was tarnished by the tawdry, commercial surroundings. We left to find our lodgings at the 'Hoo.' This was a lovely old home with stained glass windows, a lush, almost tropical garden and an Amazonian rainforest bird, 'Wally' that spoke English and Japanese reflecting the couple that owned him.

Squeezed on the Ferry
Back at Fern Cottage for our last night on the IOW, our landlady provided a welcoming cuppa' and our laundry freshly washed, dried and folded waited on our beds. Apart from the cramped washroom, our accommodations were comfortable and familiar.

After sharing breakfast time with a couple in Ryde training to become music therapists for nursing homes, we loaded up and I went back in the house to pay the balance of our bill. Sandra charged us £6 for the laundry, steep but understandable, although no other landlady has ever charged for laundry over my 19-year history of cycling in Britain. She also charged £10 for 'holding the room.' I knew that no one else tried to book the room—she had told me so. Few things upset me more than feeling cheated financially.

Our ferry to France didn't leave until that evening, so we had plenty of time but no particular plan for the day. Stopping first at the library to check for e-mail, I sat down at the computer bank at the one assigned to me and then with a start, realized that my neighbour was the same menacing tramp who had walked out of the Indian restaurant without paying two nights ago.

Back outside, poor weather made further cycling on IOW unappealing so we decided to take the next hovercraft and tour Portsmouth until time to board the ferry to St. Malo. David and I separately explored the city's pedestrianized streets that were filled with unappealing types and the shops and activities that attract them. It depressed me that so much of what was on offer was unhealthy for body or wallet: shoddy, ugly 'fashions', video games, betting shops, fast food, etc. Given the time of day and the age of the people I saw, most of them had to be unemployed. These were people living on the public purse and content to stay there--stark proof of the latest acronym NEETS—'Not in Employment, Education or Training.' My distress at all of this was particularly intense because it was so unrepresentative of 'My England', the country I so much want David to experience and admire.

However, David was excited when we got back together. He had made some excellent purchases at a sporting goods shop sale. I went back with him to see the massive bargains but was not in a buying mood. The only thing that appealed was a tea break but by this time, the teashops were closed and we had to choose from those quintessentially not-British restaurants: Kentucky Fried Chicken and Burger King.

After our meal, we were still early for the ferry but were quickly motioned on once we had passed through passport control. A large group of British cyclists just ahead of us had claimed most of the best bike parking sites. These were in a small corner storage room built out from the ship's vehicle parking area wall alongside the docking end of the ship. By the time we unloaded our bags, locked and secured the cycles, the adjacent vehicle area was full—of huge lorries. There was just enough space to squeeze in front of the most forward lorries but access to the companionways up to the passenger decks was impossible from that point. I felt trapped. This was the very lowest level of the ship. The air reeked with diesel fumes. David, although narrower in build, could not walk between the side of the lorry and the ship wall with his bags. He left them with me and slid through sideways. I passed him both sets of bags through the gap but was personally too thick to get through sideways myself. David suggested squatting down to squeeze through using the extra space of the wheel well. This was dirty but just wide enough. Then we were still blocked from access to the companionways on the other side of the ship by the tightly parked lorry fronts and backs.

Finally we found a spot to get through. Strung out by this ordeal and the day's disappointments, we were particularly grateful for the luxurious passenger area and facilities. Our tiny cabin was fully fitted with two bunk beds, reading lights and a complete en suite but accommodated two people comfortably only when one was in a bunk. We quickly did what we had to, and then went out to the upper deck to watch Portsmouth's disappearing lights and expand our space-constrained senses under the star-studded night sky.

For me, the final blow of the day was learning that dinner was still being served on board. I could have had my long anticipated French style 'Steak Frites' with wine instead of settling for the very poor meal at Kentucky Fried Chicken. Tomorrow had to be better!

Too Many Senior Moments

We were awakened by a pleasant, French accented sotto voce announcement that breakfast was now being served and disembarkation at St Malo was just over an hour away. Concerned that there would not be enough time to do everything necessary, we rushed through a cereal breakfast, gathered our gear and went down to the access door to the bike storage area.

It was locked. Nervous after our experience last night trying to get to into the ship, we now began imagining being unable to get out. The sounds of the ship's arrival and departing lorries made us feel trapped, forgotten and impotent to do anything about it. After a few tense moments, a deck hand opened the door on the deck below and motioned us down. We had forgotten the number of our deck!

The other cyclists and the lorries had already left. While loading my panniers I saw that my handlebar bag was missing. It contained my passport, camera and spare cash. Another panic attack—these are happening increasingly frequently in stressful situations. I ran back to the access door where we had waited nervously for the door to open—the bag wasn't there--my thoughts raced through the dire calamities that would ensue without passport or cash----and returned to tell David of my most recent screw-up. Before making this confession, I saw my bag sitting patiently, just at the entrance to the bike storage room where it had been purposely left while dealing with the panniers. Memory is definitely fading fast.

Nevertheless, based on a five-year-old memory, I was able to navigate us from the ferry to Intra Muros' main entrance gateonto the cobbled streets of this restored city. Our earlier breakfast had been hurried so I felt we should start our visit to France with a proper petit déjeuner--any excuse for food will do. We took this at a small café and then meandered through the city, exiting briefly through one of the seaside city gates to watch a group of disinterested teen-agers being coaxed through an obstacle course competition.

My plans for the day, exploring Intra Muros in the morning and cycling 70 km to a hostel near Mont St Michel, now seemed too ambitious. We decided instead to stay at the same no-star hotel in

Intra Muros that I used 5 years ago and spend the afternoon on a roundtrip along the scenic north coast D201. This was an ideal choice. The route went through Paramé, a seemingly self-sufficient suburb and onto the beach-bordered highway. Brilliant sunshine and a beautiful clear blue sky soothed and warmed our still somewhat fragile souls. Pausing only to survey the architecture at a nude beach, we went almost as far as the popular Pointe du Grouin before turning back and pausing for a leisurely beer at a dune surrounded beachside café.

That evening, David, now a temporary convert to my budget oriented approach to life, searched for the best bargain for an evening meal. After a wide-ranging survey of alternatives, we chose a set menu of lasagne, salad, a glass of wine and a crème caramel for the equivalent of C$22, gratuity and tax included. We concluded our day on the walled ramparts watching the sunset.

Dinan Hostel

Our next overnight was booked at the Dinan hostel but I our route had to be revised as we had stayed in St Malo instead of near Mont St. Michel. There was a distinct lack of road numbers and the posted town names did not correspond with my map. Hailing an older cyclist going in the opposite direction, we asked him for help. I must have looked a bit uncertain about his directions so he volunteered to escort us to the proper turning. This led us through the quiet, picturesque villages of St Jouan and St Souliac on a shorter, quieter route to Dinan. Once that far, our kind guide left us and David charged ahead as usual. So I arrived in Dinan alone and took advantage of my solitude to delay arrival at the hostel for time to revisit the medieval part of the city and enjoy a coffee and pastry with my book.

When I got to the hostel, a vaguely familiar man was outside waiting for reception to open. Slowly, I remembered that he was one of the English cycling group that had been on the ferry. They were employees of a firm in Western England on their annual long weekend at Dinan.

David arrived just as reception opened and we booked in. Earlier, at Alfriston, he discovered that he could become a member of Hostelling International and be entitled to the member's discount for far less than it costs to join in Canada. His annual membership cost was more than offset by the discounts on all his future hostel stays on this tour. I was not amused having invested in a Canadian life membership at significant cost.

David and I joined the English group for dinner at the hostel and later were their guests at a riverside pub for beers. That session and the 20-minute walk to and from the hostel, gave us plenty of opportunity for interesting conversation.

During the early hostel part of the evening, a group of mentally challenged people created fancy headgear outside in a celebratory mood. They later had their evening meal at a separate table some distance from us. Our only real interaction with them was in the unisex washrooms where their lack of capabilities and personal modesty was particularly evident. One man, perhaps in his twenties, wandered about nude before his female supervisor could get him dressed.

Frazzled Again

We had a long, hot 83 km cycle from Dinan to St Brieuc and arrived weary. Perhaps that is why my mental state was somewhat frazzled when we merged into the late afternoon crowds in St Brieuc's pedestrianized shopping area. Needing directions to the hostel, I chose a travel agency for their likely ability to speak English but had to wait several minutes through a telephone call to get a confusing hand drawn map to the Tourist Information Office. My draining mental energy was just adequate to work through the crowds to locate this office but its atmosphere and the pleasant woman who helped me were immediately restorative. I returned to David with a real map and specific verbal instructions on how to find the first street on the way to the hostel.

Confidentially, I told David that now that we knew how to get to the hostel, we could stop for a coffee and pastry—my universal solution to celebrate or to ease stress--any reason, no matter how flimsy, is sufficient. David demurred; he wanted to get to the hostel. So, on we went and I was immediately confused again. She had said 'prenez à droite, puis à guache.' We did but the specified street was not there. I stood at the intersection, motionless, trying to find some semblance of similarity between our surroundings and the map. David said, 'Maybe we should have that coffee--you are nearly paralysed.' That was really a low point in my self-esteem. Always managing on my solo trips—priding myself on self-sufficiency, I now felt incompetent as tour leader.

I went back and asked again. The solution was simple. Her 'turn right' was meant to be at the back of her building, I had interpreted it as at the front. From that point on, assisted only by a few references to the GPS option on David's iPhone, we found the hostel. David was immediately impressed by its French blue trimmed manorial appearance and more so by the private, en suite room we were given.

Joining the Group and Some Unplanned Misadventures
Today we join the group at Gourarec. Yesterday had been disastrous for my ego; today had to be better, I told myself once again. It was not to be. As soon as we headed out in the morning, the stays on my front mudguard needed adjustment, a regular occurrence. This time, however, I loosened the quick release lever to move it to a position that provided more clearance for the stay, but failed to retighten it.

David took the lead getting us out of the city again with some assistance from the GPS. Then, we agreed not to try to stay together. We both knew our destination, he was the stronger cyclist and while neither of us voiced it, we both needed some space.

The day was warm and traffic was not an issue. The route was reasonably straightforward until an intersection at the foot of a hill near Quintin where David might have turned right. I chose to go straight on but just a few metres into the ascent, my front wheel fell out, not being securely fastened. This new bike has disk brakes and I was immediately concerned that the disk would be bent making the brakes inoperable. With the wheel in one hand and the bike in the other, I moved to the side of the road to a convenient stone wall. Afraid of falling even further behind, I tried to reinstall the front

328

wheel without taking the time to unload the rear panniers. With that extra weight the rear end twisted, causing the front brake lever end to crash down, scraping my left arm. Made of light, relatively soft aluminium, the lever's end, ragged from leaning against rough surfaces, was an effective knife that left an eight-centimetre gash.

The wheel still wasn't on. I unloaded the panniers and replaced the wheel. Now as I feared, it would not turn probably because the disk was bent and simply would not rotate through its clamps. Widening the clearance allowed the wheel to rotate but effectively left me with no front brakes.

About an hour later, I found David waiting outside an attractive looking restaurant. It was lunchtime and I was definitely ready for some comestible therapy. A large wedding party was inside so the staff weren't particularly attentive to us on the outside patio. Although a little irritated by the delay, we enjoyed the sunshine, our lunch and a neighbour's dog that chose to join us for any titbits on offer. We also shared some more confidences but I don't recall what they were.

Nor can I remember what adjustments we made after lunch to my front brakes but they worked much better so apparently the disk had not been damaged. David's greater experience with disk brakes and his measured, more logical approach saved the day.

We were headed south towards Mur de Bretagne, which, I thought, based solely on memory, was on the canal, just about five kilometres from Gouarec. But my memory was of Bon Repos, not Mur de Bretagne. Apparently that single B dominated my brain. So, when we asked about the canal at Mur de Bretagne, everyone seemed puzzled. I switched to asking for Gouarec.

My new question produced answers leading us to the major highway N164, some 16 kilometres east of Gouarec. We were fortunate that, being Sunday, the speed and traffic volume were only scary, not terrifying. After a few kilometres, the right hand lane was blocked off to traffic by waist-high cement blocks, producing a safe cycling lane that we took gratefully. Ten minutes later, we came to the landslide that had closed the lane and now blocked us. We had no alternative but to carry on along the N164, as it was getting late in the afternoon and a group dinner was planned. Finally we reached a crossroads to Bon Repos and the canal towpath leading to Breton Bike's site at Gouarec.

We rode the five kilometres of the towpath silently and slowly restoring our traffic-frayed nerves to arrive at the campsite at 5.15, the last of the group. After a few quick introductions and a very welcome hug for me from Daniela, Geoff gave us our tents and other gear. He claimed that had we been ten minutes later, he would have erected our tents for us. Now, we had to do that, shower, change and be ready for the group dinner booked for seven at a village crêperie.

The Breton Bike Group

Geoff, a former teacher, left his Cornish home in 1989, moving to Brittany with his wife Kate to start Breton Bikes. Their three children were all born in France and are now totally bilingual. Kate was elected a town councillor. Her parents moved to the area soon after.

Geoff relaxed his normal group size limit of 14 for this twentieth anniversary year. As a result, our numbers grew to 17, despite a number that had to drop out for illness, their own or their partners.

Allan, a British former construction cost estimator, took pride of place as 'most frequent flyer' on previous BB trips. Allan is a trim, gentlemanly and well turned out but taciturn man of roughly 65. When not cycling, he is actively involved in the lives of his grandchildren, who live near enough for him to act as chauffeur.

Tom, from Minneapolis, is on his second tour with BB. Considering his 'always lost 'reputation from that first tour, I felt comforted that finally someone might outrank me for directional dysfunction. Slender and angular, Tom had been involved in computer software but since retirement took an 18-month course in financial planning and is now a qualified financial planner. This has been on my to do list for years but I don't have the will power or spare cash for the course.

Frank and Anne were the only couple. He just retired from the catering industry. Frank is also angular but his most outstanding characteristic was how much he sounds like Victor Meldrew in the British television comedy 'One Foot in the Grave.' This similarity extended to his actions and frequent use of the drawn out phrase 'I dooon't belieevve it.' Anne, unlike her television counterpart, bit her tongue, maintaining an outwardly and reasonably placid composure. They too, were BB veterans.

David, my travelling partner, is also slender but powerfully built, particularly his legs. He manages a clinic of family doctors and is an Associate Professor at an Ontario university. He is very technically oriented and loves electronic gadgets. We were constantly on the lookout for wifi and internet facilities. Besides attending numerous medical conferences during this sabbatical year, David managed to train for and complete a half Iron Man triathlon a few weeks before we left. His wife, Jane, is also a family doctor and one of their three daughters just started her residency in medicine.

Another Frank, a cheerfully content engineer from Edinburgh, is also a multi-tour client. Frank's physique is best described as 'spare.' He is nevertheless, a very strong cyclist but no one would accuse him of being fashion conscious. To be most gracious, his attire is best described as functional. We became accustomed to seeing his brown and yellow bath towel flying from the rear rack on his bike to dry. At the time of the tour, Frank was about to embark on a total change in life style by moving to Chicago, marrying a US citizen and acquiring two teenage daughters in the process. He still plans to return for the annual BB tour.

This was BB tour two for Gillian, a single lecturer in Marketing at a Northern English university. She is also a strong cyclist but I remember her more for her untamed hair, capacity for wine and her acerbic, self-deprecating wit. We had a number of interesting conversations about life as a university lecturer, the peer reviews, university ranking processes and the pressure to publish. She is working on a book provisionally titled, 'Growing Vegetables for One', but says that it won't count towards her university publishing requirement.

Jennie is a single, biological laboratory technician for the NHS in the north of England. She, too, has a great wit and wine capacity. She and Evelyn, a doctor with the NHS in Portsmouth, are close friends despite almost totally opposite personalities and cycling capabilities. Evelyn lacks speed but has tremendous stamina. Both of them are long time BB clients and are meticulous at breakfast time highlighting the route on their maps as well as excellent map readers, so it was always safe to follow them.

The other Robert, a single man from Derbyshire, shares the same surname as Rawdon, a current resident of Gouarec, but Irish by birth. Rob, who refers to himself as 'hollow leg' for his bottomless capacity for food, has a spare physique and a very upright cycling position. He climbs hills without apparent effort, gliding past the rest of us struggling on our way up-a product of living in the Peak District. Rob has been an off and on again BB client. He is in his mid-forties but just changed career directions from the financial to the environment industry and feels that he is starting back at an entry level.

Rawdon, also single, is in his mid fifties with a strong, solid, no nonsense physique. He has a varied career history, the bulk of it in military occupations with considerable experience in the Middle East. He acquired fluency in Arabic in the process and for a while was the British Foreign Office's expert on Aden. Just before moving back to Gouarec, he translated for the International Criminal Court in The Hague. For the past couple of years he has been training as a tracker (of humans and animals) in Africa and along the border between Mexico and the US. He now works as a freelance translator while seeking opportunities in the tracking world. In prior years, Rawdon co-led some BB tours. He is used to command and this year could not resist when some of the group went astray. This was not always appreciated.

Yassmin, a medical secretary from Kent, is another BB regular. Her husband is a senior researcher who loves rock climbing and rides a motorcycle to his research position at London University. These tours are a bit tame for him, so she comes alone. Yassmin is an amazingly versatile person. She recently completed a first class honours degree in Archaeology, creates beautiful stained glass products, is an excellent cook, is well on her way to finishing her first novel and is an accomplished artist. Each year she produces and sends a group tour cartoon to each of us. All this versatility may stem from being a bit of a hybrid with a Welsh mother and Yemeni father. Speaking Arabic is another accomplishment.

Daniela, a married German psychologist in her early forties, is a petite, attractive, very athletic woman. Apart from these qualities, she is notable for daily practising yoga, being a vegetarian and for travelling with more gear than anyone. She brought some 23 kilos of gear with her in a rucksack and carried all of that on the back of the bike. The extra gear included her own cooking equipment, special food for her diet and an extra warm sleeping bag. Daniela is used to only the best in sporting equipment and got particularly irritated when her BB supplied tent leaked. Geoff arranged for a replacement but that smelled mouldy. Early next morning, on a trip to the washroom, David discovered Daniela sleeping outside her tent to avoid the smell. Always a gentleman, he exchanged tents with her.

Jeannine, a new BB client from Denver, is a single, very jolly freelance pharmacist in her early 50s. She claims her profession is very well paid. That and the freedom to work only when she wants made it possible for her to tour Vietnam, Alaska and France this year. She joined the BB group immediately following a luxury cycle tour elsewhere in France. Redheaded, freckled and with a robust physique, she appeared to enjoy everything, including the occasional jokes about her US accent and terminology. She retaliated with exaggerated British pronunciations.

Ian, an early 40s Brit from Oxford, was our strongest cyclist, being also a three hour marathoner. His somewhat small build gave no clue to this ability. Ian is married with teenagers but given his cycling speed; I had little opportunity to learn anything else about him.

Finally Peter, probably in his late 30s, was a lot like Ian in build and as Evelyn, is also from Portsmouth. Peter was not a particularly social animal and I learned only that he is a software programmer for the

Navy. His accent, a Bristol product with several years' overlay of Portsmouth vowels, was often hard to understand.

Despite being so unbalanced by age, gender and ability, we were a generally congenial group. I was never aware of anyone losing his or her temper or behaving badly. On cooking nights we gathered in a circle for a cycle of starters, meal preparation, consumption and reminisces of previous tours that typically lasted over three hours. For some reason, these circles were often immediately outside my tent. The group cleaned up well but on my middle of the night visits to the washroom, I often had to negotiate round the ten or more empty wine bottles awaiting morning disposal.

Camp Cooking-Not for Me

As Mari will quickly affirm, my cooking skills extend no further than baked beans or scrambled eggs on toast. I have neither the patience nor imagination to attempt much else. So, when allocating cooking duties with my Breton Bikes partners, I choose to be sous chef and do the washing up, leaving meal choice, shopping and cooking to my partner.

Initially David felt much the same way but became inspired and challenged observing the skills and elaborate productions of some of the other campers. Breton Bikes supplies each pair of cycle campers with a mentholated spirits cooker and a bottle of spirits. Each cooker set has two pots for boiling water, cooking pasta, vegetables or whatever. Of course, only one pot can be on the fire at a time. For me, just lighting the fire risked self-immolation and sequencing the cooking process to ensure all meal components were hot and ready to eat at the same time required process management skills I don't possess. David, originally trained as an engineer, wanted to master it. He did, producing four or five acceptable one-pot meals with a rice or pasta base followed by a cup of tea. David had only minor complaints about the quality and speed of my sous chef performance. One evening however, I failed to turn off the fire after serving the plates only to discover several minutes later that the remaining food in the pot was burnt solid.

Geoff noticing that one of our pots was badly burnt on the outside said that it would be worth £20 to avoid Kate's wrath over its condition, since she has to clean the cooking gear after every tour. Always interested in extra cash, I volunteered to scrub the pot pristine.

Allan, Geoff's sympathetic clean up cooking partner, kindly offered me an especially robust scouring pad. Half an hour later, I returned with a shining but somewhat thinner pot and requested my £20. Typically, Geoff wiggled out of the situation by saying I had avoided a fine of £20, not earned a reward. Now, I am probably known by the group as 'pot scrubber' and fully expect that Yassmin's annual group cartoon of individual foibles will show me in that role. That isn't as bad as Gillian's likely fate. When we visited Roscoff's festival toward the end of the tour, while walking round the town she discovered that her cycling shorts were on inside out. Both Jeannine and Ian photographed her posterior for posterity. I'm sure this will be Gillian's identifying cartoon event.

Roscoff Festival

After a few days of bad weather and a poor campsite populated with migrant farmers and their dogs the previous evening, we settled into a super campsite outside St Pol de Leon on the northern Brittany coast. I set up my tent in a hedged area close to the facilities before realizing that more distant, but less practical sites, surrounded by boulders offered sweeping sea views through majestic evergreens. The camp also provided a pool, washer, tumble drier and a shop.

Geoff made a very wise executive decision to spend two nights at St Pol. This made up for the previous campsite, allowed people to sleep in and plan their rest day to suit themselves. I took advantage of the laundry facilities, delaying my petit déjeuner until almost eleven as a result.

That was cutting it close. It was a Sunday, when boulangerie/ pâtisseries typically close at noon. By the time I arrived, the choice was very limited. I joined several of the group still breakfasting at a bar on the square and as we were finishing, a group of British male cyclists showed up. Although they all sported 'maillot jaunes', they definitely were not Tour de France calibre. Their bulging waistlines were positive evidence that this was a gastronomic holiday washed down with considerable quantities of 'bière.' As is almost always the case, we enjoyed meeting fellow cyclists and swapping cycling tales.

Still hungry, I agreed to go on to Roscoff with Jennie, Jeannine, Gillian and Ian for lunch. I wanted to revisit Roscoff anyway as it had been my point of entry in 2004 and impressed me very much.

A massive Brittany ferry basked in warm sunshine waiting for its next voyage to Plymouth as we cycled past the harbour. After a very cursory walk round the town, we succumbed to the ever-present lure of the café. My tour budgets never include amounts for such mundane requirements as laundry so when those costs are incurred, other categories have to compensate. This morning's laundry cost the equivalent of a small meal so my lunch order was less than I wanted but when Gillian returned from the pâtisserie with a delicious looking cheese pastry, hunger overcame the budget. I too went to the pâtisserie.

I should have, but did not, think it strange it to be open at this hour on a Sunday. Roscoff was having a festival which apparently changed the rules. We first noted a man in period costume walking by our table but our minds, lulled by the warm sunshine, thought it was an isolated event. Then, when Louis XIV and some of his court strolled by, it became clear that something special was happening. Just down the street, 'Les Gourganes', a group of sea shanty singers, performed on the cobblestones in front of an onion-string draped ancient cycle outside a créperie. Breton onion sellers from Roscoff were a regular sight in southern England years ago.

The male singers wore loose, knee-length nappies that looked suspiciously in need of changing. Further on there were a grizzle-faced old time knife grinder, demonstrations of ancient games and groups of town elders in the Quaker-like Breton costumes. All of this seemed quite natural and at home in Roscoff's historic, human scaled architecture and meandering cobblestone streets. It was a happy atmosphere, made all the more pleasant because there was no rush to be anywhere else.

A Gruelling Day Avoided

My planning for this tour assumed our final campground would be back at Breton Bikes home base Gouarec on a Thursday night. That location would allow David and me to cycle to Morlaix (about 75 km) on Friday to stay overnight and do the remaining 20 km on to our booked Saturday afternoon ferry departure from Roscoff.

So I became concerned when Geoff told us Tuesday that we would camp at Silifiac on Thursday and not be back at Gouarec until noon on the Friday. Silifiac is nearly 20 km further from Morlaix than Gouarec. Then David decided he would prefer to spend Friday night in one of the huts at St Pol de Leon instead of in a Morlaix hotel. He liked the seaside setting of the campsite so much that he did not mind a ride of close to 110 km Friday afternoon. Geoff promised to have Kate check into hut availability but privately both Geoff and Rawdon shared my concern that such a ride would be tough and a risk, particularly with sunset now about seven p.m.

At Carhaix, the night before Silifiac, David changed his mind. He was now ready for more relaxed days and I was relieved not to have to play the wimp and opt out of his plan. Nevertheless, I didn't challenge Geoff's explanation that the huts could only be hired by the week.

Silifiac campsite was perhaps the most basic of all and immediately disappointing. It sat on a small hill across the road and above a lakeside crêperie that also housed all the campsite facilities. A very large Mongolian Yurt dominated the site, standing deserted, in the tall grass that covered the otherwise featureless site. Grumbles were heard from all corners as the group erected their tents and made the long trek to the showers.

The night was planned as a festive final evening with a special meal arranged at the crêperie. Kate, her parents and daughter, Rosie, joined us at a long wooden table. The meal was fun and solemn at the same time as we were breaking up as a group in the morning. Some were travelling to St. Malo, some to trains at St Brieuc for an onward journey to Paris. Since David and I weren't going to Gouarec, Kate brought all the gear we had left behind there at the start of the tour.

Given our long ride, David and I decided on a fairly early night so that we could get off first thing in the morning. The others lingered in the bar.

Climbing the hill back to the tents we gloried in the star-studded night sky. It was the most marvellous I can remember ever. Perfectly clear of clouds, it was just magical. I stood for several minutes silently admiring a view we never see in my part of the world.

Despite having said our goodbyes the night before, We could not leave without doing so all over. A heavy morning mist over the lake emphasized the sorrow of parting. We skipped the final breakfast, as did Daniela and Tom who had an early taxi booked from Gouarec. I left with them at 8.30, needing a head start on David. This lasted perhaps 15 minutes when he caught up with me as I was asking directions for a particular road.

David and I continued together briefly, but had agreed not to try to stay together if separated. This was soon the case and I arrived in Rostrenen alone at about 10, ready for some breakfast. The morning's mist had lifted half an hour earlier, finally revealing the particularly scenic countryside of Geoff's route. Unfortunately, the pâtisserie was closed for holidays and the bar had no croissants or anything else suitable for breakfast except for coffee. So, a 'grand café' and granola bars had to be breakfast.

Getting out of Rostrenen involved a short stretch on a major highway. After that, the route was clear, traffic was light, and the terrain was a pleasing mix of rural and/or forest. It was not nearly as steep as expected so my pace was better; the kilometres just disappeared. By lunch time I had cycled over 50 km, and thinking I was over halfway, felt quite positive.

The largely empty countryside was decidedly short of places to eat. I finally gave up looking for an appealing restaurant. At that point, my only choice was a small squalid café. However, for the first time this trip, I was able to order Croque Monsieur, one of my favourite cholesterol enhancers.

I arrived in Morlaix at 3.10, having completed 93 km in less than 6 hours of actual riding, the longest ride and the best rate of speed of the entire trip. Serendipitously, a few minutes later there was a sign directing me to the hotel Kate had booked for us. First, however, I needed to find a phone to call Mari. The time of day was just about right for her. We discussed her current state of health–never free of ailments for long—when one starts to improve, an old one comes back or a new one arrives. She really has a tough time. She brought me up to date on the news: the G8 conference, about to take place in Pittsburgh, and Gadaffi's attempt to set up his tent in New York for a UN meeting.

Afterwards, I went to the hotel; David had arrived an hour earlier than I had, and already explored the city a bit. We selected Le Grand Café du Terrace for dinner, an elegant, tiled and mirrored establishment with two storey ceilings and a majestic staircase. Dining early as we did, we had very attentive, courteous service. Afterwards, we strolled through the streets, enjoying the magical atmosphere created by spotlighted ancient buildings.

Back to England
Everything fell into place on this, our last day in France. Our final breakfast included gallettes and a cake like bread with orange juice, a pleasant change from the last 12 days. We emerged to a sunny, cool morning and an easy route out of the city on the D769 along the river entrance to Morlaix harbour. Soon, the road turned west and then north again along the Pense, another river out to the Atlantic.

Trailing David again, I stopped in St Pol de Leon at the massive SuperU market to buy some items for lunch. French supermarkets are marvellous for choice but Saturday morning isn't the time for a quick visit. I lost time exploring all the alternatives and then faced massive check out queues.

Despite this, I arrived at Roscoff before noon and claimed an empty park bench next to the outdoor patio of a café for lunch and book time. Afterwards, I visited the harbour and strolled the streets, searching for and finally finding the Hotel L'Angleterre, my stay on the 2004 tour. In the process, a British cyclist struck up a conversation, admired my bike and told me of his plans to cycle from Lisbon to Moscow with a group of six next year.

David and I met again at the ferry, boarding about 2 p.m. This time cycles were lashed to a rail along the ship walls rather than in a separate storage room. With only five bikes compared to 18 on the previous voyage and no lorries blocking us, the process was a lot less stressful.

We claimed a comfortable booth in the lounge, next to three British cyclists that we had met at embarkation. The first item on their business agenda was liquid refreshment in the form of 500 ml bottles of Heineken—the only item on their very repetitive agenda. We followed their example with a single shared beer supplemented by our remaining biscuits. I finished my book, 'Engleby', by Sebastian Faulks, an unusual novel laced with liberal doses of philosophy on the meaning of life. Then a day old *Daily Telegraph* reoriented me to life in Britain while absorbing sunshine on the deck. The interesting articles of the day covered British energy problems, their conflicts with EU directives, a scandal over MPs' expense claims, the effect of the Chancellor's use of 'enhanced easing' on sterling, and a find of Saxon treasure. Now the mind was fed but the body was hungry, I found David reading in a comfortable reclining chair and persuaded him that it was dinner time.

Finally, I could have the meal so long anticipated: steak frites with red wine and a fruit tart. The ferry line prices their meals in both sterling and euros but had failed to adjust the exchange rate to reflect the current weakness in the pound. Moving through the queue, collecting my meal, I did some quick mental calculations to decide which currency to use, considering the bargain offered in sterling, my stock of the two currencies and sterling requirements for the next few days.

Plymouth was already dark when we arrived but the harbour and adjoining area were well lit. It was still difficult negotiating traffic, deciphering a crude map to our B&B, and not being able to see street signs. Once we found our street, no one seemed to have heard of our B&B or, being well along into the liquid portion of his or her Saturday evening, really cared all that much. Perhaps, we delayed our landlord's own pub visit, as he was out on the street looking for us and chided us a bit for the late arrival, which we chose to ignore.

Salcombe Hostel and the Coast

Sunday morning traffic was uncomfortably heavy on the A 379 going east out of Plymouth until we got truly out of the urban area. Then the beautiful, rolling countryside offered sheep and cattle vistas. Some narrow, steep sections between overhanging vegetation were so dark that we were hardly visible to the traffic. I had to walk up a few.

David and I paused at a confusing intersection just about 4 km outside Salcombe to ask a local resident how to get to the hostel. Very talkative, he took a long time to deliver the required information but he claimed his directions would save climbing a terror hill.

His recommended single track road ran steeply down toward the sea between high thorny hedges and initially past huge plastic covered fields that we later learned were full of cauliflower. We rode, often scratchingly close, to the hedge to avoid oncoming traffic and used both sets of brakes continuously.

At the bottom, beautiful homes with gorgeous sea views hugged the cliff sides. The bay was alive with colourfully sailed boats. We then had a steep, long climb to the National Trust Bolt Head grounds where the hostel is located. It was too early for reception, so we locked up the bikes and took the coastal footpath to Bolt Head, making frequent stops to admire the views from outcroppings of black rocks, sample the wild blackberries and take pictures.

Our hostel roommates were both coastal walkers. One, a history graduate and former Liberal, MP candidate, currently worked for a council. He monopolized conversation at dinner and breakfast but was interesting and particularly knowledgeable about US political history. I got to 'enjoy' a different audio experience that night as he snored and broke wind repeatedly underneath my bunk. The other man, Steve, a diabetic, was on a week's holiday walking various parts of the Coastal Walkway. He used his car and local buses to get between the hostel and the particular part of the coast he was walking each day.   Steve alerted me to the Slapton Sands story described below.

Organic Totnes

There were several alternative routes from the Salcombe hostel to our next stop at Totnes, some 40 kilometres north. This whole area is part of South Hams, principally agricultural country, where honeysuckle blooms as late as October in the mildest climate in Britain. Yesterday's experience made us determined to avoid hills and busy roads. Hills came with the territory but hostel staff said we could find quieter roads by crossing over the river from Salcombe on a regular ferry. We understood that the ferry left at a specific time and pushed as hard as we could up the hills to the departure point—then had to carry the bikes down a steep set of stairs to the boarding area. As we reached the bottom, a slightly oversized rowboat approached from across the river towards a short inclined dock on our side. Surely, this could not be the ferry, but it was. Our captain of the moment, a gruff, taciturn man agreed to take the bikes and us. He clearly begrudged the delay we caused unloading the gear from our bikes so that they could be lifted into the rowboat as it was a fast, continuous facility, not a scheduled one with timetables.   While we boarded people were gathering on the other side waiting. So, we irritated him further unloading there. The entire experience probably took ten minutes.

Another steep set of stairs up to the road greeted us on the opposite shore but a Sustrans poster at the top seemed to answer our concerns about heavily trafficked roads. Sustrans is the system of cycle routes in the UK. The poster detailed Route 2 to Totnes. It seemed designed just for us. Unfortunately, there was no indication whether to turn left or right to get started. Somehow, we chose correctly and were soon rewarded with a Route 2 signpost. That was the last Sustrans sign we saw until the end of the day, just down the hill from our Totnes B&B! We found no others along the way at intersection decision points or anywhere else. The scale of our map was inadequate to the task so we followed our noses, but being male, they failed us, probably adding at least eight kilometres to our day.

Consequently, by lunchtime, we were still 30 km away from Totnes. The Boathouse, an attractive and apparently popular restaurant on the coast at Torcross claimed us. We chose a sea view table and enjoyed a pleasant meal, stopping afterwards at an adjacent WW II memorial to Exercise Tiger. Hundreds of the US military lost their lives in that 1944 operation at nearby Slapton Sands. In preparation for this exercise, some 3000 residents of the area were moved away in late 1943; some of these had never even left their village before.

Exercise Tiger was a full-scale rehearsal for the D-day invasion of Normandy, involving some 30,000. Slapton Sands was selected because it closely mirrored the geographical conditions at 'Utah' beach. Beach landings on 27 April, the first day of the exercise, were successful. However, the following morning; a group of German U boats attacked a procession of US LSTs killing 638 men. One of the British ships protecting the exercise had called in at Plymouth for repairs and, at least in part because the US and British navies used different radio frequencies, the LST commander was unaware of his reduced protection. Making matters worse, the British corvette leading the LSTs had them in a straight-line formation presenting an easy target for the Germans. One disaster followed another as 308 men died due to 'friendly fire' when landing. General Eisenhower ordered the use of live ammunition in the exercise so that the soldiers would have a 'realistic' experience. Ironically, the actual invasion at Utah Beach cost less than 300 lives. Books, films and television programs have told the story, some accurately, some disguised. Controversy still exists about whether there was a cover-up at the time. It is said that D-day plans were almost cancelled because ten officers, all of whom knew details of the pending invasion, were missing. They were subsequently found, all dead. This disaster was kept secret for years but the memorial now draws many visitors, in part because it is on the popular South West Coastal Path. (3)

Much of this area is designated an area of outstanding natural beauty (AONB). Nearby is one of England's most attractive nudist beaches. We never learned whether the appeal is the beach or the nudists as sadly, we turned away from the coast, missing the opportunity.

Wary of the effect on his digestion of shellfish, David had ordered whitefish for lunch, which turned out to be equally bad as he was soon suffering cramps. We gave up provisional plans to go into

Dartmouth for another ferry up the River Dart to Totnes. David needed to rest and the fastest way to Totnes was essential. So, we chose the A3122 and A381 but got separated just at the outskirts of town.

Easing back into a leadership mode, I went to the Totnes railway station to collect our pre-purchased tickets for the next day's journey back to Horley, reserve cycle places, confirm the departure platform and generally assess the lay of the land to avoid any potential problems.

Totnes has been a borough since the tenth century and thrived on the cloth trade in the medieval period. It sits on a steep hill above the river, boasts a 13th century castle and Elizabethan houses. The Tourist Information Centre gave me clear directions for finding Dart Villas, our B&B, but I could not find the access street, Moat Hill. I stopped in a pub (across from the second Sustrans route 2 sign) to get clarification. There, a well-oiled, very confident, military type gave me precise, totally erroneous information.

Asking twice more, finally to a very pleasant young man walking his dog. 'Can, you direct me to Totnes Down Hill?' He replied 'Sorry, I've never heard of that.' I carried on a few steps to the road he had just turned off and immediately saw a street sign, 'Totnes Downhill.' Just then, the young man called out, apologising for being so pedantic; 'I thought you said Totnes Down Hill! '--I had but wasn't aware that a space between Down and Hill had been voiced.

David had arrived with the aid of his GPS and was resting. Later, although he was still a bit queasy, we went out to explore the town and have dinner. Our B&B boasted organic status but we were amazed at the number of shops, restaurants and organizations with similar themes. In the end, David could not face a restaurant meal so we bought some snacks from an organic supermarket.

Next morning, after a delicious, completely organic breakfast, the Dutch owner told us about this unusual nature of Totnes, attributing it to natural geological forces that attracted New Age types. He also explained that his link to internet was by telephone to avoid the wireless airwaves.   This was almost too much for technical guru, David, but he graciously said 'Well, you have to do what makes you happy.'

David now felt a lot better and joined me for a trip to Edinburgh Woollen Stores, one of my mandatory stops on these tours, to collect one or two of their British country shirts.   There was a sale.   David became excited at the bargains, which were particularly good in his size. I got my shirt. David came away with two shirts, a sweater and some underwear, finding room in his seemingly bottomless panniers.

Back to Horley

My scouting expedition yesterday ensured that we went to the right railway platform, avoiding having to heave the bikes up and down the railway over bridge but that is about all it accomplished.   The attendant told us to stand at the far end of the platform for the bike car. Shortly later he advised us that our train had mechanical trouble and would be late.   A few minutes later the situation changed again-- now we were going on a just arriving train which had the cycle car at the other end.   And now, we faced three, instead of two, changes.

By this time, we felt truly messed about but on sober reflection, the attendant had kept us fully informed and helped us load the bikes. He also alerted the guard on the train to help us unload on arrival in Taunton because we had a tight connection.   At the next change in Reading, we had only five minutes between trains plus a change of platform across the tracks. We sprinted along the platform to find a lift down--dashed through the tunnel to the up lift to the other side, arriving at the train doors with 41 seconds to spare.   Pride in our success was quickly deflated as the train was now packed with school children and commuters.   This train stopped at every station exchanging passengers, never shedding them. We had to stand for well over an hour en route to Redhill for the final change. Amazingly, we arrived at Horley only 4 minutes later than originally scheduled.

We agreed that we should finish our tour with a proper pub meal tomorrow, choosing 'The Six Bells', a popular, traditional style pub. Overnight, David decided he wanted to go into London and have a theatre evening instead. I preferred to meander the quiet country lanes round Horley. After watching David disassemble and pack his bike so that I could duplicate the process with my own after my ride, we headed off in separate directions.

I enjoyed a ride of about 30 km, lunched on a barstool at a country pub, and wrestled for over two hours trying to fit my bike bits into their nylon carry case. The case is a standard size but the cycles aren't; mine has an unusually long head tube and fork; forcing them in gave the paint work a beating. Waiting to 7.30 pm on the off chance that David could not get a theatre ticket and would be back in time for dinner, I then went to the Six Bells to find it full. Disappointed, my lonely dinner had to be in a 'big box' type pub with no atmosphere.

For me, this tour was less than a success. Although, we often cycled apart as he is a much stronger cyclist, I could not have had a more congenial companion. But, you can have too much togetherness; the freedom and independence of touring solo is crucial for me. Even minor flaws in my plans were magnified because they discomforted my friend and so embarrassed me. David, however, claimed to have enjoyed the tour and generously thanked me for arranging everything. We continue to travel together with our local cycling group, so perhaps this tour wasn't that bad. I'm sure another is on the horizon.

NORTH MIDLANDS TOUR

BRITAIN

NORTH MIDLANDS TOUR

In 2010, my son Cameron suggested sharing a tour with me before I became too feeble. A touching concern but with conditions: August departure; eight to ten day duration; quiet roads; no hostels; no fast food; and no riding with luggage. Given my usual 25+day hostel-based tours with full panniers and a tight food budget, these conditions created a novel, more challenging planning exercise.

Cam's busy work schedule dictated August and the maximum trip length for him. Shropshire provided the answer to his other stipulations. Shropshire is a rural, lightly populated county known as the 'slow food' capital of England. Serendipitously, it is also home to the 'Wheely Wonderful' cycle touring company, based outside Ludlow. Their tours provide the cycles, accommodation and transport for your bags between B&Bs. We chose their 6 day Ironbridge tour that had overnights at Clun, Church Stretton, Ironbridge and Ludlow and would allow Cam the necessary travel days within his time limit. Manchester made the most sense as the airport.

I arranged to arrive with my own bike four days before Cam and to return home 13 days after he did. These two solo segments would incorporate as much of my regular touring regimen as possible and still get me home in time for our anniversary.

However, once this structure was locked in place with airline reservations made, the Wheely Wonderful tour booked and accommodation organized, I rediscovered Andrew, an English pen pal, long thought dead. During a typically ineffective attempt to clear out some of the detritus of my home office, I found a 31 year old letter from him.

Just on the off-chance, I did an internet search turning up an Andrew and Marion living at the same Lincolnshire address as my ancient letter. It had to be them; I was so excited, it was hard to wait until the next morning when our separate time zones aligned at a convenient time for a phone call. When he answered, his voice was immediately recognizable although we had not seen each other or spoken in nearly 40 years. We talked for over twenty minutes without difficulty or awkward pauses and agreed to share more details by e-mail.

Of course, we had to meet while I was in England. The most likely window would be during the final portion of my solo tour when I would be in Derbyshire, on the way back to Manchester for the flight home. Searching the British rail website produced a viable connection to Lincoln from Uttoxeter and we agreed on a date that only required one change to my already booked accommodations.

I arranged another get-together with Rob, one of the Breton Bike tour participants from last year, who lives in Glossop, near Manchester. We could at least have a meal one evening. I also outlined my plans to Daniela, a Breton Bike tourer from Stuttgart, who has been a pen pal (modern e-mail style) since we met on the 2008 tour. She and Rob had been cooking partners last year. She lives for holidays and asked to join us for a few days in the High Peaks of Derbyshire.

So, despite resolving, after the 2009 tour, that I needed solitude on these trips, only about 40% would be solitary on this one. Nevertheless, I was excited about renewing contact with my pen pals and enjoyed the added complexity of planning this tour.

Flight and Arrival
After the 'Underwear Bomber' incident last Christmas, I was sensitive to threats from my fellow passengers. So, I walked round the airport waiting area several times taking a census of visible potential terrorists calculating the odds that one of them would sit next to me. There was less than a 5% chance but my census was totally futile as sitting anywhere on a plane with a bomb is unsafe.

I could do nothing about it in either case, but it would have made more sense to count the young children that represented a threat to sleep. As it happened, I sat directly behind a family largely composed of very active children and a woman with a constant hacking cough. My real dangers were catching some virus and losing sleep.

The next sign of a bad flight was the pilot's announcement that coffee and tea could not be served on the flight because the 'boiler' was broken. That explained the 'free' bottle of water waiting in our seats on boarding.

Later, during the meal service, the man in the window seat across the aisle started loudly harassing the stewardess because she would not serve him a second meal. He became quite insultingly aggressive, 'I paid 1,200 good Canadian dollars for this flight and you can't give me another meal?' This degenerated into foul language and it became obvious that he was drunk. I began to fear that the flight would be diverted to Newfoundland to take him off the plane. Fortunately, his companion, probably his son, given the embarrassment he showed, managed to calm the man down.

The flight arrived without further distress, apart from a total lack of water and no hand towels in the toilet toward the end of the flight. I made my way to the airport railway station and bought a ticket for Manchester Piccadilly. After the stand up train journey wrestling with all my gear taking a taxi to the hostel (a twenty minute walk away) seemed a justifiable luxury.

It was far too early to check into the hostel, so I started reassembling the bike. Last year's exercise involved nearly three hours and considerable frustration but I resolved not to rush things this time—to take great care—to think through everything carefully and to organise my work space efficiently. I laid out all my tools on the picnic table outside reception and opened the cycle box on the patio. A strong sense of moisture in the air urged speed but I worked cautiously and steadily, only smiling at the few passers-by. But, I downed tools for a while to talk with an older man setting out on his bike.

He had an old Mercier with a traditionally lugged steel frame in beautiful condition and immaculately maintained. However, perhaps the most impressive aspect was that although he was doing a solo charity ride from Cape Cornwall to Cape Wrath, a journey of probably 1500 km with only spartan gear. It consisted of a handlebar bag about a third the size of mine and a very small saddle bag that could have barely held a single change of clothes. I was humbled by his grit and obvious competence but also felt a sense of cycle tourist kinship that strengthened my enthusiasm and determination. Reinvigorated by this interruption, the assembly was complete in about 90 minutes with few mistakes. After storing my case and the bike in the cycle shed, I had lunch in the dining hall looking out over the canal and its colourful barges. Today, in honour of my arrival, a squadron of Canadian geese did a fly by.

Rob, Daniela and the Snake Pass

Daniela agreed to meet me at noon the following day at Café Nero near Manchester Piccadilly station and go on to meet Rob in Glossop by train from there.   Given the time of her flight arrival, I fully expected her to be late but she was on time, accompanied by Rob who had met her at the airport. He looked a lot smarter than he had in Brittany with new glasses, a sparkling white dress shirt and a fashionable suede jacket. I was dressed for cycling and came off a decided second best by comparison and wasn't well pleased with his possessive air.

Perhaps a little envious of his assumptions and more elegant appearance, I apparently did not concentrate on the railway ticket machine process, mistakenly picking up another person's ticket that had been left behind. The conductor quickly spotted this flaw when checking our tickets early in the journey.   It was embarrassing.   It made me look a cheat in front of my friends.   I protested that the ticket had been bought honestly, paid for with my MasterCard and probably left behind. The conductor heard my story but took my MasterCard to check the truth of my story in full detail. I was grateful that modern technology was able to confirm my story and restore any damage to my reputation.

Daniela intended to hire a cycle and to stay at a campsite some six kilometres distant complicating our get-togethers but Rob very thoughtfully offered her his spare cycle and a spot to camp down in his two-up, two-down home.   Rob's financial resources are very limited as he is out of work but the cycle looked suspiciously new.

I went on to my B&B about two kilometres beyond Rob's house and they joined me there for a late afternoon cycle ride on a rail trail through some lovely country. Frequent gates broke the continuity of the trail which ran alongside patches of purple heather and a reservoir.   My mudguards provided complete protection from the frequent puddles but Rob and Daniela were badly spattered.

After a quick stop to clean up at our respective accommodations, we regrouped at the vegetarian Globe Pub for dinner. Once there, Rob introduced us to the staff and to the pub's owner. I got the impression that he was particularly proud to be seen in Daniela's company and wanted everyone to notice. We each chose the same entrée: spinach curry with rice and a pint of lager for the amazing price of £5.30.

Afterwards, we returned to Rob's home to look at his maps and plan our cycle journey for tomorrow. Rob could not come as he had a distant all day job interview and had to leave early. We parted, Daniela agreeing to meet me there at 10 am.

Rain threatened as we negotiated the High Street north to join the A57 east towards the famous Snake Pass. Within minutes we had to stop to put on rain gear as the threat materialized. Daniela was visibly irritated at this and then again by the need to take the gear off when the rain stopped almost as quickly. Apparently, German rain behaves better.

Glossop's elevation on our Ordinance Survey (OS) map was about 200 while the Snake was shown as 536. Since the map distances were in miles, I assumed that the elevations were in feet, making our vertical climb over 300 feet. By the time we had struggled up the Snake, Daniela was certain it had to be metres. She was right.

Once up there we had a lovely, gently sweeping 5 km + long ride downhill tracking the bends of the River Ashop to Ladybower Reservoir. Steep, sheep-manicured moors rising up to 630 metres towered above the river providing a magnificent backdrop for our descent. Although we had been riding for less than two hours, a lay by café claimed us on the way down for an early lunch.

We continued to the A6031 and thanks to Daniela's superior map reading skills found a minor forest road west and down to Peakshole Water and a popular village, Castleton. Over coffee there, we talked about her work in cognitive psychology and her contentment with her current level in the organisation. Branching off at Castleton, we chose the road through Winnate Pass, which was even steeper but mercifully shorter than the Snake as I had to walk most of it. Then, gradually going north west, we arrived at the busy village of Hayfield in time for a late afternoon coffee at the George Hotel that proudly proclaimed it had opened in 1575.

While locking up the bikes outside the George, a gregarious, somewhat inebriated chap crossed the road to talk. Inexplicably, he launched into a discussion of helicopter gunships but in manner and comment fell just short of saying 'isn't this guy too old for you, how about me?' If that was his courting technique, she wasn't buying; we excused ourselves quickly, escaping to the George's lounge.

The remainder of the trip back to Glossop was primarily downhill but the pleasure was marred by heavy home from work traffic. We arrived just after six p.m., having covered 62 km of very strenuous terrain at an average of perhaps 10 km/h. Rob was home and we agreed to meet again at the Globe for dinner.

The pub was a lot livelier tonight. We got a table but many people had to stay at the bar. I was intrigued by the rear view of a bar-stooled blonde who was the centre of attention. She had a gaudy ribbon in her obviously chemically enhanced hair, dripped jewellery, and sported eyelashes that could swat flies. Her pasted on fingernails rivalled Edward Scissor Hands. I went up to place my meal order and to get a closer look. Supplementing all her artificial bits were two large, apparently natural, bits virtually bursting out of her blouse. No wonder, she was getting attention.

Shortly after our meal arrived, a group of people entered in Hawaiian costume, including men in grass skirts. Apart from us, no one took any particular notice and there was no indication of any rationale for their attire. Then suddenly, without warning, my left leg cramped sharply and shot out straight under the table. This was immediately followed by an equally severe cramp in my right leg. My thrashing around to relieve the pain obviously alarmed my friends. Daniela immediately prescribed magnesium. After dinner, she made a trip to the supermarket to pick up some things for their breakfast while Rob and I went back to his place. She returned while I was upstairs using Rob's internet. Soon, the sound of giggles drifted up the stairs so I quickly finished off my e-mail and hurried down. Daniela solemnly gave me a bottle of magnesium which she bought as a gift. The giggling started again when I glanced down at the bottle and saw that the 'Wo' of 'Women's Magnesium' had been scratched out. She had not been able to find a male version.

My return to Manchester the next afternoon allowed us time to do something together in the morning. So we met again at Rob's house. Playing on their amusement last night, I said 'I had the strangest sensation coming here this morning--I had a strong desire to have my nails done.' Feeble, but they enjoyed it. We discussed alternatives in Rob's tiny kitchen, made tight by three people and Rob's two stored bikes.

Given the poor weather and my shortage of time, we chose to do a walk in Glossop's expansive Manor Park. The path tracked a stream leading into attractive moorlands. Sheep grazed and we saw some belted Galloway cattle belonging to an old widower friend of Rob's who greeted us as we walked by. I had a great sense of community feeling visiting Glossop which of course was due to being with Rob who has lived here most of his life. After a couple of hours in the park, we returned for a quick lunch at a small bistro and went our separate ways.

Wheely Wonderful Tour
Cam agreed to meet me at the Manchester railway station for our rail journey to Ludlow. I had originally booked the tickets for a 9.30 departure but then worried that a flight delay could make that too early, rebooked for 10.30, incurring a penalty charge as well as more expensive tickets. When I arrived at the station just after nine, a voice called out from the balcony 'Robert Adams, Robert Adams'. He was already there and claimed to have been since 8.05!

After settling in at the 'Mount', our B&B in Ludlow, I announced that if Cam was to share a tour with me it had to be inaugurated with a teacake session at Shropshire's best teahouse, deGrey's. Like Betty's in Yorkshire, deGrey's is upscale with smartly dressed servers and top quality offerings.

Back at the 'Mount', our host apologized that a conflict made it impossible for him to transport us the eight kilometres out to Petchfield Farm, Wheely Wonderful's location. He gave us the phone numbers of several taxi companies after our Saturday arrival but none of them answered their phones Sunday morning. When I mentioned our problem to the cook after breakfast—she gently scolded me for not having booked a taxi on the Saturday. Then, leaving me to fret, she disappeared for about ten minutes.

When she returned—the problem was solved—her son volunteered to function as a taxi. He took Cam, his luggage and my panniers while I cycled the back, less steep, road to Petchfield. Either the directions or my interpretation of them was faulty. Whatever it was, eight kilometres came and went. I stopped two elderly ladies, the last to leave a church service, for further directions. This cost several minutes as they could not agree on which way to go. I followed the dominant one's directions, not at all certain that either one of them knew what they were talking about.

The terrain did not permit fast riding—my anticipated 30 minute ride had become an hour by the time I arrived at a T-junction totally devoid of any signposts. In desperation, I flagged down a car, fully expecting some local knowledge from anyone driving on these back roads—but no, it was a family on holiday. They did not know any of the village names on my directions. Fortunately, however, they had just driven past and noticed the Petchfield farm sign round the bend.

I found Cam, fully equipped and briefed on the tour, enjoying a cup of tea and chuckling over the tour operator's comment 'your Dad must be a very slow cyclist.' I sputtered ineffectively knowing that my excuse would betray my directional issues. Wheely Wonderful's site was efficient, and well-organized. One side of the courtyard was devoted to the cycle touring operation and the other side housed the farmhouse and buildings used for more traditional farming purposes. The maps, route notes and directions were excellent.

We finally pedalled off at about 12.30, pausing at the mouth of the drive to photograph the dramatic Wheely Wonderful sign. Driven as ever by my stomach and by the knowledge that pubs generally stop serving lunch at two—I persuaded Cam to stop at the Baron of Beef in Bucknell for a traditional Sunday pub lunch when we had covered less than 15 kilometres. He was still feeling stuffed after his 'full English' breakfast but appreciated the atmosphere and stunning blonde barmaid. She did not serve us but obliged by passing our table many times.

Atypically, I deferred to youth and allowed Cam to navigate, as we had only one set of notes. As good as these were--directions, historical and scenic notes and thumbnail maps were all mixed together on the same page. The directions were numbered and indented but written in the same font as everything else. Blurred by the thick plastic of the handlebar map case made reading difficult. Consequently, we often missed turnings by reading over crucial directional instructions.

Before reaching the Baron of Beef, our route roughly followed the River Teme to Bucknell. Afterwards we tracked the River Redlake – reportedly so named because it ran red with Roman blood from the battle that was Caractacus's last stand. He was defeated, captured and sent to Rome. Now it was peaceful and idyllic—a cleft between the hills with beautiful rural scenery.

We rolled into Clun on a picturesque stone packhorse bridge across the River Clun, oblivious to the fact that we had crossed the border into Wales. Apart from a noisy Sunday afternoon crowd outside the Whitehorse Inn, Clun was quiet with no sign of the Crown Inn where we were booked in. Releasing our map from its plastic case, we could now see that we had passed it before the bridge.

Judy, our landlady, was looking after her twin grandchildren, Ella and Herby, when we arrived. They were beautiful tow heads, bright eyed, intelligent and totally unreserved. Ella looked me over, pronouncing me 'strange.' Judy was mortified and although amused, I wasn't best pleased. A little later, while unpacking my bike, Herby asked 'are you 'strong and thin'—when I said 'yes, I suppose so'—he made an unflattering comment about my skinny legs!

The three hundred year old house made few concessions to modern safety requirements--access to the fire escape was through our room. All the doors were built for much shorter people –warning signs appeared over each of them saying 'DUCK'—emphasized by wooden or ceramic ducks.

We dined at the Whitehorse, our only choice on a Sunday night, and finished this first day with a late dusk stroll across the river into a rough, moor-like park below the remains of an eleventh century castle. Climbing the footpath up to the remaining Norman keep we came across a man seated on a bench engrossed in a telephone call about ancient history. When finished, he called to his dog 'come on old girl, time for bed.' As they trotted off down the footpath we saw another man photographing the castle against an emerging moon.

For me, the setting and observed activities were serenely satisfying, representing so well my image of Britain and British life and thus perfectly ending our first tour day. I hoped the contrast with Cameron's hectic lifestyle would be beneficial and instructive for him.

Without revealing his own professional music training or his wife's PhD in composition, Cameron carried on a lively breakfast conversation with a man taking a course in music composition.

That day's countryside was perfect with some significant hills but nothing that forced us off the bikes. Arriving in Bishop's Castle, we noticed a priest, rushing out of a church surrounded by well-dressed people. The soutane garbed priest darted here and there, saying nothing but apparently looking for someone. Then we saw that he was barefooted but he moved too quickly for us to get a decent photo. Within a few minutes he returned to the church to conduct a funeral. As he entered, we were impressed by the superb scenery (two-legged female variety) at the entrance. Reluctantly we left, thinking our interest might be considered disrespectful. Our sandwich lunch was at a roadside bench outside town overlooking a wide expanse of pasture broken by the gracefully curving Ony River.

The route was designed to be the easy approach to the famous Long Mynd moor top west of Church Stretton. Given Long Mynd's reputation, the ascent was unexpectedly easy, so much so that we were suddenly surprised to find that we were there. It is perfect moorland country. A narrow ribbon of tarmac threaded through a closely cropped, rocky landscape with sheep, occasional cattle grates, bracing air and magnificent long views over North Shropshire. As always on the moors, I had a sense of being on the top of the world.

Tonight's B&B, 'Mynd House' was a few kilometres south at Little Stretton. On the way, we watched a large flock of sheep being expertly herded by a black and white border collie. He ran alongside the flock but, guided by the shepherd's whistle, quickly changed direction to round up stragglers without losing any of the main flock. The dog was in his element, doing a job well that he obviously loved. It was a joy to watch this bond of partnership and skill between man and dog.

Our B&B hosts had only recently taken over from the previous owners and were still feeling their way a bit. Their inviting, leather chair outfitted bar was closed, awaiting the results of their licensing regulations examination. Our compensation was a very spacious and well-appointed family suite.

Church Stretton had been the home of my pen pal Andrew when we first met in 1957. My brother Byron and I stayed with his family on two occasions that year and attended a harvest festival at his father's church. Then it was a Congregational church but they had merged in 1976 with the Presbyterians to form the United Reform church. I wanted to see the church again and try to find Andrew's home where we stayed. So, Cameron and I did a little exploring in Church Stretton after breakfast. We found the right area for the house but could not find it for certain and the church wasn't open.

Carrying on, we rode just over 50 kilometres north east to the town of Ironbridge, considered the birthplace of the Industrial Revolution. In 1709, Abraham Darby discovered a method of smelting iron ore with coke rather than more expensive charcoal. That, the presence of significant coal deposits, and the accessibility of the Severn River fostered large scale development here.

There is a very interesting Museum of Iron in nearby Coalbrookdale and the Ironbridge Gorge Museum is now a UNESCO World Heritage site. One of the most popular tourist attractions is the first iron bridge ever, built in 1779, which crosses the Severn in midtown.

Our B&B eluded us for some time despite being only 'five minutes' walk from the centre.' We easily found Paradise Road and Coalbrookdale Inn. This wasn't the exact name we were looking for but how could it be wrong? Easily. This inn looked deserted and a little less than what we had come to expect. So, we reexamined the map and retraced our route to discover 'Coalbrookdale Villa' written in small letters on the entrance gate side now facing us—there was nothing on the other side. The Villa is an imposing Victorian Ironmaster's home elevated well above the road. Built in 1850 in a Victorian Gothic style, its austere black-brown stone was brightened and softened by yellow-painted windows and doors. Unlike, our novice hosts at Mynd House, June and Derek had enough and were actively trying to sell the place.

June, a former barmaid, retained her pub-honed skill of carrying on lively, non-consequential chatter. Still, it was engaging enough to encourage some unusual banter on my part. Cameron said it was good for me. On our second morning there, we appeared to be the only guests and June felt obliged to keep us company throughout breakfast. If that is what is required, I could never run a B&B.

We used our full morning in Ironbridge to visit the Museum of Iron learning more about Abraham Darby, blast furnaces, the relationships between coke, limestone and iron ore. I discovered the use of the term 'sow' in an iron context. My OED provides two meanings: either it is the trough through which molten iron runs into side-channels to form pigs of iron, or it is a large block of iron so formed, that is, a big pig. Travel is sow broadening!

In the afternoon, we hiked several kilometres to see the Blist Hills Victorian village. I had visited here several years ago and had a great experience that I thought Cameron would appreciate. Since that previous visit, a very well done introductory 360 degree visual history has been added that is brought alive by the dramatic sound effects of blast furnaces manufacturing steam engines and ship hulls, etc. But, the older part of the village while physically the same as my earlier visit, seemed a bit lifeless as some of the interpreters were more interested in conversation between themselves than providing relevant interesting commentary for visitors. Some of them totally ignored the visitors forcing us to ask for information in at least two of the building exhibits. However, it must be very boring for the interpreters to tell the same story, hundreds of times daily.

During dinner that night at the 'Meadow' on the Wharfage we were quickly reminded of the power of today's technology. Cam received a call from his wife on his mobile to report that that the price of Apple had dropped sharply on the stock market. With the six hour time difference, Cam was able to contact his Chicago broker and buy a number of shares before the market closed. I don't know precisely how large his investment was but three months later his capital gain would have easily paid for most of this tour.

Next morning, extricating ourselves from June's chatter, we headed south west for Much Wenlock, a medieval market town considered to be the birthplace of the modern Olympic movement. The first Wenlock Olympian Games were held in 1850 for 'every grade of man.' Participation was broad but many of the events, such as pushing the wheelbarrow, arithmetic and knitting have not survived. Many years later, in 1881, at the age of 73, Much Wenlock's William Penny Brookes was reported in the Greek newspaper, the *Clio*, '….as endeavouring to organize an international Olympian festival to be held in Athens.' Others have claimed that his efforts were crucial in re-establishing the Olympic movement.

The next 19 km were billed as the most tiring of the tour. The views were superb and the hamlet names (Muckley Cross, Great Hudwick, and Ditton Priors) evoked Dickens like images for me. As navigator, Cameron generally rode ahead. About three in the afternoon, as I rounded a bend, he was face down in a ditch, moaning softly. With some assistance, he struggled to become upright and was immediately aware that he had banged his bad knee on the top tube when he fell off. Later, he admitted that he had been distracted by some attractive sheep in a brilliant green pasture on the opposite side of the road. Now, he likes to preface the story with that excuse just to see the raised eyebrows.

His wheels would not rotate--both front and rear brakes were locked on. I loosened them enough that he could complete the day's ride to our final B&B of the organized tour--'The Town House' in Ludlow. This was a Georgian Grade II listed house dating back to 1720 on Brand Lane. We cycled down the lane without finding any sign for the B&B which is understandable as there wasn't any. We knocked tentatively on the door of the house with the specified number and was greeted by 'Helen', I think; it could have been Ellen. It was a lovely home with wooden floors, not altogether level, but more charming for that. Our room contained a large old fashioned tub with curved feet but the adjacent bathroom had one of most modern showers I've ever seen with heating, multiple spray options, and seating. Overall, the whole house had a rich, but understated atmosphere of elegance and comfort.

We developed our own route for returning to Petchfield Farm on the final day and did not record it; consequently, I can't remember exactly how we got there. We made it, barely escaping a heavy downpour. Chris, the owner, quickly discovered the reason for Cam's brake problem. The front wheel had turned 360 degrees in his fall, twisting the cables and creating the same sort of pressure as pulling on the brakes. Chagrin would be a mild description of the embarrassment I felt at not noticing this but persuaded myself that it was a natural mistake--my front wheel can't rotate all the way round like that.

Chris graciously drove us and my bike back to Ludlow in his Renault Scenic SUV. I have a special spot in my heart for Renaults, having briefly owned one (which Cameron totalled) in the late 1980s, so I particularly enjoyed the chance to ride in a modern one. Chris claimed that it got 60 miles to the Imperial gallon but jokingly said that if he were 'King of the World', SUVs would be banned.

Our final night in Ludlow was back at the same room at the 'Mount' where we started a week ago. During our last day in Ludlow, we toured the castle, had a sandwich lunch on a churchyard bench at the sandstone Church of St Laurence where A.E. Housman is buried and walked above the River Teme on the 'Bread Walk.'

It was given this name because the labourers who built it were paid in bread to discourage spending their wages at the pubs. Concluding our day with a now pleasant familiar note, we returned to de Grey's famous tea shop with its beamed ceilings, black uniformed wait staff and first quality pastries. Our toasted teacakes were served courteously, perfectly buttered, in a silver covered dish accompanied by a superior brand of black currant jam.

Time to Part

It was six p.m., Cam and I had to part. He had a morning flight from Manchester and I was booked at the hostel in Leominster tonight. We spent our last moments together on his train platform, sheltering from the rain that had persuaded me not to cycle to Leominster. My train was scheduled to leave eight minutes before his from the opposite side. After crossing over the bridge, we tried unsuccessfully to carry on a conversation across the tracks. The ticket office had closed at five so my ticket would have to be bought on the train but we got to Leominster in ten minutes and there was no opportunity to do so.

It took half an hour to locate the hostel housed in a former stable. As I arrived, two other men were just putting their cycles away in the shed. The standard conversation began, 'How far have you come today' 'Where are you going' along with exclamations of interest in my coupled bike. When we learned that the hostel did not provide meals, Pat and Dan invited me to join them at a pub for dinner and then shop for breakfast items.

In stature, they were sort of a British 'Mutt and Jeff;' cycling companions for years, they are colleagues in an accounting firm in Dorking, Surrey. Dan is tall and extremely thin. I had to cover my mouth to suppress a laugh when he emerged the next morning wearing a Sherlock Holmes style hat and extremely short shorts from which his very skinny legs dangled like loose threads. Pat, showing his Irish heritage, was the more gregarious of the two which is appropriate as he deals with the clients while Dan is the office manager.

During the several meals we shared, as is my wont, I peppered them with questions about the British economy and the changes being proposed by the new coalition government. Both were somewhat dismissive of and uninterested in the new government, believing it could not last. Neither anticipated the size of the spending cuts announced in October.

Down Market Accommodations and My Long-lost Pen Pal

For many of the youth that stay in hostels, it is just a place to bunk after bingeing. About two p.m. on my last night in Leominster, I got up to use the lavatory only to find a young woman sprawled on the floor next to the toilet bowl while talking on her mobile. The floor was covered in paper litter and a partially eaten slice of bread. I felt disgust at her and despair for the future.

The new morning's agenda helped overcome that despair, promising new adventure as I headed north to Shrewsbury by way of Craven Arms, Little Stretton and Church Stretton. My route required extensive use of the A49 which was very scary, particularly when being overtaken by lorries that often swung back into the lane too soon, nearly clipping me.

In Shrewsbury, since I did not have a UK electrical adaptor, I left my camera battery at a shop for recharging and went in search of my B&B-the Lucroft. It faced the library which had formerly been a school attended by Charles Darwin. His statue stands proudly outside.

Climbing a set of dirty narrow steps to the Lucroft, I met the landlady who wanted payment up front, asking for £2 more per night than she had quoted on line but had no evidence to challenge her. Her unusually low on-line quoted rate should have made me wary anyway. Rubbing salt into that wound, she then directed me back downstairs and up the street to a locked but common rubbish bin area to store my bike. This unappealing storage arrangement was also highly inconvenient as I had to summon the landlady to lock or unlock the area every time I needed to get the bike in or out. This sour beginning was mitigated in the morning by the attractively decorated and apparently clean breakfast room.

After a bit of city exploring, I enjoyed a late afternoon ride along a cycle path, a rail trail and out into the country as far as Acton Burnell. It was a bright, blue sky day with a strong breeze. The undulating road scape presented cottages, sheep and farm smells. Along the way I stopped in front of the gates of a huge manor house where a plaque proclaimed that Mark Twain had been a guest in the late nineteenth century.

Lucroft bedrooms were not equipped with WCs; from my room these were reached through a fire door and down a few steps. On my final morning, headed down to breakfast, I passed a young man returning to his room from the toilet. As he passed and mounted the stairs towards the hall corridor I turned to observe and came cheek to cheek, so to speak, with his bare backside! He was only wearing a pyjama top! At breakfast, one of the other guest's head was a clutch of used paint brushes—her multicoloured hair stood on end.

Sights during the balance of my day were less jarring. My objective was Market Drayton, about 78 km away to the Northeast as a midpoint to Uttoxeter where I would take a train to visit my pen pal, Andrew. A torrential rain started about 11 km west of the town. Once there, it took an additional 6 km just to find the B&B. Then soaked, I knocked at the door and was told I had no longer had a reservation-- some confusion with e-mails had cancelled it. Fortunately, she still had a vacancy; half an hour later, she would not have been home.

Sometime later, the rain eased off long enough for me to walk a short distance to one of those franchised, big barn type pubs for an institutionalized meal. Later, I rang Andrew to confirm my intended arrival time at Lincoln tomorrow afternoon.

My mother instilled a strong and permanent aversion to ever being late for anything. So, I was nervous about being able to catch the early afternoon train from Uttoxeter, some 50 km from Market Drayton in time to connect with Andrew. I requested an early breakfast and rushed off at 8.20. Some five kilometres later, I was chased down by my landlady's husband—to retrieve my room key!

Despite a rolling terrain, I managed about 16 km/h, arriving in time for a supermarket lunch before train departure. Andrew collected me from the Lincoln station and drove to his home in nearby Nettleham to have tea in the garden with Marion.

Andrew showed me a bit of Nettleham including the teashop that he and Marion operated for many years after his retirement from teaching at Lincoln Agricultural College. My immediate impression of this small, friendly rural village was very positive. Particularly appealing was a period cottage which Andrew estimated would cost £350,000. It set behind the High Street alongside a small stream.

Our interests and careers differed greatly but despite this and 30 years of no contact, it was amazing how few gaps there were in the conversation. The following day, the three of us briefly toured Lincoln and enjoyed a canal-side coffee before I had to leave.

Longdon Hall, Ashbourne, Dovedale and Ilam Hostel

Andrew dropped me off at the Lincoln station just before the 1.40 train to Uttoxeter which stopped in Nottingham and Derby. As usual, my train left from the far platform. With only seven minutes to departure, it was fortunate to find a lift that avoided having to haul the bike up and down the railway bridge stairs.

This lift process had to be repeated at Nottingham but not Derby. Back at Uttoxeter, I needed help to find the B5013 out of town. Since most Britons know the roads by where they go rather than by number, it can be a little frustrating to get help unless you know the towns along the way to your destination. This time I struck it lucky and found a knowledgeable young woman in a bakery shop.

It was meant to be an easy 24 km to my accommodation at Old Longdon Hall Farm. That part was easy but just as I reached tiny Longdon village, rain started. There was no sign of or to the farm. I stopped in the Double Headed Swan pub and waited patiently for the barman to finish a card game before he could be bothered to help. Then he claimed never to have heard of the farm or the road on which it was located. 'I don't know, try the pub at the top of the hill.'

On my way to this second pub, I saw a sign for Longdon Hall Estate across the road. Thinking this a more likely source of information than a pub, I crossed over to find the building deserted--it was 5.30 pm on a Saturday. Next, I ventured down the adjacent Church Road approaching the first home for directions. My arrival was met by a fierce response from three very angry dogs. Next door produced the same response just with one less canine. My third attempt, across the street this time, was lucky--a dog-less human was at home. He had no knowledge of the farm but thought a lifelong resident neighbour might and offered to intercede for me.

Grateful for his help, I suppressed my irritation at being mistaken for a Yank. The neighbour did know the farm and gave me precise directions how to get there but warned me that my journey would be fruitless as Longdon Hall Farm did not do accommodation any more since the owner was dead!

Thinking it unlikely that I had made my e-mail booking with a corpse, I risked the six kilometres cycle to the farm. This time the directions were perfect ending at the Thorley's Hill address that the barman though did not exist. The farm's long, rough approach bordered a paddock of horses, ending at a rambling old brick pile surrounded by a terrace of brick cottages and a huge barn.

No one answered my knock at the door but I could hear voices round the side where I discovered mud-streaked Andy, the owner. He briefly apologized for his appearance and led me to the barn where my cycle was to be stored, propped up on bales of straw, near a monster tractor. Next, he showed me to my room in the attic. I offered a weak joke that the room must be reserved for his 'top' customers but was particularly pleased with the size and comfort of the room. Gigantic cathedral-like roof beams separated the twin-bedded sleeping area from a sitting room with two easy chairs. Across the hall was a massive private bath. Tea making facilities (with biscuits) were provided one level below. My window overlooked the horses as well as two border collies playing football, kicking and chasing it but sometimes running, holding the ball in their mouths by a ragged flap.

During our correspondence, Andy had offered to make dinner reservations at a pub for me and given the remoteness of his farm, to provide the necessary transport. His young, confident wife, Lee Anne, drove me there. On the way she confided that she was a 'townie' from Essex and despite having lived with Andy at the farm for four years was still 'settling in' to country life. As a qualified city veterinarian, she was used to a more active life and was still surprised at the amount of time on the farm spent drinking tea. Now, she practises locally part-time and runs a DIY livery at the farm for about a dozen horses on top of her responsibilities for Ruby, their 18 month old daughter. Andy collected me after my meal, proudly looking forward to Ruby's help with farm chores in a few months.

Next morning, I was the first down for breakfast in a large room next to the kitchen. Two long tables were set along the wall. One held the bowls, milk and a tremendous selection of cereals; the other housed a variety of breads and a toaster. Another two long tables running the length of the room were laid out for the nine guests. In the centre of each of these was a large lazy susan holding all sorts of jams and honeys.

Andy, looking totally refreshed and relaxed, took my order–'tea and a full English but no sausage or blood pudding.' He was cook and waiter. I asked if it wasn't a tremendous workload with both the farm and the B&B. He replied 'No, I do the B&B in the morning and the farming in the afternoon; there is always something different to do—I really enjoy it.' I also asked about the age of the house—'Well,' he said, 'it's 12th century but it was modernized in 1690. We used to have a moat.' As I left, the dogs were again playing football. The entire cost of this experience was less than that Shrewsbury dump, the Lucroft! And, there was nothing to rival the bare backsides and paintbrush hair.

However, the Lucroft's rubbish area cycle store might be preferable to the bits of straw and chicken manure that my bike collected overnight. Removing these, I set off north, largely retracing yesterday's route from Uttoxeter. Once there, I revisited the Co-op supermarket for a sandwich and chocolate milk and ate them outside on a bench near the bus shelter and public convenience.

This was a public convenience unlike any of my experience.   Its spotless white porcelain interior was graced with gleaming mirrors, floral arrangements and porcelain ducks of every description on the ledge above the wash basins and on the wall-length bank of urinals. Impressed; I took a number of pictures and made a special effort to commend the female attendant who had just returned from a lunchtime trip to the supermarket.   She held court in a tiny storage area in between the male and female sides. While nothing else in Uttoxeter met this standard, the town was unusually tidy and well maintained.

My objective was the llam hostel. Riding mainly north along the B5030 and B5032, I was soon at the village of Rocester, passing by a huge area of water, grassy areas and walking paths.   As it was a beautifully sunny day, the park was filled with people, many of whom were fishing with very elaborate equipment.   Behind all of this was a huge commercial building, identified only by the letters 'JCB.'

This merited a closer look, so I crossed the road and went round the park, becoming increasingly impressed with the beautiful landscaping, the wildlife, the modernistic sculptures and memorials and the tremendous size of it all.   A park bench couple answered my questions: 'JCB is a huge, international earth-moving equipment company.   Its founder donated much of the money for the park and worked with the town to establish it.   The lake is stocked and there are major fishing competitions every year.'

Despite the hard kilometres left to cover before reaching the hostel, I took an early tea and Sunday Times break in the town of Ashbourne, a market town known as the Gateway to the Peaks.   The remaining distance was in a marvellous countryside of rolling, velvety green carpeted hillsides and roiling, rock-strewn streams.   Towards the end of this last stage I was in Dovedale which is also known as 'little Switzerland.'   Here, the road runs between fairly low but abruptly steep hills graced with sheep and the narrow Dove River meanders, murmuring happily over its rocky bed.   Red brown cows with soft, sad eyes grazed on the banks.   It was blissfully peaceful.

The hostel is housed in a former estate, set in extensive, beautiful grounds ringed by dramatic hills. The former owner willed the estate to be a hostel. It is expensive as hostels go but is about as full-service a hostel as one can find with a cafeteria offering several different main courses, starters and sweets; a launderette, games room, internet access and a quiet room.

I was booked in for three nights and planned circular routes to explore the gorgeous countryside. Not moving on each night allowed me to leave much of my gear behind but the numerous hills would still be tough. First on the agenda was the Tissington Trail, a rail trail running north and south for several kilometres merging into the last bit of the High Peak trail that runs roughly SE to NW. Taking the trail avoided both traffic and hills. I found an entrance a few hard kilometres to the east of Ilam near Tissington Hall and later discovered an even closer access at Thorpe.

The trail varies, running through narrow granite cuttings or forest to emerge on high ridges overlooking wide swathes of lovely countryside. Today, the path was punctuated with puddles from the day before but my mudguards kept me clean and dry. A real downpour hit just as I got to the Parsley Gap rest and cycle hire station. Most of the poor souls that showed up later on hired cycles without mudguards were sodden and streaked with mud. The temperature dropped to 10C or below and the rain continued, making the day bleak and miserable. I claimed a dry perch on a rough bench near the cycle hire section and nursed a couple of large teas and a cheese sandwich over the next two hours until the rain eased.

As it was now early afternoon, I reversed direction and followed the High Peak trail south east to its final rest stop near the B5035 which I took past Carsington Water down to Ashbourne and then back to Ilam. This final stage of today's journey was just as tough and pleasant as it had been yesterday but cemented my decision to cut my stay at hostel short by a day to better handle the hard terrain and distance going further north.

I also decided to use Tissington Trail again to reduce the amount of hill climbing required. This second time, strong wind gusts swept across the trail along the high ridges and it was hard work to avoid being blown off. The sky wept intermittently; at Parsley Gap, the temperature had dropped back down single digits. I succumbed to a hot chocolate to warm up then left the trail to join the B5055 that runs north east to Bakewell.

A cold shower started almost immediately, thoroughly soaking me by the time I arrived at Monyash about half an hour later. The pub was closed but fortunately, there was a small open café next door offering shelter, warmth and lunch. I strung out that stay for nearly an hour emerging to a now dry but still cool day.

Bakewell was a must on my itinerary, primarily to reacquaint myself with the famed Bakewell tart that I had first sampled in the 1970s on a family holiday. The tart is a baked open pie with a jam lined pastry case filled with a rich almond paste. Legend has it that the pie was a mistake caused by an inexperienced kitchen maid who messed up the order sequence for the ingredients.

So, it was a priority on my agenda but having cancelled my hostel booking for tonight, the first priority to find alternative accommodation. On arrival in Bakewell, I immediately went to the Tourist Information Centre (TIC). Finding both nearby hostels fully booked, the TIC staff person started looking into B&Bs for me. I asked for a single room with a ceiling price of £35 and a preference for staying in Bakewell. Singles are hard to find most places and Bakewell proved to be too expensive or fully booked. So, he expanded the search until he found one spot about 10 km north on the A623 at £45 which I finally agreed to after initially rejecting it as too expensive. Given the amount of time and the number of telephone calls it took to achieve this, the £3 fee was reasonable particularly as I expected the B&B would absorb that fee. That used to be the practice but unfortunately, is no longer the case.

Normally, I compensate for such ravages on the budget by cutting out something else—but not my Bakewell tart! Instead I would scrimp on dinner by picking up a snack at the supermarket. A narrow, shop-lined passage across the street from the supermarket led to the library suggested an opportunity to access the internet. A promising teashop, offering my long-anticipated tarts, was along the way. I resisted the urge for immediate gratification to enhance the experience by a further delay and went first to the library. However, all their computers were in use, so I booked one for an hour later and returned to the teashop, choosing a large window table to provide adequate light for reading. The beautiful amber coloured tart covered most of the plate. It was delicious but disappeared far too quickly.

After my internet session I began the journey to the B&B. The route was mainly north on the B6465 to the A623 and then east. Shortly after starting out, feelings of déjà vu began to emerge; I had been here before—15 years ago while staying at the Castle Cliffe B&B just opposite the Monsal Head lookout. That day in 1995 had been my introduction to the old custom of well dressing in which a sculpted clay base is filled with different coloured flower petals to create a picture. Nearby Ashford in the Water held a well dressing festival that weekend. Now, it was enough to take a few quiet moments to reacquaint myself with the beauty of the broad, deep river valley below the road.

My B&B wasn't the four star establishment it claimed to be. The room was at the end of a long, narrow passage on the first floor. It was cold but being summer, the heating system was not operating. I immediately took a long, hot shower to warm up. Neither my mobile nor the television worked. Kevin, my landlord, came up and wiggled some wires on the back of the television—so it worked but there was nothing worth watching. There was no mobile signal. Giving up, I made some tea, snuggled most of me under the duvet to eat my yoghourt and huge pork pie.

First down for breakfast, I was already enjoying a bowl of muesli and a cup of tea when two older couples arrived, travelling together on a walking holiday. The landlady hovered, asking each in turn for their order. There was considerable dithering about how the eggs were to be cooked but eventually she got three decisions. I think the final woman may have been embarrassed by all the fuss and when asked 'how would you like your eggs?' simply said 'just as they come.' I could not resist saying 'they come in a shell—is that what you want?'

That seemed to break the ice allowing us to carry on with some superficial conversation.

Glossop was today's destination and I sought Kevin's advice on how best to avoid the worst hills. There were essentially two choices: up the Snake Pass or up the western route through Hayfield. Kevin thought the Snake, while tougher, was of shorter duration, so the pain would not last as long. I was also interested in seeing nearby Eyam, the famous Black Plague town, whose residents chose to remain in the town rather than leaving and infecting others. Eyam also had a recommended tea shop which always appeals. The ride to Eyam was pleasant and short but the town was disappointingly bland. There were no historical plaques or tea shop to be found. Reversing direction towards Glossop, I consulted my map carefully and chose some unmarked roads that tracked the A623 but avoided its traffic. Remembering the downhill run into Glossop from Hayfield on my Snake Pass day, I decided to ignore Kevin's advice, choosing the western route.

Rob wasn't at home when I stopped, so, wanting to leave a message, I went back to the street and borrowed a pen and paper from the corner pet shop to write a note suggesting we meet at the Globe pub at half seven. By the time, I arrived at my B&B, Rob had rung to say that he would prefer to meet at 7.00 as he was very hungry. There was still time for me to take a short nap but had barely stretched out when the landlady knocked at the door. 'Your friend just called back to say he can't wait any longer. He is leaving for the pub now.' It was just before six. Although groggy from my barely begun nap, I rushed through a shower, dressed and quick-walked the two kilometres to the pub, arriving at 6.30. Rob was outside on the beer patio, having left a message at the bar for 'the Canadian.' Walking over faith my pint, Rob was buried in a book about badgers.

During our meal Rob told me about his new job instructing and supervising volunteers surveying the state of vegetation on high moor country. Next month, he'll oversee replanting from a helicopter. We were joined briefly by an amateur music impresario acquaintance of Rob's. So, the conversation moved to various musicians they both knew, groups that had performed in the pub's upstairs auditorium and surprisingly, Rob's experience as a DJ. I must confess, my image of him has become much more positive since the Breton Bike trip last year. We parted company after dinner and I returned to my B&B.

My new day began well with a sumptuous breakfast of prunes in Greek yoghourt, scrambled eggs, sweet vine tomatoes, bacon and a whole wheat bap. Thus fortified, I ventured out up on the moors. The road was steep; a fierce, wet wind chilled me to the bone but the high, solitary and desolate landscape inspired and felt a fitting finale for a self-reliant cyclist who thrives on the bragging rights of rigorous riding. As I was capturing the bragging evidence my camera battery died simultaneously with a full memory card, providing justification to head back to Glossop for a warming coffee and pastry.

Temporarily full again, it was now time for my train into Manchester where I returned to the hostel and managed to disassemble and pack the bike in 68 minutes—a record! This added to my sense of competence offsetting a general malaise and aloofness that set in after the coffee stop. The tour is over, the play I hoped to see tonight ended a few days ago and the only alternatives are rubbish mass market US films or gay, lesbian ones showing at the cinemas.

My mid-afternoon flight the next day allowed time to visit the nearby Museum of Scientific Invention (MOSI) which features exhibits of scientific developments in the Manchester area. Quite a bit is devoted to the textile industry including recent technological breakthroughs and overall, the museum is well worth a visit.

Mari collected me at the Toronto airport and took me home to a very good dinner. We finished the evening appropriately with one of our favourite British television programs, set in Yorkshire. I'm already thinking ahead to next year's tour which is to include both Britain and France.

French Postal Bike on Boulevard St Germain, Paris

St CyprienVillage, Dordogne

OXFORD & SOUTHERN FRANCE TOUR

BRITAIN

FRANCE

OXFORD & SOUTHERN FRANCE

Prior experience has taught me that booking accommodations early is the best way to ensure you'll have a place to stay-important after a long day in the saddle. Sometimes, hostels are fully booked for a summer date as early as February, so my planning for a tour now generally starts in the autumn of the previous year. But, planning can be overdone and done too early. That was certainly the case with this tour. I booked my late August 2011 flight in November 2010 basing the return date on the end of a Breton Bikes group tour starting in Biarritz, near the Spanish border. This opened up a new area of research--bike transport on French Rail.

Although I've used British Rail successfully for years, my only experience with bikes on French Rail (SNCF) had been negative--a major hassle, the bike treated like freight and arriving a day after I did. So, the first objective was to learn if and how I could get to and from Biarritz with my bike without the previous problems while incorporating some solo touring along the way. A Paris based firm called Blue Marble that specializes in rail supported bike tours sold me a seven page information booklet for 20€--more than the cost of this book! The vital bits are summarized below—for free!

Some French trains take bikes only as boxed baggage–not particularly practical on a multi-location tour. Other, regional trains, allow bikes on a 'roll-on, roll-off' basis subject to space being available in the designated car. This space is a small area reserved for cycles unlike the British system which is intended for wheelchairs, prams or cycles. There the cycle can be lashed, still unloaded, to a rail on the wall with a bungee cord. In France the cycle space is fitted with up to four hooks. Bikes are to be totally unloaded before being hung. You can imagine how nerve-racking this would be, lugging bike and panniers separately while disembarking in a crush of other passengers getting on and off and with perhaps only two or three minutes before the train pulls out again. Having just a few minutes before a connecting train leaves from a distant platform only magnifies the stress.

Some of the famous TGV long-distance trains provide space for four roll-on bikes but only with a reservation and that reservation can only be bought in France—making on-line booking impossible. SCNF's

French language web-site is the sole source for learning whether a particular train allows roll-on, roll-off bikes or if a TGV will take bikes. The unloading, hanging, disembarking hassle can be enjoyed on both. If there are connections to be made, those trains have to be checked also. The availability of a roll-on, roll-off service dictated where I could plan the solo part of my time in France with any certainty. So, I spent hours on that web-site with my French maps, searching for possibilities that would connect well with Biarritz.

The web-site is organized on the assumption that you want to book a ticket now or for the near future. It only allows bookings a few months in advance, so information searches with long lead times like mine have to be based on earlier months you don't plan to travel. Complicating this is that train weekday and weekend timetables aren't necessarily the same. So, planning has to be fairly detailed to ensure that the service desired will be available on the day and at the time you want it. Even then, planning so far ahead can be a total waste of time if a wholesale system or seasonal change in the rail schedule occurs after your plan is set.

This happened to me in early summer 2011. When confirming my travel schedule I discovered that my planned train departure from Biarritz was altered to a later time that would cause me to miss the connection from Paris to Calais. Plan B became miss the final group dinner, leave Biarritz a day early on the night train and roam the streets of Paris until time for the Calais train. Both of these were TGV schedules, so the plan was dependent on being able to make a bike reservation on them once I was in France.

The rough outline of the tour became a solo ten days centred on Oxford followed by an overnight ferry to St Malo and another solo ten days in the Dordogne before joining the group. I allowed three additional days to get back to Gatwick airport.

For this tour, I again used the Michelin mapping site. It allows you to specify a route suitable for cyclists and to designate intermediate stops between A and B. Irritatingly, Michelin does not allow you to plan a loop trip that returns to the start--an A to A in effect. I booked the Oxford hostel for six nights to be able to make unladen, circular trips. The only way round this mapping problem was to build in several intermediate stops finishing with a B very close to A.

I won't be totally relying on Michelin again for several reasons. First, the instructions were often vague such as 'leave the city centre and continue for 1.5 km' with no indication of where in the centre to leave from or whether you should cycle east, west, north or south. Turning directions sometimes depended on being able to see street signs posted parallel to the road on buildings but nowhere near eye level. Other times the necessary road wasn't signposted.

The major drawback is the lack of flexibility. If you rely entirely on such a service, you have nothing to refer to if you get lost or if you simply want to explore some interesting alternative. Despite my long-held preference to plan everything, leaving nothing to chance, I now think it is better to provide for contingencies. Buy highly detailed (at least 1:150,000, preferably 1:100,000) maps for the area. These will show all the roads you might want to explore and reveal different ways of getting places, identify scenic routes and often historic sites. Such a detailed map will allow you to plan on the fly, assess elevation, avoid steep climbs, etc.   It unlocks your agenda, develops navigational skills and increases the potential for adventure. But, you probably will have to wait until you arrive to find them.

The Tour
My flight landed at Gatwick about 9.30 a.m.   The queue through Immigration was slow due to 'short staff' –part of Britain's new austerity measures, no doubt.   This delay meant however that my cycle was already waiting for me in the oversized baggage section. The duffel bag was not. I stood dejectedly watching the carousel go round and round until the last bag was removed. Mine wasn't there. Panic struck. The bag contained my clothes, my sleeping bag, my helmet and my bike's luggage racks. The trip seemed over before it had begun.

At the baggage office they asked for my receipts to fill out the missing luggage claim–then called the handling people to determine the carousel number and rather snidely pointed out that I had been standing at the wrong carousel. Who would have expected that two flights would arrive from Toronto at the same time?   The flight numbers and airline names weren't posted.   But, there was my bag, sitting forlornly in the corner by the correct carousel. This was not the tour's only panic attack but like this one, fortunately they all were overcome.

At my nearby B&B in Horley, I reassembled my bike in the parking lot, taking time to think carefully about the proper sequence of actions while conscious of ominous rain clouds.   The task went well until I discovered that some of the rear rack nuts and bolts were missing. The town's only cycle shop, at the far end of the High Street did not stock such mundane items but the ironmonger did.   However, a packet of 140 was the smallest quantity available—a lifetime stock of spares. Together with a tea break, this interruption delayed completion of the reassembly task until mid-afternoon. Fortunately, I had abandoned my earlier habit of cycling off after assembly and was booked to stay here overnight.

Now the panniers had to be packed. The yet unneeded camping gear for the group tour was relegated to the front bags. When a home was finally found for everything, I collapsed for a short nap before realising a multiyear objective of dining at the 'Six Bells'—a lovely old upscale pub just five minutes' walk away. Despite being a Monday, it was packed.

Henley

At 9.05, after a cholesterol laden breakfast of poached eggs, tomato, bacon, muesli and grapefruit sections washed down with three cups of tea, I cycled off to the Horley station for a northward journey to St Albans. My successful bike assembly proved immediately illusory as the front mudguard bracket rubbed against the wheel making an awful racket attracting annoyed attention from pedestrians. And, the computer registered neither speed nor distance.

On arrival in St Albans, I was to cycle 14 km to Welwyn Garden City for an overnight with long-term friends from our days of living there nearly 40 years ago.   My Michelin map route began from the city centre rather than the station and no one could tell me how to find the necessary road. After a few 'I don't speak English' or 'I've only lived here a few years and don't know my way round yet' responses to my requests for directions, I gave up and relied on my compass and now very faint but ultimately effective recollections.

Despite a very pleasant, relaxing visit with Penny and Jeff, I was eager to be underway.the following morning, Jeff took a picture of me astride my fully loaded bike to send to Mari. Starting about ten and using back lanes, I cycled about sixty kilometres returning through St Albans and continued south west to Slough for a train to Goring. Goring sits south of Oxford along the Thames and is a delightfully perfect village with pleasant cafes, good pubs and colourful activity at the locks. It has all the necessary sort of shops (another ironmonger fitted new batteries for my computer, restoring it to action. I like to know my speed and distance information is crucial if you are following the Michelin turning instructions).

I spent two nights at a slightly shabby Goring B&B. There wasn't anything essentially wrong. It was just the downmarket atmosphere. Entering and unloading my bike in a garage stuffed with in-process laundry, spare freezers and accumulated detritus did not inspire confidence, nor did my landlady's uninterested and dour manner. Over the two days, it was obvious that running a B&B was an economic necessity not a passion to please. After clearing up my breakfast, she ran a hairdressing salon in her kitchen. I never saw or heard any other members of the family but unless she was also running a laundry, there must have been some.

Nevertheless, Goring was a good spot for exploring the Thames Valley and my first excursion was to be Henley. Long, steep hills, some with broad, quintessentially English vistas of fields bordered by giant mushroom like trees, made a great ride. The day warmed up considerably becoming beautifully sunny. It was still summer, of course, and market day in Henley added a holiday feel. Aimlessly, I cycled the towpath, enjoying the swans, geese and ducks and observing a group of children learning to canoe. An elevated boardwalk took me into the middle of the river whose banks were graced with massive willows and marvellous homes. Small yachts were piloted through the locks (with some passengers swilling champagne). Lunching outside on a library bench and using their guest computer allowed me to send progress reports home. About four, I retraced my route back to Goring and adjacent Streatley for more river lock activity and had an excellent salmon dinner at the Barleycorn pub. Overall, it was a very satisfying day. I re-found 'my England' and had a great experience-at an all-in cost of $88!

Home for the next six nights was to be at the Oxford hostel. The route there was partly intentional but mainly ad hoc possibilities. I wanted to see the villages of Christmas Common, Fingest and Turville because I thought it would be fun to try to recognize any of the locations from one of my favourite television programs, 'The Vicar of Dibley.'

The day began with a downpour. I delayed my departure in hopes that it would ease off. My landlady, mellowed somewhat after being paid, offered me some maps of the area. When the downpour deteriorated to drips, I donned my waterproof gear and headed north then east towards Christmas Common and the other villages. The rain continued sporadically, never stopping for long. A country lane heading towards Ewelme seemed an interesting side trip, based on its unusual name, and possibly had tea break potential.

This part of Ewelme was one long street with homes and shops on one side and watercress beds on the other. These beds used to supply watercress to Covent Garden and were featured in a 'Midsomer Murders' episode. Covent Garden doesn't buy Ewelme cress anymore as there is concern about the water quality. As I entered my teashop inside the grocery-cum post office, the attendant was counting yesterday's till cash on the tea table. It was short by £1.50, which he pronounced 'close enough', reminding me of the many times my father was late home for dinner from the bank because the till was out by as little as a penny and staff weren't allowed to leave until it was found. This sounds more anal than it was--a penny's discrepancy might mask much bigger, partially offsetting errors.

The bell on the shop's door jingled constantly as people came in, passing me at the tea table, contributing to and chewing over the latest gossip, buying stamps or grocery items and discussing village business. Clearly, this was the village social centre. I enjoyed my tea break eavesdropping on local life while leafing through some history pamphlets.

About noon, I passed through Christmas Common and found the road to Fingest. Just at that moment, the rain started up with a vengeance. The soggy scenery could not compete with my desire to get warm and dry so I scuttled back to the nearby 'Greyhound' pub, found a sheltering tree for the bike and used the pub's washroom to dry and arrange my soaked strands of hair into some order. (A cycle helmet offers virtually no protection protects from rain.) The lounge bar had a roaring fire but the nearest table was already occupied. I made do with a window table seat which provided good light for reading but little warmth. There was a wide choice of entrées. As usual, my budget circumscribed my options but the potato-salmon cakes and salad were excellent and a pint of lager made it complete.

Fingest and Turville were a disappointment. There wasn't anything recognizable from the programs—very little sign of life at all. Now beyond the scope of the maps my landlady had supplied, it took the barely readable incomplete town name at the far edge of my own map, a road sign and my compass to get me closer to Oxford. Further on, I was directed to the 'old A40.' Initially, this was reasonably quiet and fast with a cycle lane of perhaps three-quarters of a metre width and very little traffic. Suddenly, there was no place to go but to an on ramp leading to what must have been the 'new A40.' This was a four–lane, 70 miles per hour road with no bike lane. It was scary; I just put my head down and cycled steadily as fast as I could. A rough, gravelly shoulder on my left, roaring traffic on my right--any loss of stability could have been fatal. This lasted for about five kilometres ending at the edge of Oxford.

Oxford attracts me on many fronts. Bikes and book shops abound. Important history is everywhere. Parks and river scenery offer beauty and serenity. The British academic atmosphere particularly appeals as I indulge a conceit of myself as a respected, tweed-clad don. Consequently, I spent my first Oxford day in pedestrian pleasures. A slow tour of Balliol College's chapel, dining hall, student rooms and grounds nourished my academic fantasies.

Dedicated cycle lanes, specified areas at traffic lights and access to pedestrian districts denied to vehicles make Oxford a cyclist's paradise. Exploring the multitude of cycle shops, I was excited by unfamiliar brands and models--particularly the retro styles by makers like Pashley--perhaps I see them as contemporaries. My own cycle is a custom built traditional.

I was also struck by the sheer number of outstanding female beauties in the city. Britain isn't noted for this, so it wasn't surprising that there were a multitude of complexions. Foreign tourists dominated the hostel and often came in large groups. One morning, at breakfast, the sea of blond heads suggested that Germany had finally launched a successful invasion. They were an enervated group but mostly well-behaved, slim and attractive, particularly the frauleins.

Other hostel guests appealed far less. One group of mid-twenties males booked on-line pretending to be a student group to be eligible for a discount. They were loud, rude and inconsiderate. For reasons which were never clear, several of them chose to come to breakfast in costume—Red Riding Hood, the Wolf as Grandma, and a few Ninja characters.

Oxford was my centre for a number of planned circular routes embracing Blenheim Palace at Woodstock, Witney, Bicester, Great Tew and the White Horse at Uffington. However, on my first excursion, one of the Sustrans cycle routes diverted me to an interesting canal tow path with scruffy narrow houseboat barges lining the bank. Several fishermen wrestled massive sets of telescoping poles to troll the undisturbed waters on the far side of the canal. The towpath emerged onto a cycle path north parallel to the A44. At the A4095 intersection, I went west to Witney, stopping at the Coach Inn for a Sunday buffet lunch advertised at £9.95. At that price, my budget barely allowed a pint of beer. I was pleasantly surprised but also mildly upset to be presented with a bill for £8.55 for both, net of the senior discount! My age was obvious—no documentary proof was required.

I bought the most detailed map available (short of an Ordinance Survey version) at Waterstone's book shop in Witney and headed west on the A4047 towards Minster Lovell, rolling into the village along a lovely lane. Minster Lovell consists of a five star hotel, a pub and one street of thatched golden Cotswold stone houses. The well-heeled couples enjoying riverside patio afternoon tea at the hotel seemed agitated that I might have the audacity to join them.

Turning north along lanes to Leafield then climbing east to the B4022, brought me to high, flat moorland with wide vistas and sunshine. It was joyous cycling, freewheeling fast back down to Witney and the A4095. Retracing my earlier path from the A44, I again followed the towpath back into Oxford. I had covered 75 km, almost totally diverging from today's plan.

The following day, Bank Holiday Monday, the cycle path along the A44 led into the village of Woodstock and home of Blenheim Palace where a classic car show was being held. The Palace entry queue was a stop and go holiday gridlock. I eased past the cars to the edge of the parking lot choosing only to attend the free car show. This was a delight. I wandered about, pushing my bike, chatting with proud owners of rarely seen British makes, and was pleased to be stopped by some who admired my 'classic' cycle. Having toured the palace years ago, a leisurely ride round the extensive gardens was sufficient to appreciate Blenheim's grandeur before venturing into Woodstock, Lord Randolph Churchill's parliamentary base, for lunch.

Next, following the A44 north west almost to Chipping Norton, I turned south at Enstone to explore more of the moorland lanes discovered yesterday and returned to Oxford again collecting a collation of cold items from the Marks and Spencer 'Simply Food' shop at a petrol station along the way. Then, competing for space at the hostel member's tiny kitchen table, I had my M&S dinner with a glass of hostel red.

France

My notes are curiously silent on my last two days in Oxford, apart from another day of pedestrian pleasures but on departure day, I was booked on the overnight ferry to France that left Portsmouth at 8.15 p.m. As Portsmouth is 150 km from Oxford, I split the distance, cycling 54 km to Reading and taking a train from there. It was a pleasant ride along the B480/481 passing by or through Stadhampton, Watlingford and Nettlebed. Most of this was quietly rural but riding against the clock to meet the train for Portsmouth didn't allow time to fully enjoy it.

Night channel ferry crossings excite me; I enjoy the whole process: going through passport control in the twilight, being waved aboard ahead of the cars and lorries, securing and unloading the bike, and noting the deck and door location before ascending to the passenger areas. The holiday atmosphere, the harbour lights, the fantastic meal choices in several restaurants, the cosy but complete cabin, all combine to create a change of pace and adventure.

I particularly anticipated slowly savouring a dinner of steak frites, red wine and a French pastry with my current book. First, though, I wanted to experience and photograph the harbour night scene. We were surrounded by the lit outlines of HMS Navy vessels, harbour perimeter lights and our own festively lighted decks. Passengers crowded the decks, drinks in hand. The tricolour flapped proudly from the stern, I felt already in France.

In the morning, about an hour before disembarkation, a soft but distinct voice murmured me awake in both languages, announcing our imminent arrival at St Malo. Quickly showering and packing up, I went down to prepare my bike for a speedy departure and was first off. Rolling past the customs officers, one called out 'English'? – thinking he was asking about my preferred language, my automatic response was 'yes'. A few minutes later, I thought maybe he was inquiring about my nationality to do a passport check. Well, I wasn't going back; I was eager to find the railway station, hoping to get the 9.30 regional to Rennes.

As part of the planning process, I had prepared and practised how to request this train ticket in French. When the time came, my written cheat sheet was missing. Surprisingly, I remembered what to say sufficiently well to be understood. Then, unexpectedly the friendly lady clerk inquired, 'Quel âge avez vous?' My nearly immediate response 'soixante dix', earned an age discount of almost 50%! The savings encouraged me to buy a copy of yesterday's *Daily Telegraph* and add an extra croissant to the petit déjeuner grande at the station café. Moving to the gleaming, new train, I was proud to see that it was made by Bombardier, the Canadian firm. But, I did not appreciate having to unload my bike and hang it on a hook. My irritation was increased by realizing that the scruffy tramp that I had seen bending down, presumably to admire my bike parked outside the station café, had stolen my stainless steel water bottle and its thermal cover.

Today's journey to Bordeaux required changing trains at Rennes and Nantes. So, I was subjected to the cycle loading and unloading process repeatedly. Minor additional stress resulted from the French practice of advising the departure platform with only twenty minutes notice. Murphy's or some similar law decrees that the finally designated platform will be distant and require lugging my 30 plus kilos of bike and gear up and down stairs. When lifts were available, they were so small the bike had to be crammed in diagonally, barely leaving space for me.

Despite these frustrations, by the end of the day I felt I had mastered(or survived) the French railway system. My booked hotel, chosen for cost as well as convenience, was almost directly opposite the massive Bordeaux station, the reception staff spoke English, my room was clean, modern and equipped with a bright blue washroom-- a cheery end to a mainly successful day.

In the morning, I boarded an east bound train for Bergerac; this time declining to unload or hang my cycle as no other cyclists were travelling. The bike wasn't stable and fell during the journey, dislodging the rear wheel, forcing it hard against the chain stay. So, once at Bergerac, I had to unload it anyway to reposition the wheel.

Coeds at Caduoin?
My day's final destination, about 35 km further east, was the hostel at Caduoin. Within a few kilometres from Bergerac station, I was tracking a road between the Dordogne and a parallel canal, lined with majestic plane trees providing both beauty and welcome shade. It was 29 degrees. Otherwise, this quiet road had little interest until Lalinde, a lethargic town of creamy stone buildings, pedestrian-only

shopping and a major new bridge where I crossed to the south side of the river.

Here the road narrowed and undulated, finishing up at Caduoin after two kilometres of downhill hairpins. The town has an immediately welcoming atmosphere of warm, golden stone with attractive restaurants lining the main street and a big cobblestone square outside the Abbey hostel entry arch.

The prospect of staying in this 11th century Abbey had intrigued me for months. Guests are warned that it is a co-ed hostel. I am used to hostels with separate rooms for men and women but this description conjured up images of cohabitation in the same room. Would I have female roommates—would they be young, attractive and uninhibited, or habit-clad convent types? Both disappointed and relieved, I got neither; the room, which slept five, was mine alone.

Its window, encased in a half metre of stone, looked out over the square and a large, open but roofed, stall being decorated for an imminent wedding reception. It was a friendly, informal, family affair which I observed peripherally later at ground level, enjoying the innocent delight of the colourfully dressed children playing round the stall.

It was market day at St Cyprien when I arrived about 11.30 the next day. People surged between the stalls, surveying every imaginable thing for sale—jewellery, clothing, knives, cheese, olives, fruit, and vegetables. A New Orleans guitarist sang US country and jazz music while his black Labrador dozed at his feet. I strolled, observing people, shops and their wares and lunched well on roast maigret in the coolness of a restaurant's covered back garden patio.

Disturbing noises from the bike disrupted the afternoon. Turning it upside down to reposition the rear wheel revealed that its disk brake rotor was rubbing. This could also be happening to the front wheel. It wasn't—the problem in front was more like an out-of-true wheel. With a few adjustments, the noises stopped, and the bike ran faster— for about 45 minutes. This time, I found a park and picnic bench to perform repairs and went through the entire process more thoroughly.

It was 5 p.m. before I finished so my return ride to Caduoin had to be abbreviated.

Back at the hostel, the cycle storage area was full of immaculate, expensive racing cycles when it had been empty apart from mine the night before. I was still alone in my room and did not meet the new arrivals until breakfast. It was a French group, occupying virtually all the space at the long trestle table. They squeezed together making just enough space for me. The men were fully occupied with themselves but some of the women were kind enough to pass me the coffee jug and some bread. During patchy, imperfect conversation with my neighbour, I discovered that the men cycle, unladen, while the women transport the luggage by car and prepare a midday picnic. This division of male and female activity seems to be a particularly French approach to a cycling holiday.

The next night, the expensive cycles were replaced with good quality but well-used touring bikes. This time it was a British group. Unlike the French, these men and women cycled together as equals. Our conversation flowed more easily and I even got some expert help with my disk brake problems. I also got a roommate. It was quite a shock to find a stranger, British but not one of the group, sitting at my room's window table.

His face was buried in a map reading with a magnifying glass. This and his general appearance did not appeal but it seemed churlish not to attempt some interaction. As a result, we had an interesting dinner together. Russell is 53, from London, and married to a woman whose only interests are television and romantic novels. His passions are trains and visiting hostels by cycle at every opportunity. Escaping his wife?

During dinner, not waiting for my answer to his request for permission, Russell casually pulled down his trouser waistband down slightly and injected himself with insulin. Despite thick glasses, he needed the magnifying glass for the menu. Both short and long vision are affected. It must make navigation and reading road signs particularly difficult not to mention dangerous.

During my remaining days in the area, I visited Montignac near the famous caves of Lascaux, strolled Sarlat's marvellous medieval section filled with evocative architecture and enticing restaurants, cycled to Monpazier and Belves (both considered 'most beautiful'), and past the stunning cliffs at Beynac before returning to Bergerac. My travels criss-crossed the Dordogne and Black Perigord, circling through constants of river scenery, plane trees, and golden stone buildings covering 300 kilometres mainly on cycle-friendly roads.

Pedalling further westward from Bergerac and again parallel to the Dordogne, added 73 km to get my Romagne accommodation. No one was in sight when I arrived at the farmhouse known grandly as Château de Crécy about 4.30. The door opened to a comfortable lounge displaying several bottles of wine and a bookings folder labelled 'Ce Soir.' Checking to see if my name was on the list, I found myself assigned to the 'Land and Ocean' room. The adjacent office led to a promising staircase with my room at the top. Despite feeling like an intruder, I showered, read and rested a while before the owners arrived about six.

They had been at work in their vineyards and must have expected me to make myself at home as there were no recriminations for doing so. After a warm, quick welcome, the wife immediately began dinner preparations. Her guests opted for dinner at the Chateau as it is quite distant from any restaurant. Her husband prepared a drink for me and I returned to my book awaiting dinner, promised 'a huit heure.'

At 8.30, we were ushered to the table. There were five of us: a Parisian couple in their early thirties, a middle-aged couple from Wales and elderly me. The French couple spoke English so conversation flowed smoothly—better than I could have expected given that we were all strangers. Connective threads made it easy and interesting. The French woman's English voice was heavily tinged with North American tones as a result of working in upstate New York, a mere 18 miles from my birth place, for Bombardier's French competitor. Now, she works for a bank. I finished my career in banking and my former chairman moved on to become the chair of Barclays Bank in Britain. The British woman, like my wife, is an artist. The 'six degrees of separation?'

We explored all these connections over a very relaxed dinner that began with a delicious salad of home-grown red and yellow tomatoes followed by sturgeon, boiled potatoes and grilled tomato. Cheese and a tarte completed the meal. All of this was accompanied by our choice of red and white house wines.

Returning through the office on my way to bed, I found a basket full of my finished laundry that our hostess offered to do when we first met. Next morning, settling up after an excellent breakfast, she would not charge me for the laundry and charged less than advertised for the dinner. This confirmed my long-held belief that farmhouse B&B's offer the best hospitality and value.

More Calamities

The final leg to Bordeaux was along part of a dedicated cycle trail between Bordeaux and Sauvaterre de Guyenne. One of the trail intersections was a short distance from the Chateau. This paved trail has its own route number, the D803, and posts distances to the next location. Running through forest, vineyards and open country, it provided constant change and interest. There is even a café.

After booking in at last week's hotel, I went to an internet café where I struggled for an hour with the French keyboard to update the family on my travels and remind them of tomorrow's start of the group tour.

Some interesting architecture a couple of blocks distant beckoned as I left the café. This was the Place de la Victoire, dominated by La Porte d'Aquitaine, an ancient city entrance. Adjacent Rue Ste Catherine, a busy pedestrianized street, looked worth exploring.

There the Saturday street scene surged with groups of grungy garths attracted by fast food hole in the walls and cheap clothing shops. All ethnicities were represented but mine was a definite minority. The day's heat and this encounter with humanity made the hotel's shower particularly welcome.

Sunday's first order of business was to book my afternoon train to Biarritz and the trains from there to Paris and Calais when the group tour finishes.   I knew from earlier planning that there were two options for Paris –a late afternoon and one just before midnight. The near midnight one might allow me to share the final dinner with the group and use the train as my overnight accommodation, saving on a Paris hotel bill. Panic struck when the agent told me there was no cycle space on either train.   When stressed, I don't think clearly, so I returned to the hotel to quietly and carefully outline my options, including abandoning the group tour altogether. However, since the final group tour day's distance was to be short, it might be possible to combine two day's distance into one, returning alone to Biarritz, a day early.

Mentally strengthened by my analysis, I returned to the railway station to discover that a morning cycle space to Paris was available for the earlier date. I quickly grabbed that along with a connecting afternoon spot the following day on the TGV to Calais. My relief was palpable but the price was a shock.   The ticket agent succumbed to my pleading for some age discount but the result was still nearly $200 without counting the need for a hotel.

Today's train to Biarritz was to be my first bike experience with the TGV.   On this journey, cyclists and their cycles were assigned to car 18.   Platform signs indicate where each car will be, lining them up with an alphabetic spacing painted on the platform.   As car 18 rolled towards position W, where I and three South African cyclists waited, it was clear that only a third of the car was open to cyclists. First on, I struggled through the narrow and steep TGV entry to discover that the bike space had to be created by folding up the seats and arms of chairs lining the car wall. We didn't see any hanging hooks. Removing all the panniers still left barely enough room to cram three bikes together. The fourth cyclist fumed outside in the passageway as the rest of us arranged our bikes to allow me to get off first as they were all going further south into Spain. He had to sit, holding his bike, which blocked the aisle.

Once at Biarritz, having begged an area map from a car-hire agency at the station, I set out for the designated campsite but wound up in a residential area with no idea where to go. It was Sunday, the street was empty and quiet.   The only possibility for help was a village centre with several cars parked outside. Barging in, I interrupted a meal, but was welcomed. Our command of each other's language was shaky but soon I was on my way to the airport! This sounds worse than it was, as the campsite was nearby and it only took a few more wrong turns to find it.

Biarritz Campsite

Pedalling with great anticipation into the campsite, I was cheered by some familiar voices among the dozen or so cycle tourists chatting away at reception. Their accents, mainly British, lifted my spirits as I knew my old friends were here and a new, more rugged part of my holiday was about to begin.

Tonight we will erect our tents, pack our panniers and endure primitive shower facilities. And, on the tour, our guide, Geoff, will not carry our gear, pump our tyres, mend our punctures, or follow in his tired, old Opel to offer us a lift when we're weary—which is perhaps best, given the way it's now groaning toward us, stuffed with tents, cooking gear, panniers and hauling a trailer full of Sheffield bikes.

Shaggy and cheerful, Geoff is a Cornishman of about 50, whose relative youth, along with that of a 30-year-old New York City woman, brought the group's collective age down to 55 (a comforting average, I decided since it gives me, as the oldest, the distinction of still being able to keep up, yet provides an excuse if I can't). My chocolate-brown custom Canadian contrasts sharply with the French blue bikes Geoff distributes, along with tents, cooking stoves and sleeping mats. We scout our designated area for tent sites, thread in support rods, hammer in pegs and cram clothing, waterproofs and books into our rear panniers. I, fortunately, also have front bags for my excess; the others must leave stuff behind along with their cases in his van.

There are 15 of us so far, with one more to arrive in the wee hours—the young New Yorker, whose tent I erected and adorned with a flashing, perhaps ambiguous, red bike light, so she'll be able to find her way 'home' in the dark. Although these tours attract a vocationally diverse mix (this one includes an engineer, a doctor, a communications specialist, a naval surveillance professional, and even the OED's science editor), our mutual love of cycling is a reliable foundation for wider-ranging conversation.

We were eager to toast the launch of our adventure with robust reds to accompany an anticipated selection of Basque Country culinary specialities. We also complemented our meals with a soupçon of risqué repartee. Tonight it was little light blue humour, as Allister, an irreverently witty lowland Scot, regaled us with a story about his anger when his banker demanded the purpose for a large withdrawal from Allister's account. Allister replied 'just put down that I'm starting a brothel.'

In the morning, motivated by the quality of that first meal and the prospect of strong French coffee we had packed up and were cycling back to last night's restaurant by 9 am for 'le petit déjeuner.' Typically, this means only coffee and croissant, but this establishment offered a buffet of fromage, jambon, et les oeufs durs. We traced the day's route on our maps, circling Geoff's choice of a likely lunch location. Given the vagaries of weather, terrain, and fitness levels, this became a daily routine.

On this first day, we mapped a course that will take us north east—the initial stretch of a 550-km loop through the Geronde region of Aquitaine—after which we'll traverse south west, tracing the Pyrenees foothills back to the Biarritz campsite. The entire itinerary will take 11 days, with treks beside stately plane trees, along broad rivers, over flower-bedecked bridges onto cobbled streets leading to inviting cafes, ancient cathedrals, and through seemingly deserted villages that spring vibrantly to life on market days. There will be challenging climbs but none that defeat us, given our preparatory training.

Geoff, always positive and optimistic, described two days of rain that doubled the weight of our tents and invited fat snails into them during the night as welcome heat relief. Another morning he told us that the day's change in elevation was a mere 600 metres. Later, climbing and descending the rolling terrain, we understood that we must conquer that rise several times. For me, the ascents were grindingly slow and tedious. At 5 to 7 km/h, I managed, but couldn't generate enough momentum to keep the front wheel steady on the often broken edge of the road, causing me to veer into traffic. Drivers were courteous, slowing until it was safe to overtake. But when the road narrowed, winding steeply upwards, the proximity of their engines, vibrating mere inches from my wobbling wheel, was unnerving.

Later in Tour de France territory, the Pyrenees provided a spectacular saw tooth panorama of peaks. Each long climb (col) was marked with a special blue and white road sign capped with a cartoon cyclist image. Misinterpreting the first sign's indicated 495 metres as distance, I thought—that's nothing—just a few minutes. After a kilometre, another sign appeared, again indicating 495 metres, I began to grumble.' It's a lie', I called out. It wasn't until 2 km further that we finally reached the top, where I sheepishly understood that the signs referred to elevation. The gradient must have been at least 12%.

Then, Ahhh, the descent, Like a waving ribbon, the tarmac undulated round the bends on the three-km ride down. I concentrate, change leg position, lean. It's bike to the left, body to the right, bike to the right, body to the left. Brake on the straights. Repeat! Over and over, and pray the wheels stay on. My odometer touched 54 km/h—a thrilling, scary ride that made the agony of the ascent totally worth it.

Such exhilaration contrasted with our daily routine. Each morning, we packed up and pedalled to the nearest boulangerie for croissants, pain de raisin or pain de chocolat before moving on to a bar for café au lait, where the besieged baristas humoured us—a horde of lycra-clad foreigners, fracturing the language and fumbling with unfamiliar coins.

Breakfasts were all too brief. The desire for an hour long session with my book as on my solo tour had to be sublimated. Inevitably, the master map reached me last when the rest of the group was ready to leave, causing stress as I rushed to complete my map. Thank goodness lunch was a more relaxed affair. Our afternoon meal is often the highlight of the day—a two-hour respite at moderate expense, as we sought restaurants competing for the custom of local tradesmen. The white trade vans parked outside make these restaurants easy to spot. One lucky day, we got five courses plus enough wine for two to three glasses each for a total of 13€. That said, while the fare in such places is often very good, it's hardly haute cuisine. As Geoff put it, one plat du jour of tripe sausage, was better than the Brittany version, only because it didn't smell so much 'like a pig's derrière.' But, there were few complaints, and, as always wine proved an excellent lubricant. So, limp of laughter and leg, we're fortunate that about 60 per cent of the day's distance is behind us, making the afternoon rides brief.

This allowed us time to buy camp meal ingredients, shower, do laundry, relax in the pool and start dinner, a task we undertook in pairs. Each pair had a liquid fuel cooker, a set of pots, cutlery, plastic plates and cups. I teamed up with Yassmin, the daughter of Welsh/ Yemini parents and more important, an excellent cook. She has brought her own Middle Eastern spices in tiny plastic laboratory tubes, each with a neatly typed label. By mutual agreement, my role was limited to chopping, consumption and cleanup.

Pasta was a popular choice but some were adventurous, taking great pleasure in demonstrating their culinary skills with such basic equipment. Generally we gathered in a circle to prepare the food, perching on three-legged stools, lounging in Thermarest mats converted to chairs or just cross-legged on the ground. Most contributed some 'nibbles' and wine and we munched away while boiling water or chopping vegetables. Campfire conversation typically reminisced about previous tours but sometimes we played word or trivia games. As the tour neared the finish, we became increasingly relaxed. Perhaps the residual wine in our reservoirs diluted inhibitions or maybe it was because the unisex shower stalls severely limited privacy, breaking down barriers. As we waited in queues to use them, some of the women stood around in their underwear, chatting. Later, their freshly laundered bras and knickers fluttered in the wind, drying on the backs of their bikes. Despite this strengthened togetherness, I now looked forward to being on my own again. Another new adventure beckons as I must leave a day early to claim my cycle space on the trains to Paris and Calais. I made my farewells after breakfast to cycle alone back to the Biarritz campsite for an overnight before embarking on the seven-hour trip to Paris.

From Paris to the White Cliffs of Dover

My overnight in The City of Light was a delightful transition. Geoff booked a budget hotel for me just off the Boulevard St Germain. I had only a vague idea of where the hotel was relative to Montparnasse station and had to cycle there in rush-hour traffic, but drivers were considerate and there are dedicated bike lanes and cyclist eye-level traffic signals. (France is a cyclists' paradise compared with Canada, although one of my day's train companions was a Dutch cyclist who considered the French provisions for cyclists inferior to those in the Netherlands.)

Paris is a magical city at night, particularly along the Seine. I sauntered the boulevard, crossed the river marvelling at the padlocks plastered over the wire fence bridge walls, most sporting Valentine type messages of enduring love. After observing break dancers entertaining the crowds outside Notre Dame, I doubled back across the bridge joining throngs of evening promenaders studying menus posted along the pavement. A bearded and beret-clad gent persuaded me into a weathered timber facade, noisy with the chatter of contented diners. For this meal, however, my sole company was a book, and I knew the next morning I would stroll a solitary route along the Seine.

That walk was a fun two hours, past the Louvre, through the Jardin des Tulieres and on to the Place de Ia Concorde, where the Arch de Triomphe and Eiffel Tower rise majestically in the distance. Along the way, I became the target for two young women seeking my cash. The first tried to 'give' me a bright gold ring she had 'just found' near my feet. 'It is too big for me, you must have it' she said repeatedly. I had a vague memory of a scam involving this story line and politely refused the ring over and over until she gave up, so never learned how she or her accomplices intended to extract my cash. The second woman could not speak but gave me a clipboard that explained she was collecting for similarly afflicted people. She became much less pleasant when my contribution did not meet expectations. It was an interesting morning and so it was with regret that, passing by Chanel and other famous fashion houses on Boulevard Saint Germain, I returned to my hotel, hauled my cycle up the 22-step circular stone staircase from the cellar and headed to Gare de Nord for the train to Calais and the ferry back to England.

Ironically, the ferries were the most luxurious aspect of the trip. With the Eurostar as competition, English Channel ferries have become luxury liners, with multiple restaurants, comfortable lounges, cinemas and bars. I've enjoyed sea voyages since 1957 when my younger brother and I sailed from Montreal to Liverpool on the Empress of France. Back then, I danced with a girl from Halifax, as the ship's orchestra played Vera Lynn's 'There'll Be Bluebirds over the White Cliffs of Dover.' Now, the towering cliffs awe me as we steamed into port; this crossing was all too short and there were no bluebirds.

Two days later, my tour ended at Horley, just outside Gatwick airport, following an overnight in Canterbury, some 100 kilometres cycling in the Kent countryside and an hour's train ride.

Now it is time to reminisce and start planning for next time.

TOUR ROUTES

The maps in each of the tour chapters show an overview of the general tour area but aren't very practical for those of you that might want to duplicate all or part of my tours. To overcome that problem, I've included map case sized detailed routes.

The general design is a line or two for each day. First is the name of the village where I stayed overnight. This is followed by a sequential list of some of the towns along the way and the numbers of the roads used. On the far right is a rough approximation, in kilometres, of the distance for that day.

For the most part, the details provided reflect the routes I actually took. However, in some cases my memory or my records weren't up to the task. In these cases, I have supplied a route that works—it just may not be the one I used. In some cases, the route requires use of some roads without numbers, that is, they are unnamed (UNM) lanes. When this is the case, you will have to make the link using the village names.

So, you will still need to carry a map (or bring a GPS if you aren't a traditionalist) to find how to make those connections and to see what alternative routes are available. If possible to find, I recommend maps on a scale of 1 cm per 1.5 km. This scale provides a good level of detail and often indicates roads that are scenic as well as landmarks such as churches and other useful information like the direction and severity of the road slope.

Finally, I must apologize for not being able to show proper accent marks for some of the French towns and villages on these routes.

If you wish to use these route pages, I recommend that you photocopy the page onto a plastic sheet that will resist moisture that might get into your map case. Or, you might want to cut the page out and laminate it.

END TO END TOUR

OVERNIGHT AT	VIA	APPROX. DISTANCE
PERTH	FROM GLASGOW	**
THURSO	FROM PERTH	**
LATHERON	DUNNET---JOHN O'GROATS---ULBSTER (ALL ON A9)	87KM
BONAR BRIDGE	DUNBEATH---BERRIEDALE---HELMSDALE--BRORA--EVELIX (ALL ON A9)	95KM
INVERFARGAIG	DAINAVIE, DINGWALL---BEAULY---MILTON (ON A836/A9/A862/A833)	87KM
ONICH(LOCH LINNHE)	LEWISTON---INVERGARRY--SPEAN BRIDGE--FORT WILLIAM (ALL ON A82)	95KM
INVERANAN	GLENCOE---TYNDRUM---CRIANLARICH (ALL ON A82)	90KM
KILMARNOCK	TARBET--LUSS---ARDEN--DUMBARTON--STEWARTON (ON A82/A8/A736/A735)	89KM
DUMFRIES	MAUCHLINE--CUMMOCK---SANQUHAR---AULDGIRTH (ALL ON A76)	101KM
CASTLE CARROCK	CARRUTHERSTOWN---GRETNA---LONGTOWN---BRAMPTON (ON A75/B6413)	72KM
PENRITH	KIRKSOWALD--LAZONBY (ON B6413/B6412)	35KM
BROUGHTON FURNESS	POOLEY BRIDGE--AMBLESIDE--CONISTON (ON A592/A593)	68KM
KIRKBY LONSDALE	GRIZEBECK--LOWICK GREEN--NEWBYBRIDGE--WHITTINGTON (ON A5092/A590/A6)	66KM

** By Train

OVERNIGHT AT	VIA	APPROX. DISTANCE
BOLTON	BURT'N LONSD--SLAIDBURN--DUNSOP BR--LONGRIDGE--DARWEN (ON B6245/A666)	108KM
HINSTOCK	LEIGH--KNUTSFD--MIDDLEWCH--NANTWCH--MKT DRAYN (ON A50/B5081/A530/A529)	111KM
LUDLOW	CRUDGINGTON--UPTON MAGNA--ACTON BURNELL--CH. STRETTON (ON B5062/A49)	82KM
COLEFORD	LUSTON--LEOMINSTER--HEREFORD--ROSS ON WYE (ON B4361/A49/B4428)	87KM
CHEDDAR	ST BRIAVEIS--TINTERN ABY --CHEPSTOW--BRISTOL--REDHILL(ON B4321/A466/A38)	68KM
SOUTH MOLTON	WEDMORE--BRIDGWTR-DUNSTER--WITHYPL(ON B3151/B3138/A38/A39/A396/B3224)	116KM
ST GENNYS	GT. TORRINGTN--STIBB CROSS--HOLSWORTHY--BUDE (ON B3227/A388/A3072/A39)	90KM
TRURO	BOSCASTLE--WADEBRIDGE--FREDDON (ON B3263/A39)	85KM
PENZANCE	HELSTON--PENZANCE--LAND'S END--MOUSEHOLE (ON A39/A394/B3315)	81KM
WINCHESTER	TOURING CITY ON FOOT	**
COOLHAM	PETERSFIELD--MIDHURST---PETWORTH--BILLINGSHURST (ON A272)	70KM
WELWYN GARDEN CITY	COWFOLD--CUCKFIELD--HORLEY (ON A272/B2036)	40KM*
GATWICK AIRPORT		**

* More by train **By train

PEAKS, LAKES AND DALES TOUR

OVERNIGHT AT	VIA	APPROX. DISTANCE
BUXTON	MANCHESTER AIRPORT---ADLINGTON HALL---WHALEY BRIDGE	40 KM
IIAM	LOGNOR-----ALSTONEFIELD----ALTON	74KM
ASHBOURNE	ASHBOURNE----SUDBURY-----LONGFORD	66KM
MONSAL HEAD	BAKEWELL----ASHFORD IN THE WATER	62KM
WIGAN	BUXTON ON A6 THEN BY TRAIN	25KM*
PENRITH	BY TRAIN TO PENRITH AND THEN AROUND AREA	42KM
DUFTON	TEMPLE--APPLEBY---MURTON-KEISLEY (SOME ON A66)	63KM
KESWICK	LG MERTON--BOLTON--CLIBURN--POOLEY BRIDGE---DOCKRAY(ONA592/A5091/A66)	64KM
COCKERMOUTH	BORROWDALE---HONISTER PASS---BUTTERMERE (ON B5289/B5292)	70KM
BOOT	ENNERDALE BR---GOSFORTH--WASDALE HD--ESKDALE GREEN (ON A5086/A595)	74KM
AMBLESIDE	HARDKNOTT PASS--WRYNOSE PASS---SKELWITH BRIDGE	41KM
KENDAL	HAWKSHEAD--GRIZEDALE--HAWKSHEAD--NEAR SAWREY (ON B5286/B5285/B5284)	53KM

*More by train

401

PEAKS, LAKES AND DALES TOUR

OVERNIGHT AT	VIA	APPROX. DISTANCE
KIRKBY LONSDALE	NOOK--KIRKBY LONSDALE--KEARSTWICK--SEDBERGH--MIDDLETON (ON A591/A590/A65/B6254/A683)	59KM
STAINFORTH	BARBON--BAWTHORP--DENT--COWGILL--INGLETON--HIGH BENTHAM--SETTLE (ON A683/B6255/B6480/B6479)	59KM
ASYGARTH	HORTON IN RIBBLESDALE--HAWES (B6479/B6255/A684)	75KM
ESHTON GRANGE	CAPERBY--CASTLE BOLTON--ASYGARTH--KETTLEWELL--THRESHFIELD RYLSTONE--SKIPTON--GARGRAVE (ON B6160/B6265/A65)	82KM
HARROGATE	GRASSINGTON--PATELY BRIDGE--RIPLEY (ON B6265/B6165/A61)	55KM
HARROGATE	POOL--OTLEY--BLUBBERHOUSES (ON A61/A659/A59/A61)	48KM
YORK	KNARESBOROUGH--WETHERBY--LONG MARSTON (ON A6055/B6164/B1224)	75KM
SCARBOROUGH	BY TRAIN THEN AROUND THE CITY AND TO HOSTEL	15KM
GREAT BROUGHTON	ROBIN HOOD'S BAY--WHITBY--SANDSEND--KILDALE--INGLEBY GREENHOW (ON A171/B1447/A171/A174/B1266/A171)	84KM
CARLTON IN CLEVELAND	STOKES**--GT. AYTON--STOKES**--HUTTON***--STOKES** (ON B1257/A170/B1363)	44KM
YORK	SEAVE GREEN--HELMSLEY--OSWALDKIRK--SUTTON ON THE FOREST (ON B1257/A170/B1363)	93KM
MANCHESTER	BY TRAIN	

** Stokes = Stokesley   *** Hutton = Hutton Rudby

CIRCLE TOUR

OVERNIGHT AT	VIA	APPROX. DISTANCE
STORRINGTON	WORTH--HANDCROSS--HORSHAM--SOUTHWATER--COOLHAM (ON B2036/B2076 B2110/A279//A281/B2232/A272/B2139	52KM
OVERTON	BURY--SUTTON--LODSWORTH--DIAL GREEN--LIPHOOK--ALTON--BASINGSTOKE (ON B2131/B3004/B3349/A30/B3400)	108KM
CALNE	WHITCHURCH--STOKE--OXENWOOD--MARLBOROUGH(ON B3400/B3048/A4)	75KM
BATH	STOCKLEY--GASTARD--NESTON--BRADFORD ON AVON--WINSLEY--CLAVERTON (ON B3108/A36)	76KM
CHEPSTOW	WICK--PUCKLECHURCH--NIBLEY--LATTERIDGE--OLVESTON--SEVERN BRIDGE (ON B4465/B4427/A48)	63KM
HAY ON WYE	DEVAUDEN--LLANSOY--KINGCOED--TREGARE--LLANTILIO CROSSENNY LLANGIHANGEL CRUCORNEY--LLANTHONY--CAPEL-Y-FFIN (ON A466/B4293/B4521)	83KM
RATLINGHOPE	BRILLEY--LOWER HERGEST--KINGTON--PRESTEIGNE--BUCKNELL--EYTON-- ASTERTON--WENTNOR (ON B4350/A438/B4355/B4367/B4385/A489)	81KM
CHESTER	PONTESBURY--ELLESMERE--OVERTON--WORTHENBURY--ALDFORD (ON A458/B4473/A528/B4397/B5130)	110KM
HIGH BENTHAM	TRAIN TO PRESTON --LONGRIDGE--WHITEWELL--SLAIDBURN--LOWGILL(ON B6243)	65KM
KENDAL	BURTON IN LONSDALE--KIRKBY LONSDALE--OLD HUTTON (ON A687/A683/B6254)	36KM
DENTDALE	SEDBERGH--DENT--COWGILL (ON A684)	41KM
KELD	SEDBGH--GARSDALE HEAD--NATEBY--K. STEPHEN--NTBY (ON A684/B6259/B6270)	46KM
THIRSK	THWAITE--REETH--RICHMOND--NORTHALLERTON (ON B6270/A6108/B6271/A168)	82KM

Note: Sedbgh =Sedbergh, K. Stephen = Kirkby Stephen, Ntby = Nateby

CIRCLE TOUR

OVERNIGHT AT	VIA	APPROX. DISTANCE
YORK	KILBURN--EASINGWOLD--STILLINGTON--SUTTON ON THE FOREST (ON B1363)	52KM
LINCOLN	HAYTON--GOOLE--SWINEFLEET--EASTON--E.BUTTERWICK--KEXBY-- SUTTON BY STOW (ON A1079/A613/A614/B1392/A161/B1241/B1398)	141KM
GRANTHAM	BRACEBRIDGE HEATH--LEADENHAM--BARKSTON (ON A15/A607)	48KM
RAMSEY	OLD SOMERBY--STAMFORD--HELPSTON--THORNEY--WHITTLESEY (ON A52/B1176/B1443/B1040)	101KM
CAMBRIDGE	HUNTINGDON--ST IVES--EARITH (ON B1040/A141/A1123/B1050)	64KM
CAMBRIDGE	ON FOOT	
CAMBRIDGE	BY TRAIN TO WELWYN GARDEN CITY AND RETURN	
WARLEY	SAFFRON WALDEN--FINCHINGFIELD--GREAT DUNMOW--BRENTWOOD-- (ON B184/B1053/A1057/A127/A128)	110KM
SEVEN OAKS	TILBURY--GRAVESEND(BY FERRY)--MEOPHAM--WROTHAM--KEMSING--SEAL (ON B186/A227/A25)	60KM
HORLEY	RIVERHEAD--IDE HILL--FOUR ELMS--LINGFIELD (ON A25/B2042/B2027/B2026/B2028 B2037/B2036)	60KM

404

NORTHERN ENGLAND AND SCOTLAND TOUR

OVERNIGHT AT	VIA	APPROX. DISTANCE
MANCHESTER	TOURING CITY ON FOOT	
YORK	TOURING CITY ON FOOT	**
THIRSK	SHIPTON--- EASINGWOLD (ON A19)	66KM
FRIENDS' HOME	INGLEBY CROSS---- CARLTON IN CLEVELAND (ON A19/A172)	31KM
PICKERING	CHOPGATE-- HELMSLEY-- PICKERING--GOATHLAND*** (ON B1257/A170/A169)	93KM
NEWCASTLE	MALTON-- BUTTERCRAMBE****--STAMFORD BRIDGE--YORK (ON A169/A166)	63KM*
ALNWICK	GOSFORTH--BEDLINGTON--WARKWORTH (ON B1318/A1068)	77KM
BERWICK UPON TWEED	SEAHOUSES--BAMBURGH (ON B1340/B1342/A1)	79KM
WOOLER	HOLY ISLAND--LOWICK--DODDINGTON (ON A1/B6353/B6525)	68KM
BELLINGHAM	CHATTON--CHILLINGHAM--POWBURN--ROTHBURY--FORESTBURN GATE-- KNOWESGATE--REDESMOUTH (ON B6348/A697//B6341/B6342)	92KM
CARLISLE	WARK--CHOLLERFORD--GREENHEAD--IRTHINGTON--LOW CROSBY (ON B6320/B6318/B6264)	80KM
COCKERMOUTH	WIGTOWN--MEALSGATE--BOTHEL (ON A595/A596/B5304/A595/B5292)	80KM
KESWICK	HIGH LORTON--BRAITHWAITE--GRANGE (ON B5292/B5289)	35KM

*More by train/ferry **By train *** Return to Pickering on A169 ****Malton to Buttercrambe all on unmarked roads

405

OVERNIGHT AT	VIA	APPROX. DISTANCE
KESWICK	CASTLERIGG STONE CIRCLE --KESWICK---SEATOLLER & RETURN 9ON B5289)	48KM
ALLENHEADS	PENRITH--ALSTON--CORNRIGGS (ON A66/A686/A689/B6295)	79KM
EDINBURGH	ROOKHOPE--STANHOPE--EDMUND BYRES--SHOTLEY BRIDGE--ROWLANDS GILL--	
	NEWCASTLE (ON A689/B6278/B6310)	71KM*
MELROSE	HERIOT--STOW--GALASHIELS (ON A7/A6091)	77KM
EDINBURGH	LAUDER--DALKEITH (ON A6091/A68)	64KM
WHITING BAY	TRAINS TO GLASGOW/ARDROSSAN--FERRY---A847 FROM HARBOUR	29KM*
LOCHRANZA	DOUGARIE--PIMMILL--CATACOL(ON A847)	45KM
LOCHGILPHEAD	KENNACRAIG--TARBERT--ARDRISHAIG (ON B8001/A83)	74KM
INVERARAY	LOCHGAIR--MINARD--FURNACE--AUCHINDRAIN (ON A83)	74KM
OBAN	CLADICH--LOCHAWE--TAYNUILT---CONNEL (ON A819/A85)	68KM

* More by train

OVERNIGHT AT	VIA	APPROX. DISTANCE
TOBERMORY	CRAIGNURE--SALEN--ARDNACROSS (ON A849)	37KM
MALLAIG	FERRY--KILCHOAN--ARDSLIGNISH--SALEN--ACHARACIE--ROSHVEN--LOCHAILORT (ON B8007/B861/A830)	97KM
BROADFORD	FERRY--ARMADALE BAY--KILMORE--ISLEORNSAY--SKULAMUS (ON A851/A87)	76KM
PORTREE	LUIB--SCONSER--SLIGACHAN (ON A87)	72KM
PORTREE	KENSALEYRE--EARLISH--UIG--QUIRAING***--STAFFIN--RIGG (ON A87/A855)	76KM
ARMADALE	SLIGACHAN****--LUIB--BROADFORD--SKULAMUS--TEANGUE (A87/A851)	76KM
GLASGOW	BY FERRY TO MALLAIG THEN TRAIN TO GLASGOW	**
DUMFRIES	NEWTN MEARNS--FENWICK--KILMARNOCK--SANQUHAR (ON A77/A76)	132KM
WIGAN	BY TRAIN TO CARLISLE THEN TRAIN TO WIGAN	**
PARBOLD	CANAL TOWPATH--PARBOLD--RUFFORD--MAWDESLEY--ECCLESTON--- WRIGHTINGTON BAR (ON B5246/B5250/A5209)	**
MANCHESTER	STANDISH--INCE---TYLDESLEY (ON A5209/A49)	42KM
		61KM

** By train   *** Scenic beauty spot ****Unmarked road from A87around peninsula and back to A87

CELTIC TOUR

OVERNIGHT AT	VIA	APPROX. DISTANCE
WINDSOR	TO AND WITHIN WINDSOR GREAT PARK	26KM
WINCHESTER	BAGSHOT--HARTLEY WINTNEY--HOOK--CHAWTON--EAST TISTED--BRAMDEAN (ON A332/A30/B3349/A339/A32/A272/B3404)	121KM
SALISBURY	STOCKBRIDGE--LOPCOMBE CORNER (ON B3049/A30)	47KM
STREET	SHAFTESBURY--GILLINGHAM--STONEY STOKE---CASTLE CARY---ANSFORD SOMERTON (ON A30/B3081/B3153/B3151)	95KM
MINEHEAD	PEDWELL--BRIDGEWATER---NETHER STOWEY---CROWCOMBE---WILLITON (ON A30/A361/A372/A39/A358/A39)	68KM
LYNTON	SELWORTHY--PORLOCK (ON A39/B3225/A39)	47KM
THORNBURY	BARNSTAPLE---BIDEFORD--STIBB CROSS (ON A39/B3233/A306/A388)	74KM
PADSTOW	HOLSWORTHY--STRATTON--CYCLING MUSEUM(B3314/B3266)--WADEBRIDGE (ON A388/A3072/A39/A389)	84KM
PERRANPORTH	TRENANCE--GOONHAVERN (ON B3276/A3075)	54KM
PENZANCE	THREE BURROWS--REDRUTH--PORTREATH--CRIPPLESEASE (ON B3315/B3277/B3300/B3301/B3311)	58KM
ST JUST	MOUSEHOLE--LAMORNA COVE---LAND'S END--SENNEN--(ON B3315/B3306)	43KM
ST JUST	ST IVES----CRIPPLESEASE--PENZANCE (ON B3306/A3074/B3311/A3071)	56KM
ROSCOFF	ST JUST ---PENZANCE FOR TRAIN TO PLYMOUTH	19KM*

*More by train

408

CELTIC TOUR

OVERNIGHT AT	VIA	APPROX. DISTANCE
HUELGOAT	ST POL DE LEON--PENZE--MORLAIX--BERRIEN (ON D58/D769/D14)	61KM
GOUAREC	BERRIEN--CARHAIX--TREBRIVAN--MAEL CARHAIX--PLOUNEVEZ QUINTIN (ON D14/D769/D20/D23/N164/D8)	65KM
GOUAREC	AT CAMPSITE AND WALKING IN VILLAGE	21KM
MUR DE BRETAGNE	BON REPOS BY CANAL TOW PATH THEN CYCLE PATH TO MUR DE BRETAGNE	21KM
JOSSELIN	NEULLIAC--ROHAN (ON D767/D125 THEN CANAL TOWPATH)	48KM
NAIZIN	RADENAC--ST FIACRE--REGUINY (ON D11/D117/D203)	26KM
ST NICOLAS DE EAUX	KERFOURN--PONTIVY (D319/D2 THEN CANAL TOWPATH)	43KM
GUEMENE	BIEUZY LES EAUX--MELRAND--TALHOUET (ON D1/D156/D142)	37KM
GOUAREC	LANGOELAN--LOCUON--MELLIONNEC--PLELAUFF (ON D3/D76)	32KM
VAL ANDRE	ST NICOLAS DU PELEM--CANIHUEL--LE VIEUX BOURG--QUINTIN--PLEDRAN (ON D8/D5/D4/D69/D28/D22/D34)	90KM
DINAN	PLANCOET--ST MAUDEZ (ON D17/D19/D62/D716/D61)	60KM
CAP FREHEL	PLOUBALAY--MATIGNON--LEVENON (ON D2/D786/D16)	55KM
CAP FREHEL	SABLES D'OR--PLURIEN--PLEVENON (ON D16/D34)	63KM
ST MALO	PLEVENON--PLOUBALAY--CHATEAUNEUF(ON D16/D786/D2/D28/D366/D76/D6/D301)	76KM
PORTSMOUTH		*
WINDSOR	COSHAM--EAST TISTED--ALTON--BASINGSTOKE(ON B2177/B2150/A32/A339)	85KM**

* By ferry ** More by train

409

WALES AND WYE VALLEY TOUR

OVERNIGHT AT	VIA	APPROX. DISTANCE
KEMSING	LINGFIELD--LIMPSFIELD--SEAL (ON B2036/B2037/B2038/A25)	48KM
WROTHAM HEATH	SEAL (ON A25)	40KM
OXFORD	SEA--OXTED--REDHILL (ON A25) TRAIN FROM REDHILL	45KM*
OXFORD	ON FOOT	On foot
OXFORD	BRIGHTWELL--BALDWIN--WATLINGTON--EWELME--BENSON	69KM
COALPORT	TELFORD BY TRAIN THEN A5223/A4169	15KM*
LUDLOW	MUCH WENLOCK--BROCKTON--ASTON MUNSLOW (ON B4376/B4373/B4378/B4368/B4363)	53KM
LUDLOW	ON FOOT	
NEW RADNOR	OVERTON--PRESTEIGNE--BEGR BUSH--KINNERTON (ON B4361/B4362/B4356/B4372)	53KM
LLANWYRTYD WELLS	BUILTH WELLS--GARTH--BEULAH (ON B4372/A481)	48KM
LLANWYRTYD WELLS	CEFNGORWYDD--GARTH--BUILTH WELLS--BEULAH--LLAN WELLS--ABERGWESYN	59KM
HAY ON WYE	BUILTH WELLS--- PAINSCASTLE----CLYRO (ON A483/B4567/B4594)	51KM
HAY ON WYE	DORSTONE--PETERCHURCH--BREWARDINE--HAY ON WYE---	
HAY ON WYE	CLYRO (ON B4348/B4352/B4350/A438)	51KM
HAY ON WYE	BREDWARDINE--MOCCAS--HEREFORD--CLEHONGER--DORSTONE (ON B4352/A438/A465/B4352/B4349/B4348)	75KM
HAY ON WYE	GOSPEL PASS--CAPEL Y FFIN AND RETURN	29KM

*More by train

Note: Begr Bush = Beggar's Bush; Llan Wells = Llanwyrtd Wells; Peterchr =Peterchurch

410

WALES AND WYE VALLEY TOUR

OVERNIGHT AT	VIA	APPROX. DISTANCE
GROESFFORDD	LLANIGON--VELINDRE--TALGARTH--LLANGYNIDR (ON B4550/A4078/B4560/B4558)	56KM
GROESFFORDD	BRECON--LOWER CHAPEL--MERTHYR CYNOG--LLANDDEW (ON B4520)	46KM
GROESFFORDD	TRECASTLE--NATL SHOWCAVES--DEFYNNOG--BRECON (ON A40/A4067/A40)	74KM
MUMBLES	TRECASTLE--LLANDOVERY--SWANSEA (A40 and A4067 FROM SWANSEA)	53KM*
MUMBLES	BISHOPSTON--RHOSSLI--PORT EYNON--OXWICH--BISHOPSTON (ON A4118/B4247)	64KM
BETTWS NEWYDD	SWANSEA--TRAIN TO NEWPORT--BRYNBUGA (ON A4067/B4596)	34KM
ABERGAVENNY	RAGLAN--LLANTILIO CROSENNY (ON B4233)	61KM
ROSS ON WYE	MONMOUTH--BERRY HILL--ENGLISH BICKNOR--KERNE BR.(ON B4233/A4136/B4228)	51KM
ROSS ON WYE	GOODRICH--SYMONDS YAT--COLEFORD--BERRY HILL (ON B4228)	40KM
BRINSCOMBE	HUNTLEY--GLOUCESTER--STROUD (ON A40/B4173/A46/A419)	62KM
BRINSCOMBE	MINCHINGHAMPTON--FRAMPTON MANSELL--CIRENCESTER--BIBURY--AIDSWORTH NORTHLEACH--CIRENCESTER (ON A419/B4425/A429/A419)	88KM
STOW ON THE WOLD	CIRENCESTER--BIBURY--NORTHLEACH--BOURTON WATER (ON A419/B4425/A429)	58KM
STOW ON THE WOLD	LR SWELL--UPR SLAUGHTER--BOURTON/WATER--L. RISSINGTON (ON B4068/A424)	37KM
STOW ON THE WOLD	ODDINGTON--MORETON/MARSH--CHIPPING NORTON--CHURCHILL (ON A436/B4450)	62KM
WELWYN GARDEN CITY	TRAIN FROM MORETON/MARSH TO LONDON** / THEN TO WELWYN GARDEN CITY	43KM*
HORLEY	BY CAR TO ST ALBANS FOR TRAIN	By train

*More by train

** London Paddington then cycle across city to Kings Cross for train to WGC

411

BRITTANY, AUVERGNE AND LIMOUSINE TOUR

OVERNIGHT AT	VIA	APPROX. DISTANCE
ST BRIEUC	BY TRAIN FROM PARIS VIA RENNES	**
BON REPOS	BY CAR TO GOUAREC THEN CANAL TOWPATH TO BON REPOS AND IN AREA	20KM
MAEL--CARHAIX	TOWPATH TO GOUAREC THEN PLOUNEVEZ QUINTIN--MAEL CARHAIX--TREBRIVAN (ON D8/D23/D20)	42KM
CHATEAULIN	KERGLOFF--CORROREC--PLONEVEZ DU FAOU (ON D48)	47KM
LE POULDU	ELLIAN --BRIEC--ROSPORDEN--KERNEVEL--BANNALEC--LE TREVOUX--BAYE (ON D770/D50/D150/D22/D49)	77KM
LE PARADIS	GUIDEL--PONT SCORFF--HENNEBONT--PLOUHINEC--ERDEVEN--PLOUHARNEL QUIBERON(PORT MARIA) (ON D49/D224/D162/D6/D26/D109/D781/D786/D186)	65KM
LE PARADIS	POINTE DE SANTE MARC--BANGOR--PORT COTON	27KM
LE PARADIS	SAUZON--POINTE DES POULAINS--LOCMARIA	40KM
BAUD	ST PIERRE QUIBERON--PLOUHARNEL--CARNAC--PLOEMEL--BRECH--PLUVIGNER (ON D786/D781/D119/D120/D102/D24)	50KM
PONTIVY	LA MADELEINE--PLUMELIAU--ST THURIAU (ON D203/D205/D768)	25KM
GOUAREC	ST TREPHINE--MALGUENAC--CLEGUEREC--ST BRIGETTE--BON REPOS (ON D159/D15A/D15 AND CANAL TOWPATH)	30KM
POITIERS	BY CAR	
LE BLANC	LE PEU--LA CHAPELLE--MOULIERE--ARCHIGNY---ANGLES SUR L'ANGLIN SAUZELLES--ST AIGNY (ON D20/D3/D86/D1/D3/D2E/D2/D3)	66KM
MONTIGIVRAY	BELABRE--ARGENTON (ON D10/D927)	100KM
HURIEL	BRIANTES--STE SEVERE--ST PRIEST LA MARCHE--PREVERANGES--ST PALAIS-- MESPIES--CHAMBERAT (ON D83A/D84/D917/D203/D112/D149/D71)	59KM

**By train

412

BRITTANY, AUVERGNE AND LIMOUSINE TOUR

OVERNIGHT AT	VIA	APPROX. DISTANCE
CHATEAUNEUF L' BAINS	COURSAGE--TEILLET-ARGENTY--STE THERENCE--MARCILLAT EN COMBRAILLE PIONSTAT--ST GERVAIS D'AUVERGNE (ON D151/D1089/D227)	68KM
CHATEAUNEUF L' BAINS	AROUND AREA	15KM
MERCHINAL	LA VEREILLE--ST GEORGES DEMONS--LES ANCIZES--GREGOTTIER LE BESSES (ON D227/D61/D19/D121/D39)	55KM
AUBUSSON	LA MAZIERE--CORCQ--PONTCHARAUD--STE FEYRE LA MONTAGNE (ON D28/D10/D18/D19/D982)	43KM
ST DIZIER	HUSSARD--VALLIERE--CHATAIN--LA PARADE--PARDOUX-MONTEROLES BOURGANEUF (ON D59/D36/D7/D58/D51A/D61)	68KM
CHATEAUPONSAC	ST GOUSSAUD--LAURIERE--BESSINES (ON D43/D57/D28A/D28/D27)	60KM
MONTMORILLON	CLOPS VERINES--LE MENIEUX--DROUX--LA BUSSIERE AUPIGNY--THIAT LE BREUIL--SAUIGE (ON D4B/D104/D12/D5)	68KM
POITIERS	SILLARS--LUSSAC--CHAUVIGNY--LAVOUX--BIGNOUX--MONTAMISE--FONTAINE (ON D114/D8/D139/D18/D4)	70KM
PARIS		**

** By train

413

BRITAIN AND BRITTANY TOUR

OVERNIGHT AT	VIA	APPROX. DISTANCE
CANTERBURY	HORLEY---EAST GRINSTEAD---ROYAL TUNBRIDGE WELLS---TONBRIDGE	48KM*
CANTERBURY	PEDESTRIAN TOUR	
BENENDEN	CANTERBURY---CHARING----BIDDENDEN-----TENTERDEN	75KM
ICKLESHAM	TENTERDEN---RYE----BREDE	46KM
ALFRISTON	BROADOAK--CRIPPS CORNER---BATTLE---NINFIELD---UPPER DICKER	56KM
FELPHAM	LEWES---CLAYTON---FULKING----STEYNING----WORTHING---LITTLEHAMPTON	70KM
RYDE	CHICHESTER---WESTBOURNE---PORTSMOUTH HARBOUR	54KM**
TOTLAND BAY	NEWPORT---FRESHWATER BAY---NEEDLES	37KM
RYDE	FRESHWATER BAY---CHALE---GODSHILL---NEWPORT----WOOLTON BRIDGE	47KM
BRITTANIA FERRY	RYDE FERRY TO PORTSMOUTH HARBOUR/AROUND PORTSMOUTH CITY	15KM**
ST MALO	ROUND TRIP ALONG COASTAL ROAD D201 THROUGH PARAME& ROTHENEUF	47KM
DINAN	PARAME ---ST PERE---CHATEAUNEUF D' ILLE-ET-VILLANE--SOUTH ON D29	62KM
ST BRIEUC	BOBITAL--LANGUEDIAS--PLELAN LE PETIT--LAMBALLE--STE ANNE--LANGUEUX	83KM
GOUAREC	ST JULIEN---QUINTIN----LA VIEUX BOURG---ST GILLES VIEUX MARCHE--BON REPOS	74KM
QUINTIN	ST TREPHINE---CANIHUEL----LA VIEUX BOURG	43KM

* More by train **More by ferry

414

OVERNIGHT AT	VIA	APPROX. DISTANCE
BINIC	ST DONAN--PLERNEUF--TREGOMEUR--LANTIC (ON D47/D4)	32KM
PONTRIEUX	PLOURHAN--PLOUHA--KERMARIA--PAIMPOL--PLOURIVO (ON D21/D79/D15)	39KM
LA ROCHE DERRIEN	PLEUDANIEL--LANMODEZ--PLEUBIAN--TREGUIER (ON D787/D20/D8)	50KM
LOCQUIREC	PERROSGUIREC--TREGASTEL--TREBEURDEN--LANNION--PLOULEC'H	
	ST MICHEL--PLESTIN-LES GREVES (OND6/D788)	75KM
ST POL DE LEON	LANMEUR--PLOUEZOC'H--MORLAIX--PENZE (D64/D76/D769)	55KM
ST POL DE LEON	ROSCOFF AND RETURN	22KM
LA GREVE BLANCHE	LANHOUARNEAU--LE GOLGOE--PLOUGUERNEAU (ON D788/D29/D32/D28/D32)	67KM
SIZUN	PLOUGVERNEAU--LE GOLGOE--PLOUNEVENTER--ST SERVAIS--LANDIVISIAN--	
	LOCMELAN (ON D32/D28/D32/D29)	60KM
CARHAIX	ST CADOU--ST RIVOAL--BRASPARTS--CROIX LANEGUER--PLONEVENEZ DU FAOU	
	(ON D30/D21/D48)	61KM
SILIFIAC	PLEVIN--PAULE--GLOMEL--TREGARANTEC--MELLIONNEC (ON D83/D85/D76/D764)	64KM
MORLAIX	D764 TO ROSTRENEN--MAEL CARHAIX--CARHAIX--D769 NORTHWEST	93KM
PLYMOUTH	D769 TO PENZE--ST POL DE LEON--ROSCOFF HARBOUR	32KM**
SALCOMBE	A379 EAST TO MODBURY--A381 SOUTH	39KM
TOTNES	RIVER FERRY TO EAST PORTLEMOUTH--TORCROSS--A379/A3122/A381	53KM
HORLEY		***
HORLEY	IN AREA --SMALLFIELD--OUTWOOD--BLETCHINGLY AND RETURN TO HORLEY	30km

** More by ferry *** Totally by train

415

NORTH MIDLANDS

OVERNIGHT AT	VIA	APPROX. DISTANCE
MANCHESTER	AIR FROM TORONTO	
GLOSSOP	TRAIN/ AFTERNOON LOCAL ROUND TRIP ON LONGDENDALE TRAIL	30KM
GLOSSOP	THE SNAKE	62KM
MANCHESTER	BY TRAIN	
LUDLOW	BY TRAIN	45KM
CLUN	PETHBRIDGE FARMS/LEINTWARDINE/BUCKTON/BUCKNELL	
LITTLE STRETTON	BICTON/MAINSTONE/BISHOP'S CASTLE/MORE/WENTNOR/RATLINGHOPE/ ALL STRETTON/CHURCH STRETTON	47KM
IRONBRIDGE	CHURCH STRETTON/ALL STRETTON/GRETTON/HUGHLEY/CRESSAGE/ LEIGTON/BUILDWAS	40KM
IRONBRIDGE	TOURING LOCALLY ON FOOT	
LUDLOW	MUCH WENLOCK/CORVEDALE/TUGFORD/BOULDON/GREAT SUTTON	53KM
LUDLOW	CYCLE TO PETCHFIELD FARM/RETURN BY CAR	18KM
LEOMINSTER	BY TRAIN	60KM
LEOMINSTER	LOOP B4529/A4110 TO HEREFORD/A465 TO BROMYARD/A44	57KM
LEOMINSTER	GINHALL LANE/B4360/A4110/A4113/B4385/B4370/A5112 PASSING BY	
SHREWSBURY	KINGSLAND/LEINTWARDINE/CRAVEN ARMS/WHITTINGSLOW/LITTLE STRETTON/ LONGNOR/BAYSTON HILL	78 KM

OVERNIGHT AT	VIA	APPROX. DISTANCE
SHREWSBURY	SHREWSBURY CYCLE ROUTE 3 LOOP TO BERRINGTON/CONDOVER/ACTON BURNELL	38KM
MARKET DRAYTON	B5067/SHREWSBURY ROAD/MERRINGTON ROAD/A528/A495 TO ELLESMERE/ B5063/B5476/B5065/A41/A53 PASSING BY BOMERE HEATH/MYDDLE COCKSHUTT/ WELSHAMPTON/PRES	78KM
NETTLEHAM	A53/A51/A34/B5027 TO UTTOXETER PASSING BY MAES/STONE /BY TRAIN	52KM
LONGDON	TRAIN TO UTTOXETER/B5013/B5234/ABBOTS BROMLEY/B5014	30KM
ILAM	B5014/B5013 TO UTTOXETER/B5030/B5032 TO MAYFIELD/A515 TO ASHBOURNE/ UNM TO THORPE	60KM
ILAM	UNM TO THORPE/TISSINGTON TRAIL TO PARSLEY HAY JUNCTION/HIGH PEAK TRAIL IN OPPOSITE DIRECTION TO BLACK ROCKS JUNCTION/B5023 PAST CARSINGTON RESERVOIR TO B5035 TO ASHBOURNE/UNM TO THORPE	67KM
EYAM	UNM TO THORPE/TISSINGTON TRAIL TO PARSLEY HAY JUNCTION/A515/B5055 TO MONYASH/BAKEWELL/ASHFORD/UNM TO A623 TO EYAM	44KM
GLOSSOP	A623/B6049 TO BRADWELL/A624 TO HOPE/CHAPEL-LE-FRITH/HAYFIELD	49KM
MANCHESTER	LOCAL CYCLING IN GLOSSOP/BY TRAIN	13KM

OXFORD AND SOUTHERN FRANCE

OVERNIGHT AT	VIA	APPROX. DISTANCE
HORLEY	BY AIR	
WELWYN GARDEN CITY	BY TRAIN/A1000 VIA HATFIELD	14KM
GORING	A1057 TO ST ALBANS/A414/B4505 TO CHESHAM/A416/A355 TO SLOUGH	65KM
	REST BY RAIL	
GORING	LOOP B4526 TO A4074/UNM TO SONNING COMMON TO HENLEY AND REVERSE	51KM
OXFORD	B4009 TO CROWMARSH GIFFORD/A4130/UNM TO EWELME/UNM TO WATLINGTON/ CHRISTMAS COMMON/FINGEST/STOKENCHURCH/A4120 TO TETSWORTH/A40	75KM
OXFORD	CITY TOUR ON FOOT	
OXFORD	TOWPATH SUSTRANS ROUTE TO A4095 BLADON/WITNEY AND REVERSE	75KM
OXFORD	TOWPATH SUSTRANS ROUTE TO A44 TO BLENHEIM/WOODSTOCK AND REVERSE	85KM
OXFORD	CYCLING ROUND OXFORD	19KM
OXFORD	ABINGDON/CHISLEHAMPTON/GARSINGTON/WHEATLEY	75KM*
BRITTANY FERRY	B480 TO STADHAMPTON/WATLINGTON/B481 TO NETTLEBED/READING	54KM
	TRAIN TO PORTSMOUTH	
BORDEAUX	BY TRAIN FROM ST MALO	
CADOUIN	TRAIN TO BERGERAC/D680 TO LALINDE/D660 TO MOLIERES/UNM	38KM
CADOUIN	LOOP D25/D51 TO ST CYPRIEN/D703/UNM TO BELVES/D54	54KM
CADOUIN	LOOP UNM TO ST AVITSENIEUR/D26/UNM/D53 TO MONPAZIER/D53	67KM
	TO BELVES/UNM TO SOUILLAC/D54	
MONTIGNAC	D25/D51 TO LEBUGUE/D703/D706 TO LES EYZIES/D706	53KM
SARLAT	D704 TO LA CHAPELLE ABBAREIL/D48 TO ST GENIES/D61/D47	47KM
BERGERAC	D703/D25/D29/TO LALINDE/D660	74KM

*Remainder of route lost to senior memory

OXFORD AND SOUTHERN FRANCE

OVERNIGHT AT	VIA	APPROX. DISTANCE
ROMAGNE	D32 TO ST ANTOINE/D936 TO CASTILLON LA BATAILLE/D119 TO LAVAGNAC/ D670/D128 TO BELLEFOND/UNM	73KM
BORDEAUX	BORDEAUX TO SAUVETERRE DE GUYENNE PISTE (CYCLE ROUTE)	45KM
BIARRITZ/ANGLET	BY TRAIN TO BIARRITZ--CYCLE TO CAMPSITE ADJACENT TO AIRPORT	10KM
ST GEOURS de MAREMNE	D74 FROM BAYONNE/D74/D126/D54 TO SAUBRIGUES/D71/D12	40KM
ST SEVER	D810/D10E/D150 TO PONTONX/D10 TO MUGRON/D32	52KM
ESTANG	D352/D11 TO CARNETTE/UNM TO D1 TO MONGUILHEM.D30	50KM
CONDOM	D30/D129 TO MONTREAL/D15	50KM
MARCIAC	TO MOUCHAN/D35 TO VIC-FEZENSAC/BASSOUES/D943	68KM
LESTELLE BETHARRAM	D943/D38 TO JUSTINE/D544/D50 TO LA FITOLE/D55/D6 TO VIC EN BIGORRE D7/D63 TO MONTANER/D27/D63/D129 TO PONTACQ/D412/D812	53KM 53KM
ARAMITS	D35 TO LOUVIE-JUZON/D920/D918	63KM
MOULEON LECHARRE	D918	47KM
ST ETIENNE de BAIGORRY	D918 TO D933 TO ST JEAN PIED DE PORT/D15	53KM
BIARRITZ/ANGLET	D948/D918 TO CAMBO LES BAINS/D932	70KM
PARIS	BY TRAIN	
CALAIS	BY TRAIN TO CALAIS FRETHUN--CYCLE TO CALAIS TOWN	15KM
CANTERBURY	BY FERRY TO DOVER/ A2/A256/UNM/A257	52KM
HORLEY	BY TRAIN TO TONBRIDGE/A26 /B2176/B2027 TO EDENBRIDGE/B2028 TO NEWCHAPEL AND B2037/B2036	52KM

SUMMARY OF BICYCLE DEVELOPMENT

Germany 1817	Drasine- A two wheel, in line running machine. Balance achieved by steering. Also known as 'Dandy Horse'.
France 1860s	Rotary cranks and pedals attached to front wheel of Drasine.
Britain 1870	Ordinary or High Wheeler. Over-size front wheel driven by rotary cranks and pedals. Large wheel delivered greater speed.
Britain/France 1870s	Ball bearings first developed in Wales in 1794 but patented in France in 1869 and made effective for cycles by lubrication and invention of ball bearing race in 1870s.
Britain 1879	Chain driven rear wheel.
Italy 1879	Freewheel (one-way clutch) allowed rear wheel to rotate without being pedalled (free-wheeling or coasting).
Britain/Switzerland 1880	Steel roller chain developed by Hans Renold, a Swiss who immigrated to Manchester.
Germany 1883	Technique for making precision steel ball bearings with extremely hard surfaces.
Britain 1885	Diamond shaped frame employed in Rover Safety cycle with equal sized wheels and rear wheel chain drive.
Britain 1888	Pneumatic tyres -conceived by John Dunlop but preceded by another Scot in 1846, patented in France and US. Made cycling comfortable and popular. Previously tyres made of solid iron and known as 'boneshakers'.
France 1890	Changeable tyres (tubulars). Previously tyres had to be glued on.
Italy 1930	Quick release skewer. Eased changing wheels/mending punctures.
Italy 1933	Derailleur -first prototype of variable gears.
Italy 1950	Derailleur parallelogram -similar to today's approach.

Sources: Herlihy,David V. Bicycle: The History, New Haven and London:Yale University Press,2004

Penn, Robert. Its All About the Bike, London, Penguin Books,2010

DAILY TOUR COSTS IN STERLING

TOUR	BED	FOOD	RAIL*	OTHER	TOTAL
END TO END	10.33	5.20	3.71	3.71	22.95
PEAKS,LAKES & DALES	13.21	9.75	1.97	4.41	29.34
CIRCLE	17.48	10.74	0.91	4.78	33.91
N. ENGLAND & SCOTLAND	14.42	12.88	4.13	3.63	35.06
CELTIC	15.50	12.83	3.49	7.24	39.06
WALES & WYE VALLEY	23.96	15.31	2.69	2.61	45.12
BRITTANY, AUVERGNE & LIMOUSINE	15.83	23.24	4.33	15.23	58.63
BRITAIN & BRITTANY	17.74	17.73	5.51	13.10	50.93
NORTH MIDLANDS	26.69	16.70	0.70	13.93	58.02
OXFORD &SO. FRANCE	22.80	22.49	9.99	13.68	68.96

Notes: * Rail includes ferries. Relatively high 'other' costs in final four tours reflects costs of purchased tours (Breton Bikes and Wheely Wonderful)

CYCLE CALORIE CONSUMPTION

Calorie consumption while cycling depends on body size, type of bike, terrain, and wind conditions. Speed, however, is also important and can dramatically affect the energy used in cycling because of its effect on wind resistance.

The chart on the following page shows calorie consumption estimates for different speeds. These numbers were developed for *Bicycling* magazine by physiologist James Hagberg, Ph.D. To use the chart, just select the speed that you cycle at and multiply the coefficient at that speed by your body weight (in lbs) to get the calories you will burn per minute. The chart shows the calculation for a 150 lb/68 kg cyclist.

The statistics assume flat terrain. Going uphill increases energy consumption. David Swain, Ph.D., a member of Bicycling's Fitness Advisory Board considers that it takes an extra 22 calories to climb 100 feet (30 metres). This is an average value for a cyclist and cycle together weighing 176 pounds (80 kg). Freewheeling downhill should save calories from the chart figures but not enough to offset the consumption of first going up the hill.

CYCLE CALORIE CONSUMPTION CHART

MPH	KMH	Coefficient	Calories Per Minute*
8	12.9	0.030	4.5
10	16.1	0.036	5.4
12	19.3	0.043	6.4
14	22.5	0.051	7.7
15	24.2	0.056	8.4
17	27.4	0.068	10.2
18	29.0	0.074	11.1
19	30.6	0.081	12.2
20	32.2	0.089	13.4

*For a 150 lb / 68 kg cyclist

Adapted from Bicycling Mileage Guide and Training Log published in 2002 by Rodale, Inc. Emmaus, PA 18098

GLOSSARY

BRITISH	NORTH AMERICAN
Aerodrome	A small airport or airfield. Becoming obsolete.
Aga Cooker	A heavy heat-retaining cooking stove burning solid fuel or powered by gas, oil or electricity. Continuous heating.
Answer Phone	Telephone answering machine
Anti-Clockwise	Counter clockwise
Bap	Bread roll
Barley Water	A drink made from water and a boiled barley mixture.
Barman	Bartender, barkeep
Bend	Curve as in a road. A double bend is an "S" curve.
Biscuits	Cookies or crackers. Sweet biscuits are cookies.
Bloody- minded	Pig headed: stubborn
Bob's Your Uncle	There you are! You're done.
Breeze Block	Cinder block (building material)
Brewer's Dray	A low cart without sides for beer barrels
Caravan	House trailer
Carcase	Carcass

BRITISH	NORTH AMERICAN
Cattle Grid	A grid covering a ditch, allowing vehicles to pass over but not cattle, sheep, etc.
Ceilidh	An informal gathering for conversation, music, dancing, songs and stories (usually Scottish or Irish).
Chips	French fries
Chock a Block	Crammed together, completely full
Cinema	Movie House
Cobble	Run up; put together roughly
Compere	Master of ceremonies
Coverlet	A bedspread
Cow	Can be a derogatory term for a woman. In Britain, the sense is more a coarse,unpleasant woman than an unattractive one.
Council	Literally, a local administrative body of a village, town, borough, city or county.
Council Charge	Formerly rates, equivalent to property taxes in NA
Cream Tea	Afternoon tea with Devonshire cream, which is rich, sweet, delicious, thicker than North American whipped cream, and is meant to be piled on top of the jam on top of the scones.

BRITISH	NORTH AMERICAN
Crisps	Potato chips
Crown Land	Crown land in Canada (Government land in the US).
Dale	Valley (a northern British term).
Drawing Pins	Thumb tacks
Dog's Breakfast	Unholy mess
Driver	Engineer (railway)
Eccles Cake	A flat round cake made of pastry filled with currants (somewhat like a mince pie).
En Suite	Usually used in connection with a bedroom to indicate that a bathroom is attached.
Estate Agent	Real estate agent
Estate Car	Station wagon
Fell	A hill (a northern English term).
Film	Movie
Flask	Thermos
Flying Scotsman	Historic railway engine on the King's Cross-to Edinburgh line.
Full English	Traditional English breakfast. Components may vary but will almost certainly include eggs, toast, tomato, baked beans, bacon and sausage. May also include fried bread, mushrooms, etc.

BRITISH	NORTH AMERICAN
Gents	Men's toilet in a public place
Goods Van	Railway term—freight car
Grammar School	A selective state secondary school with a mainly academic curriculum. Increasingly rare since the late 1960s when comprehensive schools became national policy.
Green Grocer	Fruit and vegetable shop
Higgledy- piggledy	A state of disordered confusion
Hoardings	Billboard
ITV	Independent Television. A television network that, unlike the BBC, permits commercials.
Left Luggage	Check room at a railway station or airport
Lemon Cheese/Curd	A conserve of lemons, butter, eggs, and sugar, with the consistency of warm cream cheese.
Litter/Rubbish Bin	Trash basket
Long Vacation	The long university summer vacation is the long vac.
Loo	Washroom, restroom, toilet. Not typically used by the British educated and literary or the lower middle class and genteel. These groups tend to use lavatory, W.C, or toilet, respectively.
Lounge	Living room

BRITISH	NORTH AMERICAN
Marks & Sparks	Slang for Marks & Spencer, one of Britain's oldest and most famous retail stores. Specialises in clothing and food products.
Midges	Gnats
Milk Run	A routine expedition or service journey. In a railway context indicates a train that stops frequently.
Mini	Legendary small car designed by Alec Issigonnis for Austin-Morris (later British Leyland). Featured a number of technical innovations and loved for its practicality and fun-to-drive personality. Now a very popular retro vehicle produced by BMW.
Mushy Peas	No real equivalent. This is a style of serving decent green peas that renders them a mushy overcooked mess.
News Agent	News dealer. Shop where newspapers and magazines are sold.
Non-Conformist	Member of a Protestant denomination other than Church of England (synonymous with dissenter).
Off Licence	Liquor, bottle or package store that is licensed to sell alcohol for consumption off the premises.
On Offer	Available, as in "what's on offer"?

BRITISH	NORTH AMERICAN
Open University	University courses offered over the television and radio. Open to the general public regardless of prior academic achievement. Satisfactory completion involves coursework submitted by post.
Pasty	A pastry case with a usually savoury filling, baked without a dish to shape it. The most famous is the Cornish pasty.
Pavement	Sidewalk
Pebble-dash	Mortar with pebbles in it used as a coating for external walls
Petrol	Gasoline
Point	Electric socket (or railway switch). Often used with an appropriate adjective, such as power or razor.
Pub	Bar. In Britain, pub is short for public houses that are more than bars. Public houses often serve meals and function as community social centres.
Pudding	Dessert, a term increasingly used In Britain. Pudding belongs more to the gentry but perhaps had its origin in a cooked sweet such as plum pudding.
Puncture	Flat tyre
Put Paid To	Finish, end.

BRITISH	NORTH AMERICAN
Queue	Line of people or vehicles waiting for something
Ring	Call (as in telephone). The British use both terms
Roundabout	Traffic circle that allows vehicles to enter when clear and exit on any of several spokes located round the circle.
Rubbish Tip	Garbage Dump
Rucksack	Backpack
Sit up and Beg	Flat, upright cycle handlebars like those used on commuter, hybrid and mountain bikes.
Smalls	Underwear
Subway	Underground walkway/passage
Sultana	Same in Canada. White raisin in US. In the US, Sultana is a trademark for a particular brand of seedless raisin.
Summer Pudding	A dessert made of crust less bread and mushed summer fruits. Served cold after the mass has soaked and congealed.
Surgery	Doctor's office. Often a separate part of Doctor's residence.

BRITISH	NORTH AMERICAN
Tea	Tea, the drink, and the meal that is taken about four pm with biscuits, teacakes or scones. But primarily the term working class and children use to mean an evening meal or light supper.
The High Street	The main shopping street in a town, often named High Street.
Tin	Airtight metal can for foodstuffs, etc.
Toff	Slang for a distinguished person, a swell; indicative of a way of life more than of wealth.
Torch	Flashlight
Trunk	Long distance. Used as an adjective to describe a telephone call or road. Becoming obsolete
Verge	Grass shoulder at edge of road

END NOTES

Foreword
1.　David V Herlihy, *Bicycle: the history*, (New Haven and London: Yale University Press, 2004),pp. 15-22

Peaks, Lakes and Dales
1.　Hunter Davies, *A Walk Around the Lakes*, (London: J M Dent, 1993), p.91
2.　Vanessa Thorpe, *Observer*, 14 March 2010
3.　*AA Illustrated Guide to Britain*, (London: Drive Publications, 1971), p. 423
4.　Tim Hughes and Joanna Cleary, *Cycling Great Britain*, (San Francisco, Bicycle Books,1996), p.119
5.　*AA Illustrated Guide to Britain*, p.427

Circle
1.　Leon Fitts,'Stone Circles', (*British Heritage*, March 1997), pp. 36-7
2.　Tim Hughes and Joanna Cleary, *Cycling Great Britain*, p. 86.
3.　Fitts, 'Stone Circles', p. 35
4.　Hughes and Cleary, *Cycling Great Britain*, p. 94
5.　Ibid., p. 95
6.　*AA Illustrated Guide to Britain*, p. 341
7.　Hughes and Cleary, *Cycling Great Britain*, p. 96
8.　*AA Illustrated Guide to Britain*, p. 410
9.　Hughes and Cleary, *Cycling Great Britain*, p. 39
10.　Wikipedia

Northern England and Scotland
1.　*AA Illustrated Guide to Britain*, p 445
2.　Hughes and Cleary, *Cycling Great Britain*, p. 130
3.　*Cycling Britain* (Melbourne,Lonely Planet, February 2001), p. 353

Celtic Cycle
1.　Hughes and Cleary, *Cycling Great Britain*, p. 78
2.　Norman Davies, *The Isles, a History*, (Oxford University Press, 1999), pp 352-3
3.　Arthur Eperon, *Brittany* (London, Pan Books 1990), p. 30
4.　Hughes and Cleary, *Cycling Great Britain*, p. 77
5.　Jean Paschke, 'The Prince's Alma Mater', (*British Heritage*, Dec. 2001 / Jan. 2002) pp. 45-49

Wales and the Wye Valley

1.   Davies, *The Isles, a History*, p.704
2.   Ibid., p. 613
3.   Ibid., pp.613-4
4.   Ibid., p. 443
5.   *AA Illustrated Guide to Britain*, p. 312
6.   Ibid. , p. 161
7.   Ibid. , p. 165

Brittany and Beyond

1.   Greg Ward, *Brittany and Normandy* (London, Rough Guides, 1992), p. 245
2.   Eperon, *Brittany*, pp 76/77
3.   Ibid., pp 76/77
4.   Ward, *Brittany and Normandy*, p. 219

Britain and Brittany

1.   *AA Illustrated Guide to Britain*, p. 306
2.   Davies, *The Isles, a History*, pp. 276-281 and Battle tourist pamphlet
3.   Wikipedia quoting *Daily Telegraph* of 25 April 2004 'The Forgotten Dead---Why 946 American Servicemen died off the Coast of Devon In 1944' and 'The Man Who Discovered their True Story' Bloomsbury 1988 ISBN D-7475-03095

Lightning Source UK Ltd.
Milton Keynes UK
UKOW04f0923140714

235079UK00001B/186/P